A Sovereign Idea
Essays on Canada as a Democratic Community

In *A Sovereign Idea*, which brings together the best of Reg
Whitaker's essays on democracy, federalism, and the state,
Whitaker analyses the paradoxes of federalism and democracy
in a society which is deeply divided by region, language, and
class. He examines the thought and action of such diverse figures
as Mackenzie King, Harold Innis, William Irvine, and Pierre
Trudeau and evaluates their impact on Canadian society. As well,
he surveys constitutional reform and the question of Quebec
sovereignty as it has developed from 1981 through Meech Lake
and beyond, and explores federalism, democratic theory, and the
practice of politics.

In the final essay, "Quebec and the Canadian Question," written
especially for this volume, he evaluates the major changes in
Canadian politics during the last fifteen years and assesses their
effect on the future possibilities for Canadian democracy. The
dominant political discourse, Whitaker argues, is increasingly
based on human rights. This, in combination with the ascendance
of free-market conservatism, the turn to continentalism under free
trade, and the resurgence, since the failure of Meech Lake, of
serious tensions between Quebec and the rest of Canada, has led to
a compounded crisis that requires an examination not only of what
Quebec wants, with or without Canada, but what Canada wants –
with or without Quebec.

Reg Whitaker is a professor and director of the graduate program
in the Department of Political Science, York University.

A Sovereign Idea

Essays on Canada as a Democratic Community

REG WHITAKER

McGill-Queen's University Press
Montreal & Kingston • London • Buffalo

© McGill-Queen's University Press 1992
ISBN 0-7735-0841-4 (cloth)
ISBN 0-7735-0878-3 (paper)

Legal deposit first quarter 1992
Bibliothèque nationale du Québec

Canadian Cataloguing in Publication Data

Whitaker, Reginald, 1943–
  A sovereign idea: essays on Canada as a
  democratic community
  Includes bibliographical references and index.
  ISBN 0-7735-0841-4 (bound). –
  ISBN 0-7735-0878-3 (pbk.)
  1. Federal government – Canada. 2. Democracy.
  3. Canada – Politics and government. I. Title.
  HN103.5.W44 1992   320.02'0971   C91-090324-7

To the memories of
Donald Smiley and Khayyam Paltiel,
distinguished political scientists,
teachers, colleagues, and friends.

Contents

PART FOUR DEMOCRACY AND
COMMUNITY

Preface

The late 1970s and 1980s were years of successive crises and profound changes in Canadian politics. An already fractious federalism rushed toward the precipice of potential national breakup with the election of the Parti Québécois in 1976. The Quebec referendum on sovereignty-association led to defeat for the *indépendantiste* option, but the strains on national unity continued to be felt between English-Canadian province-builders and centralists in Ottawa. The bitter struggle over the patriation of the British North America act eventuated in the new Canada Act with its entrenched Charter of Rights – included against Quebec's opposition. In the late 1980s an attempt to recast the constitution once again to gain Quebec's assent by specifying Quebec's status as a distinct society within Canada ran into furious opposition from many English Canadians. Amid the clamour of renewed divisions over language and culture, the threat of Quebec independence was once again on the agenda for the 1990s.

These constitutional contests over federalism and nationality were played out against a backdrop of (economic crisis.) Three decades of relatively prosperous welfare capitalism under Liberal Keynesian economic management began to unravel with a compound crisis of persistently high unemployment and inflation. New economic nostrums competed for the attention of bewildered policy makers. Wage and price controls, nationalist economic intervention, and free market conservatism succeeded one another. Class conflict over scarce resources matched the regional and community rivalries being played out at the level of the constitution. The Liberal party, dominant at the national level for over six decades, fell abruptly from grace to be replaced by the Conservatives as the new "government party," solidly supported both by business and (in a significant historical reversal) francophone Quebec. At the end of the 1980s, the Conservatives embarked upon perhaps the most far-reaching transformation of the Canadian nation in this century: continental free trade. The free trade election of 1988 was cast as a great referendum between alternative and sharply divergent visions of Canada.

With all these momentous movements on the surface of the body politic, it is easy to lose sight of the deeper and more significant changes taking place beneath the surface. Personalities and the excitements of the day captivate the present-minded media audience, but what is usually absent from these entertainments is a sense of where we have come from and where we are going. If political science is to have any value beyond that of political journalism, it should be its capacity to address these deeper currents.

These essays were published between 1976 and 1987 and address various political issues, sometimes contemporary, sometimes historical. Even the latter were, however, chosen for what I considered to be their contemporary relevance. I have always considered that political science without history is like the reflections of an amnesiac: cogitation without context and thus without much sense.

Despite, or perhaps because of, the aura of permanent crisis which hung over politics in these years, it seems to me that something quite intriguing was happening. Canadian politics, Frank Underhill long ago complained, are as dull as ditchwater and our history is full of it. This dullness he attributed to a lack of ideas. In recent years our politics have been shaken by debates over such great issues as nationalism, federalism, individual and collective rights, liberalism and communitarianism, feminism, environmentalism, war and peace, free markets and social welfare, national sovereignty and continentalism. These debates have often been primitive and confused, making up in sound and fury what they lack in thoughtful reflection, and positions have often been taken more in defence of narrow self-serving purposes than on behalf of generous conceptions of the public interest. And yet ... despite the difficulties, there is a sense that Canadians have been groping for ideas, seeking new ways to articulate their aspirations and project them on to the public stage. Canadian public debate is more clamorous, more contentious, more combative than it used to be – and it is definitely less dull. I have tried in these essays to get at some of the ideas which are enlivening public debate.

Political ideas take many shapes, but behind the appearances I believe we have been witnessing a movement toward greater democracy, or, more precisely, a struggle to find the proper forms to embody people's desire to participate more fully in the community. Debates over nationality, federalism and the constitution are debates over the form of political community. And the outcomes of these debates have consequences. The Charter of Rights has already begun to transform the fundamental relations between citizens and state and even the very nature of citizenship. The free trade election of 1988 was about economics and national sovereignty, but it was about much more than this. As Rick Salutin has said, it was an extended debate among Canadians about the nature of the Good Society.

I have chosen as a title for these essays *A Sovereign Idea*. This title seemed apposite because the idea of sovereignty is interrelated with that of democracy in at least three ways in these pages. At the root of democracy is the concept of popular sovereignty. But who are the "people"? There is always the problem of equality among citizens: here questions of class, ethnicity, gender, and other distinctions between Canadians have been raised and contested. Then there is the theme of Canadian national sovereignty: who are the "people" in an international context? First raised as demands for autonomy against the framework of British Imperial rule, national sovereignty in the postwar era has been contested in the light of the dominating power of the United States – as recently indeed as the great Free Trade election of 1988. There is also the question of Quebec sovereignty which has been more or less central to public debates in Canada for the past three decades. The idea of Quebec sovereignty challenges the idea of the Canadian people on the basis of nationality.

The question of equality within the national community is one common to all modern democratic states, even if it has taken particular forms in the Canadian experience. But the Canadian case is more distinct with regard to the latter two kinds of national questions. Few modern democracies have been as weakly defined in relation to the larger imperial hegemonies as Canada. And few have been as divided from within on a national basis for so long a period without either breaking up or succumbing to violent repression or endemic disorder.

The ironies of this Canadian condition have recently been dramatically demonstrated. Just after the finale of the Meech Lake constitutional fiasco, with its controversy over Quebec's status as a "distinct society," the summer of 1990 was dominated by the armed resistance of the Mohawk Nation at Oka and Châteauguay, Quebec, in the name of sovereignty or self-government for the native peoples, a resistance ultimately crushed by the coercive power of the Canadian and Quebec states, together asserting their superior sovereign power.

The idea of sovereignty thus remains a bitterly contested one. Sovereignty is not a fact. It is an idea, or, more properly, various ideas which struggle with one another. There is more than one road to democracy in Canada, and many arguments over which route to follow.

An underlying theme of all of these essays is the emergence of the "sovereign idea" of democracy within a specific Canadian reality. When Alexis de Tocqueville wrote his classic study, *Democracy in America*, he detected in the United States a particular embodiment of a universal ideal: equality. It is perhaps a price of being a Canadian, and at the same time a consolation, that one is not driven to seek universal application of what one finds here. I do not know if there is any extraterritorial resonance in what I describe, and in truth I do not greatly care. I do find the story of democracy in Canada to be of considerable interest in itself.

Perhaps, after the revolution in Eastern Europe in the *annus mirabilis* of 1989 (two hundred years after the French Revolution), we can say with some new assurance that there is indeed a universal spirit of democracy at work in the world. If so, the Canadian experience is one small and no doubt idiosyncratic representation of this spirit. If others should care to look to Canada, they might find an unusual example of democratic civility and tolerance in a world which is in notoriously short supply of such qualities. But my intention is not national self-congratulation. On the contrary, I am rather more interested in the imperfections and contradictions of emergent democracy, in the unfinished agenda of democratic reform.

Part 1 deals with the problem of class and class conflict in a liberal (that is to say, capitalist) democracy. The second section shifts focus somewhat to the particular Canadian questions of nationality and liberalism. Part 3 turns to the question of federalism as a fundamental aspect of Canadian democracy. Part 4 shifts focus again, both away from political theory toward political practices and away from federalism as such toward relations between state and society. Finally, in an essay written especially for this volume, I take stock of some of the major changes which have occurred in Canadian politics over the past decade and a half and assess the impact of these changes on the future of democracy as a "sovereign" idea.

The "Indian Summer" of 1990 proved that the national question is far more complex and difficult than the Quebec / Canada dimension alone would indicate. These essays do not address the hard conundrums of self-determination for native communities or nations. While this is a self-reproach, it is also a rebuke to Canadian political science which has generally not addressed this dimension of national sovereignty with the same care lavished on the Canada / Quebec issue. Native self-government must be on the agenda for the future. Although native rights are not discussed, as such, in these pages, there is a theme from these essays which may be pertinent. Sovereignty in the hard, absolutist sense; sovereignty which is both exclusivist and exclusionary; sovereignty which is intolerant of differences and seeks to impose itself upon diversity – all these notions of sovereignty are not only false and pernicious but may even be, to coin an ugly term for this usage only, *un-Canadian*.

If there is a peculiar Canadian genius in politics, perhaps it is to live with what other, more evangelical and dogmatic nations would see as a contradiction in terms: co-existent sovereignties. States which insist upon the metaphysical mission of unity – a people one and indivisible – may *appear* formidable and will, from time to time, wreack great mischief and injury in the course of enforcing that mission. But there is an old fable about the seemingly weak reed which survives a great wind which breaks the rigid and unbending tree. I have tried in these essays to explore this special Canadian strength in weakness.

PART ONE

Class and Community

CHAPTER ONE

Images of the State
in Canada

Leo Panitch's 1977 collection *The Canadian State*, in which this essay originally appeared, was a landmark in the emergence of the new school of political economy in Canadian social science, itself a synthesis of the older tradition of political economy particularly associated with Harold Innis and newer Marxist analytical perspectives. This essay is an attempt to reread Canadian history as determined by class conflict at the level of ideology. I argue that successive images of the state or the public realm reflect transformations in the structure of society but are themselves relatively autonomous factors in shaping changes in that society.

Other attempts to theorize the development of political ideology in Canada, particularly the famous Hartz-Horowitz "fragment" approach, have always struck me as too idealist and lacking a sense of the material reality of history. On the other hand, Marxism often falls into a kind of crude determinism. In this essay I tried to steer a course between these two extremes. Although some of the specific historical interpretations may be challenged by more recent scholarship, I would point to the method of this essay as its major contribution.

The essay (and the book as a whole) has been criticized by labour historian Bryan Palmer for understating the role of coercion in the history of the capitalist state in favour of accumulation and legitimation. I agree with Palmer, and indeed much of my research over the subsequent decade has been on the coercive state. If I were writing this essay again, I would stress much more the degree to which the state enforces, often quite illiberally, particular outcomes of the distribution process.

Reprinted with permission from Leo Panitch, ed., *The Canadian State: Political Economy and Political Power* (Toronto: University of Toronto Press 1977).

To understand what the state has been and is becoming in Canada it is necessary to understand what Canadians have thought the state to be. To develop a Marxist analysis of the Canadian state it is necessary to understand what the social classes generated by capitalist development have thought the state to be. To those, Marxist and non-Marxist alike, with a vulgar understanding of materialism, these statements may appear paradoxical. They are not at all paradoxical, in truth, but basic and crucial.

It is obvious that Marxist analysis must be made concrete in the historical specificity of particular nations and particular political economies. The mechanical application of concepts drawn exclusively from the European historical experience quickly comes to grief in the North American environment even at the level of economic structures. More importantly, for my purposes, is the fact that historical specificity is a *cultural*, as well as an economic, phenomenon. To analyse the objective economic interests of a class does not automatically lead to a grasp of the actual historical behaviour of that class. The crucial intervening variable is the individual perception by members of that class of their objective interests, as well as their capacity to develop appropriate collective forms of behaviour to achieve concrete objectives set by their conception of their class interests. And it is precisely at this point that cultural, ideological, and political factors assert a certain irreducible autonomy. To argue that the individual's behaviour is merely a reflection of his position in relation to the economic base is altogether unscientific, in the absence of any demonstrated concrete linkages between the base and the behaviour of individuals.

One never sees the world innocently or naïvely. How we interpret the sensory data upon which we base our actions is the product of our past experience; that experience structures and filters what we perceive. Historical specificity resides not only in the particular economic structures thrown up by particular geographic factors, historical timing, technological levels, and world market conditions, but also in the peculiarity and uniqueness of particular cultural mixes – national experiences – which prestructure the perceptions by classes and individuals of the objective economic factors. The point is that an inquiry into the specificity of any particular nation and its unique set of class forces must be approached with a truly open mind; forms of class behaviour cannot be presumed. It is instead necessary to understand the totality of determining factors, cultural, ideological, and political, as well as the material forces (determining in the "last instance" as Louis Althusser puts it[1]), which bear on any specific historical situation.

Hence the quest for "images" or conceptualizations of the state in Canadian historical development, the glass through which Canadians have looked in understanding their collective organization as a nation, their definition and delimitations of the public realm from the private, and the meaning of the public realm for their own, class, interests.

One further theoretical point must be made at the outset. O'Connor's functions of the capitalist state – accumulation and legitimation, along with the coercion function identified by Panitch in the preceding essay – do not lend themselves equally to the same forms of analysis. Coercion is a classical state function, central to the very definition of the state by Max Weber, among others.[2] It is particularly in areas outside the state system as such, in the identification of the coercive nature of market relations of production and in the subjugation of the working class to the exploitation of the labour market, that Marxist analysis diverges strikingly from liberal thinking.[3] The accumulation and legitimation functions require more specific attention.

First, for accumulation: Marxist economic science demonstrates that there is a developmental logic of capitalism and that it is possible to situate specific state activities in relation to that logic. In retrospect it becomes clear that such and such an action did, or did not, contribute to capital accumulation, and thus did, or did not, contribute to the unfolding of the logic of capitalist development in history. In this sense, when examining accumulation, the perceptions of the individual actors are of lesser significance than the actions themselves. To this extent the accumulation function is objective and measurable in quantitative terms. There is another sense in which this breaks down. For example, accumulation policies which fail to maintain business confidence, however irrational that elusive state of mind may be, will undoubtedly fail. Thus subjective consciousness becomes a factor intimately involved in an objective process, objectively measurable.

This is even more pertinent when discussing legitimation. To understand the concept of legitimation one must understand what people *believe to be true*. To understand the legitimation component of the state's interventions, we must deal with motives, beliefs, forms of consciousness, all of which means resorting to historical evidence which is squarely "ideological" in nature – what people said as well as what people did. To push the point further, what people held to be true must be taken with considerable seriousness, not because this is truth in a scientific sense, but quite simply because they believed it to be true, and acted upon it. Finally, it is manifestly impossible to separate the accumulation and legitimation functions into two insulated spheres. It is precisely in the interrelation of these functions that the specificity of the Canadian state may be discerned.

The enterprise I am thus proposing is a type of intellectual history of the successive images or conceptualizations of the state in Canada. It is intellectual history inasmuch as it rests upon articulated statements of historical actors, yet it is, I think, also Marxist to the extent that I situate these intellectual developments within the context of changing class forces and the development of capitalist market structures. Marx himself wrote that man makes his own history, but only with such materials as are at hand. Perhaps Claude Lévi-Strauss has posed the problem best: "The sense in which infrastructures are primary is this: first, man is like a player who, as he takes his place at the table, picks up cards which he has not invented, for the cardgame is a datum of history and civilization. Second, each deal is the result of a contingent distribution of cards, unknown to the players at the time. One must accept the cards which one is given, but each society, like each player, makes its interpretations in terms of several systems. These may be common to them all or individual: rules of the game or rules of tactics. And we are well aware that different players will not play the same game with the same hand even though the rules set limits on the games that can be played with any given one."[4]

Canada was in its origins not merely a *new* society, but a *transplanted* society. The so-called "fragment" theory of new societies developed by Louis Hartz and applied to Canada by Gad Horowitz and Kenneth McRae,[5] while hopelessly idealist from a Marxist perspective, does offer some insights into the importance of the inherited ideological legacy, the political baggage, which the founders of the colonies brought with them, whether directly from France, England, or America, or indirectly through the heavily imperialist socialization and educational process in the colonial era. New France, with its feudal and authoritarian structures, protected by the barrier of the French language and the hegemony of the Catholic clergy in educational and cultural matters, diverged from its earliest beginnings in significant ways from the rest of English-speaking North America, a divergence to which the English Conquest gave only a particular form. Yet as early as 1789, with the French Revolution and the triumph of bourgeois and anticlerical forces within the former motherland, Quebec was in many important ways to be isolated from the currents of thought and development in the French-speaking world of Europe. In the English-Canadian colonies, on the other hand, the influence of British culture and ideas, not to speak of the American impact, remained at a surprisingly high level throughout the nineteenth century. Thus in the case of English Canada, to which I intend to devote most of my attention, the images of the state were deeply indebted to the old world, as well as to the new world rising to the south. English Canadians saw themselves most often in borrowed mirrors.

In the English-speaking world of the late eighteenth and nineteenth centuries, the concept of the state was undergoing a major transformation under the combined impact of the political changes released first in the American Revolution and, more importantly, the French Revolution, and then in the Industrial Revolution in England. This change has been seen most characteristically, but not very illuminatingly, in liberal terms: the emancipation of the productive energies of the bourgeoisie from mercantilist economic controls and the remnants of feudal privilege, and the securing of an ever-increasing share of political liberties from the encroachments of autocratic state power. In fact, the triumph of laissez-faire and free-trade ideology in England can now be seen as the coincidence of classical political economy as a science and the interest of England as the first industrial nation, with everything to gain from maintaining other national competitors in a position of inferiority on the world market. By the late nineteenth century it was becoming apparent that the English concept of the state and its role in national economic life was peculiarly limited and idiosyncratic. Yet the "English model" was itself somewhat less monolithic from the beginning than standard liberal treatments might lead us to believe. Indeed, an important variant in the English tradition was of unusual importance in Canada in helping to shape the ultimate Canadian rejection of free trade and laissez-faire as the defining image of the state. That variant has been most often termed "Toryism."

The concept of the state as it emerged in the era of political and industrial revolution was always bound up with two other concepts, sometimes openly but more often, in England, surreptitiously; *nation* and *class*. In historical retrospect the French Revolution may as importantly mark the emergence of modern nationalism and the centralizing features of nationalist sentiment as it did the emergence of radical democratic and egalitarian ideas. The sweeping away of local particularisms by the centralist nationalism of the Jacobins and Napoleon, and the burst of political and military energies unleashed in this process, rearranged the map of Europe and set change and renovation in motion everywhere it touched. The power of the *nation-state*, the integral identity of the cultural, linguistic, and ethnic community with the apparatus of a centralized state with its unified political, economic, and military arms, was posed as an un-answerable challenge to the ramshackle edifice of particularisms which was the Europe of the time. But if the integration of the concepts of the state and the nation emerged from the French Revolution, so too did the concept of class conflict and the challenge from the dominated classes to the established order. This challenge, still somewhat diffuse and inarticulate in revolutionary France, took concrete form in England with the creation of a working class in the factories of the Industrial Revolution and the growth of indigenous working-class organizations to defend and advance the interests of workers within a capitalist system which enforced wage-slavery upon all who were compelled to sell their own labour power to the profit of the owners of industry. The appearance of class conflict, as a structural contradiction of capitalist society, posed the question of *whose* nation and *whose* state?

Despite the hegemony of laissez-faire liberalism in England in the nineteenth century, the Tory tradition differed significantly over the very questions of nation and class. Common ground within the English-speaking world lay in the fundamental distinction made since at least the seventeenth century between *society* and *state*. "Society" was not necessarily the same as "nation," but was a broader concept including the economic relations, social institutions such as church and school, and even elements of the legal system, such as common law and prescriptive rights such as *habeas corpus*. All of these were set against the concept of the state, which was a narrower construct involving the government – monarch, lords, and commons – and the administration. This distinction took concrete form in the American constitution, embodying as it did the concept that the people (society) contracted to form a government (state) while reserving for themselves certain rights which were to remain beyond the reach of the state thus created. This state-society dichot-omy tended to distinguish the English-speaking world from that of the European continent, where the idea of the state as the summa-tion of the economic, social, cultural, as well as political, spheres was more generally prevalent, as is best exemplified in the universal homogenous state in the thought of Hegel. In the English-speaking world, universalism gave way to more individualist and even particularist conceptions of man-versus-the-state.

Yet an emphasis on individualism and particularity left open a considerable range of controversy concerning the question of the linkage between the individual interest and the national interest. There is a sense in which the chief problematic in the confrontation between liberalism and Toryism in the nineteenth century lay in this question. To good liberals, schooled in the Manchester mode of classical political economy, there was the miraculous intervention of the invisible hand of the market mechanism which meshed individual and national interest into a seamless web of economic progress and political stability – so long as the state maintained strictly defined limits of activity. Tories were, to be sure, no less admirers of the market or of the capitalist mode of production; England, after all, had witnessed a smoother transition from aristocracy to bourgeoisie than most European countries were to enjoy, the transition taking the form of class merger which turned traditional conservatism into market conservatism. But what did distinguish Toryism was a less than automatic reliance on the ability of the market to regulate the society without a certain discretionary role for the state.

Moreover, while liberalism experienced no end of trouble with the concept of *class* in an era when liberal thought underwent a subtle change towards more liberal-democratic forms under the pressure of rising working-class demands, leaving unsolved a fundamental contradiction between the political values tending towards egalitarianism and the economic values of the market which were ineradicably inegalitarian,[6] Tory thinking tended to skirt this problem by a more open acceptance of the concept of inequality as a positive political value as well as an economic necessity. Rooted in the older feudal past of hierarchy and the authoritative allocation of roles in society, Tories tended to be much more explicitly in favour of class inequality as an end as well as a means. Liberals were more ambivalent and, in a sense, more deceptive about the inequality of capitalism. Hence the bad faith in which a thoughtful liberal like John Stuart Mill attempted to rationalize the subordination of the working class, a subordination which unsettled his conscience even as it spurred his apologetics.

On the question of the *nation*, liberals were again more ambivalent than Tories. Certainly the English nation was the forum or framework within which capitalist development took place, and liberalism became a sort of national ideology of a triumphant industrial England selling its high-priced manufactured goods in world markets. Yet at the same time free trade and laissez-faire did have certain internationalist implications, and there was one school of thought which saw the market as a kind of universal solvent of human differences.[7] Tories, again rooted in a more particularist past, were inclined to view the English nation as the highest stage of political development, a fusion of the social and economic hierarchy with the cultural particularity of the English language and English traditions.

It is easy to generalize too far about differences which were not always classifiable into polar camps. But the central area of contention – the question of the linkage between individual and national interest – was a serious problem of a market society, about which the bourgeoisie itself could readily disagree without in any sense calling into question the capitalist mode of production. The Tory view, reflecting the persistence of aristocratic, pre-industrial elements, with its emphasis on the need for more conscious order and control over the processes of a market society, was rather easily dismissed in the nation which experienced the first Industrial Revolution amid the sundering of the older mercantilist restrictions on trade and anachronistic feudal residues in legislation and custom. When Mill termed the Tories the "stupid party," he only echoed much respectable opinion among his educated countrymen. But in the transfer of cultural and political baggage to the British North American colonies, Toryism found an environment in which, rather paradoxically considering the absence of a feudal past, it was to play a more important role as a legitimizing ideology of capitalist development than it ever did in its English homeland. In colonial Canada, both inherited Tory images and the learned experience of development in the peculiar circumstances of that time and place led to a domination of the Tory image of the state over the more liberal laissez-faire concept prevalent in the imperial metropolis.

The first and perhaps most crucial point to be made is that in English Canada, and particularly in Upper Canada, which was to play the most dynamic role in national development well into the twentieth century, the bourgeoisie was not a class which emerged out of a struggle with feudalism and then recreated the world in its own image in the aftermath of its triumph, as had happened in Europe; the emergence of the bourgeoisie was instead itself the result of a conscious policy or plan, enacted through the agency of the imperial and colonial state apparatuses. The indigenous roots of the Canadian bourgeoisie were from the beginning linked closely to the imperialist-mercantilist framework which nurtured the exotic plant in new soil. The history of colonial Canada may be seen as an interaction of a series of plans, dreams, and prefabricated "societies" with the realities of the actual human and economic resources which alone could give concrete shape to these blueprints. As Gilles Paquet has written: "In fact the word 'dream' catches one of the basic ingredients of Canadian economic development. Canada has been significantly influenced in its evolution by a series of 'dreams' ... by a long list of these magnificent projects and ideas, many of which also proved magnificent failures."[8]

The point which needs emphasizing at a time when everyone – from popular historians of the "national dream" to self-proclaimed progressives who laud the "public enterprise" culture of Canada – has done his utmost to mystify the actual tradition of state activity,[9] is that from the earliest beginnings the dreams and plans which were applied to the raw material of British North American society had far more to do with the creation of a viable national bourgeoisie with all its attendant paraphernalia of privilege and luxury than it had to do with a "public sector." In this process the public domain had a role to play, but it was always a decidedly ancillary role.

Not only did the early Loyalist settlers bear with them the usual bitterness of émigrés towards the ideas and symbols of the revolutionary nation from which they had fled – nurturing an anti-Americanism, not to speak of anti-democratic sentiments, which were to remain persistent features of Canadian political life – but this basic strain was consolidated and encouraged by the ideological mission of the Colonial Office. As S.F. Wise has strikingly demonstrated, the new generation of colonial administrators following the American and French revolutions represented a new hardened and rationalized conservatism.[10] Faced with the radical and democratic implications of the French Revolution in particular, English opinion turned sharply rightward, especially during the Napoleonic wars when a blanket of McCarthyite-type conformism and anti-revolutionary zeal settled over political debate. The colonial administrators came to Canada armed with a mission to build a conservative, un-American, and undemocratic society in the northern half of the continent. In this mission the conservatism of Edmund Burke, who had alerted the opinion of right-thinking Englishmen, noble and bourgeois alike, to the dangers inherent in the revolutionary enterprise in Paris as early as 1790, proved to be a most valuable resource.

To understand the power of Burkean conservatism, it is first necessary to disabuse oneself of much conventional nonsense on the subject. Burke was in no sense a traditionalist who harked back to a defunct feudal past. On the contrary, it was Burke whom Adam Smith singled out as the only man to have come independently to the same conclusions about the workings of the market economy as Smith himself. Indeed, Burke was a Malthusian enthusiast for the abolition of all state charity and the final triumph of the "great wheel of commerce" as the sole organizing principle of economic life.[11] But Burke also quickly discerned the inherent contradiction concerning liberty and equality concealed within the assumptions of market society, and became the most influential opponent of the egalitarian and democratic tendencies within the French experiment in liberal revolution. Burke's solution to the dilemma was to resurrect the idea of traditional authority ("the bank and capital of nations and of ages") as a kind of shell, within which the new subordination of wage-labourer to employer would be masked by the customary subordination of peasant to lord ("the coat of prejudice" as Burke, nicely put it).[12] Although Burke himself was rarely quoted directly, it was the spirit of his rationalized, hard-nosed philosophy with its fusion of market liberalism and anti-democratic conservatism which served early colonial Canada as a blueprint for the nature of the society to be created.

The "better America" to be erected to the north of the United States would be one which pursued economic growth with all the enthusiasm of market man unbound by tradition, yet at the same time sought, as a positive goal of public policy, the creation of a hierarchical society where privilege was resistant to the demands of those less fortunate. The "state," such as it was, would be an instrument of economic development, understood always as both the growth of production and the consequent differentiation of society into classes specializing in the different aspects of the productive process, with vastly differentiated rewards. The conventional wisdom of the colonial administrators and the dominant local forces in strictly political terms was the so-called balanced Whig constitution of the eighteenth century, with its division of power between monarch, lords, and commons. In fact, it quickly became apparent that, given the "immaturity" of the frontier population, the subordination of the colony to Britain, and the thinness of local "aristocracy," the balanced Whig constitution would turn out to be rather unbalanced in the direction of the executive. Upper Canada thus began its constitutional history in an atmosphere of considerable executive authority, buttressed by deep ideological hostility to the principle of popular representation and the urgent sense of a need to create a dominant class of privilege and power to which colonial interests could be entrusted. In the blank slate of North American frontier development, this obviously meant a bourgeoisie without any particular stamp of tradition or birth – capital and wealth alone would be its emblem. In the particular circumstances of Canada it further meant a bourgeoisie which would be parasitic upon the colonial state apparatus from which its privileges arose. It was a peculiar combination.

Land distribution policy was a major instrument in the implementation of this Burkean blueprint. Land was, of course, at this time the chief economic resource of a frontier colony and the chief attraction to draw immigration from Europe. Both the reservation of extensive tracts of land to the clergy (as a means of providing an economic base for an established church which would act as an authoritative centre of control over moral and educational development) and the attempt to maintain artificially high land prices (to help create a landed bourgeoisie), had the long-range goal of creating a landless proletariat which would have to sell its wage labour to the nascent bourgeoisie. As Marx pointed out in refutation of the land theories of Gibbon Wakefield, a figure of some significance in colonial Canadian thinking, the necessity of colonial regimes to intervene in the land market to keep the lower orders landless was "the secret discovered in the new world by the Political Economy of the old world, and proclaimed on the house-tops: that the capitalist mode of production and accumulation, and therefore capitalist private property, have for their fundamental condition the annihilation of self-earned private property; in other words, the expropriation of the labourer."[13] Proclaiming the secret from the house-tops was an activity quite congenial to the dominant Tory figures in the colony who never made much attempt to hide their design for creating hierarchy and preventing equality. But shouting does not in itself achieve the purpose. The land scheme turned out to be one of the failed social blueprints, of which there were to be many more. The intractably mobile nature of the population, the inability to control a factor of production as abundant as land in the new world, the failure of the emergent bourgeoisie to provide employment for landless labourers, and not least the decided tendency of the privileged "aristocrats" to turn land into a quick and easy source of profit by selling their landed interests to the highest bidder, all contributed to the early demise of the entire scheme, as it was at first envisioned.[14]

By the 1820s and 1830s there had emerged in Upper Canada a locally based ruling clique attached to the state apparatus. The Family Compact was a summation of both economic and political power in the rudimentary forms in which these elements appeared. By no means lacking in political talent, in the person of such conservative operatives as Bishop Strachan (the Richelieu of colonial clerical politics) and John Beverley Robinson, the Family Compact was not averse to economic enterprise, especially of an infrastruc-

tural nature such as the Welland Canal project or the Bank of Upper
Canada. Despite the romanticizations of liberal and left-wing
historians, the unanswerable fact remains that the Tories were able
to mobilize popular sentiment and votes just as often as their opponents. The image of the Family Compact as an unpopular minority foisting itself upon a hostile mass of citizenry simply does not fit
the facts. Toryism had roots in the population; the Tory image of the
state had resonance and persistence, not simply among the ranks of
the privileged but among the poorer citizenry as well. The emergence of a ruling alliance of political and administrative notables
with nascent mercantile and commercial capital, the latter dependent
upon the former and often synonymous with them, with widespread popular support from below, whether based on ethnic-
religious identification – as in the case of the Irish Protestants
mobilized into the Orange Lodges – or on a deferential interpretation of economic self-interest, all begin to give flesh and blood to a
type of Tory hierarchical society which, while different from the
original blueprint, was nevertheless strikingly divergent from the
American model.

Toryism thus demonstrated a kind of Hamiltonian model of
national economic development, within an imperialist framework, at
the very time when Hamiltonianism was crumbling under the
assaults of laissez-faire capitalist development in the United States.
Politically, moreover, the Tory model specifically called for a state
apparatus and a governmental superstructure which would directly
reflect the inegalitarian social structure which capitalist development
was slowly consolidating, in sharp contrast to the rise of Jeffersonian and later Jacksonian democracy to the south.

Toryism was not reducible simply to an economic doctrine
masquerading as a philosophy. The Tory mind involved certain
elements which fitted it well for the exercise of national economic
development, even while undermining the effectiveness of Tories in
industrial Britain. The emphasis on *control* of the processes of
national development, the element of the collective will of the
dominant class expressed through the public institutions of the state,
while seemingly anachronistic in an increasingly laissez-faire Britain,
was crucially relevant to a thinly settled frontier colony struggling
on the fringes of a growing economic and political power to the
south. A quotation from a letter written by Bishop Strachan in 1830
on the subject of an established church perhaps indicates best the
quality of this Tory paternalist mission: "In regard to Christianity, it
may be remarked, that the spontaneous demand of human beings
for a knowledge of its truths, is far short of the actual interest which

they have in them ... it is just as necessary to create a hunger as it is to minister a positive supply ... Nature does not go forth in search of Christianity, but Christianity goes forth to knock at the door of nature, and, if possible, to awaken her out of her sluggishness."[15] In short, Toryism began with an acceptance of man's fallen nature which led to a type of activism on the part of national leaders to counteract this entropic nature by control and direction. It is in the will and purpose of the leading elements that the state and the nation find definition.

The emergence of a ruling group around certain privileged economic interests was bound to rouse the opposition of elements which felt excluded from the process. The fact that opposition reached such proportions by 1837 that an attempted revolution was mounted is certainly evidence of discontent. Yet the rapid and, it must be said, somewhat ignoble collapse of the "revolutionary" forces points in another direction, one which sits very poorly with the current revisionist school of left-wing nationalist history. The class base of the grouping led by William Lyon Mackenzie and his associates is not easily placed within a simple framework of social conflict. Small property-holding farmers and landless elements from the towns and villages employed as artisans or labourers appear to have made up the ranks. Yet these class elements themselves were drawn from the larger population in a somewhat complicated manner. Cross-cutting cleavages of religion and ethnicity, not to speak of locality, do little to clarify the picture. An examination of the ideas with which the rebels armed themselves results in yet more confusion. Mackenzie himself, now a hero of the nationalist left, managed to lead a strike-breaking cartel of employers against an attempt by his own printers at his newspaper to organize themselves, as well as to call for the virtual annexation of Canada to the United States in 1838. In fact, the ideological incoherence of Mackenzie is such that, like Thomas Jefferson, he can be quoted every which way on every issue. It would not be difficult, although scarcely illuminating, to devote an entire volume to selections of his writings which would create an image of his thought altogether opposite to that put forward by some currently fashionable selections.[16] At best one may surmise both from Mackenzie himself, and from some of the popular resolutions and other documents which emerged at the time of the rebellion, that the radicalism of Upper Canada centred around a Jeffersonian subspecies of laissez-faire, based on a perception of a simple market economy of independent commodity producers striving for self-sufficiency but ensnared in the meshes of financial and merchant capital and the privileges of those whose class positions allowed them close association with the state apparatus. There were indeed powerful reasons for making such a case. The fundamental basis of any rejection of Tory capitalist hegemony in the new colony would naturally rest on the one significant class force whose interests could not be accommodated within the projected scheme of economic and class development: the independent family farmers, who made up the vast bulk of the colonial population and who were the crucial factor in the colonial mode of production, which was mainly agricultural.

To the extent that 1837 represented the first and most violent confrontation between the grande bourgeoisie and the petite bourgeoisie, it set the tone for a century of class conflict in English Canada. Mechanical replications of particular European class struggles tend to miss the specificity of this peculiarly North American situation.[17] The frontier theory of North American development has long since disclosed its limitations, but an emphasis on the frontier does point to one crucial factor for Marxist analysis: the development in a context where land was inevitably cheap and labour inevitably dear – at least by European standards – of a mode of production reliant on the family farm as a productive unit and thus on the farmers as the most significant subordinate class. Ideologically, this class confrontation took on a form which was altogether different from the European experience. Since the struggle was mainly different *forms* of property rather than between the propertied and the unpropertied, the complexities of ideological conflict are particularly difficult to disentangle.

More importantly, one may distinguish a crucial and profound ambiguity in the world-view of the farmer, derived directly from the ambiguity of his class position as both proprietor of his own means of production and the source of the labour required for production. The farmer in a sense combined the class antagonists of capitalism within his own person. To the colonial farmer this ambiguity was manifested in his vulnerability to the money economy and the penetrative power of financial and mercantile capital over his simple market society. From the beginnings of colonial agricultural production, the credit market was a factor tending towards class conflict. Farmers were more often than not debtors. The money economy was thus the fatal flaw in the idealized image of the yeoman colony. Paper currency, manipulated by a shadowy and privileged class of finance capitalists, was a mechanism whereby the fruits of the labour of independent farmers were appropriated by idle speculators and predatory pseudo-aristocrats. An obsessive concern with currency questions has always been a characteristic of petit-bourgeois radicalism in this country. When Mackenzie's draft constitution for an independent Upper Canada included a clause forbidding mercantile and banking corporations, this in a sense summed up the strivings of independent commodity producers attempting, albeit in a mystified manner, to gain full control over the conditions of their own production within a restored simple market economy.[18]

Yet to the extent that it was financial capital and the state, rather than capitalism itself, which they identified as the enemy, the farmers could never hope to control the real forces which held them in thrall. Witness the débâcle in the United States, where the Jacksonian Democrats destroyed the Bank of the United States – a Hamiltonian fusion of economic power and political privilege – under the banner of hard currency theories and petit-bourgeois resentments, only to bring about the proliferation of state banks whose inflationary paper currencies not only contributed to destabilizing business cycles but formed the basis for the triumph of unchecked speculative capitalism. Mackenzie himself, in American exile following the defeat of 1837–8, conceived a strong revulsion against the face which Jacksonian democracy presented by the 1840s. The point is that the farmers were confused, and that their confusion arose more from their class position than from their own tactical mistakes. This ambiguity is further demonstrated by the weakness of the revolutionary mobilization, and the deep cleavages which ran through the subordinate class. In Lower Canada, the reinforcement of ethnicity and culture transformed the struggle into a much more serious patriotic upheaval of the French against their English conquerors. In Upper Canada the lines were not drawn so clearly, and in the absence of a "national" struggle by a local mercantile elite against restrictive imperial controls over commerce – as had happened in the Thirteen Colonies to the south in 1776 – class confrontation which would transform the political economy could not take shape. In the Maritime colonies there was not even a movement, let alone an actual armed struggle. Toryism emerged triumphant from Canada's one near-revolutionary situation.

The triumph of Toryism in Lower Canada meant the defeat of liberal French-Canadian nationalism and the reconfirmation of the reactionary elites which had dominated Quebec society in alliance with the Tory merchants and the British administrative class. It also meant a reconfirmation of the tacit bargain struck between these English and French elites following the Conquest, whereby economic development was left to the English capitalists and the spheres of culture and education were left to the Catholic church, which could be expected to preach political quietism and a safe inward-looking cultural nationalism that left the structures of English economic and administrative power untouched. More specifically, this bargain contributed to a long-standing distrust of the state among the Quebec masses. Given the identification of Quebec nationalism with political reaction, the state would appear in two contradictory guises: either it was an instrument for the maintenance of English power and oppression, or if it fell into the hands of the French Canadians it could do no more than protect the place of those non-state institutions, particularly the church, whose task was to preserve French culture and identity. In neither case could the state have a positive role in directing the society; it could never be a vehicle for the collective realization of popular national goals. On the other hand, the merchant class of Montreal saw the state confirmed as an instrument for their conquest of the "empire of the St Lawrence."

In Upper Canada, the defeat of the rebellion once again demonstrated the power of conservative elitism, although in this case an elitism which had stronger popular roots than the English upper class of Quebec. The emergent concept of the state was one in which accumulation took priority, since the forces which had directed their energies towards the goal of capitalist development around the state as an instrument had been victorious. The Reform demand for economy in government with its somewhat Jeffersonian image of that government which governs least governing best had been expelled from the political stage. In its place was an ideology which benevolently gazed upon the distribution of special privileges, pay-offs, and other forms of corruption, through the instrumentality of the state, to the emergent capitalist interests as a means to accumulation. In one sense, accumulation was legitimation. The two functions cannot be separated in the nineteenth century. The Tory triumph also involved a great deal of secondary non-economic legitimation as well: British loyalty, the identification of conservative elitism as British, and reform as American and hence treasonous. Toryism moveover was illiberal: the state under Tory auspices would be willing to practise coercion at a high level. Indeed, there is a Hobbesian flavour about the Tory notion of the state and the nature of state sovereignty. The power of Toryism was such that there has always been a distinctly Hobbesian flavour to the English-Canadian concept of the state as well. Certainly the readiness of the Canadian state to exercise illiberal powers – as witness the War Measures Act – has deep roots in early colonial history.

This state, focused on accumulation, would play a central role in continental economic development, but the border between the state system and the political system in Miliband's terms, is exceedingly difficult to draw in this period. The personnel of the state and the personnel of capitalist enterprise were often enough the same. Public office and private profit were two sides of the same phenomenon. One need go no further than Gustavus Myer's *History of Canadian Wealth* to discover how difficult it was to disentangle the "public" from the "private" spheres. Given the task of creating a national bourgeoisie, this state of affairs is scarcely surprising. Yet to the extent that such a bourgeoisie was actually developing, a certain amount of differentiation and specialization of labour may be discerned. In the light of Miliband's maxim that in capitalist societies the ruling class rules but does not govern, Canadian experience is paradoxical. While the state was helping bring to birth an indigenous economic ruling class, the state itself was slowly becoming a branch of this same bourgeoisie. In his study of pre-Confederation Canadian bureaucracy, J.E. Hodgetts points out that the leading state personnel in the persons of ministers of the Crown were mainly lawyers by profession. Journalists and businessmen were a poor second. Businessmen were too dogmatic and self-righteous to be successful in politics: "the businessman was not embarrassed by his dogmas but clung to them with such tenacity that he was distrusted, even ridiculed, by the lawyers who always outnumbered him in the cabinet. The businessman was always convinced that the problems facing Canada could be easily solved by the application of a few standard policies ... The subtleties and subterfuges of the legal brotherhood who largely dominated the political scene were beyond his comprehension. He did not understand that in Canadian politics the shortest distance between two points is not a straight line."[19]

The point is hardly that the state was neutral or independent of business, but rather that there was a functional division of labour involved. At the same time lawyers in politics often used their state positions to gain entry into the higher levels of the bourgeoisie. Moreover, in examining this specialist role for the state in economic life it is important not to mistake the appearance for the substance. The state as such was far too poorly organized, far too ridden with political patronage and inefficiency, and far too enmeshed with the private sector, to allow for an autonomous role in direct economic activity. Instead, the state offered an instrumentality for facilitating capital accumulation in private hands, and for carrying out the construction of a vitally necessary infrastructure; for providing the Hobbesian coercive framework of public order and enforcement of contract within which capitalist development could alone flourish; and, finally, for communicating the symbols of imperial legitimacy which reinforced the legitimacy of unlimited appropriation in a small number of private hands. The basic engine of development in Canada was to be private enterprise, but it was to be *private enterprise at public expense*. That is the unique national feature of our Tory tradition.

The hegemony of mercantile and financial capital after 1837 did not enjoy a serene reign. Most important, the British were in the very process of abandoning their colonial agents. The campaign against the Corn Laws and the victory of free trade was a devastating blow for the Montreal merchants, as they watched the entire mercantile imperialist framework being casually torn to shreds by the motherland itself. Moreover, the gradual growth of responsible government and the continued resistance of the French-Canadian representatives in the legislature of the united Canadas to assimilation meant that the internal position of Toryism was weakening at the same time. When the Baldwin-Lafontaine Reform ministry was called to office after winning a majority in an election, it was the Tory merchants of Montreal who in 1849 rioted and burned the legislative buildings. They then demonstrated their deep allegiance to the British Empire by seeking annexation to the United States.

Despite the apparently darkening horizon, the merchants protested too much. Neither the abandonment of protection by Britain nor the acceptance of responsible government meant the end of capitalist domination. North American colonies when ethnic deadlock in the united Canadas, military fear of the United States, and, above all, the crisis in the capital this time as a modernized version of the old party with strong popular roots both in English Protestant Canada and in French Catholic Quebec. Perhaps the best single characterization of the Macdonald Conservative party is that of Frank Underhill: "government of the people, by lawyers, for big business."[20] In any event, it was this party, and its traditional Tory concept of the state, which emerged as the instrument of confederation of the British North American colonies when ethnic deadlock in the united Canadas, military fear of the United States and, above all, the crisis in the capital markets which demanded a consolidation of all the colonial debts and a political framework which could guarantee future British investments, together called for a fundamental reconstruction of the colonial situation.

The major features of the British North America Act which bear on the shape of the federal state are as follows. The federation was to be highly centralized, in contrast with the United States which had just experienced a civil war. In this connection almost all important economic powers were given to the federal government, as well as all important sources of revenue. Its major role was to provide economic infrastructure, especially railways. The federal government would in addition have significant constitutional superiority over the provincial governments, including the right to veto provincial legislation. The economics-culture trade-off with French Canada was consolidated in the new Confederation. The recognition that there would be two languages and two cultures had important implications for the concept of the Canadian state. The federal government, as the instrument of national development, was primarily concerned with economics; Canadian nationalism, as such, would be economic nationalism more than any other kind of nationalism. The BNA Act gave official form to a fact which had already been accepted in practice: the Canadian state and the Canadian nation were not one and the same.

The weakness of the instruments of national power may be seen in another way. The manner in which the BNA Act was passed speaks volumes about the political legitimacy of the new "nationality." There was, of course, no democratic or popular authority. Canadians never expressed their preferences in the matter; indeed any recourse to popular ratification was assiduously avoided. Only in the province of New Brunswick was there anything like a referendum on Confederation and here the Confederationists lost. This expression of popular will was promptly ignored. There were no "we, the people" as the authors of state sovereignty. Instead, the BNA Act was an act of the British Parliament, passed on the advice of a small elite of colonial politicians. In fact, the overwhelming bulk of these colonial politicians were strikingly anti-democratic in sentiment, viewing democracy as an American heresy. Macdonald perhaps summed up best the conventional wisdom of the dominant political elites with his clever aphorism that "the rights of the minority ought to be protected, and the rich are always fewer in number than the poor."[21] The basic source of authority and legitimacy for the new nation was to be found in the traditional Tory notion of historic continuity with the British Crown. While the Americans had founded a new nationality out of a revolution against the Crown on behalf of popular sovereignty, there would be no such break in Canada. In striking contrast to the Lockean declaration of "life, liberty, and the pursuit of happiness" as the inalienable rights for which Americans had rebelled against tyranny, the BNA Act in its general grant of powers to the federal government spoke instead in authentically Hobbesian terms of "peace, order, and good government."

The political working-out of the constitutional arrangements of Confederation was entrusted to Macdonald's Tory party. To Macdonald a near one-party state would be the best device for integrating the provinces into this heavily centralized system.[22] Patronage, under the personal direction of the prime minister in Ottawa, would be the instrument for building an integrated Tory party and the latter would be the instrument for channelling energies and interests towards the national state. The old Tory notion of a strong central authority linking the private self-interest of the wealthiest and most influential citizens with the national interest would thus be accommodated within the federal state operated by the Conservative party.

The first phase of this plan was the political unification of the colonies. The second, economic, phase was inaugurated with the National Policy of 1878–9. Within a world context of growing challenge to the domination of Britain, which about this time was assuming the form of tariff protection and extensive government activity in Prussia and France, Canada openly broke with British free-trade dogma under a protectionist national development plan which saw the sponsorship of an east-west economy linked by a national railway, industrialization being protected by tariffs, with a captive market in the western prairie hinterland which would provide foreign exchange through wheat exports. Political patronage, pay-offs, and corruption were all central parts of this strategy. For example, tariffs were raised in response to campaign fund donations from manufacturers, thus linking party and state in a single development strategy.

The National Party represented a clear rejection of liberal laissez-faire in two important senses. The refusal to accept the free-trade dogma of Manchester liberalism was predicated on the grounds of national interest. Macdonald had read and rejected the ideas of the classical political economists. Tories were never in fact sycophantic to liberal Britain when the interests of the Canadian bourgeoisie conflicted with those of the capitalists of the imperialist metropole. A strategy for the industrial development of an emerging economy could not be based on free trade; even the United States had adopted protectionism. Second, the Tories rejected the Victorian liberal conception of public morality, intimately bound up with the notion of the strictly delimited state. To the Grits, the Tories were the "corruptionists." A case can be made that to Macdonald corruption was not so much an end in itself but a means to an end, that of national development. Corruption served the function of accumulation.

The Tory state was thus tinged by peculiarities of the Tory tradition, the strengths of which may help to explain the extraordinary success of that party throughout the late nineteenth century. There was a significant strain within the Liberal party which saw the world as a grim Newtonian universe of inexorable laws, mainly derived from the Manchester school of the dismal science of economics. To Macdonald it was rather a universe of contingencies, one in which men could make their own history, in defiance of the "inevitable" laws of historic development. It was that element of will and purpose which perhaps commended Macdonald to the electors of a developing nation.

The system which Macdonald helped create was given its ultimate compliment when the Liberals under Laurier assumed national office in 1896: they simply took it over and in fact made it work better than it ever had under the Conservatives. World conditions happened to be more encouraging at this time, and the Liberals benefited from this happy circumstance to extend the National Policy into a wider imperialist framework, with an imperial preference system as an added inducement to industries to locate in Canada in order to sell to the extensive hinterland regions of the empire under preferential rates. By the turn of the century such was the extent of the industrialization and prosperity that Laurier could echo a mood of naïve national confidence: "the twentieth century belongs to Canada." A more inept prediction could scarcely be found anywhere in our history.

Although Canada did not dominate the twentieth century, the National Policy was nevertheless a qualified success; it did, however, have some unexpected consequences. As a "national" policy it failed to develop a nationalist basis for the state system. And as a strategy for the consolidation of a secure national bourgeoisie it generated, as a dialectical result of its very success, significant class opposition from the farmers and the emerging working class.

The singularly *economic* basis of the instruments of the new nationality which emerged out of Confederation has already been noted. The forced recognition of French language and cultural autonomy and the accommodative relationships established between the political elites of English and French Canada through the dominant party and the federal cabinet – albeit a very unequal accommodation from the point of view of Quebec, bearing in mind the nature of the tacit bargain struck – involved a central ambiguity in the national definition. But this was only one side of the problem. That the new nation remained in a state of partial subordination to Britain and a part of the British Empire meant that in its external status it was equally indeterminate. The Canadian "nation" was thus curiously indistinct both internally and externally. Yet every attempt to define the nation more clearly in either its internal or external dimensions tended to be decisive.

The first major demands for a new nationality came from the Canada First group. The call for a new identity which would lift the minds of Canadians beyond crass material considerations to a higher cultural plane came mainly from displaced class elements such as artists and intellectuals, many of them attached directly or indirectly to the state apparatus. This later became a major strain of Tory social criticism, amplified into the Imperial Federation movement of the late nineteenth and early twentieth centuries. Again, the leading figures of this movement tended to be those in positions which were "ideological" – ministers, teachers, writers, such as G.M. Grant, George Parkin, and Stephen Leacock. Economic nationalism and the sordid pay-offs associated with it did not excite the imagination of intellectuals, nor did it offer a secure and prestigious place to those who worked with their minds. But when the Imperialists looked to a cultural or national identity above materialism they looked to their Britishness and their place within a world-wide empire.

Their attempt to found a sentimental or cultural nationalism on imperial ties involved a concept of nationalism which could only alienate French Canada. The emphasis on legitimation through the historical tradition of British rule was bad enough, but much worse were the claims for British racial superiority and the celebration of militarism and the longing for war which characterized much of the imperialist writing and agitation.[23] In advocating some form of imperial federation the Imperialists placed Canada within a larger system of sovereignty. Even if, with the misplaced confidence of the time, they may have believed that Canada would one day rival Britain within the empire, this scheme still left the national question in a state of ambiguity. At the same time, the symbols used to raise national sentiment at home were the very symbols calculated to repel French Canadians.

On the other side of the national question in English Canada in this period, the situation was even worse. Goldwin Smith's *Canada and the Canadian Question* (1891) may be taken as the most reasoned expression of the continentalist response to imperialism. Smith was if anything even more racist and anti-French than the imperialists. Indeed, one of the most striking charges he could find against the idea of imperial federation was the inclusion of Anglo-Saxons in a system which teemed with non-whites. Smith's alternative was some form of union with the United States which would finally sink the French Canadians into a powerless minority status and pave the way for an eventual "moral federation" of all the white English-speaking peoples of the world. The Imperialists' overblown sense of the superiority of the British way of life and of British institutions may have blinded them to the advance of American influence through branch-plant investment; Smith positively welcomed the absorption of Canada by the American Empire or at least its reduction to the status of Scotland within the United Kingdom. Neither the imperialist nor the continentalist argument saw Canada as an autonomous and distinctive nation in its own right. What is just as striking is the lack of strongly and consistently argued nationalist positions in this latter sense. Paradoxically enough, the closest one can find to a truly nationalist position in the national debate came from Henri Bourassa, excoriated as a traitor and a seditionist by the self-proclaimed patriots of English Canada during the Boer War and the First World War. Repelled by the anti-French sentiments of his English-Canadian countrymen, he looked to a binational, bilingual political association which would be free of foreign entanglements and divisive external loyalties. Such an association would comprise a federal state system based on a fundamental cultural duality.

What is most interesting about the various schools of thought in the national debate is the underlying structural similarity of almost all the arguments. The *nation* and the *state* were not coterminous concepts in Canadian discourse. The concept of cultural nationality and the concept of political or state sovereignty were distinct and analytically separate. Moreover, the idea of differing cultural nations coexisting under a wider political sovereignty – whether French and English within Confederation, or Canada within a wider empire, or the "moral federation of the English-speaking peoples" – was at the root of most thinking about the national question. Integral nationalism in the European sense, or even in the American sense, in which state sovereignty is synonymous with a single cultural, ethnic, and linguistic nationality, never took decisive shape in this country. The Canadian national state thus lacked one of the most powerful reinforcements known to the modern state – national sentiment and collective cultural identity. What weakened the Canadian state yet further was the fatal trap that every attempt to grasp such a collective definition only drove the internal divisions yet deeper. Even within English Canada itself, the late nineteenth century witnessed a growing regionalism and a drawing-away from national integration under the banner of "provincial rights."

The complex of factors came to a head in the 1911 general election. The defeat of reciprocity and the Liberals by a resurgent Tory imperialist wave of jingoism was aided by the Bourassa *nationalistes* in Quebec, the latter financed with New York money. Six years later there was fighting on the streets of Quebec City when the same Tories, in conjunction with Unionist Liberals, imposed conscription upon an unwilling French population. Tory imperialism created the worst internal crisis in Canada since the Riel affair in the 1880s. At the same time, Bourassa *nationalistes* drove English Canadians to an anti-French fury by their insistence upon the bicultural and bilingual nature of Canada. The political force which finally emerged out of this chaos was the Liberal party led by Mackenzie King who was unswerving in his determination to avoid any political innovation or initiative on the part of the federal state if there were the slightest hint of possible division on English-French lines.

The 1911 election was a watershed in another sense as well. The beginnings of massive class confrontation were manifest in the circumstances of an election in which the manufacturers intervened decisively to defeat an attempt at reciprocity with the United States and to reconfirm the National Policy. The full emergence of a national bourgeoisie, not merely financial and commercial but industrial as well, was indicated by the determined manner in which this class threw its weight behind the Conservatives and drove the suddenly heretical Liberals from office. Yet while its fears were centred around the development of free trade and a north-south pull to the east-west economy of the National Policy, the bourgeoisie was at least equally concerned about the rise of western farmers as a viable and vociferous force of opposition to the hegemony of this central Canadian ruling class. In fact, the defeat of the traditionally free-trade Liberals when they finally attempted a move towards reciprocity after fifteen years in office only demonstrated to the farmers that traditional party politics were hopeless. When Union government in 1917 further demonstrated the sham of party rivalry, the farmers were ready to make an epochal break with the old parties and begin the long tradition to third-party protest politics in this country.

It is important to place these development in some perspective, since so much of the writing on third-party politics has been obscured by the liberal urgency to call these movements "regional" or "protest" or "deviant" – or anything but what they most importantly represented, *class* politics in rejection of the so-called brokerage two-party model. It is also important to realize that the development of class opposition to the national bourgeoisie did not emerge out of nowhere. Rather it emerged from the same process which had created the bourgeoisie itself. The National Policy had envisioned the settling of the prairies and the development of a wheat economy. The creation of a vast agricultural hinterland in the prairies producing a staple export commodity meant the creation of a large concentrated farm population engaged in similar activity with similar interests – the latter distinctly at variance with those of the central Canadian bourgeoisie who wished to exploit the hinterland for its staple crop and for its captive, tariff-protected market for the finished manufactured goods of industrial central Canada. Moreover, to the extent that central Canada – and its hinterland satellites like the mini-metropolis of Winnipeg – did industrialize, at the same time an industrial working class was created which would inevitably develop forms of class consciousness to call the dominant values of the capitalists into question, as well as challenge their interests directly through trade union organization and action. If the Canadian bourgeoisie did not exactly dig its own grave it certainly gave shovels to its opposition. None of this is, of course, in any way surprising from a Marxist perspective. But the elements were worked out in a unique way within the specificity of the Canadian political economy in the peculiar circumstance of historical timing.

The first point is to reiterate the importance of the independent commodity producer class as the major opposition force at this historical conjuncture. Urbanization was steadily cutting into the dominance of rural over urban and agricultural over blue-collar occupations in the labour force. Ironically, at the very moment when the farmers burst on the political scene as an organized force at the end of the First World War, they were just dipping below the urban labour force as the leading sector. Indeed, in Ontario, where rural depopulation had become a major concern to the farming sector, the United Farmers of Ontario came to office in 1919 as the representatives of a class whose back was pushed to the wall and which was fighting back out of desperation – a familiar enough role for petit-bourgeois elements in Europe, often with pernicious connections to fascism and authoritarian movements. But this obscures the fact that on the western prairies the farmers were not being pushed into the cities but were the leading class element uniting an entire region around grievances of a colonial nature vis-à-vis the dominant external forces of central Canada. Particularly in the West, the farmers developed a remarkably lucid and wide-ranging ideology which represented their specific class position. The same arguments suggested earlier in this essay, for the particular position developed by independent commodity producers who idealize a simple market type of economy in which the owner-operated farm is the model of property relations, remain valid for this most fertile period of farmers' movements. Besides the characteristic obsession with monetary control by bankers and financial capital over lands and equipment, which gave a mighty thrust to the emergence of Social Credit as an expression of the farmer ideology by the 1930s, there was by now an additional element: demands for the collective control – either through co-operative enterprise or by state owner-ship – of the various factors intervening between the farmer and the marketing of his staple product, that is, grain elevators, railways, grain exchanges, and the tariff structure.

The farmers' movements also developed a political theory of far greater ideological coherence than that of the farmers' revolts of 1837. The political theory was in fact radically divergent from that of the dominant forces in Canadian life, which had used representa-tive and parliamentary governmental institutions to divide and mystify the subordinate classes. The farmers' attack on the party system was an attack on all the instruments which distorted direct democratic expression. Such ideas as initiatives, referenda, and recalls were innovative devices to short-circuit the manipulation of government by wealth and influence. Moreover, the farmers looked beyond this to a form of group government which would replace cabinet groupings. The farmers, due to their unique position as owners of their means of production and as workers of their own fields, had, it was widely believed, a special role to play in bringing about class co-operation between capital and labour. The weakness of this theory arose just as certainly from its class origins as did the strengths. The failure to understand the dynamics of the world capitalist system and the inevitable penetration of the power of monopoly capital into the simple market economy of the western farmer left them helpless before the onslaught of corporate might. Yet their own position prevented them from becoming radical opponents of capitalism as such. They were, after all, themselves property-owners, however small. Their insistence on co-operation as a means as well as an end and their fundamental hostility to a disciplined party as the arm of the movement rendered them politically impotent in the face of the continuing partisan coherence of the Liberal and Conservative parties.

As economic development and class differentiation continued apace, new elements entered the political stage in loose alliance with the farmers. The specialization of the professions led to a new middle stratum. Many of the professionals, particularly lawyers, doctors, and engineers, played a role which was largely ancillary to and supportive of the hegemony of capital. But there were also elements, particularly to be found among the teachers and preachers, whose ambiguous class position, suspended between the dominant bourgeoisie which had associated itself with all the symbols of the "cultural heritage" and the people whom they served on a day-to-day basis, left them in a state of ideological ambivalence. Although many continued to play the traditional role of agents of political socialization and bourgeois hegemony, there were a few who became loose, agitational elements, ideological leaven in an already fluid situation. The Social Gospel movement, with roots in English Methodism, became a vehicle for the expression of radical, sometimes even anti-capitalist, sentiment. The Social Gospel was the dominant ideological hegemony of capitalism turned upside-down. Instead of individual salvation and political quiescence, Social Gospellers preached social salvation and political activism. Instead of turning the attention of the poor towards the afterlife, Social Gospellers turned them to this life and its tasks. Social work, social science, and social engineering were the staples of this movement, within which they may be discerned the germ of the social-democratic image of the "social service state," an apparatus operated by technical experts motivated by a desire to do good and tuned to the amelioration of the conditions of modern life.

At the same time, there were deep contradictions embedded within the Social Gospel ideology, which reflected deep contradictions in its social base. Both its strength and its weakness came from its fusion of cultural conservatism and political radicalism. Nowhere is this contradiction more manifest than in the feminist movement which was closely associated with Social Gospel preaching. Nellie McClung's feminism arose directly out of a wholehearted acceptance of the Victorian image of woman as more "spiritual" and "civilizing" than the male; she turned this image upside-down and argued that if women were indeed morally superior they should be allowed to vote and take a leading role in political life in order to elevate the debased standards set by men. Since the movement touched on all the fundamental symbols of ideological hegemony – Christianity, the family, motherhood – but gave them a radical twist, there was a certain difficulty in confronting the challenge; yet, by the same token, the challenge was self-limiting. This cultural conservatism made it difficult for the early feminists in Canada to theorize the sexual liberation of women as well as to their political enfranchisement. Given the vote, women simply drifted back into familial and maternal quietude. Moreover, the Social Gospel, always a minority movement within Christianity, was never able to free itself from a contradiction inherent in Christianity itself: the confusion between social reformation (possibly eventuating in socialism) and moral reformation of the individual (most often taking the form of an idiosyncratic obsession with the prohibition of alcohol). Finally, the weak class position of the Social Gospel, its base in the middle-class professions, left it extremely vulnerable to changes in the more important class confrontations. When the farmers' movements dissipated themselves and labour radicalism declined in the 1920s, the Social Gospel underwent a prolonged deterioration. Marginal middle-class elements were not enough to sustain a major radical confrontation of the established order. In this sense the Social Gospel movement was strictly an ideological vehicle for deeper rooted class antagonisms, giving a particular form of expression to these antagonisms.

The significance of this ideological vehicle for the formation of socialist opposition in Canada can be seen by an examination of the first major challenge posed by the emergent labour movement to the power of capital which also took shape in this same period. Canada's industrial revolution from the 1890s through the first decades of the twentieth century, accelerated by wartime industrial production, telescoped stages of industrial development which took place over longer periods of time in the United States and Britain. For example, the introduction of assembly-line production and the mechanization of the work place, with the consequent degradation of workers from craft status to mere semi-skilled labour, was largely coincident in Canada with the minor surge of industrialization. When labour, pent up by wartime restrictions on wages while inflation raged unchecked, finally burst onto the stage in 1919, it was in the unforgettable form of the Winnipeg General Strike, the single most important working-class confrontation of capitalism ever staged in this country. This, together with sympathetic strikes in other western cities, posed the spectre of socialist revolution to the capitalist state. Yet the major ideological thrust of workers was much more social democratic and trade unionist than revolutionary. The leadership of the strikers was heavily drawn from the Social Gospel movement. Sincere dedication to the cause of the working class and a commitment to social democracy did not in itself lead to revolutionary politics when it was expressed through doctrines of class harmony and Christian fellowship. In another sense, radical working-class action was emerging at the very moment when the larger confrontation was being carried out between the grande bourgeoisie and elements of the petite bourgeoisie, especially the farmers. In this struggle, which found its expression in the 1921 federal election when the Conservatives were reduced to third-party status by the farm-based Progressive party and in a series of provincial elections in Ontario, Alberta, and Manitoba which brought farmers' parties or farmer-labour coalitions to office, the working-class elements seeking participation as a class in the political process had to choose between sides already formed. Too weak organizationally, demographically, and ideologically to act decisively on their own, the workers had to choose the side of the petite bourgeoisie under the ideological guidance of middle-class leadership elements whose views were in some senses much closer to the independent commodity producers than to wage labour. Thus a historical conjuncture of class forces with profound consequences for the development of socialist opposition was struck at this crucial moment.

Whatever the exact class conjuncture, it was the class question itself which had been unmistakably posed by the subordinate classes in revulsion against the concentration of power and wealth in the hands of the national bourgeoisie. This challenge to the domination of central Canadian capital precipitated a political and ideological crisis of such proportions as to call for revisions of the dominant ideology. Moreover, the transformation of nineteenth-century entrepreneurial capitalism to modern corporate capitalism, with monopolistic or oligopolistic control over the market by a few highly organized and bureaucratized giant corporations, created an internal dynamic within capitalism itself towards "modernization" and "rationalization," which, as in the case of the United States during the so-called Progressive era, would inevitably lead to a growing role for the state as a device to consolidate and stabilize the market on behalf of corporate capital. The nationalization of private power companies in Ontario by a Conservative provincial government in the first decade of the century was a leading example of the state acting on behalf of one section of capital against another in the long-term interests of a rationalized power grid system as industrial infrastructure.[24] Robert Borden as national Conservative leader espoused "progressive" policies of state intervention and national conservation of natural resources. The first major intervention of the federal state into direct ownership came with the nationalization of private railways into the Canadian National system under a Tory administration. Borden also presided over the modernization of the federal state apparatus itself with the introduction of the merit system of appointment and efficiency studies of government operations, at the direct behest of his capitalist supporters who demanded a strong and effective state apparatus to act as their agent, especially in external trade and the search for foreign markets.[25] In short, the logic of capitalism was tending to increase the role of the state at the same time as class opposition to bourgeois domination was making political demands on the state for policies more appropriate to the subordinate classes. It was a fateful conjuncture which presented capitalism with a crucial historical opportunity.

The bourgeoisie itself was incapable of seizing this opportunity; the state, under enlightened leadership, could play a certain entrepreneurial role in acting on behalf of the larger interests of capitalism even against particular interests. The coming of William Lyon Mackenzie King, grandson of the rebel of 1837, to the leadership of the Liberal party in 1919 was an important step in this political solution to the crisis of capitalism. With King's victory in 1921 the class struggle generated by the process of capitalist development entered a new stage: thesis, antithesis ... mystification. King represented another face to the middle-class radicalism of the Social Gospel with which he flirted. A university-trained political economist who was willing to sell his skills to the highest bidder, whether this was the federal bureaucracy in Ottawa where he had been the first deputy minister of the fledgling Department of Labour, or the private empire of the Rockefellers for whom he had acted during the war as a labour relations consultant during the bloody Colorado coal-mining strike, King represented a new kind of twentieth-century man: the technocratic intellectual. Drawing on the Social Gospel rhetoric of social service and Christian conscience, he at the same time developed a theory of the integration of class opposition into the capitalist system and a leading role for precisely the kind of "expert" which King fancied himself. His book, *Industry and Humanity*, leapt past the conjuncture of 1918 to a future when the petite bourgeoisie had passed from sight and the fully industrialized world was divided fundamentally into capital and labour. Like Galbraith, King attempted to break down the functions of ownership and control by distinguishing a managerial technostructure allegedly separate from capital. He then introduced the state as a neutral bridge between capital, management, and labour, emphasizing the role of the state as a legitimizing force for the stabilization of class harmony. Since organized economic groups were directly represented within the processes of decision-making, with the political state only one of the four "partners to industry," one is justified in terming this a liberal-corporatist theory, although King himself never used the term corporatism, which had then distinctly Catholic and non-Anglo-Saxon origins. State and economy tend to fade into one another in this scheme, and the process of conflict becomes bureaucratized and thus denatured.

The state has demonstrated its capacity to intervene with direct coercion against working-class opposition in the smashing of the Winnipeg General Strike. Against the farmers and middle-class progressives it would instead shift its forms of legitimation. The coincidental identity of King's liberal-corporatism with the class cooperation theory of the farmers' movements allowed the new Liberal government the ideological capacity to slowly swallow the Progressive members of Parliament to the point that the party was a spent force within one term. It is indeed an ironic commentary on the weakness of the farmers' movements that they should have been thus co-opted by a man who cared so little for their world. Yet King was also able to draw the support of enough trade union elements over the long years of his stay in national office to decharge much of the momentum of the labour movement as well. One must not, however, confuse King's legitimizing ideology with actual restructuring of the state apparatus. Corporatism was to be symbolic, not structural. Capital at this stage showed little enthusiasm and strong elements of the labour movement, to their credit, have always been suspicious of such an arrangement. More importantly, the continued, albeit declining, influence of petit-bourgeois elements did not offer the real economic and class base for a corporatist bargain. Furthermore, this same persistent influence also militated against the adoption of social welfare legislation which was a concern for working-class people but only of marginal importance to farmers who were more self-sufficient by nature of their occupation. Thus the only social legislation passed by the Liberals during the decade of the 1920s was the old-age pension program, virtually forced down King's throat by J.S. Woodsworth at a crucial time for the minority Liberal government.

Yet however much the King Liberals were engaged in reshaping the image of the state without changing the substance, there was a long-term change in the role of the federal state which dates from the period of crisis at the end of the war. Some observers have identified a new national policy, emphasizing regional pay-offs and a slow turn towards welfarism as a phase succeeding that of the old National Policy with its emphasis on continental development and economic growth.[26] There was such a shift, in part, but it is somewhat misleading to point away from the accumulation function. Pay-offs to regions and classes were the *price* which capitalism was willing to pay for the social and political peace which would allow accumulation to continue. The focus on the class question in the post-war years also obscured the older national question. It was not that the Liberals were anti-nationalist so much as their preoccupation with settling class conflict which blinded them to the takeover of the Canadian economy by American capitalism. Indeed the pork-barrel involved in the new national policy could be paid for out of the dividends of new foreign capital investment. Thus, once again accumulation and legitimation came together, with disastrous long-term results for the Canadian nation.

The Great Depression renewed the crisis of capitalism which had seemingly lessened during the 1920s. Canada, as a nation strongly dependent upon primary export production, was particularly hard hit by the world-wide decline in prices. The evident failure of capitalism to produce the goods was just as surely a failure of the capitalist state to carry out its accumulation function. On the one hand, Canadian capitalism was divided and confused about the nature of the crisis; on the other, the state system, battered by a profound fiscal crisis brought on by enormously increased relief expenditures at the same time as tax revenues were drastically declining, was apparently incapable of generating ideas, let alone responses. Political opposition was just as weak and confused. It must be remembered that the depression had very *uneven* effects: since prices were falling, those who retained jobs were often able to maintain a standard of living which was equal to or even surpassed that which they had enjoyed earlier; while those who were unemployed suffered inconceivable hardship without adequate state welfare.

The birth of a social-democratic party alternative, the CCF, was an ambivalent event, incorporating as it did elements of working-class radicalism, western farmer populism, and the Fabian socialism of eastern university intellectuals. The CCF critique of capitalism was largely premised on the assumption that the system had failed in practical terms – an assumption which was to cost the party dearly when capitalism later recovered – and leaned very heavily on the idea of central economic planning and centralized social engineering by elite corps of technical experts in the bureaucracy as the solution to the crisis. In other words, with the CCF came the full emergence of the modern social-democratic image of the state in capitalist society: public ownership of key sectors, extensive regulation and control of economic activity, a welfare minimum, and the integration of the organized working class within the structures of the state system, all this to be accomplished by peaceful, evolutionary, and parliamentary means without recourse to coercion. The state, and particularly the federal state, took on an aura of neutrality, as an instrument which could allegedly be used against capitalism's excesses and on behalf of its victims. The myth that any extension of state activity is a victory of "socialism" was fostered both by reconstructured fundamentalists of business and by the partisans of social democracy. The traditional Tory image of corporate state welfare could slide into the so-called "Red Tory" image of the welfare state for all, with few realizing the optical illusion, and the mystification, involved.

In any event, even this ambiguous new turn was, during the depression at least, a minor event. The farmer and populist elements within the CCF itself remained somewhat restive about the trend towards *étatisme*, and in many parts of the country agrarian discontent drifted into other political forms, from a return to traditional party politics in Ontario to the emergence of right-wing monetarist populism in Alberta with Social Credit. Both the Conservative and Liberal governments in Ottawa in this decade did extend the role of the state to a degree, particularly in direct ownership of transportation and communication infrastructure (CBC and Trans-Canada Airways) and regulation and control through such devices as the Bank of Canada. Contrary to the social-democratic belief, however, it was not so much popular pressure from below which was largely responsible for these ventures into "socialism" as the logic of capitalism and its needs. For example, the Bank of Canada was necessary to stabilize financial operations as well as to create a mechanism for national monetary policy, none of which was contrary to the interests of Canadian bankers. Indeed R.B. Bennett's Bank of Canada was literally a "bankers' bank" directed by the directors of the chartered banks. The Liberals, with greater sensitivity to the need for public mystification, changed it into a supposedly neutral state institution, although its role continued to be highly supportive of financial capitalism.

It was the experience of the Second World War which brought the crisis to at least a temporary resolution with a new role for the federal state emerging out of both the needs of capitalism and the sudden appearance of strong popular pressures. The perception on the part of the subordinate classes that laissez-faire economic policies during the depression had meant unemployment and misery while extensive government controls and mobilization of resources for the war effort had brought about full employment and stability, meant a dawning fear of the end of controls following the war and the re-emergence of depression conditions with the restoration of the old order. The CCF enjoyed a sudden upsurge of popularity, even the Communist party won a few seats here and there, and public opinion swung sharply to the left, evidenced in polls which suggested majority support for the nationalization of industry.[27] At this conjuncture both the accumulation and legitimation functions were thus in question. "Reconstruction" involved a package of economic, social, and constitutional policies which formed the basis of a successful transition to a peacetime economy, a period of renewed economic growth of capitalism, a revised and highly centralized federalism, and the continued hold of the Liberals on national office. It was Keynesian economics which formed the logic of the policies while at the same time allowing for a vastly expanded role for the federal state. In effect, the new apparatus of fiscal and monetary control guaranteed accumulation through the maintenance of full employment and the protection of a stable economic environment which would attract capital investment, much of it American. At the same time, Keynesian policies offered a neat solution to the legitimation crisis. Welfarist policies of redistribution, such as the famous family allowances scheme, placed purchasing power in the hands of the people, which provided demand for the goods and services of capitalist enterprise, which in turn kept employment up. It is interesting to note that not only did the national state emerge much stronger out of this transformation, but the state itself played a certain autonomous role in bringing these policies into being, even against the opposition or indifference of some elements of Canadian capitalism. One might cite in this regard the lack of any important voice from the corporate sector in the framing of the new policies which originated entirely from within the senior civil service with some input from important Liberal party officials as well. One might also point to a certain amount of alienation exhibited by big business towards both major political parties in their moderate leftward policy turn.[28] Certainly the senior civil service of the 1940s and 1950s maintained a fund of expertise and technical mastery over details of economic management which far surpassed earlier stages of bureaucratic development and which certainly outweighed the provincial administrations. As capitalism regained its equilibrium, and under the deadening blanket of anti-communist Cold War ideology, the social-democratic image of the state became obscured within a Liberal state which appeared to offer apolitical, technical, bureaucratic solutions to the problems of conflict within capitalist society.

It is necessary to pause before this "end of ideology" image of the Liberal state. A number of considerations call the image into serious question. First, there is the undeniable fact that once the pressure of popular demands abated with the Liberal victory in 1945, almost all initiatives in social welfare legislation ceased: the curious death of the national medical plan is the best example. In considering the long career of Mackenzie King as prime minister one judgment at least is clear: the Liberal state would be moved just so far as popular demands forced it, and never a step further. Minimal legitimation was always the maximal program. Second, as a study by David Wolfe has documented, capitalists remained highly suspicious of Keynesian economics and accepted the new role for the state only so long as economic growth continued. Stabilization and thus accumulation, were still the focus of business interest.[29] Finally, accumulation was maintained largely through the importation of American direct investment, the ownership aspects of which were beginning to reach critical proportions by the 1950s, and by the headlong rush into the exportation of unprocessed raw materials.

The Liberal party, like the Conservative party before it, fashioned its own profitable relationship with the capitalist sector out of its domination over political office. To the extent that the state intervened on a wider basis in the private sector, it became intimately involved in purchasing goods and services from the private sector on a contractual basis. The Liberal party financed itself by levying a percentage on government contracts, or by straight patronage rake-offs where tenders were not involved.[30] In short, the Liberal state, even at its zenith of prestige, begins in retrospect to appear as little more than the old Tory state writ large, but no longer in possession of any directing national principle other than economic growth at any cost, even if the capital accumulation from the profits of growth accrued more to American multinational corporations than to the Canadian national bourgeoisie. The old weakness of the Canadian state, the lack of national identity, was even more pronounced in an era when even the economic aspects of state activity became as involved in the logic of American capitalist profitability as in the national elements of Canadian development. The Liberals had bested the Tories by their superior understanding of class conflict and of the techniques of co-opting left-wing opposition generated by the success of the old National Policy, and by their ability to integrate the Quebec political elite into the state system. They ended by losing sight altogether of the loss of national integrity consequent on their pursuit of accumulation at any cost.

During the brief Diefenbaker interlude of 1957–63 and the renewed Liberal domination since, one may discern with little difficulty a general unravelling of the system built up in the 1940s. Some of the major developments salient to the history of the state system in Canada since the late 1950s may be summarized as follows: the increasing domination of the industrial and resource sectors of the economy by American direct ownership with the consequent weakening of the national government's ability to control and manage the national economy; the continued peripheralization of the economy towards regional resource-based economies with north-south connections with the United States surpassing east-west connections within the Canadian economy; the striking failure of Keynesian economic policies which became obvious earlier in Canada than elsewhere but which is now a general phenomenon of the Western world, reflected in the persistent association of inflation with unemployment; the inability of federal programs to generate significant economic growth in poor regions of the country; the emergence for the first time of a sustained basis of trade union militancy which, beginning in the mid-1960s, raised the man hours lost through strikes to unprecedented levels and began to bring pressure to bear on the profit margins of capitalist enterprise; the transformation of Quebec nationalism into an *indépendance* movement organized around a political party with widespread support among the political, administrative, media, and professional elites of Quebec, thus directly challenging the elite accommodation basis of the Liberal party's Quebec connection. All these factors taken together have altered the basis upon which the Canadian state system rests and have tended, although not without contradictions, to contribute to a deterioration of the importance of the federal state, and the emergence of stronger provincial state power amid a general balkanization of the Canadian nation.

The picture is a complex one. One demand made by the logic of corporate capitalism in the 1960s tended towards a renewal of federal strength. A rationalization of welfare plans on a national basis would be of benefit to corporate capital which was increasingly mobile: prosperity in the mid-1960s seemed to offer the economic surplus from which social security rationalizations and extensions could be financed. Welfarism also seemed to be a popular legitimation policy. But provinces could not be expected to undertake isolated initiatives in such areas without other provinces following suit. Thus a certain innovative role in the introduction of such schemes as medicare, the Canada Pension Plan, national minimum standards, and increased transfer payments from rich to poor provinces, was undertaken by the federal government. But the limitations of welfarism as legitimation became apparent when the increase in labour militancy demonstrated that class conflict, far from being defused, had been instead inflamed. When the present economic crisis struck the Western world in the early 1970s, the overall fiscal position of the state deteriorated and consequently its social security programs fell under attack. Thus both the legitimation and accumulation functions were seriously undermined at the same time. In the wake of this crisis there appears to have been a definitive abandonment of the welfarist role of the national state. With continued inflation and rising pressures from corporate capitalism for retrenchment, the federal government has ceased any significant extensions of welfare programs, is cutting back on others, and has most recently been attempting to turn back to the provinces responsibility for financing some of the very programs which the federal government had earlier persuaded, and in some cases virtually coerced, provinces to undertake.

The rise of labour militancy has had the effect of drawing the federal state into direct confrontation with the working class. The demands that federal action be taken against inflation had become so irresistible by 1975 that the Liberal government was forced to reverse its own campaign policy of 1974 and institute the so-called "anti-inflation" program. It is important to realize that the labour militancy has been almost entirely apolitical, being largely focused on industrial relations and wage negotiations with employers and scarcely at all upon global political demands which would develop a broader ideological critique of capitalist society. Even the social-democratic NDP, with its direct organizational affiliations with industrial unions, has been unable to better its political position significantly. The intervention of the federal government into the worsening relations between capital and labour was in a sense a "nationalization" of labour relations on behalf of capital. The focusing of wage demands on the state rather than the employer might seem to constitute a politicization of the labour struggle. There were indeed marked tendencies in this direction, the most spectacular being the 14 October 1976 national day of protest, the first nation-wide grass-roots labour action in the history of this country. The moment appears to have passed, however, and the most likely results at this time are either a general defeat for the working class with resultant apathy and resignation, or the securing of some sort of liberal-corporatist arrangement between the CLC, the federal government, and big business – which form a socialist perspective is scarcely preferable to the first alternative. It remains to be seen whether long-term delegitimation of the state in the eyes of the working class will result from the wage control intervention.

Working-class pressure on profits will undoubtedly push the federal government towards intervention, even to coercion if the crisis of capitalism demands illiberal measures. At the same time the current shift in federal spending priorities away from health and welfare programs towards defence projects – under the pretext of a Soviet "threat" to Canadian sovereignty – indicates a further abandonment of legitimation policies and a deepening of the emphasis on state activities directly beneficial to industry.[31] One may confidently expect that the thunderous orchestration of propaganda through the mass media in recent years attacking "big government," "bureaucracy," and "waste and inefficiency" will not be extended to a massive growth in armament expenditures.

There is another aspect to the anti-government propaganda which bears examination. Much of the campaign, whether inspired by the giant corporations or by such ideological excrescences as the small businessmen's association, has focused almost exclusively on the federal state. The Conservative party had adopted this assault on Ottawa as its prime partisan obsession along with the demand for more give-aways and tax bonuses to big business. The identification of the federal government as the source of economic deterioration is understandable at one level, given the primary role played by Ottawa in the post-war world. But the failure to include the provincial governments within the same *obiter dicta* suggests a less innocent orientation. There is strong reason to argue that the major thrust of contemporary capitalist development in Canada, primarily in the extraction of natural resources, is towards the weakening of the national state system and the balkanization of the country into regional dependencies of the American Empire. The Conservative call for the "decentralization" of Confederation, clothed in the self-serving rhetoric of freedom and local initiative, has now been given further impetus by the spectre of the Quebec *indépendance* movement enshrined in office in Quebec City and the precipitous crisis of Trudeau's federalism. It may well be that "decentralization" is an ideology whose time has come, with very powerful interests in support.

Visions of the total dismemberment of the nation are no doubt overdrawn. The national state manifestly performs functions still necessary to capitalism, which provincial states cannot perform on their own. Moreover, the question of centralization versus decentralization within the context of constitutional federalism tends in one very important sense to obscure the main issue. The state system in Canada, of which the federal and provincial governments are merely aspects, has become a complex, many-layered, and multi-dimensional phenomenon. Federal-provincial conferences and particularly the growth of vast, and literally uncharted, machinery for intensive and sustained interbureaucratic consultation between levels of government has created what some observers have called a new branch of the state. Perhaps the disintegration of the central political authority may be discerned in the weakness of any central command over this fragmented and unwieldy apparatus, where horizontal accommodations between loosely interdependent bureaucratic empires may be more important than control from Ottawa. Needless to say, such a situation offers increasing opportunity for fractions of the bourgeoisie to capture parts of the apparatus and to carry on conflicts with other fractions through the competing sections of the state system – the conflict between Alberta and Ontario over oil prices is one example. Yet the same example indicates that some unification will also be necessary for capitalism – the interests of the whole bourgeoisie – and thus some central co-ordination of oil price policy is undertaken by Ottawa. A point made by Panitch in the preceding essay may usefully be reiterated again: the fact that such decisions are taken at levels of inter-bureaucratic and intercorporate negotiation remote from any direct popular influence – levels literally *irresponsible* to the voters even under the normal definition of responsibility in liberal democracies – means that capitalist dictation to the state is even further insulated from possible oppositional class criticism.

At another level the state system in Canada has been moving towards yet closer relationships with the private sector. Senior civil servants are now encouraged as part of an official career planning program to spend periods of time in the corporations; the old career civil service model followed in the days of the Liberal mandarinate in the 1940s and 1950s is being replaced by a "cross-pollination" between executive positions in both sectors. There is the proliferation of advisory councils to departments made up of big business executives with interests closely connected with the particular department concerned. And, perhaps most significant of all, there has been a very conscious move towards blurring the line between public and private enterprise. The Canada Development Corporation, originally the nationalist brainchild of Walter Gordon, has become instead a device for taking Crown corporations out of the direct ownership of the state and into a curious half-life of mixed public-private control. The development of government-corporate consortia, such as Panarctic, is another device for integrating the capacity of the state to mobilize capital investment with the desire for profit by capitalist enterprise. And, of course, such devices are ideal for the capitalist whose profits will be guaranteed by the state itself as a partner. Only those mesmerized by the myth that state intervention is a form of "socialism," or those who perpetuate the Canadian folklore that socialism is the highest stage of Toryism, should react with shock and indignation when the suggestion is made, as it was recently, that since Canadian National has finally made a profit, after over a half-century of subsidization by the taxpayers, it should be turned over to the private sector. That is directly in the Canadian tradition – the state exists to mobilize financial support for necessary but unprofitable enterprises. Even in those areas where direct ownership has been undertaken, especially transportation and communication infrastructure, the normal pattern has been for public–private sector duality, not state monopoly: CN competes with CP, Air Canada with Canadian Pacific, the CBC with CTV. And even within the state sector itself this dualism is perpetuated, with regular departments paralleled by Crown corporations whose operations are encouraged to be as much like private corporations as possible.

The gradual merger of the state and corporate sectors ought not to surprise anyone conversant with the dominant image of the state in Canadian history. The Syncrude deal suggests a kind of archetype of state capitalism for the future: an arrangement made under the gun of the multinational oil companies involving the federal state and two provincial governments with divergent economic bases together forming a stabilizing minority interest in a foreign-controlled project for the extraction of a crucial non-renewable natural resource. The old Tory image of the state remains operative: private profit at public expense. The rationale of the old Tory image has, however, been discarded by events. A bourgeoisie has indeed come to birth long since, has even reached maturity (in some cases senility), but it is a national bourgeoisie only in part, and its private interests are not linked with the national interest, even if one defines this in the minimal terms of liberal capitalist concepts of the national interest. Even bourgeois nationalist figures like Walter Gordon and Eric Kierans have departed political life, unable to acquiesce in the further destruction of the bourgeois basis of a national state.

The fatal continuity of the image of the state from nineteenth-century Toryism to twentieth-century Liberalism, a continuity founded on capitalism without a viable national basis, is deepened by the weakness of an alternative, socialist, image. At this stage in our history there is little point in discussing a Marxist revolutionary critique as a dominant aspect of mass working-class politics. Marxism exists more importantly as an analytical tool and an academic mode of interpretation, as in this book. Yet even the social-democratic image, however ambivalent and accommodative with capitalism it has proved to be in countries where social democracy has been electorally successful, is extremely enfeebled and rests on a profoundly fragmented base. The defeat of the NDP government of British Columbia after a single, and by social-democratic standards innovative, term is a haunting sign of the political impotence of social democracy. The failure of mass working-class opposition to wage controls, especially the astonishing ideological confusion of the trade union leadership, is even more disquieting.

At this conjuncture, the election of the strongly social-democratic and union-backed Parti Québécois in Quebec on 15 November 1976 is an event fraught with the deepest irony for English-Canadian socialists. The rise of integral nationalism in twentieth-century Quebec finally destroyed the old monopoly of the national identity by the traditional elites. The bourgeois renovation of the structures of Quebec society under the Lesage Liberals' so-called Quiet Revolution in the early 1960s established the demand that middle-class Quebec become *maîtres chez nous* through the instrumentality of the Quebec provincial state. With the traditional aversion to *étatisme* thus broken, events were set in motion eventuating in the release of some of the most militant working-class energies yet seen in Canada. There is no doubt that the Parti Québécois represents the more progressive elements of Quebec society, with a strong working-class constituency. This constituency is, however, only one of its bases, and it is balanced by the same new middle-class technocratic-bureaucratic *étatiste* elements which gave thrust and direction to the Quiet Revolution. The overarching commitment to nationalism, which may be seen not so much as a goal opposed to class politics but rather as a vehicle for the class interests of the new middle class, may very well serve to submerge working-class interests once again. Yet even if the progressive aspect of social-democratic *indépendantisme* is not lost, the tragic irony for English-Canadian socialists is that even a partial victory for progressivism in Quebec may be bought at the price of the breakup of the Canadian nation.

The outlook is not bright. Yet the task for socialists in Canada must be to understand reality, as a first step to changing that reality. We must strive to understand the capitalist state in its Canadian specificity, to purge the mystifying layers of ideology from the image of the state and see it for what it really is. Toryism built it, Liberalism consolidated it, social democracy misjudged it. With our backs turned to the future and our eyes fixed upon the wreckage of the past, the question is, as always: what is to be done?[32]

NOTES

1 "Ideology and Ideological State Apparatuses," in *Lenin and Philosophy* (London 1971), 127–88

2 It is interesting that Weber specifically cited Trotsky in formulating his

definition. Weber, "Politics as a Vocation," in H.H. Gerth and C. Wright Mills, eds., *From Max Weber: Essays in Sociology* (New York 1958), 78

3 See C.B. Macpherson, *The Real World of Democracy* (Toronto 1965).

4 *The Savage Mind* (Chicago 1966), 95

5 Hartz, *The Founding of New Societies* (New York 1964), especially articles by Hartz and K.D. McRae; Horowitz, *Canadian Labour in Politics* (Toronto 1968), chap. 1

6 Macpherson, *Real World Democracy*, and his *Democratic Theory: Essays in Retrieval* (London 1973)

7 See Tom Nairn, "The Modern Janus," *New Left Review* 94 (Nov.–Dec. 1975), especially 8–11, for a Marxist interpretation of the fate of this concept.

8 "Some Views on the Pattern of Canadian Economic Development," in T.N. Brewis, ed., *Growth and the Canadian Economy* (Toronto 1968), 41–2

9 Herschel Hardin's *A Nation Unaware: The Canadian Economic Culture* (Vancouver 1974) is the most fully developed statement of the argument.

10 See his "Upper Canada and the Conservative Tradition," in Ontario Historical Society, *Profiles of a Province* (Toronto 1967), and "Conservatism and Political Development: The Canadian Case," *South Atlantic Quarterly* 64 (1970), 226–43.

11 D. Barrington, "Edmund Burke as Economist," *Economica*, NS XXI, 83 (1954). Burke's economic views come out most clearly in his "Thoughts and Details on Scarcity" and "Speech on Economical Reform" in *The Works of Edmund Burke* (London 1826), III and VII.

12 Burke, *Reflections on the Revolution in France* (London 1907), 95

13 *Capital* (New York 1967), I, 774

14 Gary Teeple, "Land, Labour, and Capital in Pre-Confederation Canada," in Teeple, ed., *Capitalism and the National Question in Canada* (Toronto 1972)

15 J.L.H. Henderson, ed., *John Strachan: Documents and Opinions* (Toronto 1969), 109–10

16 Greg Keilty's *1837: Revolution in the Canadas* (Toronto 1974) is a good reflection of the left nationalist image of Mackenzie. Rick Salutin's script for the Theatre Passe Muraille's performance of *1837: The Farmers' Revolt* is another example of this currently fashionable interpretation. Margaret Fairley's *Selected Writings of William Lyon Mackenzie* (Toronto 1960) is a more scholarly collection and one reflecting an older left-wing image of the rebel of 1837.

17 Stanley Ryerson's *Unequal Union* (Toronto 1968) tends, in my opinion at least, to see the conflict in somewhat exogenous terms.

18 The clause in question reads: "There shall never be created within this

State any incorporated trading companies, or incorporated companies with banking powers. Labor is the only means of creating wealth." S.D. Clark, *Movements of Political Protest in Canada, 1640–1840* (Toronto 1959), 429

19 *Pioneer Public Service* (Toronto 1955), 67

20 *The Image of Confederation* (Toronto 1964), 25

21 Bruce Hodgins, "Democracy and the Ontario Fathers of Confederation," in Hodgins and Robert Page, eds., *Canadian History since Confederation: Essays and Interpretations* (Georgetown, Ont. 1972), 27

22 Ramsay Cook, *Provincial Autonomy, Minority Rights, and the Compact Theory, 1867–1921* (Ottawa 1969), 9–13

23 See Carl Berger's masterful intellectual history, *The Sense of Power: Studies in the Ideas of Canadian Imperialism, 1867–1914* (Toronto 1970).

24 See Viv Nelles, *The Politics of Development: Forests, Mines & Hydro-Electric Power in Ontario, 1849–1941* (Toronto 1974).

25 J.E. Hodgetts et al., *The Biography of an Institution: The Civil Service Commission of Canada, 1908–1967* (Montreal 1972), 46–7; Paul Stevens, *The 1911 General Election: A Study in Canadian Politics* (Toronto 1970), 69–70

26 V.C. Fowke, "The National Policy – Old and New," in W.T. Easterbrook and M.H. Watkins, eds., *Approaches to Canadian Economic History* (Toronto 1967), 237–58

27 Reginald Whitaker, *The Government Party: Organizing and Financing the Liberal Party of Canada, 1930–1958* (Toronto 1977), 137–43

28 Ibid.; J.L. Granatstein, *The Politics of Survival: The Conservative Party of Canada, 1939–1945* (Toronto 1967)

29 David Wolfe, "Political Culture, Economic Policy and the Growth of Foreign Investment in Canada, 1945–1957," MA thesis, Carleton University, 1973

30 Whitaker, *Government Party*, 102–11, 402–6

31 See the *Financial Post* special supplement, "What Canada's New Defence Policy Means for Business," 19 Feb. 1977.

32 The final image is drawn from Walter Benjamin's extraordinary vision of the "angel of history": "his face is turned toward the past. Where we perceive a chain of events, he sees one single catastrophe which keeps piling wreckage upon wreckage and hurls it in front of his feet. The angel would like to stay, awaken the dead, and make whole what has been smashed. But a storm is blowing from Paradise; it has got caught in his wings with such violence that the angel can no longer close them. This storm irresistibly propels him into the future to which his back is turned, while the pile of debris before him grows skyward. This storm is what we call progress." Benjamin, *Illuminations* (New York 1968), 257–8

CHAPTER TWO

The Liberal Corporatist
Ideas of Mackenzie King

This is an exploration of the early thought of one man who was both an intellectual – an "expert" on labour relations – and the most successful politician in twentieth-century Canada. The role of ideas in politics becomes sharply focused when someone with ideas has the chance to exercise political power.

There is a voluminous literature on King as politician, but little attention is paid to his ideas. King's ideas are worth close attention to the degree that they point up fundamental conflicts within liberalism generated by industry and industrial class conflict. King was one of the first to seriously address the consequences for democratic politics of Canada's development as an industrial nation. His solution, a form of liberal corporatism, has remained one option proffered by politicians and capitalists unwilling to tolerate the economic and political consequences of class conflict. This was especially the case during the Liberal regimes of the 1970s, when this essay was written. During the 1980s, corporatism fell out of fashion as Thatcherism, Reaganism, and their somewhat less forthright Canadian reflection, Mulroneyism, sought to beat back unions and get government off the backs of business. With the eclipse of these hardnosed variants of global competition from Japan and Europe, new forms of corporatism may well emerge as the preferred option for national survival. In this case, the contradictions evident in King's early twentieth-century vision of corporatist capitalism will still be very much with us.

After this essay first appeared, a lengthy riposte to my interpretation was published in the same journal by Paul Craven (*Labour/Le Travaileur* 4 (1979): 165–86). Craven did not disagree with my textual analysis of King's *Industry and Humanity*, but he did question my reading of the historical

Reprinted with permission from *Labour/Le Travail: The Journal of Canadian Labour History* 2 (1977).

context which shaped King and the characterization of King as a "great villain" which he claimed to find in my article. There is no space here to engage this critique, although to the charge of disliking Mackenzie King, I must plead guilty. I do think that his ideas had effects, and I would point to a tendency of liberalism in this century to grasp fitfully at the wisp of harmony between the class elements of the capitalist economy in the illusion that this constitutes the grail of true democratic practice. There is actually a hidden kinship here with much of the populist tradition of the non-Marxist Left, to which I turn in the next essay.

In 1904 the young deputy minister of labour, William Lyon Mackenzie King, was reading Sir John Willison's biography of the Prime Minister, Sir Wilfrid Laurier. King noticed that after Laurier had become Liberal leader in the late 1880s, his speeches lost all originality and became a mere repetition of the ideas of his youth. "This is perhaps inevitable," King reflected, "once launched as a leader the day for gaining intellectual capital is past." Characteristically, King drew a personal moral: "I must learn this, I must learn now is the time to become prepared or the day will pass and the opportunity not be known."[1] Fifteen years later, King became Laurier's successor as Liberal leader, and his own time for intellectual capital accumulation was past. His subsequent record as Canada's most successful politician has tended to obscure from view the early King, whose general reputation among contemporaries was that of a bright young man with advanced ideas.

Political biographers may argue about King's personality, but quite apart from this is an interest in what King did and said in these early years of "gaining intellectual capital." More than twenty years ago Ferns and Ostry, in a pioneering attempt to uncover the ideological thread which underlay his early activities, came to hostile yet strangely respectful conclusions.[2] More recently the suggestion has been made that King's ideas as embodied in his book *Industry and Humanity* (1918) should be taken more seriously than they have been, given the early and rather prophetic appearance of concepts of government-business-labour relations which are close to the currently fashionable notions of corporatism in advanced liberal democracies.[3] It is in connection with this attempt by King to work out certain innovative concepts of class harmonization and the integration of interest groups into liberal democratic structures that his work and ideas take on a contemporary relevance.

One must avoid the opposite trap of taking King's ideas too seriously. It would be preposterous to claim that Mackenzie King is a hitherto undiscovered Machiavelli of industrial politics or, even with the opening of his voluminous confessions a Rousseau *manqué*. Yet a case can be made that King was acutely sensitive to the currents of thought and sentiment of the age in which he was formed, that he had a deep sense of the enormity, if not the exact meaning, of the malaise of industrial capitalism facing class conflict, and that his attempts to resolve the material contradictions on the ideological plane reveal some of the basic processes at work in advanced liberal democracies. That he was lacking in true originality of mind is thus an observation of secondary significance. King is interesting more for what he reflected, in sharp focus, than for what he himself generated.

Any attempt to make Mackenzie King's mind a unified and harmonious whole is akin to squaring a circle. King reflected the contradictions of the work into which he was born on many levels. King lived these contradictions out in the form of a "very double life," King's own revealing phrase chosen by C.P. Stacey as the title of his recent biography.[4] The man who would become famous for the formula, "Conscription if necessary, but not necessarily Conscription," was already so famous at the University of Toronto during the student strike of 1895 that he was immortalized in a *Varsity* cartoon depicting him as the King of Clubs, calling out "let us boycott lectures" on the one side and "let us return to lectures" on the other.[5] This political ambiguity was not merely studied, it was instinctive. King without contradiction would be like Canada without conflict. Thus young King could never quite make up his mind whether he was a conservative or a radical, an economist or a spiritualist, a teacher or a preacher, an academic or a bureaucrat, a thinker or a doer. He finally, and with conspicuous success, settled for the profession which utilized other men's weaknesses and contradictions as its very currency: he became a politician.

A second point to be remembered is King's social origins. His own exaggerated sense of lineage stemming from his grandfather William Lyon Mackenzie, the rebel of 1837, often bordered on the grotesque. Yet King did not in fact have the social position to which he felt entitled. His family was neither particularly wealthy nor especially prestigious in the eyes of high society or the corporate boardrooms of St. James and Bay Street. Indeed the King family was something of a classic case of small town gentility swamped by the rising tide of new money which came with the industrialization of the country in the late nineteenth century. He was thus the type which Richard Hofstadter identified as the "Progressive" man of that era in the United States.[6] And in a fashion similar to many young men of the Progressive era, King moved upward through the professions, as a member of the "new middle class." Although his family connections did give him some help at certain points, particularly in introducing him to Sir William Mulock who was later to invite him to Ottawa as editor of the *Labour Gazette*, they were distinctly secondary to his own attainments and skills in self-advancement. In the vast confrontation which he saw taking shape between the wealth and power of capitalism and the desperate force of numbers of the side of the dispossessed working class, the middle class intellectual like King had everything to lose and little to gain. The only resources of the intellectuals in this confrontation were, as Christopher Lasch has put it, "argument and exposition"; they thus had a "class interest in nonviolence for its own sake." The solution was to substitute education for force, which as Lasch suggests, " sometimes seemed only to rationalize a crude will to power on the part of the intellectuals themselves."[7] It is thus not very surprising to find King in 1906 quoting with approval his late bureaucratic colleague, and youthful soulmate, Bert Harper, to the effect that:

The true rulers of the nation are outside of our parliaments and our law courts, and that the safety of society lies in informing those who form public opinion ... The poor downtrodden have more to hope from men who, having a specialized training in the operation of social forces, apply themselves to the proper remedy, then from all the windy, ultra-radical demagogues.[8]

What exactly was the "specialized training in the operation of social forces" which King acquired in his university days? The University of Toronto in the 1890s was not a source of many of King's ideas. A few professors made some impression on him. The most significant was James Ashley, professor of Political Economy, who resigned the year after King arrived to take up a position at Harvard, where King eventually followed. Ashley was a critic of many accepted tendencies of classical political economy, who had attached much laissez faire dogma as rationalization of injustice and an insult to the working man. Ashley represented a trend in economic science which had begun in Germany and was gathering strength in the United States at this time: a shift away from the abstract deductive method to an historical, statistical, and inductive method of analysis. This school looked to public policy supported by facts rather than theory, and in Germany it had gone hand in hand with a much more *étatiste* approach to economics than English liberalism had allowed. Goodwin credits Ashley with founding the Toronto tradition of integrating economics with history and political science, later to be so characteristic of the Political Economy Department under Harold Innis.[9] In Germany the historical school had been associated with a deeply reformist, sometimes outrightly socialist, strain in which the gathering of facts led directly to recommendations for reform without much theoretical mediation.[10] In its transmutation into the American institutionalist school by which King was to be much influenced, this strongly reformist strain was watered down considerably, but left its mark nonetheless.

The most significant impact on young King while at Toronto did not come from the lecture halls but from his discovery of the writings of an English economist and social reformer of the previous decade. Arnold Toynbee the elder, who had died at an early age after a brief but illustrious career as an economic historian, a lecturer in working men's educational associations, and a founder of a social settlement for the poor, Toynbee Hall, bowled King over by his ideas and the example of his life. Upon reading Toynbee's *Industrial Revolution in England* in the summer of 1894, King confessed in his diary that "I was simply enraptured by his writings and believe I have at last found a model for my future work in life."[11] Toynbee was a liberal critic of laissez faire who wanted a humanized or moralized political economy which would retain the market and individualism but with a dedication to Christian duty impelling capitalism toward more moderate redistribution of resources to the poor. To Toynbee the historical method of economic analysis revealed the injustices which capitalism had created during the Industrial Revolution. The exposure of exploitation and injustice would serve to arouse public opinion to push toward reform. In industry, Toynbee looked to the extension of joint boards of conciliation seating owners and workers together as the means of bringing about class harmony and co-operation.[12] It was above all the application of Christian sentiment to the problems of economics that attracted King to Toynbee. Unswerving in his fundamental belief in Christianity, King was obsessed by the problem of evil in a world created by a God of love. The undeniable existence of misery and exploitation in the material world would never lead to a crisis of religious faith, but rather to a crisis of secular belief in the accepted verities of bourgeois society. Thus a figure like Toynbee who had attempted to Christianize capitalist economics, both in academic work and in personal life, was precisely the model for which King was striving. The crucial point is that at this stage in his development it was not mystical otherworldly solutions which appealed to him but rather secular resolutions of the material problems of Christian capitalist civilization, which he saw as the working out of God's will in the material world, with a little help from worthy young middle class reformers imbued with both a moral conscience and technical knowledge of how the capitalist market actually operated. Toynbee remained a dominating influence on King's mind. Over twenty years later when he was working on *Industry and Humanity*, he once again returned to "the finest influence on my life" and "derived much amusement from the attack Toynbee made on Ricardo."[13]

When King went to the University of Chicago to pursue graduate studies, it was with a Toynbeean double purpose in mind: academic advancement in the understanding of political economy and involvement in the Hull House social settlement founded by Jane Addams. The major intellectual influence he felt at Chicago was that of Thorstein Veblen, whose lectures on socialism King pronounced "the best I have ever listened to." Indeed, King concluded that Veblen's course "has influenced me greatly. I believe that Socialistic tendencies are coming to be the prevailing one." It is not altogether clear in retrospect just where Veblen stood with regard to socialism, although he was, of course, the most mordant and biting critic of the mores of the American bourgeoisie. Certainly he was the most penetrating commentator on Marxist thought at this time in the English speaking world. Veblen understood and respected Marx at a time when there was general ignorance in the Anglo-American academic world of the spectre haunting the European continent. King had read Marx's *Capital* as part of Veblen's course. He found the early section on use value and exchange value very difficult reading – it took him two hours to cover 26 pages – but eventually he found it "very logical after getting into it." Engel's *Socialism, Utopian and Scientific* elicited the following tribute: "there is much in it. There is something about Socialism which interests me deeply – there is truth in it – it is full of truth, yet much that is strange and obscure."[14] It is in the last phrase, "much that is strange and obscure," that we glimpse the real reason for King's ultimate lack of interest in Marxism. The barrier was essentially a cultural one: materialist explanations of the world could draw King's attention only to a point, but when they went so far as to offer an alternative *Weltanschauung* to Christian idealism, King simply lost his intellectual moorings. In fact, after Veblen's course, King never returned to the writings of Marx and Engels, and there is no evidence of any lasting impact of this reading on his thought. Nor, for that matter, did he ever return to Veblen's own writings: perhaps the cynicism and irony of that great critic of American civilization were equally alien to King's earnest moralizing taste, despite the undoubted effect of his brutal rationality on the impressionable young student.

King has already developed some familiarity with socialist politics at a practical level, through contacts with the Socialist Labour Party and other working class militants in Toronto. Indeed, the student strike at the University of Toronto, in which King played a leading role, was precipitated by the refusal of the administration to allow socialist speakers on the campus. Through his work at Hull House, he developed some first hand knowledge of the social conditions in the working class slums of industrial Chicago. As a reporter for the *Mail and Empire* in the summer of 1897, he investigated sweat shop conditions in Toronto and wrote muckraking exposés. Thus while still a student he had gained both theoretical and practical knowledge of socialism and the social conditions of the working class. Out of this background he developed a genuine social conscience, but one which was quite different from the kind of social democratic commitment which J.S. Woodsworth would develop out of a much closer familiarity with the conditions of poverty and misery spawned by industrial capitalism.

What King's early studies and observations did provide him with was a fairly sensitive understanding of the potential power of an aroused industrial working class. Late in 1897 he was writing in his diary that "I fear revolution in the country yet, another 1793 as in France – growing Democracy vs. growing Wealth and tyranny of rings and combines. A few very rich and the many very poor."[15] The fear of revolution was, of course, never far from the excited minds of the possessors of wealth themselves. It was not King's fear of revolution which demonstrated any particular perspicacity, but rather his conviction of how to avoid the eventuality that showed some insight into the social forces at work. Even if his reading of Marx had left him with little concrete appreciation of the revolutionary dialectic of capitalist class structures, he understood one crucial weakness in Marxist thought, the problem of class consciousness. King, idealist that he was, knew that all the material mechanisms of history could not serve automatically to bring about the rise of revolutionary class consciousness on the part of the proletariat. The instinctive resort of reactionaries threatened by revolution – repression – was not much to King's taste, since it left someone like himself with little role to play. Instead, from the beginning, one can discern in King a growing conceptualization of a mediating role between rich and poor, capitalist and worker, in which technical knowledge and skill at *ideological* manipulation of the consciousness of both sides become valuable resources.

It was Harvard University which provided him with his greatest intellectual stimulation, and it was Harvard which reciprocated with the greatest recognition of his abilities. Already King had published some articles and book reviews in the *Journal of Political Economy*, edited by Veblen (factual historical accounts of trade union organization in the United States which read as rather dull, uninspired, although careful compilations).[16] But he never did acquire a degree from Chicago, an institution about which he entertained somewhat mixed feelings. At Harvard, on the other hand, King found himself very much at home. The most important influence on him there, along with Ashley from Toronto, was Frank Taussig, leading American economist and always a great example and guide to his students. Taussig was something of a transitional figure between the older classical political economy and the newer doctrines making their way from the continent. In 1896 Taussig published an examination of the celebrated wages fund doctrine which had animated political economy for some time, and King spent much effort as Taussig's student puzzling over the intricacies of the controversy. The moral which King eventually drew from Taussig's discussion was the eminently orthodox one that labour is dependent upon capital for production, that labour is thus dependent upon a "wages fund ... which is in the hands of the capitalist class. Their money income is derived from what the capitalists find it profitable to turn over to them."[17] This soundly conservative lesson of classical political economy was one which King maintained throughout the rest of his career, and was a fundamental weapon in his intellectual armoury against socialism. Reinforced by his reading at Harvard of the classics – Adam Smith, Ricardo, Malthus, J.S. Mill, Cairnes, Jevons, Bohm-Bawerk, and Marshall – King developed a firm belief in the legitimacy of profit as a return to a necessary factor of production, thus further distinguishing him from Marx's thought. On the other hand, King often enough permitted himself to question the *distribution* of wealth in contemporary capitalism, expressing his doubts "as to the advantages of great accumulations of capital. I cannot see why smaller accumulations in the hands of a number should not have as good an effect, if not better on Industry."[18] Obviously, King never altogether lost the traditions of *petit bourgeois* protest which his grandfather had championed.

An important event to King was the arrival at Harvard of Archdeacon William Cunningham of Cambridge as a visiting lecturer on the industrial revolution. In Cunningham's lectures King caught some of the inspiration he had derived from Toynbee, and for much the same reason. Cunningham was interested in an empirical analysis of the origins and significance of the industrial revolution, the single modern development which fascinated King most deeply, and he was a Christian who devoted considerable attention to the relationship between political economy as a science and the moral imperatives of religion. King respectfully termed Cunningham a "Christian economist," and went on with a flattering comparison: "the Harvard men present the Utilitarian point of view most strongly. Taussig is a strong Utilitarian. Cunningham shows Christianity necessary for complete view."[19] As with Toynbee, Cunningham was once again consulted with pleasure when King was composing *Industry and Humanity* some twenty years later.

The absorption with writers like Toynbee and Cunningham point to one of the keys to King's thought. King was a dualist, whose perception of a fundamental contradiction between his material existence and his idealist strings was so acute, indeed so extreme, as to create a permanent tension in his emotional as well as in his intellectual life. His ability to play the very practical game of politics, with persistent success and indefatigable enthusiasm for so long a career, is evidence of more than mere toleration of the secular world. Yet his diary bears interminable witness to his obsession with things spiritual, an obsession which was later to grow into a broad mystic streak with the attendant trappings of occultism and personal oddities. What we see is a young man torn by profound religious strivings and tormented by the problems of how the spiritual world can be reconciled to the sinful material world. As a product of the post-Darwinian generation, King refused to be drawn into reactionary or obscurantist defences of an outmoded world view. Huxley's lectures on evolution he approved unreservedly, and he greatly admired Henry Drummond, a popularizer of Darwinism of somewhat dubious authenticity, who had argued that evolution was teleological process pointing toward the ultimate perfection of God, with altruism and charity incorporated into the struggle for survival. Drummond's attempts to discover a natural basis for morality struck a responsive chord in King, who remained rather uncritical of the suspect basis of the popularization. When King wrote in his diary that natural law and spiritual truth must be the same, that "all life must be under the one law, it appears to be so, the more we see of the universe and understand of man the more we see the unity of all things, a one underlying will, a supreme Intelligence directing all things in accordance with invariable law," we perhaps see more the hand of wishful thinking and yearning faith than of a rational philosophical foundation.[20]

It is difficult to take King's pseudo-philosophical strivings seriously. Nor is it surprising that in later life he should have fallen into outright occultism. Not content to be simply a mystic by night and a practical politician by day, but lacking a firm foundation for reconciling the two worlds, it was perhaps inevitable that to preserve his faith he would end by finding "evidence" of the penetration of the material by the spiritual in séances with the dearly departed and the interpretation of coincidences of every day life as "signs." The point here is that this faith in the underlying unity of the material and spiritual, in the essential order and pattern in the material world which could be discovered by human science but which was founded in a divine purpose which itself transcended the material world, was the basis upon which King built his political and economic ideas.

King capped his academic career with a travelling fellowship from Harvard which he used to visit England, France, and Germany at the turn of the century. The most interesting observation about King's European trip is what it revealed of his evolving social and political philosophy, in particular his growing alienation from the doctrines and practice of socialism with which he had earlier flirted. Already at Harvard his classical economic training reinforced a hardening personal conservatism. When he met Eugene Debs in 1898 he felt contemptuous of the Socialist leader's lack of a "trained mind," even if his heart were in the right place.When on the same day he received a letter from Debs and from a wealthy Canadian friend of the family, he mused significantly in his diary: "A labour agitator and a millionaire. To know both and understand their interests, sympathies and points of view. This is well." A little later he wrote flatly that "I am becoming more conservative and less a believer in radicalism." His reading of Spencer and other social Darwinists confirmed his belief in the individualist basis of human progress and the view of socialism as a hopeless flying in the face of the law of survival of the fittest. The evidence of political corruption in the United States unearthed by the muckraking journalists did not so much add to King's reformist zeal as deepen his conservatism:

I never read this sort of thing but I see the end of all schemes of self-government such as Socialism presents, till the heart of man and his morality has changed, external changes whatever they be will neither end corruption nor misery. I find myself becoming ever stronger against government action, except for making restrictions, regulations, etc., chiefly because of the deteriorating effect it tends to have on human character, giving wider scope for favouritism leading to idleness etc., in those employed, and a favouring sycophancy on the part of those seeking it.[21]

In England his deepening dislike of socialism was confirmed. He called on the Webbs and was adopted by them for a time, being brought along to Fabian meetings and to lectures at the London School of Economics. The Fabians as a group appeared to the increasingly ambitious King as being "rather on the edge of things as it were." The Bohemian element in the Fabian society, especially among the women, predictably enough disgusted him; they were, he wrote with a misplaced colonial snobbery worthy of Vincent Massey, simply the wrong "sort of people," lacking in the proper social manners and refined education. "There is a sort of 'soreheadedness' among a good many of this sort, a soreheadedness arising from some misfortune in their own lot or because others have failed to sufficiently recognize them."[22]

Just as his disillusionment with socialism was waxing, he discovered the co-operative movement in England, which pleased him greatly. Co-operation as a channel for working class energies did not directly challenge capitalism, but rather saw itself as a parallel movement for workers' ownership. To labour militants it was simply class collaboration. Certainly it was designed to appeal to King's distinctly *petit bourgeois* instincts since it suggested a means whereby workers might develop a small "share" in the existing system of private property. Most of all, King liked the anti-statist and pro-business elements of co-operative philosophy: "Co-operation has in it all the virtues claimed for Socialism, without its defects; it is individualistic, all self help, self initiative, and self dependence, no government protection. I am greatly taken with the movement as the best thing seen yet to put the working classes on a high level, to make them good citizens and men, and to raise them above the plane of industrial strife which destroys and enslaves." The co-operators, in short, had a "wider view" than socialists – they saw things from the capitalist as well as from the labour side.[23] Although King never maintained any deep interest in or connections with the co-operative movement, and certainly did nothing as a political leader in Canada to further the aims of a flourishing co-operative movement centered in the farm population, the spirit in which he praised what he saw in the movement in England is very revealing of his basic concept of class co-operation in capitalist society. As a different level of economic and political structures, the concept of co-operation applied to class relations was to be a crucial element in *Industry and Humanity*.

The turn away from socialism, with its attendant indifference to the possibility of any type of positive state intervention in the productive process, finds a parallel in the kind of reading which King followed after his college days were ended. As editor of the *Labour Gazette* and deputy minister of the newly formed department of labour, King immersed himself in the literature on labour relations mainly of the factual, descriptive and policy-oriented type characteristic of government reports and institutional-oriented academic monographs. This was precisely the kind of economics which had most appealed to him as a student. On the other hand his interest in theoretical work in political economy waned directly with the lifting of the enforced discipline of university courses.

At this same period one also notices from King's diaries a waxing interest in the spiritual and inspirational type of literature. As always with King, he showed a certain lack of discrimination in this regard and took some works seriously which no one with any taste or intelligence ought to have wasted time on. But he also found value in some more significant writers as well. Chief among these were the Victorian critics of materialism. Ruskin he had been familiar with from his youth. Then in the early years of the new century he discovered the works of Matthew Arnold and Thomas Carlyle. Arnold's attack on middle class philistinism, *Culture and Anarchy*, he much appreciated despite the fact that some of Arnold's targets might have been uncomfortably close to home. Arnold's poetry struck him with the force of relevation. The sense of faith under attack by materialism and of the apparent chaos of the industrial world were emotionally akin to King's own state of mind:

> And we are here as on a darkling plain
> Swept with confused alarms of struggle and flight
> Where ignorant armies clash by night.

From Arnold he derived a kind of crude Hegelian notion that the religious ends of life were immanent in historical and material forces. Thus he interpreted the labour movement as "the effort of the great mass of the people to realize the capacities of their natures, to fulfil the end of their being. The evidences of the order of the universe being goodness and truth, as seen by the impossibility of having public opinion favour a known wrong, etc."[24] Carlyle, the author of *Heroes, Hero-Worship and the Heroic in History*, and the great advocate of a return to paternalism of feudal institutions as a way out of industrial class conflict, was to King "in his rugged, earnest, honest, truthful way ... the greatest soul the British Isles have yet produced." Carlyle's *Past and Present* impressed him with its spiritual fervour and its emphasis on the work ethic.[25] It was presumably the emotive, thunderous prose, the powerful sentimentality of Carlyle to which King responded and not to any specific proposals which were largely wanting in Carlyle's works.

His admiration for Carlyle reveals the profound social and cultural conservatism of King. While his interest in the mechanisms of the material world, and in specific solutions to disequilibrium in these mechanisms made him a liberal, as did his populist heritage from his grandfather's tradition and protest against privilege and aristocracy, he was in his personal and social life a fierce defender of the status quo and the conventional wisdom – which often enough meant the conventional hypocrisies. King was quite aware of the ambiguity in his mind and attempted to resolve it by means of tidy definitions of liberalism and conservatism.

A Toryism which will conserve law and order and institutions that have helped to maintain society on a stable foundation, as, for example, the sanctity of marriage; of the home; of a day in seven for rest, etc. etc., is a Conservatism in which I believe and which is much needed in our time. The maintenance of privilege against all sense of rights is Toryism. There is a big distinction ... Privilege is always blind and will never make way for justice save by some force which will overthrow it; that is why I hate Toryism with all my heart.[26]

Reading Willison's biography of Laurier moved King to the following philosophic speculation:

Human nature has two directions – one self that distrusts itself, seeks refuge in tradition, authority and control from without, and the self that believes in itself and the nature of its creation, loves freedom, liberty, and the right to follow an inner vision wheresoever it leads. The former is naturally Conservative and hates change; the latter is by nature radical and seeks progress. The fault through excess of the one is bigotry, prejudice and oppression, of the other, license and revolution. As forces controlling each other each plays a useful part, of active forces in the cause of Humanity Liberalism is the best.[27]

Christianity made King a natural conservative; the optimistic temper of his theology made him a liberal. Both wedded him inexorably to the world as it was, whether as the cultural traditionalist or as the midwife of the logic of God's design in history.

If King defined himself in old-fashioned terms of political philosophy, his liberalism differed in one striking particular from that of
Laurier and the old party which he was about to inherit. In discussing labour policy with the Prime Minister one day, the young
deputy minister sadly concluded that Laurier had little basic sympathy for the working class: "I think he is strong in his antagonism
to race and religious differences, but not so in class differences (that
must be the next great stratum of political foundations)." Even the
primordial Canadian schism between English and French was to
King a more ambiguous and complex relationship than it might
appear. When Lord Milnor asked him about English-French conflict
in Montreal, King impatiently dismissed the "old story": "I explained that this was largely because some of the social people in
Montreal had made money rapidly, and the French not being as
wealthy, the division had become one of wealth rather than of race,
though to appearance it might seem a racial difference."[28] King was,
of course, later to demonstrate an acute sensitivity to ethnic and
cultural politics, but his understanding of the economic and class
aspects to political conflict distinguished him sharply from fellow
Liberals who lived more in the nineteenth than in the rapidly
industrializing twentieth century with its growing class divisions
and politicization of class conflicts. It was this understanding which
gave King a special touch of modernity which other Liberals lacked.

Some of the ambiguities surrounding King's concept of labour
and its place in the capitalist political economy were clarified when
he settled down to the job of creating Canada's federal labour
policies as deputy minister and minister of labour from 1900 to
1911. This is not the place to review King's role as labour mediator
or the shape which the new department took under King's direction.[29] What is significant is the ideology which his actions embodied. King's activities and his reflections about his activities all
point to one supreme central tenet in his conception of the role of
the state in labour relations: industrial "peace" at all costs. It is
scarcely an exaggeration to suggest that to King a work stoppage
was a sin against the holy ghost. When his beloved mother lay on
her death bed in 1917, King earnestly attempted to comfort her for
having produced a son "who has helped somewhat to improve
conditions for labour and to avert some of the loss that comes
through strikes and lockouts and other forms of industrial strife –
loss of life possibly, loss of happiness certainly, and who can say
what else!"[30] This extraordinary passion for preventing a single
stutter in the hum of production may in part have stemmed from

the perspective of a developing economy with a worship of economic growth even more unquestioning than today. But King's desire for peace at any price also derived very logically from the liberal philosophy which we have already traced in his intellectual development. There is an underlying order and harmony in the universe which reflects a divine harmonic design. Conflict in the material world is an impediment to the unfolding of this design. The resort to force deepens class consciousness and thus creates an escalation of violence which may end in reaction or revolution. The role of middle class reformers is to mediate between the two conflicting classes to restore the natural equilibrium in the political economy. Since there is no fundamental conflict of interest – both capital and labour are legitimate factors of production with their respective returns regulated by the market – conflict is essentially a problem of communication, of consciousness. Mediation between the two sides involves the manipulation of consciousness to cultivate the common ground and promote agreement. Mediation is therefore a *political* problem with political resolutions.

The mechanisms of mediation, or conciliation as King preferred to call it, rested heavily on the idea of investigation and publicity. The state would intervene to collect the facts involved in an industrial dispute and publish them. As an early annual report of the department of labour claimed, the "knowledge that all such disputes and differences are made the subject of an official inquiry by the department, have had a decided influence in deterring parties from hasty action preliminary to a strike or lockout, and of helping to bring to a termination disputes which had already arisen."[31] The 1907 Industrial Disputes Investigation Act which King authored and which "firmly established the major principles that have underlain Canadian industrial disputes legislation," in the words of one labour relations expert, placed central stress on investigation, with the additional power of compulsory delay of work stoppages while investigation was proceeding. A tripartite Board of Conciliation and Investigation was empowered to bring down recommendations concerning what "ought and ought not to be done by the respective parties concerned."[32] The impact of this legislation was to establish the federal government in a position of direct intervention in labour relations which was far more extensive than that obtaining in the United States. Moreover, King, who believed that "machinery is nothing, personality is everything," personally intervened in a surprisingly wide variety of labour disputes during this period.[33]

Stuart Jamieson, a scholarly and dispassionate student of labour relations, has concluded that many of King's interventions as deputy minister and minister of labour may have paradoxically bought short term peace at the cost of exacerbating long term conflict, for the simple reason that organized workers were stymied in their demands and eventually broke out later with yet greater strength and militancy.[34] Indeed, the notion that the exposure of the "facts" of labour disputes to the public will compel the two sides to agree is by now an antiquated relic of the past. Yet there is a larger sense in which King's legislative handiwork and his practice as a conciliator had a profound and long lasting impact of industrial relations in Canada. The central role of the Canadian state was established just when Britain was reducing the role of government in industrial relations. Later federal legislation, such as PC 1003 during World War II and the Industrial Relations and Disputes Investigation Act of 1948, as well as much provincial labour legislation, continued to embody this interventionist role of the state. The relative success rate of specific interventions within this legislative framework is perhaps less important than the fundamental acceptance by the labour movement of the state as a central actor in industrial relations. This implies a certain acquiescence on the part of labour in the image of the state's "neutrality" which King had been at such pains to cultivate.[35] Yet one does not have to probe very deeply to discover how mythical this "neutrality" is. That the state should intervene to seek continued production at all costs would inevitably reinforce capital in its struggle with labour. Even beyond this rather obvious point, King's activities may be seen as distinctly contrary to the most fundamental interests of the labour movement with which he claimed to sympathise.

In considering the anti-labour colouring of King's activities, it is important to note that King steadfastly refused to accept the basic industrial self-determination of workers: he refused to recognize their voluntarily chosen unions as having any necessary legitimacy in bargaining with their employers. Much of the labour unrest and industrial violence in this period stemmed from the refusal of owners to recognize unions as bargaining agents. The strike for union recognition was a relatively common occurrence, and King would have none of it. Here a basically paternalistic attitude comes to the surface of King's philosophy. To King there were legitimate unions and illegitimate unions, legitimate union leaders and illegitimate union leaders. The former were those who were willing to co-operate with capital and with the state; they were to be actively encouraged by employers and by government and thus enhanced in the eyes of the workers. The latter were to be fought with every weapon at the concerted disposal of and the state. Strikes for union recognition were wholly illegitimate and must be stopped; collusion between government and employers to foster company unions was altogether admirable and in the public interest. The alternative was to hand over the working class to the socialist and syndicalist agitators. King visited British Columbia on more than one occasion on missions of conciliation, and he was shocked by the very un-North American degree of labour militancy and socialist agitation in that province. "All of Canada can learn from B.C." he admonished, "the province speaks a note of warning in strongest terms against the dangers of a labour democracy. Industry will be fettered, and the source of wages and wealth left undeveloped, if change does not come. Where men without a stake rule those who have everything to lose, or at least to risk, the alarm is great."[36] King was out of the country while the Winnipeg General Strike was being contested in 1919, but while in the United States he was much frightened by the Seattle General Strike, which led him to comment:

Either the trade unions will have to become more conservative themselves, and be dealt with by employers ... the labour movement will slip away from any kind of organized control and into the worst kind of revolutionary unrest. The Bolshevist movement has shown the need, where numbers of men are employed, of some form of organization and of some close contact between the leaders of such organizations and the business managers, in a way that will bring out the unity of the interests between them.[37]

The Russian Revolution demonstrated the need for a "union of the organized forces of labour and capital, against a common enemy which menaces all human society."[38] Such a united front could only be made up of labour unions acceptable to capital, that is to say, company unions.

The exact nature of King's stance in relation to the labour movement appears in stark relief with his work as labour relations consultant to the Rockefeller empire during World War I. This page in King's career has been the cause of some embarrassment to his apologists, and even to King himself. The Rockefeller interlude was not, by any generous stretch of the imagination, an edifying or inspiring example of Mackenzie King's professed dedication to the working class or to liberal principles of fair play and equity. The bloody and tragic events of the Colorado coal "war," culminating in the infamous Ludlow massacre in which women and children were killed by troops, called forth one of the first major essays in corporate image building. This was an era when the robber barons of American capitalism generally took the position with regard to public opinion expressed by Cornelius Vanderbilt: "the public be damned." The Colorado affair was simply too much for moderate middle class opinion in the Progressive era. An official federal commission of investigation was headed by a populist who hated the Rockefellers and was intent upon bringing the wrath of an outraged citizenry down upon them. The Rockefellers responded in what has now become the classic behaviour of the capitalist corporation under fire – they sought to improve their public image. To this end John D. Rockefeller, Jr., hired Ivy Lee, a pioneer in the field of public relations and advertising, and Mackenzie King, a technical "expert" in labour relations. In accepting the Rockefeller post with alacrity, King demonstrated that as a middle class professional, his talents were for sale to the highest bidder, whether it was the public bureaucracy of the Canadian government or the private bureaucracy of the Rockefeller empire. He was, in truth, the kind of academically trained technocrat who would willingly become the "servant of power."[39]

Two facts are particularly pertinent to King's role in this affair. First, the entire strife in the Colorado coalfields had been brought about by the company's refusal to recognize the United Mine Workers as bargaining agent for the employees, who were existing under abject conditions of subordination to a feudal species of corporate domination – company towns, company stores, no collective negotiations, etc. The Rockefellers were adamant that they would never bargain with the union chosen by the majority of the workers. Moreover, King was told of this position in no uncertain terms by the Rockefellers, father and son, when he was being interviewed for the job, and he raised no objection. Indeed, he explicitly agreed with them in this, although he went on to suggest that the company was wrong in allowing such working conditions as existed in Colorado to prevail.[40] This was King's "moderate" position between the "extremes" of corporate autocracy and union militancy. He had no compunctions about breaking the United Mine Workers union. To King, the UMW was outside the pale since it based its actions upon the idea that the working class should be sovereign in its choice of its own collective organizations. In carrying out the Rockefellers' orders, King characteristically attempted to justify himself in high sounding liberal terms. In a veritable triumph of formal and empty liberalism, he argued that the men could join whatever organization they wished, but that the employer was equally free to choose with whom he would bargain:

The question of making an agreement with a particular union was one thing, and the question of allowing men to join any organization they pleased was another ... Briefly stated, the crux of this union matter seems to me to come down to this: the demand on the side of the union that this agreement should be entered into with them, permitting only the employment of union men, is an extreme position on the one side. Each is an unfair abridgement of a fundamental human right.[41]

What was done instead in the Colorado case was to organize a company union around alleged patterns of worker participation in the affairs of the mines. It is true that conditions were materially ameliorated by this device; this too was part of King's liberal philosophy, for without a concrete improvement of conditions, he knew that the UMW would remain strong. In the short run this co-optive liberalism worked. The UMW was broken and a company union established with which the Rockefellers could live amicably. Some twenty years later the "Colorado plan" as it was grandiosely touted by the Rockefeller public relations apparatus was officially outlawed by the United States Congress in the Wagner Act.

There are a number of points which emerge from this episode salient to King's developing ideas on class in industrial society. First, the profound paternalism of King's attitude toward the working class is manifest. I choose that word advisedly, for King was always most anxious to steer the Rockefeller empire away from any public suggestion of "paternalism" in labour relations. King knew very well that an increasingly restive working class striving for a greater share of economic democracy to match the rhetoric of political democracy which was so pronounced in North America in this era, would view paternalism on the part of employers and the state as merely another guise for domination. Even in his own diary, King scrupulously avoided tainting himself with the odour of paternalism. Yet what other word can one give to an approach to labour which refused steadfastly to recognize voluntarily chosen collective representatives of the workers and looked to company-inspired pro-management organizations to avoid worker sovereignty even within the confines of capitalist ownership of the means of production? That King's mission was essentially paternalistic is confirmed by the extravagant praise he heaped upon Rockefeller, Jr. and his executives, "the best men in America" he termed them, adding significantly, "and true friends." He clearly viewed young Mr. Rockefeller's inherited riches as a trust, to be administered with *noblesse oblige*, for as he told his boss, "men of power or position, however attained, have a special obligation to secure justice to the many who were in a relatively weak position."[42] The master of image politics inadvertently let the cat out of the bag when under questioning before the Commission on Industrial Relations. When he was asked to state his views on whether the American people were not the most responsible force to compel the Rockefeller interests to better conditions in Colorado, King egregiously replied:

If you are speaking of the immediate force and immediate influence, I think that the conscience of Mr. John D. Rockefeller, Junior, is more powerful on that, and will affect social justice quicker than any other single force that you could bring to bear. I think he realizes there is a great work to do there, and he intends to have it done.[43]

The publicity storm which broke over King's head following this blunder drove him to paroxysms of self-righteous indignation. Sinking into self-pity he lamented that

It is an easy thing to publicly champion the cause of the poor and miserable, and to talk to the world about their injustices. One gets nothing but abuse and misunderstanding for attempting to do this on behalf of a millionaire ... The public is governed by its prejudices, not by a regard for the working out of immutable moral laws in the affairs of men ... [I] shall await with extreme satisfaction the day when this incident of standing for right and justice and fair play as regards the wealthiest man in the world is going to serve to make my voice heard on behalf of some of the poorest against the aggressions and tyrannies of wealth.[44]

King had worked assiduously at cultivating an image of enlightened, responsible capitalism for the Rockefellers, emphasising the personal charm of young Rockefeller, and stressing the philanthropic and charitable dispensation of the family billions. A socialist UMW leader, John Lawson, was unimpressed. "It is not *their* money," he asserted, "that these lords of commercialized virtue are spending, but the withheld wages of the American people."[45] In that one sentence, Lawson laid bare the paternalism of King's *apologia*. The alleged middle course which King attempted to steer between the "extremes" of capital and labour was a fraud, for he denied the sovereignty of the working class to choose its own effective representatives to bargain with capital, and at the same time justified an autocratic and irresponsible right of capitalists to distribute the surplus resources of the economy in any way they saw fit, guided only by their sovereign Christian conscience. Underlying King's pretensions to modernity in political philosophy, one quickly detects a much more old-fashioned liberalism than would appear on the surface.

One final note of interest to emerge from King's Rockefeller period, as well as from his service as deputy minister and minister of labour: it was not some arcane "technical" skill in labour relations which was King's selling point as a consultant for hire, it was in a very real sense simply his *political* skills at the manipulation of men's minds, precisely the same skills which were to serve him so well in future years as prime minister of Canada. When a corporate empire like that of the Rockefellers found itself in labour difficulties, which were compounded by political difficulties in an era of muckraking journalism and middle class social conscience, it required the services of someone with at least minimal understanding of labour union organizations and of the prevalent directions of thought among labour leaders, along with a finely-tuned sense for what would "sell" to the public. King as a mediator in labour disputes showed consummate skill at playing union leaders off against one another, at undercutting their credibility and legitimacy with their members by making direct appeals to the latter over their heads, and at presenting the employers in the best possible light. In the Colorado affair, King hit upon a happy stroke of genius by separating the ownership (the Rockefellers) from the management, and blaming the local managers for all the company's mistakes while building up Rockefeller, Jr., as the enlightened capitalist who would set things aright once he had been given wise counsel (i.e., from King). When all was said and done, it was sheer political skill which saw King through these labour disputes; his reputation as a labour relations expert was more in the nature of public relations trumpery than actual substance. To be fair, King himself had a theory to explain this. When the president of Harvard took him to task for failing to provide a "fundamental" contribution to the question of labour relations, King simply replied that "the whole question of industrial relations was essentially one of human relations, and that the method of dealing with it lay along the lines of considering the significance of the personal contacts in industry."[46] Inasmuch as King was in fact playing the familiar game of liberal interest group politics, it is well to note that his activities are in fact subject to the same criticism that this sort of politics has generally attracted. He was highly successful in the short run at reestablishing peace and consensus, but his short term solutions did little to build the basis for long term agreement, indeed in most cases they served to exacerbate the fundamental conflicts.

What we have observed up until now is the progress of a relatively intelligent, ambitious, and politically adroit young man on the make, whose academic training was carefully utilized as an instrument for personal advancement – the very model of the upwardly mobile new middle class man of the early twentieth century. If that were all there were to King, the investigation of his career would merely be of interest to students of political engineering. But that there was more to King is evident from his book *Industry and Humanity*, which emerged out of his work for the Rockefeller Foundation. This much-despised book, impenetrable, pompous, tedious, as overstuffed as a Victorian sofa and as interminable as a sermon on moral uplift, is nevertheless, with all its undoubted faults, an important statement of liberalism in twentieth-century Canada. Indeed, taken in comparison with the flood of books on the "social question" which emerged in Canada during and just after the war, with authors ranging from tories like Stephen Leacock to farmer and labour radicals like W.C. Good and William Irvine, King's book, style and structure aside, stands out as among the most farsighted and insightful. What is perhaps most surprising about *Industry and Humanity*, considered in relation to what we know of its creator, is its fundamentally *visionary* quality.

Despite the suspicions on the part of some observers that the book was merely a campaign document to help King win the Liberal leadership, it is clear that to King himself the book was far more. Rockefeller, Jr., who always entertained serious doubts about the entire project, suggested to King that he could make more money and do more significant and concrete work by freelancing as a labour relations consultant for American corporations than by devoting himself to the writing of an abstruse tome. King was adamant: "the book would have a far-reaching influence ... it would have the principles which should be applied and could be applied all along the line ... my subsequent work would be the application in a practical way."[47] Yet it is also clear that from the beginning King saw his task as more than simply writing a textbook on the principles of labour relations. The title itself conveys the extraordinary breadth and scope which the author wished to cover. Moreover, the infamous diagrams appended to the end of the volume, which caused Rockefeller some embarrassment and have afforded subsequent generations much amusement, were not an afterthought intended to give pseudo-philosophical form to King's written ramblings; rather the author began with the diagrams and later worked out the text to accompany them. This point is of more than passing significance considering the grandiose, metaphysical nature of these diagrams with their cosmologies of the world, industry, mankind, and the natural laws of peace, work, and health. In other words, in King's own mind, the specific policy aspects of labour relations were only applications of an overarching interpretation of man's place in the universe.

To be precise, King actually began his work for the Rockefeller Foundation with the development of his diagrams, well before the book was an active project. Early in 1914, King was spending some time at Harvard and outlining a chart of industrial relations. "It was a delight," King enthusiastically reported in his diary, "and I went at the work as a sculptor or painter would, with the rough outlines and the gradual marking in of proportions and symmetries." Within a few days more diagrams followed. The quote from Louis Pasteur on the competing "Laws" of "Blood and Death," and of "Peace, Work and Health," with which the book was eventually to open came to King's mind at this early stage as a key to unlocking the secrets of the industrial problem. Since these "laws" are the worst kind of pseudo-science, nobody has paid them much heed. Intrinsically, they certainly require no serious attention. More interesting is what the use of these "laws" reveals of King's deeper purpose. When the Pasteur quote occurred to King, he saw it as revealing a parallel between medicine and industrial relations.[48] At first glance, this seems an odd parallel to draw, until one realizes that King wished to find a "scientific" basis for an *organic* theory of society.

As his diagrams took shape, King consciously drew upon the implications of an organic concept of society. By analogy to the human body, King saw all of humanity governed by the heart or the stomach, instruments which answered to the two goals of human relations, the "domestic" (market relations of material satisfactions). "To begin at this point," King wrote, " is to lead to readjustment in one's whole outlook on life. It is to see what Christ meant when he spoke of man not living by bread alone (the needs of the stomach) but by every word which proceedeth out of the mouth of God (the needs of the heart). Both are interrelated and interdependent. The art of living is an understanding [of] how to produce harmony between them," King does not pursue this organic conception as literally as John of Salisbury, but it underlies his drive to "bring out strongly the position of society as a whole ... that co-operation towards a common ideal, the well being of the whole, must supplant the idea of domination of one of the parts, over other."[49] The rhetoric appears egalitarian, until one considers the significance of the organic mode of thought, which is inevitably hierarchical inasmuch as the mind must rule the stomach, as the heart (moral sense) must rule the mind. The *organic* role of the working class is thus of a lower order than that of the directing principles of capital and management.

In *Industry and Humanity* King quotes with approval the left wing of Social Darwinism which had argued that "Mankind as a whole is the complete social organism ... A world of peace ... each part-co-operating with the others and effecting a co-ordination of effort aimed at destroying every obstacle to perfect manhood, would reveal a social organism rendering itself fittest to survive."[50] Yet only a few pages earlier, King had used Sir Henry Maine's argument about modern society moving from "status to contract" with evident enthusiasm, since he sees contractual relations between capitalist and worker in Lockean terms as presupposing "equality of the parties before the law" (p. 79). Thus "if the *cash nexus* has broken the bond of personal security, it has broken also the yoke of personal subordination." Is King thus hopelessly suspended between contradictory assumptions or organic collectivity versus contractual liberalism? There is no doubt that King fails in the end to resolve the contradiction: he wishes to remain a liberal, but with organicist roots. Yet the answer must be qualified by the precise specification King gives to his organic model. In fact King is here drawing (without acknowledgement) from his old mentor Toynbee, who had argued that the industrial revolution, by destroying the old relations of feudal subordination, had created the basis for a new and more equitable partnership between employer and employee, based precisely upon a contractual, as opposed to a customary, link. The move from status to contract in an *industrial* world laid the foundation for an organic society in which the roles were truly divided on a *functional* basis. The division of labour and the returns to production were decided by the mechanism of the market, which by its impersonality, could not be accused of favoritism or corruption. This provided the basis for a truly *just* organic structure of roles and rewards.

Epistemologically, King had no doubt about the validity of deriving all-embracing laws of human behaviour from metaphysical postulates. Defending himself against those who would see the "Law of Peace, Work, Health" as a "mere abstraction," King rather ingenuously replied that it was no more so than the law of gravitation, or the law of evolution:

In the case of each of these so-called "laws," Science has ventured to explain certain facts of the material universe by means of hypotheses which make these facts intelligible and reasonable. In each case she has put forth a proposition in accordance with which it is possible to give sequence, orderly relation, and meaning to what otherwise would be unrelated and inchoate elements. If the physical universe is rational and can be understood, is it not reasonable to suppose that, in the field of human relationships, as respects human right and obligation, there are also laws which govern conduct in accordance with previous thought?

A universal cosmic order which is wholly rational and law-abiding is the fundamental assumption of all science. It assumes that those propositions are true which are necessary to make the facts of life intelligible and reasonable ... The Law of Peace, Work and Health is a part of the larger Order which sustains a divine creation, and which evidences a universe begotten of a beneficient Deity, not a world the outcome of Chance, nor even of Intelligence, limited to the direction of Matter and Force.[51]

This argument bears less resemblance to a chain of logic than to a revolving door. King enlists natural science in the cause of social science, but the entire relationship rests on faith alone. What we do find here is the key to King's veritable mania for *simplification*,[52] that underlying the complexities and diversities of the sensual world, the basic structure is clear, orderly, and simple. King's lack of interest in philosophy is explicable in this light. The problem to him was not philosophical, but practical – how to implement in a sinful world what was obvious to any morally informed intelligence.

The organic basis of human social relationships is to be *discovered* as a material reflection of the Mind which orders the universe. The "law" of "peace, work, and health" suggests that industrial peace allows for economic production by the co-operating units which in turn results in the organic "health" of the social collectivity. King, in writing during the carnage of World War I, is careful to extend this from the industrial to the international plane. In doing so, King boldly confronts the objection that his argument is irrelevant to the real world. There is a competing law at work, that of "blood and death." King, after all, is a Christian, not a Pollyanna. Mankind has fallen from grace and must earn forgiveness by triumphing over evil. Promethean man's very reaching for perfection disturbs the natural order, even while giving proof of his position between God and beast. Thus the imagery with which he begins the first chapter on "industrial and international unrest," the imagery of Frankenstein, the creation of man turned into an uncontrollable monster of death and destruction. This Gothic image of the industrial revolution is striking enough in itself as evidence of a failing faith of the North American middle class in the comfortable certitudes of inevitable progress. "Surely, Industry is something other than was intended by those who contributed to its creation, when it can be transformed into a monster so demoniacal as to breed a terror unparalleled in human thought, and bring desolation to the very heart of the human race!"[53] More importantly, this imagery suggests the power which King attributed to the industrial revolution as a universal solvent of social tradition and customary ways of life. Marx too laid epochal significance on the transformation of man by the processes of modernity, but to King it was not the market system nor the rise of the capitalist bourgeoisie which were the crucial factors. King is much more of a technological determinist than Marx; it is the material transformations rather than the changing relationships among men which are the turning point. Here King is within a Canadian tradition, from T.C. Keefer's *Philosophy of Railroads* to George Grant's *Technology and Empire*, a tradition which sees technique as the key to historical change, whether for better or for worse. And not merely the key, but the *universal* key.

The stress which King laid upon the industrialization process as the transforming factor, to the exclusion of class development and class conflict gives further support to the hierarchical nature of his organic society. Class divisions are to King necessary and natural phenomena of all conceivable political orders. There can be no concept of a "universal class" in King's thought. There are only interdependent classes, performing specialized tasks functional to the organic whole. King has no doubt that industrialization has altered class relations, and in one sense, for the worse. The very facts of class conflict and industrial strife are evidence of the disturbance which has taken place. He is also aware of the enormous disparity between capital and labour of the "inherent ubiquity of capital," its "mobility" and "fluidity," its internationalism, "with no definite occupation or home," and of the crucial political influence derived from wealth, as opposed to the powerlessness and insecurity of labour, its confinement within national and cultural borders, its psychological as well as material weakness. He is also aware that just as capital seeks to overcome the insecurity of the market by mergers, cartels, and monopolies, so too workers "exist as atoms in a human tide so vast, and subject to such ceaseless ebb and flow, that the effort to secure collective stability becomes the first requisite of existence itself."[54] Like J.S. Mill, King harbours doubts about the supremacy of capital:

For the preferential treatment Capital has thus far received, there is no defence possible on grounds of democratic theory or fundamental justice, only an explanation. Capital has been able to wait; Labour has not. Capital, through its ability to wait, has been in a position to compel a voice.[55]

King's solution is one of co-partnership between capital and labour.

In light of his actual activities as a mediator, and his Rockefeller duties, it should not surprise us to find that this is, from labour's point of view, very much a junior partnership, if that:

Partnership is essentially a matter of status. It does not involve identity of function on the part of the partners, or equality of either service or rewards: but it does imply equality, as respects the right of representation, in the determination of policy on matters of common interest.[56]

We have moved from status to contract back to status again. In other words, as to the actual division of the resources of the industrial economy between capital and labour, King remains silent. At another point, he speaks of an "adequate" return to the worker, and then immediately defined this as the market value of his productivity. At another point, he falls back on Mill's distinction between production and distribution as offering an opportunity to redistribute without altering the productive system. But he does little with this; he is much more interested in the old North American tradition of economic growth as an evasion of class conflict. With more being produced, invidious comparisons about the distribution will presumably be lessened.[57]

An emphasis on economic growth leads to an emphasis on productive efficiency, and thus on industrial peace. We are thus back again at King's *idée fixe*. Where capital confronts labour directly, the conflict will inevitably tend to be over resources (profits versus wages) and hence a zero-sum game. To solve this basic industrial disorder, to bring about the partnership he wishes to see, it is necessary for King to step outside this bipolar conflict model and seek external forces for compromise. It is here that King's book borders on some originality.

His concept of the "four partners of industry" attempts to widen the scope of industrial politics in two directions. First, his emphasis on the separation of capital and management was not merely a sign of some sensitivity to the prevailing currents of opinion, but also showed an acute understanding of the *political* significance of demonstrating the existence of a "technostructure" (in Galbraith's later term), distinct from the capitalists themselves. As King argues, state socialism might expropriate individual capitalists, but "in actual practice, 'political managers' would be substituted for 'capitalist managers'. Though differently controlled, the capitalist form of large organization of Industry, with its division of labour, its division of industrial processes, and its divisions of industrial areas, would still remain." The political moral was clear: "It is not against the *form*, but against the possible *abuses*, of industrial organization, whatever the system, that protests should be uttered."[58] Galbraith himself could not have stated it better a half century later.

After management, the fourth partner to industry is the "community." It is by no means clear just what King understood by this. At times it would seem to be some Rousseauean collectivity in possession of a general consensus, if not a general will. More often it seems to be simply the government. This interpretation is obviously strengthened by King's own role as an interventionist bureaucrat. A few points may be made about this role for government. First, it may be noted that labour is reduced to a one-quarter partnership. The employer has two voices, capital and management. King is careful to specify that governments in capitalist societies are essentially supportive of business ("What is ninety-nine percent of the expenditure of Government in normal times, but outlays in the nature of investment in Industry: investment in property and services of one kind or another which alone makes possible the vast co-operation and co-ordination of effort which is the very life-blood of Industry?"[59]) It is thus apparent that labour is decidedly a minority; King's behaviour as mediator certainly offers no evidence to dispel this impression.

More striking yet is what this concept reveals of King's attitude toward government. So deeply does he believe in "industry" as the key to human conflict, that traditional government structures are quite secondary. When he contemplates the idea of industrial peace, he adds as an afterthought that "the existence of such a perfectly adjusted industrial order would be found to disclose a perfectly organized political order as well. For if, in all the relations within industry, there existed perfect adjustment, the habit of mind of communities would be such that, in the domain of politics, variation from the laws applicable to Industry would be unnatural." King goes further than this to suggest that the four partners for a "Directorate" which would control industry in the common interest, "just as, in a Cabinet, expression is given to the common interests of a nation."[60] We thus have an extension of governmental forms in industry; what then of the traditional state? King is carefully ambiguous:

Whether political and industrial government will merge into one, or tend to remain separate and distinct, the one being supplementary to the other, is a moot question. The probabilities are that for years to come they will exist side by side, mostly distinguishable, but, in much, so merged that separateness will be possible in theory only.[61]

If the "directorate" of partners corresponds to the cabinet, King unflinchingly draws a parallel between industrial management and the political executive, which is particularly revealing of his political ideas. After briefly discussing the conventional theory then current of the separation of politics and administration, only to drop it in favour of a more realistic notion of the important role of the administration in policy making, King makes clear that the directorate would function "with Management advising, and often dictating to the other constituent elements, just as under the British constitution, the Prime Minister and his Cabinet, and under the American constitution, the President and his Cabinet, not withstanding that their primary function is executive, advise, and, within bounds, dictate to Parliament and Congress respectively."[62]

The integration of labour within industrial decision-making structures; the gradual merger of the political and industrial "governments"; a determining voice for the managerial technocrats: thus the outlines of what can only be described as a *corporatist* vision of the future. King does not draw out all the ramifications; many questions are left pointedly unanswered. But King himself was quite aware that his ideas represented a shift away from traditional liberalism towards "collectivism."[63] This "collectivism" was in no sense socialistic, since it involved no change in the ownership of the means of production. But it was collectivist inasmuch as it saw society composed of organized groups, and saw individuals having significance only as members of such collectivities. Politics becomes the ordering of relationships between organized groups; indeed, the structures of accommodation appear to supersede government altogether. Since organized interests are represented in the interior processes of decision-making, they are collectively responsible for the decisions. King's faith was that the clash of interests characteristic of capitalist societies was not inevitable, as pluralists would have it, but could be brought to a definitive end.

Philippe Schmitter has drawn well the contrast between pluralist and corporatist views of interest groups:

The former suggest spontaneous formation, numerical proliferation, horizontal extension and competitive interaction; the latter advocate controlled emergence, quantitative limitation, vertical stratification and complementary interdependence. Pluralists place their faith in the shifting balance of mechanically intersecting forces; corporatists appeal to the functional adjustment of an organically interdependent whole.[64]

King's corporatism appears to correspond to Schmitter's category of "societal corporatism," as opposed to the "state corporatism," usually associated with fascism. That is to say, King's corporatism remains liberal, to be based not on authoritarian compulsion but on the ability of an enlightened technostructure to bring about the integration of the organized interests into governing structures through the leadership and education of public opinion. King's statement of corporatism remains visionary, and his book is filled with careful circumspection on the possibility of realizing the vision. This circumspection is itself evidence of his fundamental liberalism; he would work with the forces of society as they were and not try to force the issue. To push too quickly would only arouse the opposition of powerful forces and thus exacerbate conflict. Short term peace, whether in industrial relations or in politics, was always King's major concern. Moreover, King's book was visionary in more ways than one. So far as the Canada of 1918 was concerned, *Industry and Humanity* ignored the class conjuncture of the time and leaped ahead to a future when the farmers and other *petit bourgeois* elements had ceased to be of real economic or political significance. The actual Canada which King inherited as prime minister in 1921 was one of which the main political conflict was between the *grand* and *petite bourgeoises*, and King devoted his efforts to placating the agrarian Progressives, a group given not a line in *Industry and Humanity*. The class conjuncture which he envisioned in the book was thus prophetic, but not entirely relevant to its own age.

King's corporatist vision was not simply Utopian. He did have a theory of social change which, while scarcely activist, was not entirely quietist:

The renovation of nations, says William James, begins always among the reflective members of the State, and spreads slowly outward and downward. The thinkers, the teachers, the spiritual and political leaders, the practical idealists in business, hold a country's future in their hands. How to transmit the force of individual opinion and preference into public action has been described as the most difficult and the most momentous question of Government. Intricate as it may appear, in the midst of dire necessity and surrounded as we are by the controversy of contending forces, we must "find a way or make it."[65]

Thus the role of King's book. On these grounds it must, of course, be judged a failure. Its length, its style and its inaccessibility prevented it from renovating the nation, even by extension. Yet to give King his due, it must be admitted that his liberal corporatist vision had, for its time, an astonishingly prophetic quality. Taken in conjunction with his legislative imprint on Canadian industrial relations with its central role for the "community," King's corporatist vision indeed has some concrete manifestation in the real world of the 1970s. Corporatism as the alternative to socialism and an answer to labour militancy is moreover the conventional wisdom of much of the Western world today. That the Canadian Labour Congress, sixty years after King's book, can think of nothing better as an alternative to class conflict in a capitalist society than corporatist "tripartism" (only management removed from King's scheme) is itself a tribute to the modernity of the early Mackenzie King.

What is interesting about King's intellectual odyssey toward corporatism is what it reveals of the basis of this currently fashionable concept. Corporatism was not inimical to liberalism, but instead grew out of a crisis of liberal capitalist democracy and offered an apparent solution to that crisis which would not challenge the basic structures of the capitalist political economy but would instead consolidate them. Corporatism would freeze existing class inequalities by institutionalizing them and incorporating them into the structures of the state. Corporatism was above all an *ideological* solution to a *structural* problem. It was no accident that King held to an organic view of society which derived from an idealist metaphysics. It was only at the ideal level that the organic structure of precapitalist society could be obtained in the cash nexus world of industrial capitalism. The achievement of corporatism was not so much a material problem as a problem of *consciousness*. Yet the intractably inorganic and alienated nature of the real world presented a fundamental contradiction. King's failure to resolve this contradiction ought not to surprise us, for his failure is the failure of his successors a half century later. In 1918 King struck the prophetic stance of a liberalism yet to come. Both in the theoretical accession to traditional liberalism and in the weakness which that accession obscured, King was, like a good liberal, just slightly ahead of his time.

NOTES

This is a modified version of a paper presented to the Annual Meeting of the Canadian Political Science Association, Fredericton, N.B., June, 1977. Many people have commented on the paper – among them: Ramsay Cook, Russell Hann, Greg Kealey, Bernard Ostry, and Leo Panitch. These and others I would like to thank for their helpful criticisms.

1 Public Archives of Canada, William Lyon Mackenzie King Papers, Diary, 21 February 1904.
2 Henry Ferns and Bernard Ostry, *The Age of Mackenzie King* (1955: new edition, Toronto 1976).
3 See my review of the 1973 reprint of *Industry and Humanity* in the *Canadian Journal of Political Science* 7 (March 1974): 166–7; K.J. Rea and J.T. McLeod, *Business and Government in Canada* (Toronto, 2nd ed., 1976), 340; Leo Panitch, "The Development of Corporatism in Liberal Democracies," *Comparative Political Studies* 10 (April 1977): 61–90 and "The Role and Nature of the Canadian State," in Panitch, ed. *The Canadian State: Political Economy and Political Power* (Toronto 1977): my article, "Images of the State in Canada," in Panitch, *Canadian State*; Jack McLeod, "The Free Enterprise Dodo is no Phoenix," *Canadian Forum* 56 (August 1976): 6–13.
4 C.P. Stacey, *A Very Double Life: The Private World of Mackenzie King* (Toronto 1976). See also my own, rather different, approach to the problem of contradiction in King's personality, "Mackenzie King in the Dominion of the Dead," *Canadian Forum* 55 (February 1976): 6–11.
5 Diary, 22 February 1895.
6 Richard Hofstadter, *The Age of Reform* (New York 1955), 131–73. The question of King's relationship to the American Progressives has been perceptively explored by Keith Cassidy in a paper delivered at the Mackenzie King Centennial Colloquium, University of Waterloo, December, 1974.
   My thanks to Prof. Cassidy for providing me with a draft copy of this paper. On the new middle class see also Wiebe, *The Search for Order 1877–1920* (New York 1967), 111–32.
7 Christopher Lasch, *The New Radicalism in America, 1889–1963: The Intellectual as a Social Type* (New York 1965), 169.
8 King, *The Secret of Heroism* (Toronto 1906), 114.
9 Craufurd D.W. Goodwin, *Canadian Economic Thought: the Political Economy of a Developing Nation 1814–1914* Durham, N.C., 1961), 160–1, 176–7.
10 Joseph Schumpeter, *History of Economic Analysis* (New York 1954), 800–24.
11 Diary, 11 July 1894.
12 Arnold Toynbee, *Lectures on the Industrial Revolution in England, Popular Addresses, Notes and Other Fragments* (1884; new edition, New York 1969), with introduction by T.S. Ashton. On Toynbee see also Melvin Richter, *The Politics of Conscience: T.H. Green and His Age* (London 1964).
13 Diary, 27–9 June, 1916.
14 Diary, 12 May and 18 June, 1897. Veblen's article, "The Socialist Economies of Karl Marx and His Followers," *Quarterly Journal of Economics* 20 (1905–6): 575 and 21 (1906–7): 299, demonstrated a perceptive grasp of

the Hegelian foundations of Marx's thought and of the limitations of
the mechanistic determinism of post-Marx Marxists who had distorted
the teachings of their master. O.D. Skelton, himself an intelligent critic
of Marxism, cited Veblen as "The most objective and clearsighted
student of Socialism." Skelton, *Socialism, A Critical Analysis* (Boston
1911), 249.

King's copious notes on Veblen's lectures can be found in the King
papers. See also Diary, 21–8 May 1897, 13 August 1897.

15 Diary, 3 November 1897.
16 "Trade-Union Organization In the United States," *Journal of Political
Economy* 5 (1897): 201–15: "The International Typographical Union,"
Journal of Political Economy 4 (1897): 458–84.
17 F.W. Taussig, *Wages and Capital, An Examination Of the Wages Fund
Doctrine*, (London 1896), 319–25. On Taussig, see Schumpeter, *History
Of Economic Analysis*, 870–1. Diary, 5 December 1898.
18 Diary, 19 January 1898.
19 Diary, 18 March 1899. For Cunningham's discussion of economics and
religion see his *Christianity and Economic Science* (London 1914).
20 Diary, 23 March, 11 November 1898; 15 January 1899. On Drummond
and other popularizers of Darwinian "ethics," see Richard Hofstadter,
Social Darwinism In American Thought (2nd ed., New York 1955), 85–104.
21 Diary, 27 October, 1 November, 8 December 1898; 26–7 January, 28
February, 19 April, 26 June, 5 and 11 July 1899.
22 Diary, 18 October 1899; 2–3 and 22 January 1900.
23 Diary, 27 January 1900.
24 Diary, 7–8 September, 15–16 October 1901. The verse quotation is from
Arnold's "Dover Beach."
25 Diary, 10 January 1901; 6 April 1908.
26 Typescript diary, 25 April 1915.
27 Typescript diary, 18 February 1914.
28 Diary, 12 February 1904; 11 April 1908.
29 See Ferns and Ostry, *Age of Mackenzie King*, 46–145; Jay Atherton, "The
Department of Labour and Industrial Relations, 1900–1911," MA Thesis,
Carleton University, 1972.
30 Diary, 6 February 1917.
31 Quoted in Atherton, "Department Of Labour," 123.
32 Stuart Jamieson, *Industrial Relations In Canada* (Toronto 1957), 105–6.
33 Diary, 2 January 1903.
34 *Times of Trouble: Labour Unrest and Industrial Conflict In Canada*, 1900–66
(Ottawa 1968), 70–1, and 112–21.
35 See Bradley Rudin, "Mackenzie King and the Writing of Canada's
(Anti) Labour Laws," *Canadian Dimension* (January 1972).
36 Diary, 19 November 1901.

37 Typescript diary, 8 February 1919.
38 Quoted in Ferns and Ostry, 310.
39 Loren Baritz, *Servants of Power: A History Of the Use Of Social Science In American Industry* (Middletown, Conn., 1956).
40 Typescript diary, 1914–15, pp. 15, 121.
41 Typescript diary, 7 and 13 September 1915.
42 Typescript diary, 1914–15, p. 42; diary, 24 October 1916.
43 Quoted in F.A. McGregor, *The Fall and Rise of Mackenzie King, 1911–1919* (Toronto 1962) 167.
44 Typescript diary, 17–25 May and 26 May–4 June 1915.
45 George S. McGovern and Leonard F. Guttridge, *The Great Coalfield War* (Boston 1972), 320–1.
46 Typescript diary, 27 January 1915.
47 Typescript diary, 7–9 March 1917.
48 Diary, 6, 13, 20–1 October 1914.
49 Diary, 13 October, 1914.
50 *Industry and Humanity* (Toronto, new edition, 1973), 86.
51 Ibid., 109–111.
52 A point nicely made in an unpublished paper by Barry Cooper on *Industry and Humanity*. I wish to thank Professor Cooper for showing me this paper.
53 *Industry and Humanity*, 15.
54 Ibid., 43, 456, 158.
55 Ibid., 238.
56 Ibid., 236–7.
57 Ibid., 76, 174–5, 178.
58 Ibid., 76.
59 Ibid., 238.
60 Ibid., 269.
61 Ibid., 246.
62 Ibid., 272.
63 Ibid., 268.
64 "Still the Century of Corporatism," *Review of Politics* 36 (January 1974): 97.
65 *Industry and Humanity*, 276.

CHAPTER THREE

William Irvine and the Farmers in Politics

This essay was originally written as the introduction to a new edition of William Irvine's 1920 book *The Farmers in Politics*. Irvine was an early twentieth-century political thinker and politician, but a very different one from Mackenzie King. Irvine represents two important strands of radical politics. One, now a historical relic, was the movement of farmers into politics as part of the post-World War I revulsion against urban industrialization, big business, and old-line partyism subservient to big business. The second was the more enduring tradition of social democracy. Irvine tried to theorize the relationship between agrarian protest and social democracy.

Although farmers' movements are no longer politically relevant, I argue in this essay that Canadian social democracy was decisively shaped by a historical conjuncture of class forces which has given it a certain specificity and a unique identity. Social democracy in this country emerged out of a synthesis of British labourist and Fabian themes, along with some Marxist strains, and an indigenous agrarian radicalism which Irvine analysed from an unusual perspective. This essay gave me the opportunity to re-examine some of the themes developed by an earlier generation of political scientists in explaining the farmers movements, the CCF-NDP, and Social Credit, including those raised in *Democracy in Alberta* by my old teacher and intellectual mentor in political theory, C.B. Macpherson.

The farmers' movements generated some searching populist critiques of the party system and the capitalist model of economic decision-making. In the early 1990s we appear to be witnessing once again the decline of the old parties and the sudden emergence of new parties. The most successful of these, apart from the nationalist Bloc Québécois, has been the

Reprinted with permission from William Irvine, *The Farmers in Politics* (Toronto: McClelland & Stewart 1976).

Reform Party, which has its base in Irvine's Alberta and espouses a radical critique of the existing process of party government. Although Reform is more right-wing than left-wing in its economic program, its program for political reform offers a striking testimony to the continuity of a certain strain of prairie populism throughout this century.

Subsequent to the publication of this essay, David Laycock, a young political scientist at Simon Fraser University, published *Populism and Democratic Thought in the Canadian Prairies* (Toronto: University of Toronto Press, 1990) which places Irvine, as well as other Western populist figures, within a convincing framework of evolving democratic ideas. I urge any interested readers to consult this very useful work.

Canada, according to the familiar legend, is a country singularly without political ideology. Political ideologies are believed to be, like venereal diseases, the result of moral decay, and characteristic of the decadent areas of the world, such as Europe. Here, in the clean frontier atmosphere of North America, there seems little evidence of such weaknesses. Instead of ideology, the Canadian password has been *pragmatism*. Our politics have been those of brokerage parties which seek to aggregate the largest number of disparate interests behind the most nebulous platform possible, and political decision makers have been guided not by dogma but a practical appreciation of what will work in a given situation.[1] So the legend goes.

There is, of course, a large element of truth in this image. Few would deny that Canadian politics have been lacking in ideological clarity. There is also an uncomfortable awareness, even among those who laud the rejection of ideology, that our politics have been without principles and moral commitment.[2] Yet the picture is overdrawn, on both sides. The simple two-party model of contending factions distinguished only by their status as either "Ins" or "Outs" still have the ring of reality about it. At the same time, third parties basing their existence on an ideological rejection of the major parties have been a permanent feature of the national and many provincial scenes since the end of the First World War, and have attracted the considerable attention of social scientists for many years. Moreover, the use of the label "pragmatism," like a coat of paint, may conceal a host of sins, in this case ideological sins. The politics of pragmatism in many cases prove to have been the politics of mystification, serving particular interests while piously denying that politics is about the advancement of certain interests against others.

A number of revisionist works have described the domination of Canadian public life by the interests of corporate capitalism, utilizing a panoply of ideological weapons, including "apolitical" or "pragmatic" politics, to consolidate this domination.[3] This in turn suggests a further dimension to the question of ideology. Ideological politics inevitably implies *class* politics: contending ideologies arise from differentiated social and economic classes within a given society, representing differing images of how the resources of that society should be divided, and of the kind of human relationships considered desirable. Hand in hand with the denial of ideology has gone a denial of the class basis of Canadian society. The myth of classlessness, which has been recently subjected to such devastating attack as to be no longer defensible,[4] served the dual historical role of obscuring both the actual perceptions of the weaker classes of their own situation, and of mystifying in retrospect the real impact on Canadian politics of class issues and class ideologies.

The great upheaval in Canadian politics at the end of the First World War is at the same time the most startling example of the power of class politics in this country, and the most extraordinary example of the ability of the pragmatist school to argue away the material evidence of class and ideology as important factors in our politics. The end of the old two-party system, the rapid and highly successful organization at both the federal and provincial levels of a new party around a distinct class base and in support of a set of ideas whose radical divergence from the conventional wisdom of the old parties certainly justifies the term "ideology" – these are facts of some significance in assessing the nature of political development in this country. The sudden explosion of the farmers into politics, with consequences the reverberations of which are still heard today, was a crucial event in the shaping of the Canadian political culture.

THE ROOTS OF FARMER RADICALISM

The first, and undoubtedly the most important, analytical approach to Canadian political economy is the staples model of economic development associated with W.A. Mackintosh, Harold Innis, and others, and the Laurentian school of historical development which is connected to it. The staples model, emphasizing single resource extraction (fur, timber, cod, wheat) within an imperialist framework, has become part of the wider literature on economic development, constituting perhaps one of the most important contributions of Canada to international scholarship. The decline of this approach in the 1950s and 1960s coincided with a general decline in the entire concept of political economy, as distinct from either economics or political science.[5] In the present decade, there has been a revival of this older tradition of scholarship which looks to the interrelationship of economic and political factors as the basis of historical development. One of the most important strands in this revival has been a tendency on the part of younger scholars to fuse the staples model with the class concepts of Marxism.[6]

However much the staples approach has taught us about the basis of economic development, it has also generated a certain metropolitan and upper class bias to the understanding of the political responses to economic changes, as so conservative a scholar as W.L. Morton long ago pointed out.[7] Locating the dynamic of development squarely in the metropolitan merchant class of the St. Lawrence, or in its successors in the Toronto-Montreal financial and industrial bourgeoisie, is a crucial step in identifying the source of capitalist development, but the focus tends to miss the reactions of those on the receiving end – reactions, which have been very important factors indeed in the shaping of the Canadian political economy. Marxist analysis, as a method, recognizes a dynamic, or internal logic, in the development of capitalism as a system; and it sees this dynamic in terms of class differentiation and conflict. To employ a much misused term, this type of analysis is *dialectical*; that is, it attempts to comprehend both actions and reactions and to locate the specificity of a particular political economy in the interplay of these factors.

To say that North American society has developed differently from Europe is to state the obvious. Yet simply because the classic Marxist class conflict between the organized working class and the capitalist owners of the means of production has been much more pronounced in Europe than on this continent is no reason to assume that class conflict has been absent from North American politics. The question must rather be posed in terms of which classes have been important in North American economic development, and whether their interests have been significant factors in structuring the politics of the time.[8] In Canada, the relative weakness of the working class as an autonomous agent of political change is not seriously to be disputed – at least in relation to Europe, although perhaps not in relation to the United States. But this does not mean that class has been without significance, certainly not with regard to the dominant classes, as the literature of the merchants and financiers of the central Canadian metropole clearly indicates, but no less with regard to the dominated classes.

It was a universal comment in the nineteenth century that in Europe land was dear and labour was cheap, but that in North America, land was cheap and labour dear.[9] This establishes a crucial point of divergence between the two continents in class terms. It was difficult to keep people in the labour force and off the land in the new world. Despite ill-conceived Tory schemes for creating landed aristocracies and established churches backed by clergy reserves in the early colonial history of Canada, the country developed a largely agricultural economy with the family farm as the typical unit of production. Not until the 1921 census did the urban share of the Canadian population finally rival the rural proportion. The 1901 census showed that 89 percent of all farms in Canada were operated by their owners.[10] In Marxist terms, this meant that there was by European standards, a very large and economically significant group of independent commodity producers – a "petite bourgeoisie," standing apart from either capital or labour.

As early as the 1820s and 1830s some of the elements of class conflict between the independent farmers and the growing commercial and financial interests of the dominant groups (symbolized by the Family Compact and the Chateau Clique) were apparent. Although numerous other factors, such as religion and ethnicity, were germane to the political conflicts which flared into open rebellion in 1837–38, very specific class issues as perceived by small farmers were featured in the manifestos and political programs of the rebels. The complaints of the farmers tended to concentrate on political and economic grievances, among which the problem of credit was particularly prominent. It is of course impossible to generalize about the economic situation of the small family farmer over the whole of the nineteenth century, but some factors stand out. The question of the capital necessary for investment in land and equipment was crucial. It was at this point that the "independent" producer became vulnerable to financial capital through the credit market. The price of the produce was of course subject to the vicissitudes of the market, and storage, transportation, and marketing were additional areas where the farmers' control over their return became subject to powerful outside forces.

To the extent that the dominant forces of capitalism were successful in the late nineteenth century in their attempts to industrialize the country, the agricultural sector was doomed to relative decline and depopulation. Along with the consolidation of farms, and heavier capitalization, agricultural production was drawn ever more tightly into the web of the wider capitalist market. In the long run this is exactly what did happen, but there was an important counter-trend. The National Policy of the Macdonald Conservatives, later extended and broadened by the Laurier Liberals, had as one of its central tenets the incorporation of the western prairies into the national economy as a producer of agricultural exports to gain foreign exchange in world markets, as well as to provide a domestic market for the protected manufacturing industries of central Canada. Out of this policy was formed a vast agricultural hinterland, with wheat as its staple cash crop, in an inferior and subservient position to the central Canadian metropole. The seeds of agrarian radicalism in the west thus grew in a soil of class resentment enriched by regional identity.

If capitalism destroyed the feudal order in Europe, and with it the landed aristocracy and the peasants who worked the fields, it created a new dialectic of class antagonism with its development of a landless labour force filling the mines and factories of the Industrial Revolution. In Canada, there was no feudal past and no peasantry. Nevertheless, capitalism created its own antagonists, through the logic of its own growth. The beginnings of an industrial working class and the development of a large independent commodity producer class, both in an economic and political position of domination by corporate capitalism, set the stage for the emergence of professions, particularly teaching, preaching, and journalism, which were in a somewhat problematic relationship to the dominant forces of capitalism, and were feared by these forces as unruly and untrustworthy agitational elements.[11] The rise of the "Social Gospel," the radical left wing of Christianity spread by men consciously imbued with feelings of solidarity towards the lower orders, and the increasing salience of such issues as feminism in mobilizing the interest and support of sizeable sectors of the population, indicated that by the time of the First World War Canadians were in a process of reappraisal of their underlying social and political values.

The war itself greatly accelerated the changes already initiated by the rapid industrialization of the previous two decades. By war's end, there was such pent-up frustration and desire for change that a sense of impending upheaval was pervasive throughout the society. The outpouring of books and pamphlets on the "social question" at this time was unprecedented in a nation little disposed toward introspection and social criticism.[12] This intellectual concern was matched by political activism and grass-roots militancy on a scale never before witnessed. From the explosion of the farmers into political prominence to the Winnipeg General Strike, the lower orders, hitherto reasonably passive, were on the move – although in what direction no one could positively say. Abroad the picture was even more disconcerting to those familiar with the certitudes of the nineteenth century: the convulsion of world war had brought in its wake the Russian Revolution, and the year 1919 saw a series of revolutionary uprisings across Europe. The old world was coming adrift from its moorings.

In the end, the storm passed, and the old order reasserted itself, albeit in a modified and modernized form. Out of the political upheaval in Canada came not revolution, but William Lyon Mackenzie King and the Liberal party. Capitalism had faced the challenge, and the mid-1920s, the forces of radicalism seemed spent on all fronts. Yet a decade later, by the 1935 election, with capitalism reeling from the effects of the Great Depression, it had become clear that the simple two-party brokerage system had been lost forever, and that a social democratic third party, the CCF, had arrived on the scene, thus distinguishing Canada from the United States, where the Socialist party had disappeared from national politics, never to return. Both the weakness and the tenacity of the radicalism generated in the early twentieth century must be taken into account in the historical balance sheet. Radical political action fell far, far short of transforming the structure of the Canadian political economy, yet it did leave an imprint on the shape of Canadian politics.

To understand the specific nature of radicalism as it actually developed in Canada, it is first necessary to analyse the concrete class forces which went into the left-wing upsurge. The fact that the most impressive political confrontation of corporate capitalism mounted in this century came not from the organized working class, as occurred in Europe, but from the aroused farmers is of signal importance in the shaping of radical thought. The Winnipeg General Strike of 1919, the sympathetic strikes carried out in other western cities, and the emergence of some elements of labour political representation in both federal and provincial politics did indicate the appearance of a class consciousness among industrial workers. But this was very incomplete and tentative; moreover, the industrial working class was simply not large enough at the end of the war to be of such strategic importance to the Canadian economy as was the working class of more advanced industrial nations. The farmers were a different story. Larger in numbers, strategically placed both in economic and political terms, and demonstrating a high degree of solidarity and collective purpose, the farmers were poised at an historical moment of great potential for political change.

The world view of the farmers, the ideological image of the well-ordered society derived from their particular class position and life experience, was one which allowed a significant divergence from the orthodoxy propagated by the dominant forces of capitalism and accepted by the mainstream of society. The farmers' movement did involve the vision of a better world that was indeed radical by the standards of the time. It would be false to suggest that all the farmers held such a view; even the leaders of the movement were deeply divided on its goals. Like any large social movement of radical tendency, there were many motives and many expectations assembled under the same umbrella. The point is that advanced ideas were generated by advanced thinkers; such ideas were not simply disembodied rhetoric but found resonance in the larger movement. The *movement* was precisely that: a group of people in motion, in search of a better life, open and questioning. It is in this situation that the true seedbed of radical social and political thought is to be found. Just as in Europe, where periods of revolutionary change such as the English Civil War and the French Revolution have been the periods generating the greatest contributions to political philosophy, so too the period of political unrest and agitation at the end of the First World War in Canada, while far from a revolutionary era, nevertheless generated some original ideas about reforming and transforming the Canadian political economy.

The crucial importance of the farmers at this point of political and ideological flux can scarcely be overestimated for the shaping of left-wing political ideas. The most politically advanced elements of the working class movement were forced to choose sides in a struggle predominantly featuring the large bourgeoisie of central Canada, along with its middle-class allies, against the petite bourgeoisie led by the independent commodity producers of the western wheat provinces and rural Ontario. Not surprisingly, they chose the side of those farmers struggling for what was called "economic democracy," under the leadership and ideological hegemony of a class whose interests and outlook were significantly different from those of the organized working class. There has been a certain tendency on the part of present day Marxists to decry this historical conjuncture as having drawn the working class movement away from its proper socialist path and towards an inappropriate petit bourgeois mentality. Yet to dismiss the farmers and their world as of no interest is an injustice. They were people with a way of life, traditions, culture, and their own hopes and dreams. They went down before the implacable onslaught of the market, of industrialization and urbanization, but they went down fighting, with some dignity and not a little imagination in their stand against the forces oppressing them.[13] Certainly they and their leaders mounted a more impressive counterattack than the organized working class or its leaders have ever mounted against some of these same forces.

As Mackenzie King knew well, the forces of technological liberalism and the capitalist market had indeed doomed the farmers to eventual extinction as a significant political force. His book, *Industry and Humanity*, leaped forward across the decades to a time when the independent commodity producer class had virtually disappeared, and the major confrontation in society was squared between capital and labour, to a society in fact in which this axis of conflict had become so decisive that the entire political structures of decision-making were to be transformed to embody these collective interests.[14] Yet King himself spent his first years in office as Prime Minister driven by the necessity of finding compromises and common fronts with the representatives of the farmers while the labour question was far down the agenda. And when a social democratic party finally came to birth in the early years of the depression, it was as a farmer-labour alliance, and its founding convention was held in Regina, in the midst of an almost entirely unindustrialized, wheat growing province. Many have argued that this alliance imparted a particular tone to the new party, which has helped shape its philosophy since. On the other hand, the same class of independent commodity producers also turned rightward in politics in other places and other times. The sudden reversion of Ontario farmers back to traditional two-party politics by the mid-1920s, Social Credit in Alberta, the conservatism of the United Farmers government in Manitoba, the Tory populism of John Diefenbaker on the prairies in the 1950s and 1960s, all demonstrate the ambiguity of the farmers' perception of politics, the curious oscillation of views from left to right, the Janus-faced conservative-radicalism of the farmers in politics.

It is precisely at this point, where the farmers' movement overlapped with radical, labour politics that the ideas of William Irvine become highly relevant. An examination of Irvine's career and the evolution of his thought helps cast considerable light upon this complex historical question.

WILLIAM IRVINE, 1885–1962

William Irvine was born in the Shetland Islands and left school early to serve an apprenticeship as a carpenter and boatbuilder. A brief sojourn in the United States, where he worked on the construction site of the St. Louis World's Fair, ended in his return home, where he turned to the Methodist ministry while assimilating a good deal of labour and socialist literature. Recruited by the father of J.S. Woodsworth, later the first leader of the CCF, Irvine came to Canada in 1907 and graduated from Manitoba and Wesley Colleges in 1914 in theology. The author of a recent personal sketch of Irvine suggests that even at this stage in his career, he was "more interested in the social gospel of such teachers and friends as J.S. Woodsworth and Salem Bland than he was in theological dogma."[15] His socialist activities led to a heresy trial and his resignation of his ministry in a small Ontario town in 1916.

Irvine moved to Calgary to take up an offer from the Unitarian Church, which specified that he was to spend 10 per cent of his time on the religious needs of his congregation and the remaining 90 per cent on community work.[16] This was exactly the proper mix to suit Irvine, who threw himself into the seething cauldron of radicalism that was the West in those days with an enthusiasm, dedication, wit, and intelligence matched by few others. One of his first activities was journalism, as he helped found a sparkling radical newspaper called *The Nutcracker*, later the *Alberta Non-Partisan*, later still the *Western Independent*. It was an exciting time of new ideas and burning social criticism: during the same period, Calgary also supported another "underground" newspaper of lively and mordant wit – the celebrated, though much less political, *Eyeopener*, edited by the flamboyant and somewhat dissolute Bob Edwards.

The farmers of Alberta had been smarting from the defeat of reciprocity and the victory of protectionist Toryism in the 1911 election, along with a host of other grievances centering around the marketing, storage, and transportation of grain, and the ubiquitous credit system with its high interest rates and foreclosures on mortgages. Irvine's first direct political intervention was as secretary of the Alberta Nonpartisan League, an offshoot of the left wing farmers' movement in North Dakota, which had swept into office in that state in 1916. The League acted as an initial impetus in Alberta for direct political action by farmers, two members being elected in the 1917 provincial election. As its name implied, the League focussed its attacks on the party system, and looked to a non-partisan "business" government in which delegates voted according to the wishes of their constituents and not at the behests of party whips.[17] This importation of political principles which were apparently more appropriate to the American division of powers, where the executive did not depend upon the partisan support of the legislature, than to the British system of cabinet government, was to have a long and paralyzing influence on the farmers' movement in both provincial and federal Canadian politics.

The Nonpartisan League did succeed in drawing the United Farmers of Alberta (UFA), originally a non-political farm organization, into direct political action, despite the reluctance of Alberta farm leader Henry Wise Wood, with whom Irvine had some serious disagreements. The UFA took over from the League as the political arm of the farmers, while Irvine continued to agitate for farmer-labour unity, eventually gaining election to the House of Commons as a "Labour" candidate with UFA backing. Despite his crucial role in encouraging UFA political action, Irvine left Alberta for seven months near the end of 1920, to organize for the farmers' movement in New Brunswick. It was in his absence that *The Farmers in Politics* appeared and was reviewed in the western press, thus keeping his name and ideas before the people of Alberta. Upon his return to Calgary, he threw himself into feverish political activity as the UFA swept to provincial power in the 1921 election, and he himself won a federal seat a few months later.

Coming as it did only a year after the stunning victory of the United Farmers of Ontario in that province's general election, and on the eve of the Alberta victory, followed by a farmer government in Manitoba in 1922, and just before the displacement of the Conservatives as the second largest grouping in the House of Commons by the farmer-based Progressive party in the 1921 national election, *The Farmers in Politics* was obviously a topical book. It endures as one of the most lucid statements of a distinctive class and ideological approach to Canadian politics, which with passion, wit, and relentless vigour seeks to demolish the great Canadian myths of classlessness and pragmatism. It has, moreover, much to say about the historical problem of the relationship of the farmers as a class to the development of radical and socialist politics. The latter point is somewhat paradoxical, since Irvine himself was neither a farmer nor of farming background. As an outsider and an intellectual, Irvine may have overstated the case for the group which he claimed to represent. Certainly, many of the farmers themselves were far more conservative and moderate than Irvine's picture would tend to suggest. Yet at the same time, this defect may have been a virtue, in the sense that Irvine was able to draw out with considerable clarity some of the inarticulate assumptions of the farmers' movement that perhaps only an outsider could discern.

The book did play a modest role in the events which reshaped Western Canadian politics. Yet, even if one is sceptical of the ultimate importance of books in changing the world, it must be said that this is a book which reflected a current of political activism which did in some ways change the Canadian political world. Coming at the full tide of the farmers' politicization, the book is less a theoretical treatise than an expression of the fusion of theory and practice: the articulation of the more advanced ideas associated with a genuine mass protest movement. This places it firmly within the Canadian tradition of political writing, for until very recently Canadians have been very little given to abstract theorizing about the political order and have confined themselves to reflecting upon practical political activities. What *The Farmers in Politics* does demonstrate is that this genre need not be lacking in imaginative innovation. It did involve a serious attempt at a social and political theory which rather outdid the most advanced sections of the farmers' movement.[18]

Richard Allen has written that the "most striking aspect" of Irvine's book "was not so much the exposition of his concept of group government, as the mixture of his political and economic arguments with the religious concepts of the radical social gospel."[19] In fact, compared to such social gospel tracts as Salem Bland's *The New Christianity*, Irvine's book is rather more striking for its dominantly secular tone. Aside from an obligatory section on the "new religious spirit," the argument constructed by this late minister of the church depends not at all upon religious conviction, except perhaps in a political optimism which might only be sustained by faith. In fact, Irvine never returned to the church in his former capacity; *The Farmers in Politics* would appear to mark a transition in his own thought towards a more materialist and secular form. In this he only anticipated the eventual movement of the Canadian Left away from its social gospel origins.[20]

The book begins with a vivid, if perhaps somewhat overexcited, depiction of the new age rising irresistably within the bosom of the old. Old values are crumbling; new values take their place. Profit is replaced by morality, competition by co-operation, individualism by the co-operative commonwealth. Irvine's view of the world is dialectical: competition and co-operation are opposites, yet are united by an evolutionary process which will transcend both in a greater synthesis. There are laws of society, which are natural laws, discoverable by scientific inquiry.

Irvine's analysis of the law of co-operation is an interesting case study in his dialectical method. Co-operation, he argues, arises directly out of the basic human condition of competition. The original state of nature to Irvine was a Hobbesian war of all against all.

In order to protect themselves against the constant insecurity of this state, men organized themselves into tribes. Paradoxically, this development both encouraged co-operation within the tribe, while organizing and intensifying competition with other tribes, through warfare. Similarly, the nation state offered wider scope for collective action, yet had at the same time raised warfare to new levels of savagery. The free market economy saw similar developments: capitalists abolished competition among themselves, by mergers, monopolies, and cartels which organized and rigged the market. Yet this allowed them greater scope for carrying on economic warfare against other groups, such as farmers and labour. When the latter groups organized themselves, greater group co-operation would lead to more intense conflict between economic interests. The thrust of this analysis is that an inevitable logic leads to higher and higher stages of co-operation precisely in order to carry on competition at a more effective level. Yet this process can end only when competition digs its own grave by organizing itself out of existence. Self-interest is thus a motor force which ultimately transcends itself. The argument is an ingenious, if sketchy, extension of Hobbes within an Hegelian developmental framework. Religion and morality, *pace* Allen, have nothing to do with the immanence of the new and better society, which, paradoxically, arises out of the basest of material motives.

To Irvine, political forms are the reflection of underlying economic realities. "Government forms," he wrote, "are no more permanent than industrial or educational forms. Governments take their forms from the economic basis upon which they rest, and for which they function" (55). The governmental form being rendered obsolete by the rise of new forces from below is the two-party system. Originally based on the economic struggle between the decaying feudal aristocracy and the rising bourgeoisie, the Conservative and Liberal parties, particularly in the Canadian context, no longer reflect any real balance of forces, but linger on as a "fetish," uniting those at the top through the linkage of control by campaign fundings, and manipulation of opinion, while dividing those at the bottom along irrelevant partisan lines. Nor does this mystifying party system have any basis in individual psychology: every person has liberal and conservative characteristics, inextricably mingled together. The point is that the economic organization of workers and farmers offers an alternative: occupational representation along class lines. Pointing to concrete signs of the decay of the two-party system and the emergence of new group representation in provincial legislatures, Irvine argued that his alternative model was a fact, not a theory.

Party organization is itself the enemy of democracy, whether the party in question is an old line organization, or one which purports to represent radical ideas. Here Irvine spoke with the authentic accents of the anti-party traditions of the Canadian West: political parties were eastern, business-dominated systems of corruption which smothered regional and class minorities under the device of parliamentary discipline. Irvine would have agreed with Robert Michels' "iron law of oligarchy" as applied to socialist parties attempting to embody egalitarian and democratic principles in their own organization, but Irvine drew a sharp distinction between *party* organization and *economic* organization. In a complex, class-divided, capitalist society, the former is inherently anti-democratic, since it mystifies different class interests by lumping them together in evanescent electoral coalitions. Economic organization based on productive units is inherently democratic, on the other hand, since it directly expresses true *self-interest*, unmediated by shifting secondary associations.

There is an apparent paradox in this argument: if democracy means only the expression of self-interest, how can collective decisions emerge from the clash of various self-interests? Irvine's solution is by no means entirely satisfactory, but neither is it as simplistic or naive as some of the attacks on the party system which had appeared at that time, or which have come forward more recently in Canadian history. Irvine begins by redefining democracy: "a very popular term – chiefly because nobody knows what is meant by it." The political actions of the masses have hitherto been those of the mob, a rabble of individuals manipulated by the ruling class. Universal adult suffrage does not in itself indicate democracy:

A mob is a mob whether it is engaged in a lynching operation, or in throwing little pieces of paper into a ballot box. A mob might be defined as a number of people acting on an idea which does not belong to them; whereas a number of people acting on an idea, which, by a synthetic process involving a compounding of the different ideas of all the individuals concerned, is theirs, would be a democracy. (152)

Democracy must start at the lowest level, which is that of the productive unit. Group solidarity and co-operation in the workplace is the school of democracy, for it is here that individual self-interests are organized around the common economic goals, where each man's interests are advanced by collective action with those engaged in similar productive activity. Political *ideas* are merely part of the superstructure, and thus transitory. Economic *interests* are primary, and form an enduring basis for collective human activity. Interests lead to organization, and ideas emerge from the latter. To reverse this process is to mystify the natural order of things, which is precisely what top-down "non-class" parties have done, by imposing political ideologies from without – on behalf of ruling class interests, of course. The Farmers' Platform[21] is, on the other hand, a genuinely democratic production, in that it emerged from democratic groups of farmers organized around their economic interests. "It is," Irvine affirms, "the first democratic utterance of political significance to be heard in Dominion Politics" (168–9).

Having established democracy at the level of the productive unit, Irvine still faces the problem of how collective political decisions can emerge from the competition of these divergent economic interests. Syndicalism might build on the basis suggested by Irvine: a revolutionary overthrow of capitalism through direct mass action, with the economic organizations of the masses forming the nucleus of the organization of the post-revolutionary society. Irvine, however, rejects Bakunin and the revolutionary anarchist tradition. He similarly rejects Marx, whom he identifies with Russian Bolshevism, as representing the opposite extreme to anarchism: state bureaucratic control by a revolutionary elite. Instead Irvine looks to the British school of evolutionary guild socialism as a middle way. His rejection of revolutionary socialist models does not rest primarily on moral grounds, or on liberal scruples, but rather on a materialist assumption about the organization of society. In developing this assumption, Irvine demonstrates that his guild socialism is more than merely a derivative idea grafted onto the Canadian system, but an idea of some originality.

Class and class interests are the result of the division of labour in society. This division of labour is along functional lines and will exist irrespective of the form of organization of the society. A socialist society will continue to divide people into functional groups, just as capitalist society does. While this might appear to indicate the irreducibility of group interests and thus of group conflict, Irvine assumes that the functional division of labour represents a potential harmony of interests through mutual dependency for the exchange of goods and services. Society should be like an efficient factory, in which the myriad of individual tasks are co-ordinated within a complex, yet natural, organizational blend which would be based not on hierarchy and authority, as in capitalist industry, but on co-operation, the enlightened form of self-interest. This is, to put it mildly, a somewhat heroic assumption, involving as it does the transposition of the Platonic conception of justice (each unit of the community performing its proper function in co-operation with others) to an industrialized capitalist economy without, moreover, any place for a caste of philosopher-kings to oversee the spiritual health of the Republic. The Platonic analogy is, however, merely superficial, despite Irvine's insistence on the harmonic basis of the just social order. For in Irvine's basically Hobbesian universe, harmony emerges precisely out of an intensification of self-interest and of class conflict. Only when each productive group openly recognizes its own group interests as primary, and organizes itself politically around this self-interest, will the true basis for social co-operation be laid bare. When all the cards are on the table, when there is an honest recognition of class selfishness as the motive power of human action, but with *all* classes represented openly and frankly, then the Platonic conception of justice can be effected, as each group recognizes its dependency on every other through a rational calculus of enlightened self-interest. For this organic stage of co-operation to be achieved, it is necessary that all intermediary associations between the economic group and the decision-making process be eliminated, particularly political parties, which will be replaced by functional representatives, acting as direct delegates of their economic constituents.

An apparent weakness in this group government doctrine, especially as handled by some of the farmer philosophers themselves, such as Henry Wise Wood, was its confusion of classes with producer groups. Indeed, C.B. Macpherson makes this a central part of his critique of the social theory of the United Farmers of Alberta.[22] For Macpherson, this confirmed his thesis concerning the petit bourgeois nature of the Alberta farmers' ideology, in its characteristic refusal to see the class basis of capitalist society deriving from the petite bourgeoisie's own ambiguous class position between capital and labour. Macpherson is undoubtedly correct in his critique of the broad position of the farmers' movement as a whole, and Irvine himself did fall into the same confusion. Yet, perhaps because he was an outsider, or because of his education in European labour-socialist thought, it is interesting to note that Irvine at the same time pointed to an intriguing and imaginative way out of the dilemma he himself had set.

The dilemma, briefly, is this: class solidarity cuts across the lines of division among producer groups, and *vice versa*. A class conscious working class will unite miners, transport workers, and steel workers around their common position as wage labour in the employ of owners. Producer consciousness will on the other hand unite the workers around their own industrial interests, which may divide them, as *workers*; that is, higher wages for transport workers may reduce the return to miners by raising the cost of the product. Higher wages to miners may increase the cost of steel production and thus reduce the capacity of steel workers to gain wage increases. Producer groups, moreover, may well involve inter-class solidarity along industrial lines: owners, managers, and workers function together in a corporatist arrangement against other industries. There is indeed little in the group government doctrine as expounded by the farmers to indicate whether ownership and management of productive units were to remain unchanged under the new governmental arrangements. It was not an issue about which farmers concerned themselves, since it was a problem with which they themselves did not have to deal, given the family farm as the basic unit of agricultural production. It is also a question about which Irvine, as a socialist, is rather pointedly vague, perhaps evasive. At one point in *The Farmers in Politics*, he argues in good corporatist fashion as follows:

Reformers, to be successful, must be able to give the positive presentation of their case. Instead of saying: "Upset the government," "Down with capital," "To hell with the system," etc., they must say: "We come to fulfill the highest functions of these." Capital must be used to greater advantage for the common good; it must be made to serve. Capitalists will not be destroyed; they will be called to the higher service of managing capital for national well-being. (96–7)

Similarly, two years later in the House of Commons, Irvine refused to be drawn into a debate over the merits of public versus private ownership of railways, saying that he was more interested in *how* an enterprise was run than in *who* owned it, and then called for cooperative management of the CNR to include representatives of the workers as well as the public.[23] At another point in his book, when he looks to the shape of the new society which will "replace capitalism," he goes on to talk about the right of self-determination of classes: "All classes must be recognized. The real classes are the industrial groups, and of these there are as many as there are industries" (232).

These statements would seem to preclude altogether any Marxist conception of class as deriving from the basic ownership of the means of production. Yet Irvine is not at all unaware of this conception, and indeed falls into a loose Marxist framework on occasion. There is an inconsistency here which no amount of gloss will cover. Irvine's mind was, above all, eclectic: caught between his labour-socialist background on the one hand, and his advocacy of the farmers' movement on the other, he found himself caught between two contradictory conceptions of the social and economic order. He does not resolve the contradiction, by any means, but his tentative solution is certainly original.

When he falls back into what I would call a loose Marxist conceptual framework, he sees the modern capitalist economy divided into three basic classes: the capitalists, the workers, and a middle group of independent producers, of which the farmers are the chief representative. The conflict between capital and labour, when put into these naked terms – shorn of the industrial identifications which otherwise obscure this fundamental division – seems on the face of it, antagonistic and irresolvable. Both sides had organized, and the rise of labour militancy had already manifested itself in Canada through the Winnipeg General Strike, as it previously had on a larger scale in other countries. The stage was set for a terrible struggle. Here Irvine departs from Marx, although in curious parallel with him. Where Marx saw the proletariat as the "universal class" which, since it had no lower class left to exploit, could only emancipate mankind from class exploitation by overthrowing its own exploiters, so too, Irvine looked to a "universal class." In Canada, this was not the proletariat, but the farmers. They are the last to organize themselves, and they are also the most important class, in terms of numbers. The farmers, as a "universal class," have a special mission to end class rule. "The farmers alone," Irvine writes, "have discovered the higher law of co-operation. While other groups exist by co-operation, they do not see that co-operation must be applied between competing groups." In a remarkable synthesis of Marxism and agrarian guild socialism, Irvine argues that:

The farmers are in a position to do great national service, not only because they woke to consciousness in the midst of a changing world, but also because their aims are synthetic. Although fathered by oppression, the farmers' movement has escaped that bitterness of feeling against capital, and that extreme rashness both of expression and action, so characteristic of labor. *The farmer, in reality, combines in his own profession, the two antagonists. He is both capitalist and laborer.* He knows that production is not furthered when war is going on between the two. He sees, also the hopeless deadlock between organized capital and organized labor in the world of industry and commerce, and is thus led to the discovery of co-operation as the synthesis without which progress cannot be made. In this way the United Farmers have become the apostles of co-operation: they have captured the imagination of the nation by combining true radicalism with scientific moderation, and it is safe to say that they are the most hopeful factor in Canadian national life today. (101–2, emphasis added)

Thus the farmers will act as the special class with an historic mission to reconcile the antagonistic class forces of capital and labour. Marx's universal class, the proletariat, would abolish class conflict by abolishing class divisions. Irvine's universal class would abolish class conflict by instituting co-operation between continuing classes.[24] Marx's ultimate stage of communism would also be one in which co-operation was the basic form of economic relationship, but this co-operation is an end, not a means. To Irvine, co-operation is both end and means.

This then was Irvine's considered statement of political philosophy at the high tide of the farmers' mobilization amid the radical aura of post-war agitation – but before the returns had begun to come in on the effectiveness of these ideas and of the political movement as a whole. It is, as Irvine himself was aware, an untidy, unfinished work: but it reflected an untidy, unfinished political movement. The freshness of mind, the optimism, the vigor, and good humour with which the argument is pursued, make it a work typical of that rather innocent moment of radical confidence – soon to be drained and dissipated by the unexpected strength and tenacity of the old order and its old values. As Nellie McClung later recalled of the feminist movement, its militants went "singing up the hill." For all their sunny optimism, many were to find that the top of the hill was a graveyard for their radical dreams.

Even in *The Farmers in Politics*, the seeds of self-destruction can be discerned. The banking of radical capital on the farmers was a dangerous gamble, for all of Irvine's assiduous theoretical efforts to prove the contrary. The obsession of the analysis with political forms, to the exclusion of any probing of the economic structures, meant that most of the radical energy of the movement was to be directed toward the attack on the party system and the establishment of group government. How this was to be achieved in the face of the British system of cabinet government and party discipline, especially when the structure of group government had been left so vague as to be merely utopian, was not at all clear. Finally, the contradiction between the producer group theory and a more conventional class analysis was left largely unresolved, despite Irvine's ingenious attempt to link the two through the universal class role of the farmers.

In Ontario, Alberta, and Manitoba, farmer parties assumed office in traditional manner, with cabinet posts reserved for their supporters – which in Ontario included some Labour members. In these legislatures, cabinet government functioned more or less as it always had. In the federal House of Commons, the large Progressive contingent refused to act as the official opposition, thus allowing the shattered Tory forces to maintain appearances, and perpetuate the two-party image of Parliament. Irvine's attempt to alter parliamentary procedure to allow the government to hold a confidence vote after losing on a substantive issue in the House, and to carry on if that confidence motion passed – a device to break party discipline and make the House of Commons more like the American Congress – failed when the combined forces of the Liberal and Conservative parties defeated his proposal. An attempt to change the electoral system to Proportional Representation, moved by Irvine's Ontario Progressive colleague and friend, W.C. Good, also failed, thus dashing hopes of altering the voting system along lines more favourable to functional, or group, representation.[25] Interestingly, in the closing section of *The Farmers in Politics*, Irvine pessimistically contemplated the consequences if his ideas failed of achievement. "There is only one constitutional alternative to group representation in parliament," he admitted, "and that is to continue the party system." If the farmers choose the path "which leads to party government," "little of value will be attained, and the whole democratic fight will have to be fought over again." In a rare show of conservatism, Irvine then avers that "it may take thousands of years to accomplish co-operation." If the people are not ready for group government, then "civilization will have to wait until they are" (223, 226). Group government did fail to find realization, and in its place the farmers' movement had no alternative political plan, and an embarrassing void where a searching economic analysis of capitalist society should have been. Worse yet, it quickly became apparent that many of the Progressive leaders, including the national leader, T.A. Crerar, were merely Liberals in disguise, more than ready to return to the fold. The story of how Mackenzie King swallowed the Progressives one by one is edifying in terms of political shrewdness, although not in terms of radical ideals.

Irvine, as a Labour member, co-operated where possible with the Progressive members, but grew increasingly critical of their failure to follow through on their promise. Eventually, he and his leader, J.S. Woodsworth ("I wish to state," Irvine cheerfully informed the House, "that the honorable member for Centre Winnipeg is the leader of the Labour group – and I am the group"[26]) formed the "Ginger group" with the more advanced Progressive members, a group which became the nucleus of the CCF party in the 1930s. But

the hopes of the immediate post-war period, and the exalted historical role assigned to the farmers by Irvine in his book, dribbled
unheroically away. In 1925, Irvine publicly put his feelings on
record in parliament:

I regret to find no bright hopes in the Progressive party so far as labour is
concerned, and I abandon my hopes of it very reluctantly. Many forward-
looking people to-day see in the Progressive party as it now is a fitting
epitaph for the tomb of a lost opportunity ... The flood time has passed, the
ebb has now set in, and the Progressive party is now grasping and wrig-
gling like a fish left stranded on the beach before the receding tide. There I
will leave them.[26]

To Irvine the failure was of the Progressives, not of the concept of
group government itself. As late as 1929, Irvine published another
book, *Co-operative Government,* in which the case for group organization of government was restated in even more far-reaching terms,
this time involving the elimination of constituency voting, with
replacement by a quota system of a fixed number of representatives
from each group, no matter how small. The number of representatives was to be determined by "the value of the service rendered to
the community, and not the numbers employed ... Function and
numbers, rather than territory and numbers, should be the factors
considered."[27] This was travelling pretty far down the road to
corporatism. Indeed, there might appear to be much in common
with the liberal corporatism of Mackenzie King's *Industry and
Humanity,* which Irvine was given to citing now and again. But King
did nothing whatever to establish the ideas he had so broadly and
sententiously enunciated in his book, despite his position in national
office, while Irvine was a powerless backbencher well outside the
mainstream of Canadian politics. It is perhaps not surprising that
Irvine was particularly bitter towards the Liberals and their leader,
who was the master of co-optation of left wing dissent.

As a member of Parliament, Irvine was best described as the
proverbial gadfly. He made his maiden speech in the House on the
eighth day of his first session; instead of praising the beauties of his
riding in the traditional manner, he began by citing Hegel, and then
launched into an attack on the party system and the banking system.[28] From then on, Irvine was regularly heard on all sorts of
issues. The only times when he was silent were when he was
defeated and out of Parliament, as he was in 1925, from 1935 to
1945, and after 1949. Gerrymandered out of a seat, Irvine could
come bouncing back in again from elsewhere. Over the years he

represented three different constituencies, including one in British Columbia. Although he had few illusions about the usefulness of Parliament, it did give him a job, and a forum for his eloquence and fertile political imagination. His name became associated not only with lost causes, such as group government, but with liberal ideas in advance of their time, such as the abolition of capital punishment and the reform of the divorce laws to put wives on an equal footing with husbands.[29] Irvine, along with Woodsworth and A.A. Heaps also acted as a three-man pressure group to draw public attention to labour issues and the grievances of the working class. The most spectacular example in the early 1920s was the crisis in the Cape Breton coal mines, when the British Empire Steel Corporation slashed the wages of the workers by a third, while the Liberal provincial and federal governments acted to jail union leaders and support the company.[30] On issues such as this, Irvine was unfailingly on the side of the workers.

One issue with which Irvine forcefully associated himself during the 1920s, not without ambiguity to his ideological position, was advocacy of Social Credit. In lieu of either a Marxist critique of the structure of capitalism or of a fully developed social-democratic critique of the economic practice of capitalism. Irvine's economic thought was somewhat eccentric. Although he was never a monomaniac on the subject, as the true believers later proved to be, Irvine did place considerable weight on the views of monetary reformists, particularly those of Major C.H. Douglas, founder of the Social Credit movement in England. Premised on an "underconsumptionist" theory of business cycles, Irvine's views ran strongly towards social control of the credit system and the provision of sufficient purchasing power in the hands of the people to maintain effective demand for the goods and services produced. Production was not itself the problem and could, Irvine believed, be carried out effectively either under capitalism or socialism. The real problem was distribution, and the source of the problem was the *money* economy. Instead of being a social or collective service, geared to the common good, the financial system had, under capitalism, fallen under the control of finance capital, in the form of socially irresponsible bankers. Following Hobson and Lenin, Irvine further suggested that the growing power of finance capital, along with the underconsumption endemic to industrial societies, had generated imperialism in search of markets for surplus goods and investment, and thus exacerbated the chance of war through inter-imperialist rivalry.[31]

Social Credit, in its broadest and most basic meaning, that of the ability of a nation to use credit on the assumption of future economic growth returning a social surplus is, as Robin Neill has pointed out, a developmental strategy for a new nation differing from the National Policy strategy only in its "institutional instruments and the implications for the distribution of the results of accumulation": as such, it had deep and indigenous roots in Canada extending back well into the nineteenth century.[32] Irvine succeeded in referring a motion to investigate the credit system to the House Committee on Banking and Commerce in 1923. Irvine, working closely with W.C. Good, had a number of witnesses called to present unorthodox views. George Bevington, an Alberta farmer of proto-Social Credit views, testified at some length, and was later followed by Major Douglas himself, who came from England for the occasion. Also called were leading bankers and academic economists. The hearings thus present a valuable insight into the state of thinking in the country on monetary questions at this time. It must be said that much of the left wing attack on the bankers and orthodox economists reads very well from a respectable post-Keynesian perspective. Indeed, much of what appeared to be radical and crankish notions to the conventional wisdom of the early 1920s seems to be merely unexceptionable good sense today. The notion of government script replacing private bank notes as the sole legal tender, the idea of a central bank, the demystification of the gold standard, the recognition that banks create credit through loans and that the actual amount of currency in circulation is a small percentage of the total money supply – all these have become the conventional wisdom of a later day. Irvine's sharp intelligence demonstrated itself time and again when confronting the pillars of finance or of academe. One of the barons of Bay Street, Sir John Aird, was reduced to pleading that "we do not want theories introduced into banking. If you get into theories you are on dangerous ground."[33] It might also be pointed out that Irvine's thesis of underconsumption, although deficient in itself, did suggest what one mainstream economist has called the "characteristic radical groping towards the formulation of important economic principles and concepts," including a "close Canadian approach to a Keynesian basis for fiscal policy ... one of the earliest statements of principle to capture the spirit, if not the letter, of the 'national employment budget,' the concept of the 'gross national product,' and the role of the government in the achievement of high and stable levels of employment and income."[34]

Unfortunately for Irvine, despite his avowals that so far as the Douglas system of Social Credit went he was "merely a student of the subject ... not a propagandist,"[35] the popularizing of Social Credit was an activity with disastrous and ironic consequences for an Alberta socialist. Social Credit was an idea which had immense scope for organizing the western farmers in a manner which could only spell trouble for convinced socialists. To the farmers, the major villains of capitalism, as manifested in everyday life, were the banks and loan companies, the distant manipulators who foreclosed on mortgages, and charged fixed interest without regard to the very unfixed distribution of rainfall, temperature, and world price for wheat. The bankers were the fly in the ointment of the yeoman republic of independent producers, a constant reminder that the farmers' property was not really theirs, that the fruits of their labour were already expropriated in advance. When the Depression deepened this already difficult situation, the Social Credit promise of money to each individual in the form of Social Credit script had just the right touch of demagogic simplicity to sweep the electorate. Finally, Social Credit offered a peculiar but devastating mixture of radicalism and conservatism: a single, simple adjustment theory of what had gone wrong, which offered the easy comfort of cultural continuity and the familiar moral verities along with a painless reform which would affect only an unpopular lot of bankers mainly resident in distant Toronto and Montreal. The evangelical fundamentalism in Bible Bill Aberhart in the charismatic campaign which swept Alberta in 1935 was in a sense a parody of the social gospel which had given such impetus to the earlier socialist and reform movement at the end of the war.[36] In another sense, it was merely a *reductio ad absurdem* of the weaknesses of the social gospel and the reformism based upon it. Irvine's views in the 1920s *could* issue in Social Credit, just as the ideology of the farmers' movement always bore that possibility. In the event, the vicissitudes of time and circumstance threw up Social Credit in Alberta, and a social democratic farmer-labour party in Saskatchewan. Irvine, who as late as the eve of the Socred sweep in Alberta was moving a Social Credit amendment to the federal budget,[37] was horrified at the reality of the monster brought to birth under the name of Social Credit – "the most extraordinary will-o'-the-wisp that has ever been projected into political discussion in this country," as he was later to characterize it.[38] It was particularly ironic that it should be in Alberta, Irvine's own province, where Social Credit took hold as an alternative to agrarian socialism. From 1935 on, Irvine was fated to continue his CCF activities in an arid political wilderness, while his chosen political vehicle went from success to success in the province next door.

With the demise of the Progressives and the dissipation of the thrust behind the farmers' movement, the rationale of the group government concept was lost. Not all the adherents of the idea gave it up – as late as 1933 W.C. Good was continuing to advocate the old concept in a memorable exchange with Frank Underhill in the *Canadian Forum*[39] – but Irvine, with his characteristic openmindedness and flexibility, appears to have abandoned interest in the idea. Despite his earlier strictures about the corrupting influence even of reform or radical political parties on their members, if they were to be organized as electoral parties, he threw himself with great gusto and dedication into the task of building a farmer-labour political party in the 1930s. The famous meeting of left wing MP's which set in motion the founding of the CCF party was held in Irvine's office in the House of Commons. Of course, the new party, although clearly organized as an electoral party attempting to attract the support of various groups, across occupational lines, and quite willing to employ such heretical devices as party discipline in the legislature, was not quite what the old line parties had been. There is no doubt that from the beginning the CCF was more democratic in its structure and more principled in its approach to the electorate. In Walter D. Young's terms, it was both a political party seeking electoral success and a social movement seeking to change the moral climate of the country. In its latter guise it did continue to bear some of the features of its antecedents of the 1920s. As the movement aspect diminished while the party aspect waxed stronger, the old voices of anti-partyism could still be heard – and sometimes among them was William Irvine.[40] Yet it had become clear to him that however much the party system might offend his sensibilities, the only possible way for the workers and farmers to fight back against class oppression was to organize themselves as a political party and to make compromises in their own organization for the greater good of the idea of socialism. Irvine was a realist. Ends and means could not always match perfectly, in an imperfect world. When they did not, it might be necessary to adopt means that were not entirely consonant with the ultimate goals. Party organization and party discipline were among such means.

An example of how far this thinking had changed is to be found in a play which he wrote in the mid-1930s, *The Brains We Trust*, which was performed in Toronto and Edmonton.[41] It is a satire of the 1935 election, with a Socialist party filled with well-meaning idealists and led by a saintly figure obviously representing J.S. Woodsworth. In this play there is an interesting section in which socialist strategy is discussed by the new party's leaders. The party, it appears, is beset by moderates who wish to disguise socialism as something acceptable to non-socialists, to talk in populist terms which people understand, while avoiding Marxist concepts such as "surplus value" and "economic determinism." The issue is resolved on the basis that socialism must be based on a movement, not a political party – votes must be real. Socialism cannot be won without winning elections, but elections can be won while socialism is lost. Irvine clearly was trying to resolve the contradiction between his old and new view of political organization.

His devotion to the new party cannot be questioned. Defeated in 1935, and out of Parliament for the ten years following, Irvine did not seek employment which might offer him some economic security, but instead turned his attention full time to organizing and propagandizing for the CCF, on a salary so intermittent and low that his personal finances were wrecked. That his activities were centered in Alberta, where Social Credit had virtually pre-empted the entire potential vote for the CCF, is further confirmation of his dedication against depressing odds. In 1940 he was reduced to begging national headquarters for a loan of a few hundred dollars so that he could build himself a modest home in which to live. "If I had a place of my own," he wrote David Lewis, "however small and humble, it would give me a sense of security which I now lack and besides I could get along on a very small income if I didn't have to pay rent ... it won't be very long until I will be unable to carry on the rough and tumble of organization work. Then what? The thought of an old man pennyless, and in poverty is not a good thought to live with during a sleepless night."[42] Lewis tried unsuccessfully to raise the money, and Irvine's problems grew worse. Somehow he carried on, and in 1945 managed to get himself back in Parliament for the last time. The house was built, and Irvine and his wife lived in it until his death.

The idea of socialism to which Irvine showed such selfless dedication was, to the end, an eclectic, indefinable blend of British Labourite thought, North American populism, agrarian radicalism, anarcho-syndicalism, and quasi-Marxist concepts.[43] He picked up considerable intellectual baggage along the way, and most of it showed. It would be futile to attempt to neatly categorize this astonishing collection of ideas under any convenient label. There is no doubt that he remained a social democrat, in the sense that he never believed that revolution was necessary nor that a dictatorship of the proletariat was either a sensible or desirable concept. Marx provided some good ideas to Irvine, but never a comprehensive world view which would exclude any other. On the other hand, his fierce devotion to the underdogs of society, his congenital open-mindedness, and his constant radical questioning of accepted verities, all tended to place him on the left wing of the CCF. He was, in the end, a party man in the best sense, of loyalty and work, but he remained his own man in terms of ideas and principles.

This obstinate individualism drew him into great difficulties with the party in his last years. Irvine was not stampeded by the Cold War atmosphere of the 1950s to change his lifelong aversion towards armaments, militarism, and "patriotism" as the last refuge of scoundrels. Although, unlike Woodsworth, he was not a pacifist, he maintained throughout his life a deep distrust of those who wished to project political conflict away from the internal class issues of capitalist society and onto foreign "enemies." Moreover, the specific ideological thrust of the Cold War, the mobilization of class solidarity under capitalism against the "menace" of communism, was correctly perceived by Irvine as a blow against progressive forces throughout western society. The mindless celebration of "our way of life" along with the hysterical assault on anything or anyone considered radical could only redound against a social democratic party, however moderate its policies might be in reality. It was thus with increasing misgivings that Irvine watched the CCF eagerly line up behind the Cold War bandwagon. Nor were these foreign policy developments entirely unconnected to the rightward drift of party policy as a whole throughout the 1950s. In 1956 the party replaced the Regina Manifesto, the original platform of 1933 which had called for the eradication of capitalism, with the Winnipeg Declaration which scarcely mentioned public ownership and expressly recognized a place for private enterprise. Irvine was not happy: "we are born in the manger of poverty and the old capitalists are still the same."[44] To Irvine the domestic and foreign policy trends were clearly linked. The Cold War rearmament had, he argued, prevented the reversion of the capitalist economies to large-scale unemployment and depression following the end of the Second World War. Irvine's old underconsumptionist theory of business cycles was thus maintained, but the Western world's artificial and dangerous answer to the problem left the basic question unresolved: if the instability of capitalism could only be evaded by preparations for war, a radical solution to the problem became even more urgent than before, now that atomic weapons raised the spectre of the destruction of the planet itself. The challenge was for social democracy to develop a position distinct from either capitalism or communism. Irvine's logic was simple: "social democracy either has a position which is different from both, or it has no position at all."[45]

That he may have entertained despairing thoughts that social democracy has indeed no position left is one possible interpretation of his last significant political actions: visits to the Soviet Union and the People's Republic of China. Irvine's visit to the Soviet Union in 1956 along with some fellow Alberta CCFers, nearly got him expelled from the party to which he had devoted his life. Irvine had never been a doctrinaire opponent of the Canadian Communist party, unlike some CCFers. On occasion he had co-operated with the Communists in joint ventures or common fronts, but this was for tactical reasons.[46] On the other hand, he wished to see the Soviet Union for himself, rather than through the eyes of the Western media. When the Tass news agency quoted Irvine as commenting favourably on the existence of economic democracy in the Soviet Union, the CCF executive reacted violently. A press release under the signature of the national leader, M.J. Coldwell, told the Canadian press that "on his return to Canada, Mr. Irvine will be queried with respect to any statement he may actually have made. If there is any suggestion at all of approval by him of a one-party dictatorship, it will be immediately and completely repudiated by the CCF."[47] Irvine's position as Alberta party president appeared to implicate the party in a pro-Communist stance from which it had been trying desperately to distance itself, in the face of right wing, anti-CCF propaganda. Irvine was, however, unrepentant upon his return. Although his expulsion from the party was seriously discussed on an informal level, it was thought wiser to leave him alone, not only because in the words of the national secretary, "We must recognize the very special place which he had in our movement, the long years that he has contributed to and sacrificed for it and the fact that it would break his heart to be tossed out at this late stage in his life by those with whom he worked so long," but also because he still had, "even in spite of his recent folly, a tremendous number of followers in the movement": his expulsion would cause a "major schism."[48]

Irvine had been genuinely impressed with what he had seen in the Soviet Union, and had no intention of remaining silent on the subject, despite complaints from party colleagues that he was making speeches "indistinguishable from those of Tim Buck." Despite the impression of naivety which he gave to anti-communist CCFers, Irvine was not unaware of the "warts" in the Soviet way of life. When he published a book about his Russian experiences in 1958, *Live or Die With Russia*, he had made a conscious decision that anti-Soviet propaganda had to be counteracted, and that the "warts" would not be emphasized.[49] It was above all his concern for coexistence and peace which animated this decision, yet it is difficult to read this book without sensing an uncritical quality in Irvine's enthusiastic description of his guided tour. Like a long line of

Western radicals, such as the Webbs and Lincoln Steffins, Irvine's good will somewhat outran his critical faculty when confronted with the Soviet system. The Soviets were sufficiently impressed with the book to have it translated into Russian. In any event, the Alberta CCF executive supported him, and some of its members involved themselves in the Stockholm Peace Congress, labelled a Communist front by the national party. Unbowed, Irvine then went on a trip to Mao's China which, if anything, was considered even farther beyond the pale at this time. In 1961, a year before his death, yet another book was published, *The Twain Shall Meet*, written by Irvine and some of his companions on his China visit. As the title indicates, it was an appeal for understanding between east and west.[50]

In 1961, Irvine was a delegate to the founding convention of the New Democratic party, the successor to the CCF, and then helped organize the Alberta NDP.[51] His party loyalty remained to the end. He died in 1962, completing a political career as interesting and as colourful as any in Canadian history.

Is there any thread of unity in this long and eclectic career? *The Farmers in Politics* provides a clue to the underlying continuity not only of Irvine's thought but of the social democratic left in this century. Any attempt to root Canadian socialism in the reality of the Canadian political economy necessitated the recognition of the crucial importance of the rural population and way of life. That it was the farmers who were in the vanguard of the first major class confrontation with capitalism in this century set the tone of ideological conflict for generations to come. Irvine, perhaps more than any other political figure, attempted to work out the implications of this for radical politics. In drawing the underlying assumptions of the farmers as a class force out into the scrutiny of rational analysis, he also demonstrated the ambiguities and contradictions inherent in farmer-labour alliances. Yet his tenacious insistence upon the cardinal importance of this class alliance as a progressive force is equally important. In other countries, the petit bourgeois rural population has sometimes turned into a bulwark of reaction, or even the electoral backbone of fascism (as in Weimar Germany). Social Credit did exhibit some of these tendencies, but even it never became authoritarian or anti-semitic on the European scale. On the other hand, agrarian socialism took firm hold in Saskatchewan, and the western farmer has always been a factor of significance in both the CCF and the NDP. That the farmers have continued to act as a radical force on occasion – although not always, by any means – has been of particular importance to the Canadian Left. On the other hand, the influence of the farmers on the social democratic party has no doubt contributed to its populist, non-Marxist ideological bent, and its petit bourgeois political instincts so decried by Marxist critics, such as the now defunct Waffle wing of the party expelled in the early 1970s.

In the late twentieth century, the independent commodity producers have declined to the point of near extinction as a significant factor in the Canadian economy. Preservation of the family farm and the rural way of life in the face of corporate farming and agribusiness seems to be a losing battle. Despite its predominantly labour foundations, the NDP continues to maintain its old traditions by supporting the disappearing family farm against the Liberal celebration of consolidation and "modernization," and still gains electoral support in rural Saskatchewan and other prairie locations. The National Farmers Union maintains the radical – and non-partisan – traditions of agrarian protest with such tactics as product boycotts and tractor blockades of highways. It is, however, obvious that the major focus of class conflict has shifted toward the industrial sector and the confrontation between organized labour and corporate capitalism. In this sense, Irvine's book is a summation of an era which has now largely passed. It is none the less important for it is a vivid and lively statement of a thoughtful political figure from a crucial era in the development of radical thought and practice in this country.

NOTES

1 Perhaps the classic statement of this liberal pluralist view is to be found in J.A. Corry and J.E. Hodgetts, *Democratic Government and Politics* (Toronto, 1969).

2 Foreign observers of Canadian politics have been quick to note the unprincipled and even sordid nature of political bargaining. See André Siegfried, *The Race Question in Canada* (1907; new edition: Toronto: Carleton Library No. 29, 1964), and Viscount Bryce, *Canada, an Actual Democracy* (Toronto, 1921).

3 Gustavus Myers, *History of Canadian Wealth* (1914; new edition: Toronto, 1972) is the earliest example of this genre. More recent examples include R.T. Naylor, *The History of Canadian Business*, 2 vols. (Toronto, 1975); Robert Chodos, *CPR: A Century of Corporate Welfare* (Toronto, 1973); John Deverell, *Falconbridge: Portrait of Canadian Mining Multinational* (Toronto, 1975); Larry Pratt, *The Tar Sands: Syncrude and the Politics of Oil* (Edmonton, 1976).

4 John Porter, *The Vertical Mosaic* (Toronto, 1965); Wallace Clement, *The Canadian Corporate Elite* (Toronto: Carleton Library No. 89, 1975).

5 For an overview of these developments see D. Drache, "Rediscovering Canadian Political Economy," paper delivered at the Canadian Political Science Association, Annual Meeting, June, 1975. For an appreciation of the staples model from a main-stream American economic historian, see Glenn Porter, "Recent Trends in Canadian Business and Economic History," *Business History Review* 47, no. 2 (Summer, 1973): 141–58.

6 There is also a muckraking strain, in the Myers tradition, which is not necessarily Marxist. Naylor's work exhibits this characteristic.

7 W.L. Morton, "Clio in Canada: the Interpretation of Canadian History," *University of Toronto Quarterly* 15, no. 3 (April, 1946).

8 I have developed this more fully in "Images of the state in Canada," in Leo Panitch, ed., *The Canadian State: Political Economy and Political Power* (Toronto, 1977), 28–68.

9 The early theorist of colonization, Gibbon Wakefield, made a major point of this relationship. Some of the implications are brought out by Marx in vol. 1 of *Capital*, chapter 33. Haliburton had Sam Slick utter it as an obvious piece of conventional wisdom. T.C. Haliburton, *The Clockmaker, First Series* (Toronto, 1958), 27.

10 K.A.H. Buckley and M.C. Urquhart, *Canadian Historical Statistics* (Toronto, 1965).

11 Michael Bliss, *A Living Profit: Studies in the Social History of Canadian Business, 1883–1911* (Toronto, 1974), 117–24.

12 Among the flood of such works, one might single out – in addition to the Irvine book reprinted here – Mackenzie King, *Industry and Humanity* (1918; new edition: Toronto, 1973); Stephen Leacock, *The Unsolved Riddle of Social Justice* (1920; reprinted in Alan Bowker, ed., *The Social Criticism of Stephen Leacock*: Toronto, 1973); W.C. Good, *Production and Taxation in Canada* (Toronto, 1919); Salem Bland, *The New Christianity* (1919; new edition: Toronto, 1973).

13 Raymond Williams has recently attempted to reassess the traditional Marxist antipathy to "rural idiocy," *The Country and the City* (London, 1973).

14 I have discussed King's thought at greater length in "The Liberal Corporatist Ideas of Mackenzie King," *Labour/Le Travailleur* 2 (1977).

15 Tony Mardiros, "A Man to Remember: William Irvine, 1885–1962," *The Nutcracker* 1, no. 7 (May, 1975): 4–5. Richard Allen, *The Social Passion: Religious and Social Reform in Canada, 1914–28* (Toronto, 1971), 46; Allen interviewed Irvine a year before his death.

16 Tony Mardiros, "William Irvine: Heretic in Politics," *NeWest Review* 1, no. 3 (October, 1975): 1–2. My thanks to Professor Mardiros for supplying me with copies of this article and the one cited in fn. 15, above.

17 Paul F. Sharp, *The Agrarian Revolt in Western Canada: A Survey Showing American Parallels* (1948; reprinted, New York, 1971), 77–104. C.B.

Macpherson, *Democracy in Alberta: Social Credit and the Party System* (second edition: Toronto, 1962), 25–6.

18 Macpherson, *Democracy in Alberta*, 28–61, offers the most comprehensive and interesting analysis of the social and political theory of the UFA thinkers, including Irvine.

19 Allen, *The Social Passion*, 208.

20 In 1940, in desperate financial straits, Irvine could still show little enthusiasm for a possible offer of a Unitarian ministry in Ottawa. "My heart is not in the Church as you know," he wrote David Lewis, "but in the CCF. To have to go to the Church for a living would be unfair to the Church and most difficult for me." National Archives of Canada, CCF Records, v. 97, Irvine to Lewis, no date (1940).

21 The Farmers' Platform was a program promulgated by the Canadian Council of Agriculture and ratified by the Council's member associations meeting in convention during 1917. It was revised in 1918 under the title of the "New National Policy." L.A. Wood, *A History of Farmers' Movements in Canada: The Origins and Development of Agrarian Protest, 1872–1924* (1924; new edition, Introduction by Foster J.K. Griezic: Toronto, 1975), 345–6.

22 Macpherson, *Democracy in Alberta*, 34–8.

23 House of Commons, *Debates*, 1923, 1953–4.

24 It might be noted in passing that the concept of a "universal class" has obsessed numerous other modern political thinkers. To the early liberal thinkers, the bourgeoisie would take on this role; to Hegel, it would be the bureaucrats; to Frantz Fanon, it would be the peasantry and lumpen-proletariat of the Third World. None of these universal classes, including Marx's proletariat, have ever quite lived up to their advance billing. Irvine was thus only essaying a North American variant of a familiar quest, with as much success as other such attempts.

25 House of Commons, *Debates*, 1923, 208–44; 389–434.

26 Ibid., 1925, 1963.

27 *Co-operative Government* (Ottawa: 1929), 220. The book begins with a curious foreword by Henry Wise Wood, who states that he knows the author, but has not read the book!

28 House of Commons, *Debates*, 1927, 211–34.

29 Believers in intellectual progress may note sadly that the current debate on retention of capital punishment could have been lifted almost *verbatim* from the debate generated by Irvine's abolitionist bill in 1924, a half century ago. Only the statistical "evidence" has changed: the arguments remain unaltered. See *Debates*, 1924, 1265 ff. Irvine's bill was defeated by a vote of 92 to 29.

30 Kenneth McNaught, *A Prophet in Politics: A Biography of J.S. Woodsworth* (Toronto, 1959), 173–9.

31 Irvine aired his monetary views in a number of forums, one of which was a two volume pamphlet issued in 1924, *Purchasing Power and the World Problem* (Dominion Labor Party, Labor Temple, Calgary). An unpublished graduate paper by David Laycock, "Socialism and Social Credit in the Political Thought of William Irvine" (Department of Political Economy, University of Toronto, 1977), provides a useful inquiry into that question.

32 R.F. Neill, "Social Credit and National Policy in Canada," *Journal of Canadian Studies* 3 (1968): 3–13.

33 House of Commons, Committee on Banking and Commerce, 1923, *Proceedings and Evidence*, 379. The head of the Canadian Bankers Association was similarly stymied by Irvine: "Very difficult to answer. You really might ask a question that Sir Isaac Newton could not answer and I am not Sir Isaac Newton; I am a practical man, that is all. I am not a master of economics." Ibid., 320.

34 Irving Brecher, *Monetary and Fiscal Thought and Policy in Canada: 1919–1939* (Toronto, 1957), 94 , and 54–5.

35 Banking and Commerce Committee, *Proceedings and Evidence*, 1047.

36 Macpherson, *Democracy in Alberta*; John A. Irving, *The Social Credit Movement in Alberta* (Toronto, 1959); William E. Mann, *Sect, Cult and Church in Alberta* (Toronto, 1955).

37 Frank Underhill characterized a 1932 speech by Irvine in Toronto in behalf of the new CCF as "pure social credit." Walter D. Young, *The Anatomy of a Party: The National CCF, 1932–62* (Toronto, 1969), 34.

38 House of Commons, *Debates*, 1947, 1288. The flavour of Irvine's contempt for the religious obscurantism of Social Credit is caught in a letter he wrote to David Lewis concerning Aberhart's successor as premier, Ernest Manning: "Mr. Manning is young, rather well liked and oozes the blood of the lamb over everything. He proved by science, in three lectures on the air, that the whale swallowed Jonah and said that, if the bible had said that Jonah had swallowed the whale, science could prove that too. That is the sort of thing most people like. He will be more popular than 'Abby.'" CCF Records, v. 74, Irvine to Lewis, 3 June 1943. Irvine's mature views on Social Credit can also be found in a letter to W.C. Good, reprinted in Good's autobiography, *Farmer Citizen* (Toronto, 1958), 215–17.

39 August, 1933. The exchange is reprinted in Good, *Farmer Citizen*, 184–95.

40 Young, *The Anatomy of a Party*, 113.

41 (Toronto: Thomas Nelson and Sons, 1935). He wrote another play the following year, *You Can't Do That*, which was performed in Wetastikiwin (Letter to another from Tony Mardiros, 23 May 1976).

42 CCF Records, v. 97, Irvine to Lewis, 19 August 1940.

43 His 1945 pamphlet, *Is Socialism the Answer? The Intelligent Man's Guide to Basic Democracy* (Winnipeg: Contemporary Publications, 1945), includes a veritable pot-pourri of influences from American New Dealer Maury Maverick to Karl Marx.

44 Young, *The Anatomy of a Party*, 128.

45 From an unpublished manuscript, "Challenge to the 'Free Private Enterprise' Capitalist Way of Life," CCF Records, v. 300. The manuscript appears to have been written in 1956; that it was not published by the party is scarcely surprising, considering its direct challenge to the views then dominant in the national executive.

46 Young, *The Anatomy of a Party*, 262. Ivan Avakumovic, *The Communist Party in Canada: a History* (Toronto, 1975), 105, 128. In 1943, Irvine assured David Lewis apropos of Communist leader Tim Buck, that "I have never communicated with the gentleman in my life." CCF Records, v. 74, Irvine to Lewis, 16 Nov. 1943.

47 CCF Records, v. 97, CCF Press release, 19 July 1956.

48 Ibid., Lorne Ingle to Elmer Roper, 9 August 1956.

49 Ibid., Roper to Ingle, 11 Sept. and 3 Nov. 1956. Mardiros letter, 23 May 1976.

50 Edmonton, 1961. Irvine came off badly with his prediction that "common humanism" would prevent a Sino-Soviet split. He even suggested that the Russian-Chinese alliance would outlive NATO, 132–3.

51 Mardiros, "A Man to Remember," 5.

PART TWO

Liberalism
and Nationality

"To Have Insight into Much and Power Over Nothing": The Political Ideas of Harold Innis

Harold Innis, Canada's preeminent social scientist from the 1930s to the early 1950s, is here reinterpreted in terms of his underlying political ideas, especially his complex and despairing defence of Canadian autonomy against American domination. This essay was originally written for a conference on Innis held at Simon Fraser University in 1978 (and published five years later, after some peculiar adventures with Canadian publishers and journals). The conference was itself evidence of renewed interest in Innis by various academics since the 1960s.

Innis has been claimed and/or amended by more than one school, but the one with which I have the closest intellectual kinship is the new political economy, with its left-nationalist perspective. Yet, however important Innis was in inspiring my generation's intellectual resistance to the imperialism of American social science, I was not altogether happy with the dominant economistic reading of Innis as staples theorist, and I found the characterization of him as a "nationalist" too simplistic. Too little attention had been paid to his later writings on communications, where he ranged widely across time and space and civilizations. I was very much attracted by John Watson's pathbreaking interpretation of the influence of classical scholarship on Innis, especially on Innis's emphasis on a dialectic of power and knowledge as a universal theme of human history. Within this context I believe that the paradox of Innis as nationalist and anti-nationalist can be resolved.

It is a tragic resolution, and I found this re-reading of Innis to be a moving, if saddening, exercise in self-knowledge as a Canadian. The coming of Free Trade and the powerlessness with which nationalist Canadian academics, writers, and artists have watched the inexorable process

Reprinted with permission from *Queen's Quarterly* 90, no. 3 (Autumn 1983): 818–31.

of continental integration and national disintegration offers confirmation
of Innis's pessimistic forebodings of four decades ago.

Harold Innis was an historian and political economist, not a political theorist. Although he dealt with political questions and pondered political relationships among men and between nations, he
very rarely isolated political matters from the broader economic,
social, and cultural context within which they arise. This may be one
of his strengths. At the same time it places a burden on the interpreter of Innis who wishes to do what Innis himself was so loath to
do, that is, to focus on the political aspect of a multifaceted thought.
My analytical project is to abstract some of the elements of a political theory from Innis' thought, but only for the purpose of dissolv-
ing this theory back into the more comprehensive body of his
thought. In so doing, I would hope that some clarification of Innis'
writings will result.

My point of departure is the revisionist interpretation of the later
Innis by A. John Watson in his article "Harold Innis and Classical
Scholarship."[1] Watson's argument, highly compressed, is this: the
key to understanding the later Innis' communications work is to be
found less in the extension of his earlier staples studies than in his
intellectual relationship with certain members of the University of
Toronto classics department in the 1940s, especially C.N. Cochrane
and Eric Havelock, and in his discovery, through the classicists, of a
compelling theme of antiquity – human society is a product of the
interplay, or dialectic, between power and intelligence. It is this
dialectic, itself subtle and complex, which is the real dynamic in
Innis' theory of history, rather than the more mechanical and
deterministic interplay of durable and non-durable media, or of
time-biased and space-biased media presented by most interpreters
of the later Innis.[2] Intelligence furnishes power with its technique;
intelligence requires power for the order within which it may
flourish. The intellectual, whose independence of thought is crucial
to man's cultural progress, is fixed in inevitable conflict with
political power, which is exclusively self-interested, hence anti-
intellectual, and yet at the same time is based on monopolies of
knowledge. Intellectual man is thus lonely and alienated, as the very
products of his imagination have come back to weigh upon his
freedom as oppressive nightmares. Havelock's image of Prometheus,
the bringer of fire and thus technology to man, bound down forever
to tortuous punishment by the power of Zeus, who attempts to
monopolize control of technology, is the mythic image which helped
crystallize Innis' grasp of the tragic dilemma of western history.

Innis' particular contribution, as a colonial intellectual viewing empire from the periphery, and as an economic historian following the staples approach to resource extraction over extended frontiers, was to disclose a materialist mediation for the historical development and dissolution of particular monopolies of knowledge in the communication technologies of empires. The success of an imperial system implies a balance at the center, just as the very dependence of the peripheries implies imbalance. This central balance will be embodied in an equilibrium between complementary media; an imbalance at the center implies political instability and the decay of cultural creativity. In Innis' own words:

Concentration on a medium of communication implies a bias in cultural development of the civilization concerned either towards an emphasis on space and political organization or towards an emphasis on time and religious organization. Introduction of a second medium tends to check the bias of the first and to create conditions suited to the growth of empire. ... The ability to develop a system of government in which the bias of communication can be checked and an appraisal of the significance of space and time can be reached remains a problem of empire and of the Western world.[3]

Watson's reading of the later Innis has two particular virtues. First, to re-read the communications studies in the light of the classical dialectic of power and intellect is to find many previously opaque and difficult aspects suddenly clarified, to discover a new and intriguing pattern in the eclectic mosaic of fact through which Innis' mind moved. I would not for a moment assert that it is the *only* pattern to be found there; Innis' thought is too rich and fertile to be subject to such reductionism. It is a particularly provocative pattern. The second value is that it points to the specifically *political* orientation of Innis' later thought. It thus helps us to understand the scholarly and theoretical basis of the increasingly political commentaries and warnings of his last years.

In these political interventions, Innis did not always make himself easily understood. This was deliberate. If he was typically cryptic it was because he has a secret message, both to convey and to conceal. As Plato has Socrates say in the *Phaedrus*, "once a thing is committed to writing it circulates equally among those who understand the subject and those who have no business with it; a writing cannot distinguish between suitable and unsuitable readers."[4] The curious combination of an impenetrable wall of empirical fact marked by sudden, unsettling glimpses into the oracular beyond in the communications studies is matched by a studied indirection and an elaborate deceptiveness in the more directly political commentaries. The key to unlocking this riddle of Innis as Sphinx may be found in his address, "The Church in Canada," given to the Board of Evangelism and Social Service of the United Church of Canada in 1947.[5] As chairman of the Department of Political Economy, Innis was the subject of constant surveillance and harassment by those who wielded political and economic power and who constantly reminded him that he "should be very careful about the way in which his views are expressed." Innis agreed ironically with this advice: "I am largely compelled to avoid making speeches in public and to resort to the careful preparation of material to be made available in print. In most cases this involves writing in such guarded fashion that no one can understand what is written or using quotations from the writings of authors who stand in great repute." The cryptic opacity of Innis the political writer is not a result of artlessness but of its opposite. The interested reader may be referred to Leo Strauss' *Persecution and the Art of Writing* .[6]

"The danger of shaking men out of the soporific results of mechanized knowledge," Innis warned, "is similar to that of attempting to arouse a drunken man or one who has taken an overdose of sleeping tablets. The necessary violent measures will be disliked. We have had university professors threatened with the loss of their positions for less than this." Paradoxically, more dangerous than the reaction of power is its indifference. Innis immediately followed the above sentences with the reflection that "I have little hope of making any impression with what I have to say." Innis "envied the freedom of my colleagues in other subjects. ... I am always impressed by the ease with which they make statements largely because no one will pay much attention to what they have to say, or because they speak about subjects which do not affect people's direct interests." Political scientists and economists who feel freer today than did Innis a quarter-century ago would do well to ponder those words.

The dialectic of power and intellect is unending and tragic. "It is not only dangerous in this country to be a social scientist with an interest in truth but it is exhausting. You will remember the remarks of the Persian at a banquet in Thebes noted by Herodotus. This is the most cruel pang that man can bear – to have much insight and power over nothing.' " Like Plato's philosopher who has emerged from the dark cave of illusions into the dazzling sunlight, Innis no longer knows how to talk to those who remain in the cave, those who cling to their shadows and to their illusions. He may be ignored as a madman, or considered as an enemy of the state, that is to say, of the cave. Socrates, after all, was put to death. Plato's solution, the coincidence of power and intellect in the institution of the philosopher-king, is a solution in words, an ideal laid up in heaven but unrealizable in practice. Worse, Innis could see in Plato's just city itself only another monopoly of knowledge, an inquisition before which Socrates himself would inevitably be brought.[7] Ironically, either in its unrealizability or in its very realization, the vision of intelligence is tragic, and thus the existence of the intellectual is permeated with pessimism and sadness. It is, moreover, a very classical sadness, unrelieved either by Christian transcendence of this world or by the modern secular faith that man can make his own history and thus make himself.

It is not surprising that Innis in later life should have been so deeply impressed by the writings of Cochrane and Havelock on classical themes. Perhaps in this introduction to antiquity, Innis experienced what literary criticism has termed the "shock of recognition" – a profound but unspecified alienation from the modern world-view was suddenly cast into resolution in the mirror-image of antiquity. I think that this resolution can best be understood in terms of a clarification of the tragic image of man which Innis was already dimly perceiving. Let us consider the difference between the classical and modern concepts of tragedy, as embodied in the myths of Oedipus and Macbeth. Both are brought from high to low estate, but in the former case it is not a fatal flaw in Oedipus' character which brings about his downfall, as it is with Macbeth's ambition. No personal moral blame attaches to Oedipus for killing his father and marrying his mother, for he did these things innocently, unknowingly. But fate is implacable, and Oedipus must suffer. Macbeth's actions are sinful, a result of his own conscious will. The "pollution" which afflicts Oedipus forms, in the words of a contemporary classicist, "the automatic consequence of an action, belongs to the world of external events, and operates with the same ruthless indifference to motive as a typhoid germ."[8] As Cochrane explained, the classical world was one in which fortune was unpredictable and indeterminate; after Christianity and Augustine, fortune becomes God's will while it is the individual personality which becomes indeterminate. It is evident that Innis felt a strong affinity for the classical view which seemed to mirror his own increasing sense of the irrationality of history's unfolding. Yet it could not be that Innis, nor any other modern, could simply go back to antiquity. Innis is, as many have pointed out, a dialectical thinker. Knowledge of the classical view serves in a sense to overcome the modern, but this overcoming is synthetic.

Let us examine this synthesis more closely. Classical man was caught in a world which he could neither control nor fully understand; at best, he could build a small microcosmos of order and meaning within a larger universe indifferent to his fate. Such was the Greek *polis*, antiquity's consummate political achievement, and such was the delicate balance which the Greeks struck between the oral and written traditions, and thus the happy balance between time and space which Innis so admired. But these precarious moments were doomed, and quickly dissolved in the rush of history, as Alexander swept down from Macedonia with his superior military technology and put an end to the *polis*. "The first of the great sledgehammer blows of technology in which force and the vernacular hammered monopolies of knowledge into malleable form had been delivered."[9] The point is that while fortune is cruel and indifferent, and while Innis cannot find in it evidence of a divine or transcendent meaning, neither is it altogether outside man's control. "The great sledgehammer blows of technology" which buffet man like cyclones are not indeed the thunderbolts of Zeus. Papyrus, parchment, paper, printing press, radio – the cataclysms which convulse man's social, political, and cultural being are catastrophes which issue from man himself, from his Promethean capacity to transform nature to his own design. Worse, it is that very faculty of man – his inventiveness, his intelligence – which Innis saw always pitted against power, which itself gave the creative impetus to technological advance, and thus to the conditions of its own frustration and enslavement. As Watson puts it, Innis sees "how the products of man come back to him in an increasingly horrifying and alien form, the more his knowledge and power of production are extended."[10] On the other hand, the modern post-Christian tradition, from Machiavelli through Marx, which stresses man's radical capacity to shape his own being in history, is closed to Innis. As James Carey has aptly written, Innis grasped "the amount of cultural loss that was attendant upon technical innovations and the degree to which given technologies, when imposed throughout social organization, finally destroy the very ends they are trying to achieve."[11]

I should like to be yet more specific on this last point. It is a danger of the power-intelligence interpretation that Innis may be read too exclusively on an idealist ideal. However much he might have deplored the contemporary decadence of the "form of mind from Plato to Kant which hallowed existence beyond chance,"[12] Innis did not attempt to become a philosopher, Neoplatonist or otherwise. Most of his communications work is materialist. In analyzing the effects of the successive "sledgehammer blows of technology," Innis moves through a mass of empirical fact to grasp the materialist basis of the concrete mediations and their consequences in successive historical epochs. What is unique to Innis' research is his argument that each dominant medium of communication so structures or biases the nature of the ideas and values communicated as to progressively destroy the cultural vitality of the civilization as a product of its very domination. Only when media of opposing characteristics are in balance can this suicidal dynamic be stopped, and then only briefly and precariously. The implications are clear. The modernist tradition from Machiavelli through Marx is simply the advancement of a new monopoly of knowledge through the conquest of space (nature). In completing this conquest, man equally loses all grasp over the dimension of time. Instead of liberating himself he has bound himself with a bias hardened into a monopoly – the chains of Prometheus. Thus Innis' Cassandra-like political stance of his last years proceeds from a radical conservatism, the classical roots of which permit him a thorough and pervasive criticism of modernity, while the modern roots permit him a certain scientific detachment from the past. When Havelock wrote that intellectual man's exercise of foresight, always and everywhere resisted by power, "brings on a certain loneliness," he could scarcely have found a better subject than Harold Innis.[13]

Perhaps the master key to history, Innis wrote sardonically, "lies in the conclusion that human movements provoke violent reactions":

Roman imperialism created by intense nationalism ended by destroying the nationality of rulers and subjects. The nationalism of the Jews left them without a country. The Catholic church renounced the world and became the heir of the defunct Roman empire. Universal suffrage heralded the end of parliamentary government. The more successful a democracy in levelling population the less the resistance to despotism. The interest of the French Revolution in humanity kindled the fire of patriotism and nationalism in Spain, Germany, and Russia. ... Stability which characterized certain periods in earlier civilizations is not the obvious objective of this civilization. Each civilization has its own methods of suicide.[14]

Just as Innis began, as early as the *Fur Trade in Canada*, to note that the history of "progress" is the history of violent disturbance,[15] so in his last years he saw the fate of modern western civilization as catastrophic. Unlike the anti-utopian visionaries of the twentieth century such as Zamiatin, Orwell or Huxley, he does not view the future in terms of a horrifying stasis, a death-in-life in which change grinds to a halt in the perfection of control, but in a great crash. This is not a personal speculation on his part, but a logical conclusion of his own theory of communication and empire. The growing monop-olization of knowledge through space-biased media of communica-tion has created an imbalance at the center of western civilization which makes collapse inevitable, if counter-measures are not set in motion. That is why the question of communications is fundamen-tally to Innis a *political* question. The ancient dialectic of power and intelligence has entered a critical phase under modern conditions of technology. The response to this crisis must be political.

The bias of communication in space implies great inequality of economic and of political power. On the former point Innis wrote of a "sponge theory of the distribution of wealth which assumes violence."[16] On the latter point, the rigid connection between the control of space and the growth of state bureaucracies is evident from all Innis' later writings. To Innis all monopolies are bad, and are unfavorably contrasted with competition, hence the constant counterposing of "rigidities" to "elasticities." The modern state is the most ominous of all these monopolies, since it makes increasing claims to all-inclusiveness, economic, social, and, worst of all, cultural and intellectual. Particularly under the impetus of the Cold War, and particularly in the new metropole of empire, the United States, Innis saw the birth of a kind of national capitalism – which was as "capitalist" (in the competitive sense) as its defeated ana-logue, National Socialism had been "socialist." "Extensive govern-ment expenditure and intervention and large scale undertakings have raised the fundamental problems of morality. A friend in power is a friend lost. A decline in morality has followed war and the growth of hierarchies in Church, State and private enterprise. Power is poison."[17] "Adam Smith," Innis wrote in 1938, "might have said of capitalists as he said of merchants: 'The government of an exclusive company of merchants is, perhaps, the worst of all govern-ments for any country whatever.' "[18] National capitalism destroys the market, the device which Smith at least believed saved capitalism from the excesses of capitalists. The national capitalist state fuses awesome economic and political power. This fatal identity can be further specified in the control of the dominant media themselves. American pulp and paper interests become newspaper monopolies with a vested economic interest in penetrating the state with a view to stirring up imperialist adventures, which in turn sell newspapers. The "free press" is a monopoly which turns the state to coercion and conquest. Mass "democratic" media lead to militarism.[19] Elec-

tronic media – of which, it must be admitted, Innis was only imperfectly aware – only intensify the reversion to force. Radio was to
Innis particularly odious, since it mechanized his beloved oral
medium and turned it into the opposite of the flexible oral tradition
of face-to-face communication, into a one-way medium for the
commands of power. Hence Innis, in sharp contrast to his *soi-disant*
disciple, Marshall McLuhan, could speak feelingly of the "cruelty of
mechanized communications."[20]

One of the worst cruelties of mechanized communication is the
mechanization of knowledge itself. "We are compelled to recognize
the significance of mechanized knowledge as a source of power and
its subjection to the demands of force through the instrument of the
state."[21] Mechanized knowledge implies the propagation of mass
"culture," the loss of the oral tradition of scholarship, the degradation of the humanities, an emphasis upon statistical and quantitative
methods in the social sciences which lose sight of humanity, a
valuation of "facts" over ideas, and the channeling of knowledge
into the machinery of the militarized state. "Political life has become
a blazing furnace burning off material which might have been used
for the development of a broad cultural base."[22]

What is particularly subtle and intriguing in Innis is his refusal to
settle for behavioral explanations of the bias of communication in
controlling cultural and intellectual life. As Carey summarizes Innis
– more clearly than the original, it must be stated:

He believed that the fundamental form of social power is the power to define what
reality is. Monopolies of knowledge then in the cultural sense refer to the
efforts of groups to determine the entire world view of a people: to produce, in other words, an official view of reality which can constrain and
control human action ...

Modern computer enthusiasts ... may be willing to share their data with
anyone. What they are not willing to give up so readily is the entire
technocratic world view that determines what it is that qualifies as a
valuable fact. What they wish to monopolize is not the data but the
approved, certified, authorized mode of thought, indeed the very definition
of what it means to be reasonable.

What Innis recognized, of course, is that knowledge is not simply information. Knowledge is not given in experience as data. There is no such
thing as information about the world devoid of conceptual systems that
create and define the world in the act of discovering it. And what he
warned against was the monopoly of these conceptual systems or para-
digms.[23]

This lengthy quotation admirably serves to suggest a curious parallel in Innis to the work of the Italian Marxist Antonio Gramsci, and particularly to the latter's concept of ideological hegemony. I call this a *curious* parallel, for Innis and Gramsci neither knew of one another nor shared many common reference points. There is thus no point in pushing such a comparison too strongly. Yet in both cases there is the same interest and concern with the non-coercive elements of ideological social control, which exists in somewhat problematic relationship to forms of coercive social control. As a Marxist, Gramsci specified a class basis for hegemony. Innis is not lacking in appreciation of Marxist analysis, but is concerned not to push such analysis systematically to its "ultimate limit, and in pushing it to its limit, showing its limitations."[24] Innis' idea of monopolies of knowledge as forms of ideological hegemony is an attempt to grasp the material basis of a systematic bias in thought which is at a deeper level than class alone, although that is involved, and which colors all thought communicated through the same media whatever its source.

This admittedly ambiguous comparison with Gramsci may serve to highlight the profound ambiguity of Innis' actual political position in relation to his own time and his own country. At one level, the political implications of his views would seem to leave him close to the kind of radical conservatism later developed in the work of George Grant. In its return to antiquity, in its plea for the time dimension, its dread of the mechanization of control over space, and its defense of Canadian nationhood, Grant's philosophy has sharp and intriguing parallels with the concerns of the later Innis. But Grant, true to his classical pessimism, *laments* things which have passed and cannot be restored. Innis in his last days was darkly pessimistic. And yet he seems never to have concluded that the circle was irrevocably closed. Innis can never be a truly conservative pessimist like Grant because, unlike Grant, he is fundamentally dialectical in his mode of thought. This dialectical cast of mind never leads him to Marx's revolutionary optimism; indeed, it leaves him so far short as to make the comparison almost comic. It does, however, leave some glimmers of light amid the gathering gloom.

Innis dialectically specifies a radical imbalance and instability in the center of the modern empire. Moreover, he has an elaborately worked-out historical theory of the rise and fall of empires over six millennia. A crucial question is that of the location of antagonistic elements which might overcome the present unstable political order. Innis is quite clear about the "tendency of each medium of communication to create monopolies of knowledge to the point that the human spirit breaks through at new levels of society and on the outer fringes."[25] Specific examples seem to indicate that Innis sees this in center-periphery terms; it is at the margins of empire that the "spirit breaks through," such as the invention of the printing press in Germany, "territory marginal to France in which copyists' guilds held a strong monopoly."[26]

The location of potential sources of resistance on the periphery of empire serves to locate Innis' own position as a scholar and as a critic. It is Innis' own marginality as a colonial intellectual which allows him to stand, as it were, both inside and outside the biases of empire. I need not reiterate on this occasion the oft-repeated and persuasive argument that the staples approach could only emerge from an economic historian in a staples-producing hinterland economy. Equally to the point is the famous Innisian dictum that "the economic history of Canada has been dominated by the discrepancy between the center and the margin of western civilization," for it is in the perception of that very *discrepancy* that a certain critical distance might be achieved. It is the same critical distance in *space*, which Innis also attempts to achieve in *time* by his return to antiquity. The dialectic of mindless power and powerless intelligence finds its analogue in the dialectic of the rigid, monopolistic imperial center and the powerless intellectual on the margin of empire. As I have stressed in my introduction of the classical theme, it is a dialectic: intelligence furnishes power with its technique; intelligence requires power for the order in which intelligence may flourish. So too the relationship between metropole and hinterland is dialectical: the marginal areas draw the very logic of the development from the economy of the center, yet that dependence stifles the capacity of the marginal areas to correct imbalance at the center. In returning to antiquity Innis remains both inside and outside the modern world: "In attempting to use other civilizations as mirrors by which we may understand our own we are exposed to much greater dangers in studying Greek culture and its successors since our own culture has been profoundly influenced by it."[27] Innis is painfully aware of the difficulties of trying to see his world whole, and just as painfully aware that he has come nowhere near success.[28] Yet, like Socrates, Innis is aware of his own ignorance, which is in itself a knowledge superior to that of the imperial social scientists who lack all knowledge of their own limitations. Innis ends a long historical discussion of the "military implications of the American Constitution" with the following ironic statement: "These remarks have been made by one who does not pretend to understand the United States." Yet more ironically, he follows this shortly with the reflection that "what we didn't know hurt us a lot."[29]

Canada is on the margin of the American empire, an imperial project which Innis viewed as violently unstable and self-destructive. A *discrepancy* between center and periphery is not a *contradiction*. A discrepancy may offer a little critical space for intelligence; a contradiction entails its overcoming. Canada is both inside and outside the American empire. To the extent that it is inside, it is colonial, penetrated by the bias of empire, and contributes to its own subordination. To the extent that it is outside it is critical, touched by elements foreign to the bias of the center and resists its subordination. To the extent that it is inside, Innis despairs of the capacity of powerless Canadian intellectuals to understand power, let alone confront it. And yet to the extent that it is still outside, Innis can begin and end his *Empire and Communications* with Canada.[30] If Gibbon actually wrote about the decay of the British empire when he wrote his *Decline and Fall of the Roman Empire*, as Innis implied,[31] then Innis actually wrote about Canada in his communications work, in the sense that it was the concerns of a Canadian which led him to see the linkages between imperialism and communications.

It is in the ambiguous context of Canada's status on the margin of empire and the dialectic of power and intelligence that we may begin to unravel the riddle of Innis as anti-imperialist and antinationalist. The antinomies of Innis' calls to resistance to American imperialism on the one side, and his unmistakable excoriations of Canadian nationalism on the other, have bedevilled his critics ever since his death, leading many to opt for one or the other pole as Innis' "real" position. I would submit that both positions are right, and are in fact commensurate with one another, when properly understood. First, Innis was not so much anti-imperialist as anti-*American* imperialism. It would be difficult to reconstruct from his *Empire and Communications* a consistently anti-imperialist bias. On the contrary, balanced empires sum up what is best in human aspiration. The American empire, on the other hand, embodies the worst tendencies of the modern epoch, a radically imbalanced and unstable conglomeration altogether out of touch with the time dimension of culture and increasingly reliant on violence and mechanized knowledge to control space. Canadian resistance is a good thing if it offers a creative alternative to this swollen Leviathan, but Canadian *nationalism*, as Innis saw it, tended to be only a marginal reproduction of what was worst in the imperial center. Thus Innis' jeremiads against the "totalitarian" tendencies of Liberal one-party dominance in Ottawa fused with a rigid bureaucracy, in turn generating regionalism and local separatism as a sort of dialectical *reductio ad absurdum* of "nationalism" eating itself. A bureaucratized and militarized national capitalism protecting its parochial and petty self-interests is as equally appalling as the imperial parent which gave it birth. If anything, it is a bit more ridiculous. "No one can be a social scientist in Canada without a sense of humour ... 'A joke is a joke but no-one wants to die laughing.' The hazards of our profession are becoming serious."[32] More seriously, this kind of national capitalist state only reproduces on a smaller scale, but with equal virulence, the domination of mindless power over powerless intelligence. It is a mark of Innis' pessimism that he felt it necessary to argue these points so cryptically and indirectly. Even the universities, the last refuge of intelligence – "With imperfect competition between concepts the university is essentially an ivory tower in which courage can be mustered to attack any concept which threatens to become a monopoly"[33] – have been so penetrated that courage is rarely mustered from within. Innis can suggest only that "we can survive by taking persistent actions at strategic points against American imperialism *in all its attractive guises.*"[34] That last phrase reveals how powerful the adversary is, how deeply the bias of the imperial center has penetrated the mind and standards of those on its margins. And it is not at all clear what Innis means by "persistent actions," other than calling in the cultural traditions of the Old World to redress the imbalance of the New, or exhorting the universities to return to their ivory towers. Like Plato in the *Republic*, Innis' position is, truly, tragic: he sees what is wrong with the world, he knows how it could be better, but he has almost no faith that anything can in fact be done about it. The very radicalism of his vision ironically deepens the tragedy: he knows better than most what it is that eludes our grasp.

To return to Innis' quotation from Herodotus which I have used as the title of this paper, we find in Herodotus that on the eve of a decisive defeat of the Persian invaders by the Greeks, Persian leaders were invited to a banquet in Thebes, which had allied itself to the invaders. Here a Persian confided to a Greek present that few of the Persians beside him would remain alive in a short time. The Greek, astonished, asked him why the Persian commanders were not warned of the impending disaster. "Many of us know that what I have said is true," the Persian replied, "yet, because we cannot do otherwise, we continue to take orders from our commander. No one would believe us, however true our warning. This is the worst pain a man can suffer: to have insight into much and power over nothing."[35]

NOTES

1 *Journal of Canadian Studies* 12, no. 5 (Winter 1977): 45–61. This article is drawn from Watson's extraordinarily interesting doctoral dissertation, "Marginal Man: Harold Innis' Communication Works in Context" (University of Toronto, 1981). See also William Christian, "Harold Innis as Political Theorist," *Canadian Journal of Political Science* 10, no. 1 (March 1977): 21–42, and Leslie A. Pal, "Scholarship and the Later Innis," *Journal of Canadian Studies* (Winter 1977): 32–44.

2 The most grievous recent example of this latter reading is in Carl Berger's Governor General's Award-winning *The Writing of Canadian History* (Toronto, 1976), 187–95.

3 *Empire and Communications* (Toronto, 1972), 170.

4 Plato, *Phaedrus and the Seventh and Eighth Letters*, trans. by Walter Hamilton (Harmondsworth, Middlesex, 1973), 97.

5 *Essays in Canadian Economic History* (Toronto, 1956), 383–93.

6 Glencoe, IL, 1952. See especially chap. 1.

7 See Harold Innis, "Charles Norris Cochrane, 1889–1946," *Canadian Journal of Economics and Political Science* 12 (1945): 97, on the "Platonic state" in the twentieth century. The image of Socrates brought before Plato's inquisition is drawn from F.M. Cornford, *The Unwritten Philosophy and Other Essays* (Cambridge, 1950), 66–7.

8 E.R. Dodds, *The Greeks and the Irrational* (Berkeley, 1951), 36.

9 *The Bias of Communication* (Toronto, 1951), 10.

10 "Harold Innis and Classical Scholarship," 50.

11 "Canadian Communication Theory: Extensions and Interpretations of Harold Innis," in G.J. Robinson and D.F. Theall, eds., *Studies in Canadian Communications* (Montreal, 1975), 51.

12 *Bias of Communication*, 90.

13 *Prometheus* (Seattle, 1968), 106. Innis himself once quoted a passage from P.W. Bridgman's *The Intelligent Individual and Society*: "The inexorable isolation of the individual is a bitter fact for the human animal, instinctively so social, and much of his verbalizing reflects his obstinate refusal to face squarely so unwelcome a realization" (*Essays*, 386).

14 *Bias of Communications*, 140–1.

15 (Toronto, rev. ed., 1956), 18–21, 388.

16 *Bias of Communication*, 76.

17 *Political Economy in the Modern State* (Toronto, 1946), XIII.

18 *Essays*, 268, 307.

19 *Essays*, 127–33, 396, 408–9. *Bias of Communication*, 29–32, 79, 189. *Empire and Communications*, 163–5.

20 *Bias of Communication*, 191.

21 Ibid., 195.

22 *Political Economy*, 78.
23 Carey, "Canadian Communication Theory," 44–5.
24 *Bias of Communication*, 190.
25 *Empire*, 117.
26 Ibid., 141.
27 *Bias of Communication*, 235.
28 Ibid., xvii, 29, 132; *Empire* xiii, 8–9; *Essays*, 272.
29 *Changing Concepts of Time* (Toronto, 1952), 43, 45.
30 *Empire*, 1–6, 169–70.
31 *Bias of Communication*, 73.
32 *Changing Concepts*, 73.
33 *Political Economy*, xiii.
34 *Changing Concepts*, 20.
35 This is a slightly revised version of a paper originally presented at the "H.A. Innis Symposium" sponsored by the Department of Communications, Simon Fraser University, 30–31 March 1978.

CHAPTER FIVE

Reason, Passion, and Interest: Pierre Trudeau's Eternal Liberal Triangle

With Pierre Trudeau we return from the fringes of politics and the ivory tower to the highest political office. Between them, Mackenzie King and Pierre Trudeau presided as prime minister for close to forty years of this century. Like King, Trudeau developed ideas about politics before he became a practising politician. Trudeau's ideas were more respectable than King's and it can be said that he had greater success in implementing them. To understand Canada in the late twentieth century it is necessary to understand both Trudeau's ideas and his politics.

This essay has a curious history. It was written in the fall of 1979 for a conference on Trudeau's thought at the University of Calgary. Trudeau had just been unseated as prime minister by Joe Clark and was in the un-accustomed (and uncomfortable) role of leader of the opposition. While I was revising it for publication, he announced his retirement, so I adopted a somewhat retrospective tone. When it appeared in the spring of 1980, the Tories had fallen, Trudeau had returned as leader, won a majority in a snap winter election, and was once again prime minister. To top off the reversals of fortune, he had just campaigned victoriously against the Parti Québécois in the Quebec referendum on sovereignty-association.

Trudeau has articulated a memorable statement of liberal philosophy, tuned very finely to the particular circumstances of Canada, especially the relations between the two linguistic and cultural communities of French and English Canada. Trudeau's philosophical liberalism generated a powerful intellectual construction of federalism as a counter to separatist

Reprinted with permission from the *Canadian Journal of Political and Social Theory/ Revue canadienne de théorie politique et sociale* 4, no. 1 (Winter/Hiver 1980). This paper was originally presented, in slightly different form, at a symposium on the political thought of Pierre Trudeau, sponsored by the Department of Political Science at the University of Calgary, 19 October 1979.

nationalism. As I argue, this achievement was undermined by liberalism's incapacity to legitimate the distributive results of the market.

At the time this was written, my verdict on Trudeau liberalism was a variant on Lyndon Johnson's cruel judgement of Gerald Ford: he couldn't talk and chew gum at the same time. Trudeau's liberalism had provided a vivid and compelling response to the conundrum of the nationalism question but had proved a failure in relation to the class question. From the vantage point of the early 1990s, I would amend the former part as well: Trudeau's vision of federalism looks far more threadbare than it appeared ten years earlier. The wave of Trudeau nostalgia which crested with the failure of the Meech Lake accord seems curiously beside the point. For reasons which will become apparent in the last essay in this collection, written in 1990, I now believe that Trudeau's legacy to Canada was noble but ultimately misconceived.

History may well record that Trudeau's dramatic and highly effective intervention against the Meech accord was an act of great *hubris* which helped percipitate precisely what Trudeau had fought against so passionately throughout his career: the departure of Quebec from Canada. If he had only exercised restraint, his legacy might have been preserved.

Considerable attention has been lavished over the years on Trudeau as the philosopher of federalism and bitter critic of Quebec nationalism. It is easy enough to assume, along with the Right and Left in English Canada and *le tout-Québec*, that Trudeau's "rigidity" and "inflexibility" on these questions has simply left him as an anachronism, passed over by the rush of events and the seemingly inexorable advance of *indépendantisme* in Quebec and decentralist regionalism in English Canada. Yet nothing is more notoriously ephemeral than political fortune. That Trudeau's ideas are presently in eclipse is apparent; that they are thereby exhausted is by no means obvious. It is a mark of the power of this man that no strong federalist position can in the near future escape the colour and quality which his expression has given to this thesis in the dialectics of centralization-decentralization and duality-separation. In this sense alone Trudeau's arguments bear continued reading: to a greater extent than many of us would like to admit, he remains close to the heart of our central dilemmas.

It is not however this relatively familiar terrain which I propose to cover once again. Journalist Anthony Westell wrote a book on Trudeau called *Paradox in Power*, and that phrase perhaps best sums up a common reading of Trudeau, especially by English Canadian intellectuals. How could a man who first rose to notoriety in Duplessis' Quebec as a "radical" defender of strikers, a passionate proponent of civil liberties and a tireless advocate of democratization of public life turn into the prime minister who invoked the War Measures Act, defended RCMP illegal acts, and brought down wage controls against the labour movement? Many, particularly on the left, simply shrug their shoulders at yet one more sorry example of how "power" turns decent progressives into vicious reactionaries. Others return to Trudeau's early writings for evidence of the original sin always lurking beneath the opportunist's costume of the day.

I think the answer to this problem is rather more complex but also more interesting than either of these alternatives. Trudeau's reflections on politics over the last thirty years, while scarcely constituting an original contribution to political philosophy, nevertheless do offer striking and sometimes illuminating insights into the strengths and weaknesses of liberal-democratic thought, insights given further pungency by his personal participation in political power. It is not so much the specific concerns of Trudeau – French Canada and federalism – which appear most interesting in this light, although they have received most attention, but the more general problems of liberal-democratic theory and practice. Let us give Trudeau his due: he has always wanted to be known for what is universal in his makeup, rather than what is culturally particular. Of course, as a social being, man must start from the particular to approach the universal. George Grant, in deploring Trudeau's "evident distaste for what was by tradition his own," goes on to admit that his "quality of being a convert to modern liberalism is one cause of his formidability."[1] What English-speaking Canadians have generally accepted as tradition, Trudeau gained as rational accession. This may account for the vigour and the freshness of his thinking, so uncommon in this era of liberal pessimism and uncertainty. It also gives us the opportunity to grasp, at the level of theory, contradictions of liberal-democratic practice which are otherwise normally engaged at the level of empirical political science alone.

"Reason over passion." Trudeau once proclaimed this as his personal motto. It is no accident that his arch rival, René Lévesque, has recently had a book published under the title of *La Passion du Québec*. But Trudeau's slogan is, in this form, scarcely more fertile or illuminating than Lévesque's affectation. No theory of liberal democracy could be deduced from the proclaimed supremacy of "reason." It is my thesis that a third, sometimes silent, partner to this relation is the ancient liberal actor, interest. It is this *ménage à trois* of reason, passion and interest which forms the more interesting dynamic of Trudeau's liberal politics. It is an eternal triangle, without resolution: a romantic liberal tragedy played out again and again. If we still applaud, it is because the plot continues to speak to our concrete political experience in the English-speaking world.

Trudeau comes to this originally as an outsider, as it were. Few have analyzed with such mordant wit and such Voltairian iconoclasm the bizarre, fantastic world of Quebec ideological life before the Quiet Revolution, as Trudeau himself in his journalism of the 1950s. Abraham Rotstein once remarked of Trudeau's thought that "it seems vaguely, in its intellectual underpinnings, *à la recherche d'un siècle perdu*."[2] Indeed, one can almost see Trudeau as once striving to be a one-man Enlightenment to a nation which had put the French eighteenth century under permanent interdiction. Yet, it is this only "vaguely," for Trudeau did not stop at 1789, and even formulated a relatively complex answer to the ambiguous legacy of the Englightenment. He is also very much inspired by the nineteenth- and twentieth-century *English*-speaking liberal tradition and this gives his thought an eclectic leaven. When examined in its uniqueness, this elective world view proves to be often surprising, and almost always interesting.

The first surprise, and one which has passed unnoticed by the nationalist and conservative critics who see Trudeau as a "rootless cosmopolitan," is to find a religious foundation to his thought. His old reputation as an anticlerical "radical" and his reluctance to publicize his religious faith for political ends have misled these critics in the same way as his fashionable technocratic rhetoric about cybernetics and functionalism. It is true, however, as he himself has admitted, that his faith is more protestant than traditionally Catholic, inasmuch as his well known reluctance to accept external discipline interferes with the acceptance of hierarchial authority. On the other hand, Trudeau very early on decided, in his perversely individualistic way, that just because the Church told him to believe in God was no reason to become an atheist. A reading of Aquinas on the relationship between morality and free choice convinced him that he could accept certain moral codes and precepts freely as a rational form of self-discipline. His Catholicism thus placed the emphasis on inner conscience rather than on external conformity to rules. And it was the Christian existentialists, Kierkegaard, Berdyaev and Mounier who influenced his developing mind the most. The personalist philosophy of Mounier's review, *Esprit*, indeed exercised a pervasive influence over the entire *Cité Libre* group. In Trudeau's case, personalism meant that the fundamental datum of the social order is the individual, not a technological Prometheus unbound from chains of religious tradition, but rather the individual as the personal reflection of humanity's origin as God's creation in His own image. It also meant that faith must be manifested not in contemplative witness, but in the social embodiment of virtue in actual behaviour (in *works* if we may use a Protestant term.) We find here the abstract basis of a social liberalism which argues that the individual is the irreducible basis of the social order, requiring the maximum possible liberty so that autonomous wills may create the spontaneous nexus allowing for creativity and progress.[3]

Publicly a defender of a secular morality, Trudeau as Minister of Justice reformed the criminal code in matters of sexual and personal morality not in terms of "permissiveness," but on the high ground of liberal principle:

We are now living in a social climate in which people are beginning to realize, perhaps for the first time in the history of this country, that we are not entitled to impose the concepts which belong to a sacred society upon a civil or profane society. The concepts of the civil society in which we live are pluralistic, and I think this parliament realizes that it would be a mistake for us to legislate into this society concepts which belong to a theological or sacred order.[4]

To trust to personal conscience matters which do not call into question the liberty of others is not merely a liberal principle *à la* J.S. Mill; in Trudeau's case it reflects a respect for the value of the individual conscience which itself has a religious rather than a secular basis. Hence his reasoned rejection of capital punishment in parliament began with a theoretical discussion of the Christian concepts of justifiable self-protection and the just war as moral bases for taking a life, then argued that the question of capital punishment as a "justifiable act of collective self-defence" could only be answered by "factual data and logical induction, not moral philosophy," and called for a "practical rather than a moral judgement." Having then rejected the death penalty on these "practical" grounds, Trudeau concluded that, under these circumstances it was therefore immoral for the state to deliberately take a man's life. That he in effect places the burden of proof on the state rather than the individual cannot, I think, be dissociated from the *sacred* value embodied in the individual. This becomes especially clear in his angry dismissal of the argument that the state should "experiment" with the death penalty to determine if it actually deters murder. In a rejection which also applies to all calls for revolutionary violence against individuals to advance some collective project, Trudeau simply asserts that we have no business experimenting with human lives.[5] Again, his well known antimilitarism stops short of pacifism: "In my political philosophy, I think that there sometimes is room for violence. In my religion I really cannot think of cases where violence is justified ... But, here again, when the religious principles, like the philosophical, are translated into reality, sometimes the reality forces violence on you, and there is no escape from it, and then I don't think it's something you should try to hide your face from."[6]

A personalist Catholic morality places on the individual a heavy burden of moral choice in concrete situations. Political philosophy is a kind of practical reason indicating a systematic basis for making such difficult choices, the difficulty of which deepens drastically when one moves from teacher and preacher to power wielding politician. We should now go on to follow Trudeau along this path of ascending difficulty, while never allowing the starting point to slip from our minds, as it has from the minds of all too many of his critics.

Once in the course of attacking a statement of André Laurendeau that liberty must be wrested from authority, Trudeau replied unequivocally that "Liberty *is* a free gift – a birthright, which distinguishes man from beast." He went on to draw the consequence that the "game of politics should consist less in wresting liberties from a grudging State than in grudgingly delegating powers to the State." He even makes a case for "inalienable rights" of the individual in democratic theory, to be guaranteed by bills of rights which are anterior in "some sense" to the very existence of the state, although he does so in rather functionalist terms which would no doubt fail to please true natural law theorists: "to assure the effective participation of all citizens in the development of public policy, these rights must remain vested in each citizen independently of the laws."[7] In 1964, expressing his contempt for the revolutionary pretensions of that era's "nationalist brood," he spoke in somewhat forlorn tones of Quebec's revolution which never took place: such a revolution could "have consisted in freeing man from collective coercions ... in the triumph of the freedoms of the human being as inalienable rights, over and above capital, the nation, tradition, the Church, and even the State." This kind of statement, along with his quotations of Acton and other writers stressing the sacred quality of man's individual dignity, have led at least one Quebec critic to decry Trudeau's exclusively and naively ethical interpretation of rationality.[8] While avoiding the error of those who view Trudeau as simply an amoral Machiavellian, this interpretation fails to do justice to the complexity of his liberalism. For while

Trudeau begins with the individual and his "free gift" of liberty, he quickly situates this datum in the real world of conflict, violence insecurity and death. If Cain used his "free gift" of liberty to slay his brother, then Christianity obviously will not save us in *this* world. We need political philosophy and law – the latter understood as both social science and social control.[9]

In allowing himself to muse on the Quebec revolution that might have been, he was allowing his irritation and anguish at the actual course of events to get the better of his own good sense. Elsewhere his writings are studded with exhortations to follow the "first law of politics ... to start from the facts rather than from historical 'might-have-beens,'" warnings that history is useful only as a guide to a future toward which we are being impelled by material reality, brilliant denunciations of the irrelevance of social and political theory divorced from social and economic facts, and appeals to *realpolitik*.[10]

Trudeau's sense of reality and of the transience of human contrivance has led conservative and nationalist critics to accuse him of mindless celebration of the triumph of modernity. Some of his rhetoric certainly suggests this; one hesitates to deny this as an element in his thought which has on occasion gained supremacy. But to assume, with George Grant, that liberalism always identifies necessity with goodness, is to oversimplify. Trudeau has often exhibited a historical sense of the impermanence of things, and of the ironies which history plays on those who seem to shape it. Speaking of Louis Riel in 1968, he wondered "how many of us understand the loneliness, the sense of futility of such a man? How many of us are willing to concede that future historians, in chronicling the events of our lives, may choose to emphasize and applaud the activities, not of the privileged majority, but of some little known leader of an unpopular minority?" More to the point is his facing up to the fact that "the nation of French Canadians will some day fade from view and ... Canada itself will undoubtedly not exist forever. Benda points out that it is to the lasting greatness of Thucydides that he was able to visualize a world in which Athens would be no more."[11] Nor can we simply take this as cheerful surrender to progress. Since the PQ victory in 1976 Trudeau has on more than one occasion publicly confronted the possibility that Quebec may indeed separate: which is to say, that everything to which Trudeau has dedicated his public life since 1965 will come to naught. Trudeau's very activism on this issue indicates that he sees history as made by men, not impersonal forces. But if the results must ultimately be accepted, this acceptance may be closer to classical stoicism than to Panglossian celebration. Once in a television interview, before he became prime minister (and before his ill-fated marriage), he quoted Marcus Aurelius: "This vase you hold in your hands may shatter, this woman you love may be unfaithful."

But if all is flux and if brute reality rules the world, Trudeau would have little resort but to retreat to a private garden of contemplation. On the contrary, the superiority of modern liberalism to classical stoicism is in its development of mechanisms for managing the tension between change and continuity. The key is to create a procedural basis for solving conflicting demands on criteria minimally acceptable to all actors in the process. Individuals compete, economically, socially and politically, in a continual process of remaking the world; the only constant is the process itself – the rules of the game, so to speak. This much is obvious and central to any genuinely liberal reading of the political process. What is perhaps less obvious is the extent to which such a reading precludes, on theoretical grounds alone, any prior acceptance of the Good, or of *a priori* moral ends of the community. Instead of the Good there can be only "goods," demonstrated to be goods only by the fact that they are demanded. If justice is the resolution of competing demands on a procedural basis acceptable to all reasoning and calculating participants, then any dedication of the community to a particular concept of the Good is, *ipso facto*, an upsetting of the procedural fairness of a liberal political order. We in the English-speaking world have thought and acted in this familiar intellectual landscape that we are often incapable of seeing it whole.[12] Trudeau, a passionate (if he would forgive the word) convert to this world-view from a cultural milieu in which such ideas were by no means familiar, raises some fundamental questions with particular clarity and force.

When Trudeau tells us that "ideological systems are the true enemies of freedom," he is telling us something which appears on the surface as little more than an appeal to North American "pragmatism." In fact he is getting at something more interesting from the point of view of his political philosophy: how to reconcile the claims of liberty and authority without allowing the answer given at a particular moment to harden into an orthodoxy which itself becomes an obstacle to future flexibility. His much-quoted remarks on creating "counterweights" and his insistence on checks-and-balances, whether in parliamentary or federal forms, are the institutional expression of his personal guide to political participation: "When a political ideology is universally accepted by the elite, when the people who define situations embrace and venerate it, this means that it is high time free men were fighting it."[13] The core of the opposition to ideological systems does not rest on some faith in pragmatism as political know-how, but on the liberal principle that only procedures, never ends, can be sacrosanct in a progressive society. Ideological systems congeal volatile elements into monopolies by transforming goods into the Good. This seems to me to be a crucial point in Trudeau's thought. As a shorthand, I will call it "procedural justice." If we see that Trudeau's focus always rests on justice as procedure, never as end, I think his thought becomes much clearer, overall.

Procedural justice remains at an unacceptable rarefied level of abstraction when argued in narrow political terms alone. To see why this is so, let us begin with Trudeau's most ambitious attempt to expound a pure political theory of democracy, his 1950s articles in *Vrai*, later gathered together in book form.[14] Faced with the *"grand noirceur"* of Duplessis' Quebec, Trudeau wishes to provide an answer to a question which he poses in a provocatively personal way: "how it is that Maurice can give orders to Pierre?" The heaviest penalty for refusing to engage in politics is to be ruled by someone inferior to yourself.* Even if madmen rule over us, it is least up to us to "see to it that we are governed no worse than is absolutely necessary." We are going to be governed, like it or not, but we must demand from political power that any exercise of authority be explained in a way which satisfies our reason, since the "nature of things" cannot explain the conventional forms which politics actually take in the world. From this late eighteenth-century *philosophe* position of radical scepticism Trudeau stakes a claim on explaining the universal principles which underlie the diversity of the real world of politics.

All the obscurantist theories of authority fall in the face of one overwhelming fact of human history: men *do* overthrow rulers, whether "divine" or otherwise. "In the last analysis any given political authority exists only because men consent to obey it. In this sense, what exists is not so much the authority as the obedience." In other words, in the long run the only sovereignty is popular sovereignty. This is not to deny that there is a "psychological disposition" to obey, history and observation will indicate (not least in the Quebec of this era) that the people will put up with a very great deal before being moved to disobedience, but it is the ultimate sanction of disobedience or revolution which is the crucial fact. After all, to shift gears to ethical terms, if the "purpose of living in

---

*Presumably the 1979 election indicates that political engagement is no proof against this eventuality.

society is that every man may fulfil himself as far as possible" and if that society serves him badly, then "he is entitled to overthrow it." This should not imply anarchy, however. It is up to each citizen to judge the value of his particular state, but the standards upon which such judgements may be made cannot be mere individual interests, since, lacking the crucial bond of social solidarity, a society of social egoists quickly becomes a society of slaves. "To remain free then, citizens must seek their welfare in a social order that is just to the largest number; in practice only the majority has the power to make and unmake governments."

There is a middle way between despotism and anarchy which rests on the device of the majority. Democracy is a mechanism of civilized peoples "whereby citizens can fight against laws they disapprove of without going outside the law or becoming conscientious objectors or political martyrs." A constitutional democracy is one in which the rule of law is interpreted as follows: "our obedience then is not to individuals but to the general will of the nation, a will embodied in laws, to whose service and execution the rulers are appointed." The particular will of the statesman must bow to this general will: "that is why the statesman must be attentive to the needs of all sectors of society, with no bias towards thwarting any one of them, and must wish only to reconcile them all and direct them towards the general interest." Understood in this context, Trudeau's Lockean espousal of the right to revolution as a logical corollary of the doctrine of popular sovereignty is, like Locke's own teaching, a conservative device to prevent the necessity of violence or tyrannicide. "If that is to have a revolutionary spirit, then I admit to it, but I must add that such a spirit is the best safeguard against revolution."

This purely political theory of democracy has the virtue at least of vigorous clarity and forceful expression. Compelled to explain first principles in a society hostile to liberalism, Trudeau does provide us with the skeleton rather than the clothes. But the very starkness of the skeleton discloses all too readily some missing linkages. A major example lies in the inadequate discussion of the social content underlying the political forms and, allied to this, the emptiness of Trudeau's concept of the state.

Trudeau's use of Rousseauian language (general will, particular interests) was, no doubt deliberately, a provocation to the clerical reactionaries and conservative nationalists of the day to whom Rousseau was a veritable red flag.[15] Yet aside from his evident desire to épater le (petite) bourgeoisie, it is not clear what Trudeau gains from Rousseau. The latter had a very clear idea of the social preconditions for the emergence and maintenance of a "general will," and very rigorous conditions they were – to the extent that Rousseau himself was left wondering if such a conjuncture would ever be possible in the real world. Above all, Rousseau had a strong sense of the distortions which the uneven distribution of property and economic interests would have on the possibility of the general will finding expression. Even if Rousseau's own solution was anachronistic and contradictory, it is somewhat startling to note that Trudeau does not even diagnose the problem, let alone suggest a solution. The closest he comes is in the above-quoted sentence in which he discusses the impotence of mere egoistic motives to effect revolution and concludes that citizens should seek a "social order that is just to the largest number." When he follows this immediately with the statement that "in practice only the majority has the power to make and unmake governments" it seems that he is suggesting only a mechanistic argument from power politics; the so-called "general will" is nothing more than a given majority. But if this general will is merely the addition of particular wills, each presumably reflecting individual "egoistic" interests, into an evanescent coalition controlling a majority of votes, then it is at least incumbent upon the political theorist to consider the particular wills in their social reality, which is to say, in their class reality. What are the classes and the class interests which go to make up the "general will" of a democracy through the mechanism of majority rule? Or, to rephrase the question in historical terms, what are the different kinds of democracy which are possible under this principle? This pure theory of popular sovereignty would seem to yield a good deal less than meets the eye. At least Locke made it fairly clear what kind of majority he was advocating.

The lack of social content to the concept of sovereignty tends to vitiate almost entirely Trudeau's concept of the state. "The state," he announces, "is an article made to measure by its citizens, according to the precise amount of obedience they are prepared to offer it." He pleads with Quebecers to see the state not as a foreign power but as something which "has been for all practical purposes in the hands of those we choose from election to election." It is all quite simple, really: "the state is by definition the instrument whereby human society collectively organizes itself and expresses itself. A sovereign society that fears the state is ... unconvinced of the usefulness of its own existence as a group." The state grew because individual efforts could not provide the society with necessary services, whereupon "the community simply decided to solve these problems communally, through the state." Quoting Karl Marx and

Saint Thomas More, he does admit that at "all times and under all systems there is a tendency for the few to use the State to enslave the many." But for this democracy is itself the sole remedy, "since it is the system in which the citizen consents to be governed by a body of laws that the majority of citizens wanted."[16] The state, as such, collapses into the democratic majority. Or, as Trudeau's *Cité Libre* collaborator, Jean Pellerin later summed it up neatly: "L'état, c'est nous."[17] Trudeau does suggest that while the state should do more, it should arouse less reverence and face more means of control and limitation. But this is merely the opposite side of the coin to the sovereignty of the people. What most strikes the reader some twenty years after Trudeau's political statement is its naive reductionism. There is almost nothing about the influence which particular interests (Rousseau's partial associations) may exercise on the formation of majorities as well as upon the exercise of power by the state, nothing about the representation of particular interests within the state. If Trudeau had set out to demystify the state in the eyes of Quebecers, he surely was setting up an equally mythical construct in its place.

He does admit two major qualifications to his theory. First is his Millsian insistence that majorities have no monopoly of truth and that the liberties of minorities must thus be protected. This of course can be explained, as by J.S. Mill himself, on progressive grounds: today's minority may be tomorrow's majority. Majorities should be liberal toward minorities out of prudence alone. At the same time the tyranny of the majority is itself in violation of the fundamental liberal concept of procedural justice. A tyrannical majority would in effect have substituted its idea of the Good for the free individual pursuit of goods. In this sense majorities are merely practical mechanisms for registering a critical weight of opinion against excesses of government, but have no value in and of themselves.

A much more serious qualification is also admitted, but only through the back door, as it were. Having described a Platonic form of the state which was in no way related to the specificity of twentieth-century liberal-democratic capitalism, he then grants that a democratic majority cannot understand the complexities of modern legislation and administration. This admission is in contradiction to the theory of the state as an "article made to measure by its citizens." The recognition of the Weberian principle of the state as a bureaucratic phenomenon leads Trudeau to a further attempt at precision which calls into question the entire concept of majority rule as a mechanism of popular sovereignty. In a well known passage, he indicates that the "electoral system asks of the citizen only that he should decide on a set of ideas and tendencies, and on men who can hold them and give effect to them. These sets of ideas and men constitute political parties, which are indispensable for the functioning of parliamentary democracy." Voters will not be asked to decide "each of the technical problems presented by the complicated art of government in the modern world." The point is made clearer yet when Trudeau posits a hypothetical benevolent despot and asserts the need for some mechanism whereby the despot would be forced to abdicate if opinion went against him – but this, Trudeau concludes is, itself the "actual mechanism of democracy." In a functioning democracy, "at each election ... the people assert their liberty by deciding what government they will consent to obey." Popular sovereignty thus means no more than the ultimate authority residing in the people at elections to recall the mandate of politicians in office. The people can judge government only by results – "real or apparent on the happiness of the group."[18]

We thus see a double reinterpretation of popular sovereignty: first, it becomes identified with numerical majorities (albeit with liberal guarantees for minorities), and second, majorities themselves are called into being only as periodic ratifications or rejections of the politicians who head the state – a state which, by indirect inference must be assumed to be a much more formidable and autonomous organism than the pure theory would lead us to believe.

Trudeau's purely political formulation was admittedly designed for a limited and specific polemical purpose. When he turns his attention to the question of the origin of the state – the hypothetical social contract underlying it – he has managed to suggest more fruitful perspectives. In an article written in the early 1960s, he drew attention to the dilemma of the individual in modern society "hamstrung by a web of social, economic and administrative institutions," unable to determine if he is being economically exploited by monopoly capital: "And even if the citizen knew he was the victim of an injustice, he wouldn't have the power to come to grips with such offenders. Therefore, if the citizen wants to avoid being commanded against his will at every turn, he must give himself as a protector a state strong enough to subordinate to the common good all the individuals and organizations who make up society."[19] Here we can readily detect the tones of an earlier theorist who was most concerned with the state as a means of protecting citizens from one another: Thomas Hobbes. The "common good" is not, in this Hobbesian formulation, the Good as a community goal, but the rules which allow a minimum of security in the pursuit of individual goods. The strong state is necessary precisely because competition in civil society renders life insecure.

Trudeau's constant appeals to "facts" and "reality" begin to make sense in this context. In the way in which Robert Dahl defines political power ("a relation among actors in which one actor induces other actors to act in some way they would not otherwise act" based on the Hobbesian combination of promise of rewards and threat of sanction).[20] Trudeau sees power as the basic datum of politics, the building blocks material, as it were, of the political superstructure of values and institutions. At first glance this seems incompatible with the rather idealist and abstracted reading of politics described just a moment ago. It depends, however, on the level of analysis. Hobbesian *realpolitik* at the structural level readily turns into idealism at the superstructural level. This is, indeed, an ideological characteristic of liberal thought. Trudeau is no exception.

One of the closing paragraphs of his *Approaches to Politics* makes the connection between the two levels quite overtly. It is worth quoting at length:

As for majority rule, the fact must be faced that it is a convention, possessing simply a practical value. It is convenient to choose governments and pass laws by majority vote, so that those who exercise authority can feel assured of having more supporters than opponents – which is itself some guarantee that the social order will be upheld. It is true that from one point of view the majority convention is only a roundabout way of applying the law of the stronger, in the form of the law of the more numerous. Let us admit it, but note at the same time that human groupings took a great step towards civilization when they agreed to justify their actions by counting heads instead of breaking them.[21]

Under the clothes of the Enlightenment which Trudeau strove to legitimate in Duplessis' Quebec we find, if not the old Adam, at least the old Hobbes, as revealed in Locke's majoritarian rendering.

My stress on the Hobbesian basis of Trudeau's reading of the foundations of the state rests on more than the pedantic desire of the historian of political thought to classify theorists into historical pigeonholes. The failure to recognize the Hobbesian assumption which Locke slipped into modern liberal discourse has arguably misled generations of students of liberal democracy into most peculiar and irrelevant notions of the "rule of laws, not men" and of the strictly limited state – notions which have worn increasingly thin in the last few decades of state capitalist development. There has always been a sense that the political culture of Canada has been rather more Hobbesian than that of America, but now the case is being made that the constitutional foundations of the United States are deeply Hobbesian as well.[22] Certainly since C.B. Macpherson's

The Political Theory of Possessive Individualism we are better able to appreciate the curious combination of possessive individualism in civil society and a policing sovereign grown more and more absolutist in the public sphere, a combination which appears to be characteristic of liberal democracies in the late twentieth-century. And since it is on grounds of his alleged "betrayal" of civil liberties in office that Trudeau has drawn most criticism from academic critics, this Hobbesian basis of the state should be examined.

Hobbes broke from classical political philosophy by denying that political rights and obligations could be derived from natural law as an ideal pattern of behaviour. Individuals alone could be seen as the source of right, and this right could be understood only in terms of the private wills of individuals. The unlimited appetite for power which Hobbes read in human nature was itself both cause and consequence of the chaotic conflict of particular private wills in competition with one another: striving for power was a striving for an illusory security resulting only in the universal insecurity of the state of nature. However, individuals in the state of nature are also rational calculators of their self-interest. Enlightened self-interest, the highest form of reason, suggests that the transfer of each individual's power to a sovereign is the appropriate means of creating secure foundations for the continued pursuit of private goods. It also suggests that the sovereign will prudently take into account the interests of his subjects for his own security, although he is not bound by the social contract to do so. Locke, and Trudeau, extend this somewhat by developing the majoritarian doctrine as a more flexible device for effecting the same end.

Trudeau accepts a great deal of this Hobbesian teaching, more than most have been willing to see. But he does not accept all of it, and it is here that he remains interesting as more than a mere interpreter. The most crucial difference between Trudeau and the seventeenth-century liberal thinkers derives directly from Trudeau's own specific cultural and intellectual background in twentieth-century Quebec, and more generally from his experience as an observer of twentieth-century world history. Trudeau has seen the reemergence on a vast and frightening scale of an element in human nature which the seventeenth-century liberals believed they had contained: the passions. To Trudeau, men are not quite the rational calculators of self-interest which Hobbes posited; they *may* be that, but they may also be passionate champions of irrational causes which, by objective standards, would not be in their self-interest as calculating individuals. What happens to the liberal theory of procedural justice when men passionately devote themselves to the application of a particular concept of the community Good even at the expense of their individual pursuit of goods? And what happens when this passion turns out to be a passion for one's Own rather than the Good, but interpreted on a collective rather than on an individual basis. In short, to speak the name with which Trudeau has identified this passion, what happens to liberalism when nationalism is let loose on the world?

Classical political philosophy had taught that the desire for material gratification was the necessary but not sufficient condition of the political order. Plato saw the money-makers as the first level of the just city, to be governed by the quality of spiritedness or courage which in turn must be governed by reason or wisdom. Christianity in a sense separated the last level from politics by placing wisdom in the City of God. The virtue of spiritedness as the governing principle of pre-capitalist society had long disclosed its limitations in the passions and warfare which constantly rent the fabric of European society. Hobbes well understand that the passionate desire for honour was disruptive of all social peace. At the same time, bourgeois property relations and the dedication to money-making were evils which could be counterbalanced to the evils of the passionate politics of princes. The calculability and predictability of a commercial society could even begin to seem as agreeable alternatives (*le doux commerce*) to the old order with its aristocratic passion for heroic virtue. Ultimately in Locke it could provide the social basis for a reliable bourgeois majority guaranteeing order. The notion of man as a calculating being pursuing his self-interest (reasoned, deliberate self-love) appeared to many Europeans emerging out of feudalism not as the bleak picture many in the twentieth century see, but as a liberating view, when interest is seen as a force counteracting the irrational and destructive passions.[23]

It should be clear that a market economy is a necessary structural precondition of the rational calculating human nature required for liberal procedural justice. Indeed the equation of rationality with market rationality or reason with calculation is so pervasive in the contemporary literature as to make their disentanglement difficult indeed. Suffice to say for now that to Trudeau practical reason is thus linked with individual calculation of self-interest. Of course philosophical or theological knowledge unconnected to the market is not denied; it is simply assumed to be the realm of that private, autonomous self, the inner person, which his personalist Catholic liberalism tells him forms the end of social and political organization. The individual is free to pursue his reason in this sense wherever it takes him, and he must be protected in this autonomous activity by safeguards against, for example, the tyranny of public opinion. But it is quite another matter for the individual to impose his private views on his community where such an imposition interferes with procedural justice. The latter can only rest on a firm basis of calculating self-interested wills; practical or political reason is the intelligent management of all these conflicting interests within a dynamic equilibrium. The art of the statesman is thus a kind of meta-rationality in the economic sense, "fine-tuning" to use a current cliché) the market mechanism. As Mandeville wrote long ago in the *Fable of the Bees*, the "skillful management of the Dextrous Politician" is the necessary condition for turning private vices into public benefits. Mandeville meant not day-to-day crisis management but the conscious elaboration over time of an appropriate legal and institutional framework. This would seem close to Trudeau's views of the role of the rational statesman.

In this light, it is no surprise to find in Trudeau's writing that the market, the industrialization which the market entailed, and finally the entire panoply of modern technology which came in the wake of industrialization, were all taken as *givens*. Bélanger adds, "le politique, à l'opposé, paraîtra beaucoup plus málleable, sujet à une construction; bref, à un certain voulu. De ce fait, il ouvrira la porte toute grande à une vision éthique de la res publica."[24] Hence the crucial disjuncture which I noted earlier between a realist reading of social and economic structure and an idealist reading of the political superstructure. But the contradiction involved in this, while characteristic of liberal thought, is all too easily apparent. Politics is hardly the realm of freedom; its relative autonomy is merely a short length of leading-strings. And these leading-strings are its own understanding of reason as calculating self-interest.

Trudeau's earlier espousal of "socialism" or the social-democratic state was indeed, in Pierre Vallières' contemptuous phrase, a mere "*étiquette.*"[25] It is a sad comment on the sheer political illiteracy of right wing journalists in this country that this "socialism" was ever taken seriously in the first place. At best, he never meant more than certain state actions to promote greater equality of opportunity among individuals, or perhaps a certain Galbraithian faith that technology entailed more state intervention and regulation.[26] "Powerful financial interests, monopolies and cartels are in a position to plan large sectors of the national economy for the profit of the few, rather than for the welfare of all. Whereas any serious planning by the state, democratically controlled, is dismissed as a step toward Bolshevism."[27] Only those haunted souls who would define the "skillful management of the Dextrous Politician" as socialistic need be alarmed by this.

Far more dangerous to Trudeau's mind than concentrations of economic power in the market was the growth of nationalist passions in the hearts of his fellow Quebecois. Passion overthrows reason again and again in the twentieth century. The relationship between passion and interest is, however, relatively complex in a concrete historical situation. It is a peculiarity of nationalism that one person's interest is another person's passion: nationalism too involves its own individual interests, but they can only be achieved at the expense of a greater irrationality, an illiberal political regime.

In his analysis of Quebec society in the 1950s, Trudeau looked for a class basis for opposition to Duplessis' *ancien régime*. Whose class interests would propel them in the direction of confronting the political autocracy and the ludicrous and irrelevant social ideologies which diverted attention from its true nature? Trudeau found his answer in the Quebec working class whose class interest in democratization had been dramatically indicated in the famous 1949 Asbestos Strike at which Trudeau himself assisted. The workers were learning that "devant un conflit d'intérêts, un gouvernement gouverne toujours pour le profit de ces secteurs qui le reporteront au pouvoir." This meant, despite nationalist pleas for ethnic unanimity, that class struggle was a positive good in which the working class would change the world through struggling for its *own* interests. This did not mean revolutionary class struggle, of course: "il faut laisser les forces sociales s'exprimer rationnellement et calmement au sein d'une cité libre."[28] Trudeau read the struggle of labour and capital in a thoroughly Hobbesian way, especially when he praised the workers' escalating demands as part of the motor of economic progress, while at the same time noting that the conflict was never solved on more than a temporary basis. The very material inferiority of the workers in the struggle was itself one of the reasons for trade unions leading themselves to the democratization of Quebec. More to the point, the labour movement represented a welcome kind of reality principle counterposed to the bizarre world of nationalist ideology; union thinking was "essentially the child of necessity, and had little opportunity to lose touch with the social realities of our industrial world." Finally, the labour movement was part and parcel of the "only powerful medium of renewal" in Quebec: industrialization.[29]

The interest of the working class in democratization was not the only element in the struggle against Duplessis. Competing for the alliance of Quebecers was nationalism, which Trudeau consistently associated with *bourgeois* interests – sometimes with the "new middle class" later to become so celebrated in analyses of the Quiet Revolution, sometimes with the "petty bourgeoisie" more generally.[30] The point at issue here is not the sociological validity of this fairly schematic explanation of nationalism, but the fact that Trudeau did not view nationalism simply as disinterested passion. It was one avenue of attack on nationalism to unmask the particular class interests which hid under its rhetoric. Indeed, it is interesting to note that at the very core of his own later bilingualism programme in the federal government was a specific appeal to the same "new middle class" which was promoting nationalism and independence in the Quebec of the 1970s: a bilingual civil service with emphasis on Francophone talent was supposed to operate as an alternative pole of attraction to the new technical-professional elite. Class interests were to be incorporated into the struggle for federalism as a counter to the same interests behind *indépendantisme*. That the strategy appears not to have worked very well may tell us something about political realities but does not diminish the theoretical significance for Trudeau's political philosophy.

Trudeau's polemical assaults on the irrationality and even insanity of nationalism, its causal linkage to civil violence and war, its socially reactionary, intellectually oppressive and culturally stifling qualities – all are too well known to be rehearsed here once again.[31] Criticized bitterly from within Quebec, these views have been widely mistrusted by nationalist intellectuals in English Canada as well.[32] Certainly, Trudeau's cry – "Ouvrons les frontières, ce peuple meurt d'asphyxie!"[33] – elicited remarkably little support from the alleged victims. Nor is there much doubt that he greatly overstated his case, turning empirical associations into causal links and treating nationalism as a reified absolute, abstracted from the concrete social circumstances which alone can give it meaning. Analysing the nationalism of a tiny Quebec struggling to maintain its language and culture in the vast anglophone sea of North America as exactly the same phenomenon as the nationalism of Nazi Germany is, on the face of it, simply bad political science. But Trudeau is not a bad political scientist. In part Trudeau on nationalism may simply offer another illustration of Lord Keynes' comment on Friedrich Hayek: how, starting from a mistake, a remorseless logician can end up in Bedlam. Yet, amid the vehement jeremiads there are no shortage of arguments suggesting a subtler interpretation.

First of all, nationalism is a brute fact, and facts, in Trudeau's Hobbesian world, must be faced. Second, his own not unsubtle reading of eighteenth- and nineteenth-century history leads him to discern a direct connection between the achievement of popular self-government in the American and French revolutions and the appearance of the idea of national self-determination. "While the erstwhile territorial state, held together by divine right, tradition and force, gave way to the nation-state, based on the will of the people, *a new glue had to be invented* which would bind the nation together on a durable basis." Any modern state needs to develop and preserve "as its very life" a consensus whereby "no group within the nation feels that its vital interests and particular characteristics could be better preserved by withdrawing from the nation than by remaining within ... And since it is physically and intellectually difficult to persuade continually through reason alone, the state is tempted to reach out for whatever emotional support it can find ... Hence, from the emotional appeal called nationalism is derived a psychological inclination to obey the institution of the state."[34] Moreover, the nation is the guardian of cultural, moral and historical qualities which "at this juncture in history go to make a man what he is." Even if these national qualities are particularistic and hence divisive, "they are a reality of our time, probably useful, and in any event considered indispensible by all national communities."[35] Light at the end of the tunnel begins to appear – just as conflicting self-interests can be linked together by procedural justice in a liberal democracy, so it may be that conflicting passions of nationalism may be linked together by another form of practical rationality. The problem is not nationalism after all, but the demand for a national state where political sovereignty is coterminous with a single linguistic cultural and ethnic identity.

"Only a few political thinkers" – Garth Stevenson has recently written, "Pierre Elliott Trudeau would probably be one of them – have endowed the concept of federalism with the heavy load of symbolic attributes more normally attached to such words as democracy, liberalism, and socialism."[36] Trudeau in fact endows the concept of federalism with what he considers the most noble task on the agenda of liberalism in the twentieth century – the management of nationalist passions to the benefit of mankind. When Prime Minister Trudeau told the American congress that the breakup of Canada would be a crime against human history, or when he has made the even greater claim that Quebec's separation would be a sin against the Holy Spirit, many Canadians, both English and French, have no doubt winced at this kind of emotive rhetorical excess. Certainly Trudeau the Hobbesian realist and stoic historicist poses his own self-criticism to this (dare we say?) passionate ideologizing of the federalist "dogma." It is crucial in understanding the man's thought to understand why he should have such a passionate commitment, one which many of his fellow citizens have come to see as an increasingly irrelevant obsession. If Trudeau has any original contribution to make to liberal theory, it is certainly here. Just as liberal procedural justice claims to manage conflicting self-interests for the greater good of the community, so too federalism according to Trudeau can claim to manage nationalist passions. The passions themselves must be accepted; the trick is to turn them to benefit. Trudeau's reading of Canadian history suggests that federalism as it has actually evolved can, with skilful management, accomplish exactly this end. It thus has an importance which transcends Canada's national status as a mere middle power.

Typically, Canada's advantage accrues not from *a priori* ideals but from a frank recognition of the facts of the case. Quebec was from the beginning a national entity too strong to be crushed or assimilated by English Canada and yet too weak to assume the status of its own national sovereignty. Confederation was a bargain in which the English Canadian majority traded off a little of its own ideal for the new nation in the face of the French "fact." Like the Hobbesian social contract, the origins of federalism are rather ignoble, but its base origins are transcended by the rationality inherent in the working out of the bargain. English and French Canada represent a "balance of linguistic forces." "In terms of *realpolitik*, French and English are equal in Canada because each of these linguistic groups has the power to break the country. And this power cannot yet be claimed by the Iroquois, the Eskimos, or the Ukrainians." These words were written in 1965. In 1971, justifying his government's policy of multi-culturalism, he told the Canadian-Ukrainian Congress that Canada's population was so balanced ethnically that "every single person in Canada is now a member of a minority group." He went on to caution them, however, that "an overwhelming number of Canadians use either English or French ... It is for this practical reason – not some rationalization about founding races – that these two languages have attained an official character in Canada."[37]

Federalism's great advantage is that the national state cannot be ultimately based on the passionate loyalties of its citizens but only on their rational calculations of self-interest. If the federal government tries to focus such loyalties in a binational country, it can only do so at the expense of one side or the other. Hence the various attempts in Canadian history to whip up national feeling – Canada First, The Imperial Federation Movement, the recycled British

monarchy in the post-war world – these only cause further alienation in French Canada. It is almost as if Trudeau is trying to allocate
passion to the provinces in a federal-provincial distribution of
powers. "The great moment of truth arrives when it is realized that
in the last resort the mainspring of federalism cannot be emotion but
must be reason."[38] Despite Conservative and PQ criticism of Trudeau's alleged centralist tendencies, his own historical reading of
Canadian federalism is redolent with praise for decentralism as a
positive good. It is the very possibility of decentralized decision-
making and local initiatives against the centralized administration of
things that commends federalism so strongly to him. These things
are much more difficult to achieve in highly unitary states, such as
France, where culture, language, ethnicity and centralized bureaucracy all combine to form a monolithic unity which is moreover all
too subject to the winds of nationalist passion, such as in the
Algerian war. Canada is, by virtue of its federalism, proof against
such passions, at least at the national level.

There are a number of observations which emerge from this reading of Trudeau. First, despite what so many nationalists have
argued, there is little direct justification for labelling Trudeau as an
"anti-nationalist" who is ideologically incapable of standing up for
Canada in relation to the outside world, especially the Americans.
There is an irony in this, for as a foreign policy maker Trudeau has
been taxed by those with an internationalist bent for reorienting
Canadian foreign policy towards the national interest. But there is
no inconsistency in Trudeau. As Bruce Thordarson concluded from
a reading of the corpus of his work, the continued existence of the
sovereign Canadian state is "central to his political thought."[39] If
federalism is a kind of rational synthesis of national passions
(accepted as facts) and liberal procedures of government, then the
federation itself is an entity to be cherished and protected. The
criticism that Trudeau's rejection of Quebec *indépendance* for continued federalism could equally be applied to Canada's ultimate
absorption into the American nation is, quite simply, invalid. The
United States, although formally a federation, is in reality a highly
unified nationalist state with a long record of brutal repression of
those minorities who do not match up to the standards of Ameri-
canism. As Trudeau wrote in 1964, we may "yet be spared the
ignominy of seeing [our] destinies guided by some new and broader
emotion based, for example, on continentalism." In a lyrical passage
in 1962, he even envisaged a messianic role for Canadian federalism,
an example to new nations rent by ethnic divisions, more compelling than the American melting pot. "Canadian federalism is an

experiment of major proportions; it could become a brilliant prototype for the moulding of tomorrow's civilization."[40]

There are some very considerable difficulties involved in this
rationalist messianism. Not the least is the fragility of reason as a
focus of popular support for national government, a problem of
which Trudeau is himself uneasily aware. One attempt to infuse
reason with some emotional colouring is his espousal of functionalism as an ideal – certainly one of Trudeau's more bizarre ventures
into the psychology of consent. Functionalism, which seems to mean
little more than the application of scientific technique systematically
to the organization of human society has, as George Grant constantly reminds us, its own inexorable dynamic in the modern world and
certainly does not need Pierre Trudeau to ensure its progress.
Nobody other than Trudeau, to my knowledge, has actually tried to
give this phenomenon the emotive status of a symbol of national
loyalty. He has always been personally committed to this as an ideal
which flows quite readily from his rationalist liberalism, from his
first article in *Cité Libre* in 1950 ('Politique fonctionelle") to his
obsessive concern while prime minister with mechanisms of administration and the need for rational policy-making machinery.[41]

The manifesto "pour une politique fonctionelle" signed by
Trudeau, Marc Lalonde and other like-minded Quebec academics
and intellectuals in 1964 gives the full flavour of this technocratic
aspiration to reduce politics to administration and predictability.
The conservatism of this view (although certainly not in Grant's
sense) in its acceptance of the "system" as a fact to which one must
adjust, its reduction of politics to problem-solving and its faith that
philosophy and the human sciences are a mere reflex of science in
the hard sense, have all been noted and criticized from both right
and left.[42] Most distressing to nationalists is the decree that "L'ordre
social et politique doit être fondé au premier chef su les attributs
universels de l'homme, non sur ce qui le particularise" and the
further statement that "les tendances modernes les plus valables
s'orientent vers un humanisme ouvert sur le monde, vers divers
formes d'universalisme politique, social et économique." No doubt
there is an unmistakeable flavour here of Hegel's universal, homo-
geneous state as the end of history, and of the identification of
freedom with technological power (elsewhere Trudeau has written
of how everything was becoming possible in Quebec in 1960 "so
wide open was the road to power for all who had mastered the
sciences and the techniques of the day: automation, cybernetics,
nuclear science, economic planning, and what-not else"[43]). And yet I
suspect that altogether too much has been made of this naive

expression of faith in technocracy by a small group of Quebec intellectuals recently emerged out of an atmosphere of clerical reaction and facing a renewed nationalist wave in the form of youthful separatism. It is assumed that the techniques exist for the efficacious management of all "problems" and the only difficulty is the failure of will to use them. Beyond this the manifesto is replete with traditional expressions of liberalism and assertions that "la règle démocratique doit être maintenue à tout prix." A faith that "science" can systematically do what liberal democracy wants done to the end that individuals can be free to pursue their own individual goods without unnecessary inefficiencies and blockages in the system is certainly liberal, but to suggest that it bespeaks totalitarianism is to stretch a criticism to the point where it wears rather thin. Moreover, as Bruce Doern has point out, Trudeau's technocratic tendencies derive in good part from a conjuncture of older ideas of juridical mind and Montesquieu's checks and balances.[44]

What is most remarkable about Trudeau's "functionalism" is his grotesque notion that this arid technocratic dream can be a basis for counter-passion to nationalism: "If politicians must bring emotionalism into the act, let them get emotional about functionalism!" Since this issues from the same man whose clarion call to Quebec intellectuals in 1950 was *"froidement, soyons intelligents,"*[45] one must assume either that reason has become Trudeau's own passion or that he has become increasingly uneasy about a legitimacy of federalism based on reason alone. If the latter interpretation is correct, then waving the flag of functionalism has been ironically mistimed to coincide with the apparent failure of technocratic liberalism to solve the very technical problems which the technocrats had set themselves – and with the resulting general legitimation crisis of capitalism which in Canada has pressed hardest of all upon the national government and the federal system itself.

The exercise of political power for any length of time is bound to wear away at the confidence of the philosopher, and darker strains of pessimism and even bewilderment have begun to appear in his prime ministerial musings and rationalizations. Speaking to the no doubt perplexed Liberal organizers and constituency officials of Vancouver on May Day, 1971, the philosopher-king described the disjuncture in the modern world between technological development and our cultural awareness: "We stand at this juncture in history in as great a need of a philosophy of technology as did the world in the seventeenth century need a philosophy of a science and mathematics just prior to Descartes' *Discourse on Method*." He went on to admit that "in the absence of a philosophy at this age we must give the appearance of a generation gone mad." Then, astonishingly, he posited the need for a "sense of wonder and awe [which] has been permitted to exist beside the regimentation of reason, to prevent what Kenneth Clark describes as a 'new form of barbarism' resulting from the 'triumph of rational philosophy.' "[46] Was his audience aware that this was nothing less than self-criticism of his own past faith? Later the same year in an interview with James Reston he responded to a question about the decline of "moral leadership" in liberal democracies by suggesting that, in effect, liberalism had served to destabilize societies in the late twentieth century, with the individualist ideal expressed in terms of selfishness without political consensus. It was inevitable, he warned, that the pendulum would swing away from this insupportable society of egoists to one of authoritarianism in which, perhaps, the peer group will become the deity to which individuals become enslaved – a future in which divisive and passionate group loyalties make liberal democracies at the same time both ungovernable and unfree. The theme of heightened expectations and disenchantment toward the political process – the now familiar thesis of "ungovernability" which has spread throughout western political science in the last decade – began to crowd out Trudeau's "participatory democracy" slogan of 1968 almost as soon as he was elected.[47] A purely cynical response to this has a surface plausibility yet fails to recognize that there may not have been disillusionment solely on the part of Trudeau's 1968 enthusiasts, but on the part of Trudeau himself. The tools did not seem to work, politics became day-to-day crisis management, demands were being made by powerful sectors which could not be accommodated together with other demands, the fiscal crisis of the state forced a pervasive negativity on the actions of government ... The optimism of the manifesto for a functional politics must have appeared merely naive.

The imposition of wage and price controls was the symbol for much that had gone wrong in the earlier vision. This was, in effect, more than an exercise in Hobbesian state sovereignty. It suggested that the economic system could not be taken as a given but was itself the problem – a very disquieting prospect for a liberal. Yet when Trudeau drew the appropriate conclusion that the free enterprise system had not been working and that changes would have to be made in it, the outcry was of tidal wave proportions.[48] Three years later Trudeau went down to defeat at the hands of a Tory party dedicated to the ideological proposition that everything wrong with the economy was the fault of the state and that the answer is to "privatize" public activity. A greater irony: wage controls finally precipitated the labour movement into close and open electoral support of the NDP, while identifying Trudeau, once of Asbestos Strike fame, as the primary enemy of the Canadian labour movement. Trudeau's liberalism has been bested not by conservatism nor by socialism, but by an unreconstructed faith that the free market and minimal state can save us, while he has himself offered no basis for a critique of the functioning of the capitalist system which might transcend its present crisis.

The problem is, in a sense, within Trudeau's own assumptions. To begin with a Hobbesian reading of human nature in action, to call in the state as a mechanism to resolve the conflicting demands of groups and classes, to reject any notion of the collective Good as different from the configuration of individual demands for good is, in the end, to leave the politician in a position of blindness and impotence. All that counts is effective demand; Trudeau can in fact be read as always having told groups without real power to either make their demands effective or stop complaining. But however realistic the advice, it is simply to ratify the intensification of conflict and instability. When demands reach a volume and level that overloads the system (to use the "ungovernability" argument), we begin to see a further complication of Trudeau's eternal triangle: self-interests are pursued so passionately as to bring into question the rationality of the system. When the crisis deepens, the political leader has the choice of coercive intervention or of preaching moral reformation to the passionately competing individuals. Trudeau has tried both. While the former works better in the short run, it creates long term opposition. The latter, as with Trudeau's pleas to Canadians to "lessen their expectations" has a forlorn quality about it from the beginning, especially in a political culture which has drawn deeply on optimistic individualism, and where such appeals can readily be dismissed as the class-biased preaching of the privileged.

Obviously the notion of positing the functional activities of the national government as its legitimation in a federation where cultural and nationalist loyalties rest at the provincial or regional level has proven to be weak indeed. Nor has the idea of the federal government as a guarantor of individual civil rights through constitutional provisions raised much groundswell of support: Trudeau's juridical mind here seems very detached from the concerns of ordinary citizens. All this suggests that Trudeau's most cherished ideal, a rational federalism, is in considerable difficulty, especially when faced with what after all was his original *raison d'être* for entering politics: the threat of Quebec secession, now in a most imminent form. As William Mathie has argued, if the reason which underlies Trudeau's federalism is without ends of its own (this is my interpretation as well), then the will expressed by the nations which make up the federation is "altogether legitimate"; there can thus be "no appeal against a non-rational will to secede."[49] Since alternative props have been pulled out, Trudeau finds himself in a tenuous position. Yet however precarious his argument has become, his response to the challenge of the PQ shows a certain liberal tenacity, not to say dignity.

We can best understand this by contrasting his behaviour since November 15, 1976, with his actions during the October crisis of 1970. The excesses of that latter episode need not detain us, as they have been very fully expounded by others. I do wish to suggest that, contrary to conventional wisdom, there was nothing *in principle* (police execution of others is another matter) in the use of the War Measures Act which violated Trudeau's own liberalism. Against a terrorist group which threatened the lives of citizens (and diplomats who fell under the protection of the laws, and which sought thereby to create a "parallel power" challenging that of the state, there was no question that a Hobbesian liberal like Trudeau should have called upon the state to intervene with its full coercive power. Importantly, Trudeau did in the immediate aftermath of the crisis make it clear that this would *not* be his response to a constitutional challenge to federalism backed by a democratic majority: "the country is held together only by consent, not by force of arms ... if a whole province decides that it is happier outside the country, then it will leave."[50] The PQ project, however distasteful to Trudeau in content, is premised on the expression of democratic will and on orderly procedures and due process. The transformation by the PQ of sovereignty into reality must be accepted, so long as it follows the rules of procedural justice. Inasmuch as he views politics as an essentially Hobbesian power struggle, a majority for independence would be a kind of fundamental fact which would have to be faced. More importantly, because his own concept of federalism cannot permit an overriding notion of the Good, a democratic majority with the Quebec nation for sovereignty would constitute an expression of will which would be unanswerable by reason and would have to be accepted as legitimate. That certain Toronto nationalists convinced themselves that Trudeau was always planning another October action, this time against the PQ, tells us a good deal less about Trudeau than about the Toronto nationalists.[51] For his own part, the former prime minister on more than one occasion made it clear that he was "not the man to lead Canada into civil war." In fact, any other position would be a violation of his liberal principles.

Yet even if the dignity and sincerity of his ideas has been maintained, at least in this case, the failure remains. The eternal liberal triangle of reason, passion and interest once again fails to resolve itself. Before we leave this now somewhat isolated figure in search of a better idea, we had best pause to ponder the fate of his ideas. Are there any among us who could remain entirely unmoved by his appeal after the PQ victory, that Levesque had surrounded himself with blood brothers, but that he, Trudeau, wished to speak to us of a loyalty which is higher than to blood alone? Which critic of his mechanistic liberalism could tell us, in good conscience, of a community Good which could replace the individual pursuit of goods, without entailing the kind of civil conflict which Trudeau has always sought to avoid? The very liberalism of the PQ itself – not to speak of the much cruder liberal ideology of the Conservatives who replaced him – cautions us against criticism which is not also, at some level, self-criticism. Even George Grant has admitted that "despite the disintegration and contradictions of our regimes, liberal principles are the only political principles we've got."[52] Coming to terms with both the strengths and the failures of Pierre Trudeau in his extraordinary passage across our intellectual and political life means coming to terms with some of the central values and central conundrums in the present crisis.

NOTES

1 George Grant, "Nationalism and Rationality," *Canadian Forum* 50 (January, 1971): 336.

2 Abraham Rotstein, *The Precarious Homestead* (Toronto, 1973), 110.

3 George Radwanski, *Trudeau* (Toronto, 1978), 36, 39; Trudeau, *Conversations With Canadians* (Toronto, 1972), 7–10; André Carrier. "L'idéologie politique de la revue *Cité Libre*," *Revue canadienne de science politique* 1 no. 4 (décembre, 1968): 416.

4 Quoted in Radwanski *Trudeau*, 96.

5 Canada, House of Commons, *Debates*, 15 June, 1976, 14500–1. Trudeau's horror of capital punishment goes back a long way. See his "L'affaire Coffin," *Cité Libre* 21 (juillet, 1958): 46.

6 *Conversations*, p. 67. A good example of his earlier antimilitarism is "La guerre! La guerre!" *Cité Libre* 42 (décembre, 1961).

7 *Approaches to Politics* (Toronto, 1970) 50, 84. Although these words were written in the 1950s, Trudeau as prime minister in the 1970s has pursued the notion of a charter of human rights, this time buttressed by the further functionalist argument that such a charter would provide a

focus for individual loyalties to the federal government which would transcend provincial group loyalties. For a discussion of this point see William Mathie, "Political Community and the Canadian Experience: Reflections on Rationalism, Federalism and Unity," *Canadian Journal of Political Science* 12, no. 1 (March, 1979): 3–20.

8 *Federalism and the French Canadians* (Toronto, 1968): 205, 159, 181; André-J. Bélanger, *Ruptures et constantes: Quatre idéologies du Québec en éclatement: La Relève, la JEC, Cité Libre, Parti Pris* (Montréal, 1977), especially 99–100 and 127.

9 Radwanski, *Trudeau*, 59.

10 *Federalism*, 192. See also 172–6 on the nation as an unfortunate but undeniable fact of life, and *The Asbestos Strike* (Toronto, 1974), especially 12–16, 25, 330, and 349.

11 *Conversations*, 45; *Federalism*, 177.

12 George Grant, *English-Speaking Justice* (Sackville, New Brunswick, 1974).

13 *Federalism*, xix–xxiii.

14 *Approaches to Politics* (Toronto, 1970). This and the following two paragraphs are drawn from this source.

15 When two right-wing nationalists attacked him for quoting Rousseau, Trudeau wittily replied: "But to tell the truth, I know when I quoted even the most inoffensive phrase of Rousseau's that I was setting a snare for all the watchdogs of reaction. I might have known that I would find Mr. Dagenais in it, on all fours along with Leopold Richer." Ibid, 57.

16 Ibid., 50, 42, 44, and 86.

17 Jean Pellérin, *Cité Libre*, 81.

18 *Approaches*, 89, 76–7, 45–7. See also Radwanski, *Trudeau*, 126 for more recent restatements by Trudeau of the difference between "participation" and "decision-making." Two writers who have drawn attention to Trudeau's plebiscitory majoritarianism and its contradictions are Denis Smith, *Bleeding Hearts ... Bleeding Country: Canada and the Quebec Crisis* (Edmonton, 1971), chapter five, 82–105; and Henry David Rempel, "The Practice and Theory of the Fragile State: Trudeau's Conception of Authority," *Journal of Canadian Studies* 10, no. 4 (November, 1975): 24–38. The paradoxical results of the 1979 federal election should have brought home to Trudeau in the most personal way the limitations of his treatment of popular sovereignty as electoral majoritarianism in a functioning parliamentary democracy. After all Trudeau was forced to yield office to a man whose party actually garnered about 4 per cent *less* of the popular vote than Trudeau's party: a curious "mandate" for change. More curious yet is Trudeau's own silence on this fact.

19. "Economic Rights," *McGill Law Review* 8 no. 2 (June, 1962).

20 Robert Dahl, *Modern Political Analysis* (Englewood Cliffs, N.J., 1970), 17.

21 *Approaches*, 88.

22 See my own argument for Canada in "Images of the State in Canada" in Leo Panitch, ed., *The Canadian State: Political Economy and Political Power* (Toronto, 1977). For an American reading I am most indebted to Frank M. Coleman, *Hobbes and America: Exploring the Constitutional Foundations* (Toronto, 1977).

23 The argument of this paragraph owes a great deal to Albert O. Hirschman's *The Passions and the Interests: Political Arguments for Capitalism before Its Triumph* (Princeton, 1977).

24 Bélanger, *Ruptures et constantes*, 87.

25 Vallières, *Nègres blancs d'Amérique* (Montréal, 1968), 293.

26 See his "Un manifest democratique," *Cité Libre* 22 (octobre, 1958) and 'Leçon de science politique dans un parc qu'il s'agirait de préservet," ibid. 25 (mars, 1960).

27 Economic rights."

28 "Réflexions sur la politique au Canada français," *Cité Libre* 3 (décembre, 1952.

29 *The Asbestos Strike*, especially "The Province of Quebec at the Time of the Strike," 1–82 and "Epiloque," 333–52.

30 *Federalism*, 109, 173, 208–11; *Asbestos Strike*, 31.

31 See especially his articles "New Treason of the Intellectuals" and "Separatist counter-revolutionaries" in *Federalism*.

32 Two Quebec nationalists who have dealt seriously with Trudeau are Pierre Vadeboncoeur, *La dernière heure et la première* (Montréal, 1970), and *Chaque jour, l'indépendance ...* (Montréal, 1978), 43–53; and the late Hubert Aquin in "La fatigue culturelle du Canada français" (1962), reprinted in Aquin, *Blocs Erratiques* (Montréal, 1977), 69–103. Camile Laurin's speech on the second reading of Bill 101 in the National Assembly also constitutes a virtual point-by-point disputation with a number of Trudeau's theses. English Canadian distrust is best expressed in James and Robert Laxer, *The Liberal Idea of Canada: Pierre Trudeau and the Question of Canada's Survival* (Toronto, 1977).

33 "L'aliénation nationaliste," *Cité Libre* 35 (mars, 1961).

34 *Federalism*, 184–9.

35 Ibid., 177. Mathie ("Political Community,") has read Trudeau more carefully on this than have most critics.

36 Garth Stevenson, *Unfulfilled Union* (Toronto, 1979), 4. Another is the nineteenth-century French anarchist, P.-J. Proudhon, whose *The Principle of Federation* has recently been translated by Richard Vernon (Toronto, 1979). Curiously, in his otherwise interesting introduction which takes extensive notice of Canada, Vernon makes only one passing reference to Trudeau. Another passionate federalist is Canadian

anarchist George Woodcock, "Up the Anti-nation," *The Rejection of Politics* (Toronto, 1972), 72–82.

37 *Federalism*, 31; *Conversations*, 32–3.

38 *Federalism*, 194.

39 Bruce Thordarson, *Trudeau and Foreign Policy: A Study in Decision-Making* (Toronto, 1972), 57–65. Mathie makes the same point very well ("Political Community").

40 *Federalism*, 196, 178.

41 *Cité Libre* 1 (juin, 1950) and 2 (février, 1951). G. Bruce Doern, "The Policy-making Philosophy of Prime Minister Trudeau and his Advisers," in T.A. Hockin, ed., *Apex of Power* (Scarborough, 1971), 127–34.

42 *Cité Libre* 67 (mai, 1964): 11–17. An intelligent left critique is Fred Caloren, "The War Measures Act and the Politics of Functionalism," *Our Generation* 7, no. 3 (October–November, 1970).

43 *Federalism*, 206.

44 Doern, "Policy-making Philosophy," 34.

45 *Federalism*, 197; "Politique fonctionelle," *Cité Libre* 1.

46 *Conversations*, 27–8.

47 Ibid., 39–40, 77–9.

48 Laxer and Laxer in *The Liberal Idea of Canada* have made this the centre-piece of their argument that Trudeau has in effect betrayed traditional liberal ideology. There is a point here worth making, although their own insistence on American economic domination as the precipitating factor seems a bit parochial. "Killing expectations" have, after all, become an international ideological phenomenon in the West in recent years.

49 Mathie, "Political Community," 10–11.

50 Quoted in Smith, *Bleeding Hearts*, 174. *Conversations*, 69. Smith's argument that Trudeau's actions in 1970 had undermined Levesque's options and forced a polarization between Trudeau's armed federalism and Pierre Vallière's armed separatism (133) seems a poor prognosis indeed in terms of what has actually happened since. Armed separatism was defeated by the superior power of armed federalism, thus clearing the way for the Parti Québécois. This is tacitly admitted in Vallière's *L'urgence de choisir*, (Montreal, 1972).

51 See, for example, Abraham Rotstein, "Is There an English-Canadian Nationalism," *Journal of Canadian Studies* 13, no. 2 (Summer, 1978): 117–8.

52 Review of J.S. Mill's *Essays on Politics and Society* in *The Globe and Mail*, 6 August 1977.

PART THREE

Federalism
and Democracy

CHAPTER SIX

Federalism and Democratic Theory

Pierre Trudeau raised federalism to the status of political theory. Political scientists, on the other hand, have generally viewed federalism as little more than a particular set of institutional arrangements with little or no philosophical resonance. As a Canadian political scientist I was rather forcibly struck by the disinterest of most of my colleagues in the relationship between two of the most significant features of Canadian political life: democracy and federalism. In this essay I seek to rethink the concept of federalism in relation to the concept of democracy and to vindicate federalism as a democratic practice of government.

In pursuing the relationship between democracy and federalism in modern political thought, I concluded that the concept of sovereignty had to be seriously contested. Perhaps it is especially easy for a Canadian to call sovereignty into question since, one way or another, it has always been a contested concept in this country. Sovereignty, like nationalism, is one of those chameleon ideas which take on a very different colouration depending upon the context. Sometimes it is a progressive concept, challenging imperialism and oppression; yet in the next instance it can become an instrument of oppression itself. Taking federalism seriously is a way of "deconstructing" sovereignty.

Taking federalism seriously also allowed me to become rather more sympathetic to regional distrust of centralism than my location in central Canada would suggest. I am rather pleased, looking back, to realise that in this and the following essay, both published in 1983, I anticipated the Western call for an elected senate with equal regional representation.

Readers may note that in this essay I make passing but rather scathing

Reprinted with permission from Queen's University, Institute of Intergovernmental Relations, Discussion Paper 17 (1983).

reference to the practices of Soviet "federalism." Subsequent events in the disintegrating Soviet empire call the high degree of centralization of the USSR into question. But I do not think that these events call into question the analysis I offered here. Because the USSR, despite the official rhetoric, was neither democratic nor federalist, the recent emergence of genuinely democratic aspirations and the decay of authoritarian rule from the centre have resulted in fierce, and often violent, peripheralizing and disintegrative nationalistic forces. Whether a genuine democratic federalism could have averted what may well be a catastrophic implosion is an academic point. But I would strenuously argue that a polyglot and multinational empire such as that of the USSR could only be governed through some form of democratic federalism. Of course, as with the case of Canada, the necessary condition for survivability may not be the sufficient condition.

A century and a half ago, Alexis de Tocqueville set out to examine the "great democratic revolution" which was sweeping the New and Old Worlds alike, and affirmed that the rise of the democratic principle was universal and lasting, that "it constantly eludes all human interference, and all events as well as all men contribute to its progress."[1] Yet Tocqueville himself was examining the United States as a system which was not only democratic, but federal as well: the first modern political democracy and the first modern federal state.

Today, when " democracy" has become the formal banner under which almost all nations march, to whatever tunes, there is a vast literature on democratic political theory. There is also a more restricted and specialized, but still large, literature on federalism, its meaning and its functioning. There is, however, surprisingly little reference to federalism among democratic theorists, and perhaps even less consideration of democratic theory among students of federalism.[2] This is, on the face of it, odd. After all, a number of leading liberal democracies are themselves federations, and this latter form has been replicated in a number of new Third World nations opting for Western models. Even the Soviet Union, which claims to be an economic democracy, is a formal federation of republics. Moreover, when Tocqueville investigated the United States as a prototype of the coming democratic state, he was very well aware that American federalism was equally as innovative as its democracy, and that the two were inextricably interconnected.

I advance the hypothesis that democratic theory and federalist theory are not only intertwined at the point of origin of the modern science of politics, but continue to offer illumination one to the other, and that neglect of the relationship between these two theories has tended to blur an important dialectic at work in the development of modern democratic politics. However irresistible the rise of the democratic principle, it is a curious observation that democratic theorists have expended much heat, and some light, on justifying limitations on that very principle. The tyranny of the majority, the iron law of oligarchy, polyarchy, elite theory, the administrative state, checks and balances – all these concepts and more have been advanced to rationalize the necessity of popular sovereignty being limited, constrained or even reduced to a mere rhetorical formality. Some democratic theorists rather regret this, while many seem content to view democracy as a kind of instructive theoretical principle which tends to self-destruct in practice.[3]

Modern federalism is an institutionalisation of the formal limitation of the national majority will as the legitimate ground for legislation. Any functioning federal system denies by its very processes that the national majority is the efficient expression of the sovereignty of the people: a federation replaces this majority with a more diffuse definition of sovereignty. It does this not by denying the democratic principle, as such, but by advancing a more complex definition of democratic citizenship. As a result, individuals find political expression and representation in dual (sometimes even multiple) manifestations which may even be contradictory and antagonistic. This poses some severe theoretical challenges to democratic theory. At the same time, I would argue that it casts light on what may be inherent weaknesses in democratic practice.

I propose in this paper to explore some of the problems raised by the relationship between federalism and democracy. I look to the history of political thought to clarify some of the crucial concepts involved in this exploration. First there is the concept of sovereignty, examined with an eye to its possible meaning in a federal state. There follows a discussion of the emergence of the idea of democratic sovereignty, with particular attention paid to Rousseau's direct democracy as counterposed to the model of representative democracy operative in western societies. It is argued that many of the limitations of democratic sovereignty sometimes ascribed to federalism are in fact inherent in the representative form itself, as indicated by Rousseau. I then proceed to examine some historical attempts to theorise democratic federalism, beginning with the American Constitution, the Federalists, Calhoun, and Proudhon, and suggest some lasting conclusions which can draw from these sources. In the final section, I conclude with some reflections on federalism as a form of democratic polity, and offer a qualified defence of this form.

One of the oldest controversies surrounding the theory of federalism has to do with the question of sovereignty. Indeed it is no exaggeration to suggest that the rise and persistence of federations has been a leading factor in the decline of the concept of sovereignty from the height of its prestige in the sixteenth to eighteenth centuries. Functioning federations seem a kind of standing reproach to the notion that a sovereign power, absolute, indivisible and inalienable, separate from and supreme over the society, is a necessary element of any polity.

What is less well known is that at the very period when Jean Bodin was developing the concept of monarchical sovereignty to oppose the chaos of decaying feudalism, another theorist, Johannes Althusius, was developing a very different approach which may, with little violence, be called proto-federalist. Twenty-seven years after the publication of Bodin's *Six livres de la République* in 1576, Althusius published his *Politica Methodice Digesta* (or *Politics*), which, instead of seeking a theoretical justification for absolutism, attempted to constitutionalize the existing political fragmentation of Europe in a multilayered combination of functional and territorial jurisdictions within a commonwealth where sovereignty rested in the whole, rather than in a supreme authority.[4]

It is instructive, in light of future federalist thought, to note that at the basis of his politics were "symbiotics," or consensual associations (voluntary private associations based on functionalism such as guilds or corporations; and public associations based on territorial jurisdictions, from the cities and provinces to the commonwealth as a whole). Sovereignty is the symbiotic life of the commonwealth taking form in the *jus regni*, or fundamental law of the realm.

The universal power of ruling is called that which recognizes no ally, nor any equal or superior to itself. And this supreme right of universal jurisdiction is the form and substantial essence of sovereignty ... When this right is taken away, sovereignty perishes ... The people, or the associated members of the realm, have the power of establishing this right of the realm and of binding themselves to it ... This right of sovereignty does not belong to individual members, but to all members joined together and to the entire associated body of the realm ... And what they once set in order is to be maintained and followed, unless something else pleases the common will. For as the whole body is related to the individual citizens, and can rule, restrain, and direct each member, so the people rules each citizen.[5]

In one sense Althusius was not challenging Bodin's idea of sovereignty: "The power of the realm is always one power and never many, just as one soul and not many rules in the body." But he goes on to assert that since the administration of this power may be divided, citizens can individually share in the function of governing, while the plentitude of the power rests with the commonwealth or realm as a whole, which is to say, the people in association.[6] And this associative commonwealth moves from the particular through the local to what we would call the "national." It is not exactly what we mean by federalism post-1787) but some of the basic elements are there. Nor is Althusius strictly speaking a democratic theorist. Yet there is in his thought an attempt at sketching an alternative view of sovereignty which rests as an attempt to build the universal on the existing particularities, and on an idea of sovereignty resting with the people in proto-federal association.

In the English-speaking world it was Hobbes' enunciation of absolutist sovereignty which set the tone for the seventeenth century. Even in Locke's majoritarian restatement, the Hobbesian insistence on sovereignty resting in a single ultimate and supreme location remains. To Hobbes, the sovereign power must be indivisible since overlapping jurisdictions automatically return the commonwealth to a state of war. The ideologists of the Whig constitution post-1688 got around this difficulty not by denying it, but by claiming that sovereignty was seated in the supremacy of Parliament, understood as an institutional unity of the leading elements or estates of English society: monarch (the Crown), aristocracy (the House of Lords), and property (the Commons). Even if less awesome than Hobbes' "mortall God," the Crown-in-Parliament was a formidable enough embodiment of the idea that sovereignty was a power supreme over all others, located in a single synthetic institution, although not in a single person, or even an assembly acting as a single person.

As Althusius already hinted, however, there is a deep, probably fatal flaw in the absolutist idea of sovereignty. A critique of this idea, with reference to Hobbes, has recently been put brilliantly and devastatingly by M.M. Goldsmith:

The argument is persuasive, but fallacious. If it were correct, the constitutions which divide, separate, or distribute the powers of sovereignty would not merely be tricky to operate, requiring adherence to constitutional rules and acceptance of the separate jurisdictions of the officers empowered by the constitution in various spheres, they would be impossible. The fallacy is contained in holding that the logically necessary characteristics of an independent system of authority must be possessed by some identifiable part of the system. It is as simple an error as holding that because clocks tell time, the power of telling the time must be a characteristic possessed by some identifiable part of a clock. For a system to be an independent and absolute one, it is only necessary that there be no appeal outside it – that it should not be (normatively) dependent, closed, complete and conclusive system merely requires that there should be a final decider (set by the rules of the system – its constitution) in any sphere, for any issue or controversy that may arise.[7]

We may conclude that sovereignty can be, and is in fact, divided among different holders of the attribute, under the authority of a set of rules which is supreme, without calling into question the external sovereignty of the polity as a whole, or necessarily raising the spectre of a reversion internally to a state of war. This recalls the legal positivist view of sovereignty developed in this century by Hans Kelsen. Legal norms can only be derived from legal norms, but since infinite regress is not logically permissable, Kelsen posited a *Grundnorm* which is subordinate to no other but to which all others are subordinate. The Grundnorm which names the sovereign (be it an autocrat or the people) cannot be challenged from within the system in which it occurs, although it is testable outside the system. In the case of a federal state, Kelsen argued that a two-level theory identifying, *faute de mieux*, the national government with the whole, was inadequate. Instead he posited a total federal state or *Gesamtstaat*, a summation of the other levels of government, including the national, which was the ultimate ground of the legal norms of the federation.[8] The *Gesamtstaat* concept has, it is true, a weak record of legal recognition in actual federations, but it contains a theoretical distinction which is intuitively satisfying, one given a plain spoken expression in a Canadian constitutional decision regarding federal-provincial distribution of powers: "The constitution of Canada does not belong either to Parliament, or to the legislatures; it belongs to the country and it is there that the citizens of the country will find the protection of the rights to which they are entitled."[9]

Harold Laski argued that the 'pure theory' of sovereignty is inherently statist and, in his early writings at least, expressed himself as a "frank medievalist" in harking back to a pluralist/federalist matrix of particularist sovereignties.[10] The pessimism of the early Laski that federalism was only a step on the road to unity and that the future lay with centralist statism might have been tempered by a somewhat subtler understanding of sovereignty. As one contemporary writer has put it, all sovereigns have claimed some higher justification, thus sovereignty must be seen as a right according to the law. In a liberal society, the real principle is that there be no legal subordination to *persons*. Persons holding or wielding sovereign authority can be many: all that really matters is that in each case there is some authority, prescribed by law, whose decision is final, but in accordance with law. Thus the state as an institution cannot be sovereign, but the state understood as the whole political community can be.[11] A further refinement is offered by W.J. Ree who restates the concept to extract three distinct "expressions" (I would prefer to interpolate the word "moments") of sovereignty: the "legal," the coercive," and the "influential." The belief that sovereignty is indivisible is correct in that only one ultimate decision is made in each case, but different questions may be settled by different sovereigns. For example, in a representative democracy, the popular majority is the "influential" sovereign, whose influence is exercised over the "legal/coercive" sovereign (parliament and the judiciary), but which does not itself possess the legal or coercive moments or expressions of sovereignty,[12] a point to which I will return presently.

The reason for traversing this chequered field of debate on sovereignty is not to stir up once again the embers of the old quarrel over divided sovereignty into federalism. Dicey long ago laid that question to rest with a straightforward formulation: "Unitarianism ... means the concentration of the strength of the state in the hands of one visible sovereign power, be that power Parliament or Czar. Federalism means the distribution of the force of the State among a number of co-ordinate bodies each originating in and controlled by the constitution."[13] This simple but clear statement may serve as a summary of our previous discussion. However, my real interest is to discuss, not sovereignty in general, but democratic sovereignty in particular. It is when the ultimate, or "influential" moment of sovereignty, (to revert to Ree's terms) shifts away from either "Parliament or Czar" and comes to rest in the people, constituted as a voting body, that very real, and intriguing, questions arise in relation to federalism. Succinctly, if federalism divides sovereignty under a constitutional arrangement of powers, what are the implications when the sovereignty so divided is in fact the sovereignty of the people?

The historical transformation of sovereignty into popular sovereignty has about it the aspect of an optical illusion. There is an ambiguity about the very idea of popular sovereignty, as embodied in any form of representative institutions. As Bertrand de Jouvenel explains, "it is no matter for surprise that the transition to democratic legitimacy required ... so long a time. This was especially true as the new principle settled the attribution of sovereignty only to outward view, the lawful owner being merely a fictive character who must entrust to others his right of government" – such delegation can be to a Bonaparte, an "elected aristocracy," or it may be fragmented.[14] Yves Simon suggests substituting a 'coach-driver theory' for 'popular sovereignty.' Power is transmitted to a government for limited purposes: "What characterizes the democratic condition of sovereignty is that, in a democracy, sovereignty is never completely transmitted."[15] What is retained is only latent, embodied in public opinion, except when referenda call the people into a semblance of a deliberating assembly. Dicey, grappling with the particularly vexed problem of the sovereignty of Parliament in a democracy, admitted that electors are a part, indeed, the "predominant part of the politically sovereign power." Thus, if Parliament remains de jure sovereign, it is certainly the case that the people retain an indirect, de facto, sovereignty, given that Parliament's formal sovereignty is "limited on every side by the possibility of popular resistance."[16]

Every discussion of the ambiguities of popular sovereignty in Western thought is haunted by a spectre – the direct democracy of Rousseau. The theory of democratic sovereignty in fact presents itself to us in a contradictory dual form. Let us look more closely at this two-headed theory.

At the risk of some oversimplification, let us assume two polar models of popular sovereignty. The first is a direct democracy, or a Rousseauian community of equals constituted under conditions which allow the determination of the "general will." Here the sovereign is united, indivisible and the attribute of sovereignty is inalienable; by the same token, the community is small and decisions are taken in a face-to-face setting. The second is the representative democracy, where adult citizens exercise their sovereignty only by choosing their rulers in an election, that is to say, by a "collective" decision constituted by the statistical result of individual voter choices between rival organized groups of candidates. Here sovereignty is delegated or mandated from the people to a group (party) which constitutes itself as a government – either directly through a national presidential election, or indirectly through a parliamentary majority. Such a system may be based on a very wide territory and large population. The former model exists nowhere, although perhaps glimmerings of some of its elements may have been present in those brief and transitory phenomena of workers councils or soviets which have from time to time emerged in periods of great crisis and collapse of government. The latter model serves as a general description of the wide variety of specific governmental forms which exist throughout the western world.

It may reasonably be questioned what theoretical value is to be found in juxtaposing two polar models, one of which is a kind of Platonic construct of the imagination, and the other an empirical description of elements common to existing states. This methodological problem should not be ignored, but keeping both models in mind has manifest advantages. Rousseauian direct democracy offers a persistent theoretical critique of the limitations of representative democracy in actually embodying popular sovereignty. Representative democratic practice offers a concrete reminder of the severe practical limitations to direct democracy which Rousseau himself admitted. Above all, the two models serve to clarify some ambiguities in the relationship between federalism and democracy. "Democracy" must be first specified before being put into play.

Jean-Paul Sartre in 1973 was led to argue that

Universal suffrage is an institution, and therefore a collective which atomizes or serializes individual men. It addresses the abstract entities within them – the citizens, who are defined by a set of political rights and duties, or in other words by their relation to the state and its institutions. The state makes citizens out of them by giving them, for example, the right to vote once every four years, on condition that they meet very general requirements – to be French, to be over twenty-one – which do not really characterize any of them.[17]

Sartre offers a further perspective on public opinion as serial: "They are *serial ideas* which are expressed through my vote, but they are not *my ideas*. The institutions of bourgeois democracy have split me apart: There is me and there are all the Others they tell me I am (a Frenchman, a soldier, a worker, a taxpayer, a citizen, and so on) ... Who am I, in the end? An Other identical with all the others, inhabited by these important thoughts which come into being everywhere and are not actually *thought* anywhere? Or am I myself? And who is voting? I do not recognize myself any more."[18]

Sartre's critique of representative democracy is squarely Rousseauian (although not acknowledged as such), in the same spirit in which Rousseau wrote that sovereignty cannot be represented: "The English people thinks itself free. It greatly deceives itself; it is so only during the election of members of Parliament. As soon as they are elected, it is a slave, it is nothing. Given the use it has made of its brief moments of freedom, the people certainly deserves to lose it."[19] Robert Paul Wolff echoes this argument in a cogent present-day attack on the legitimacy of representative democracy.[20] The Rousseauian argument ultimately rests on two assumptions: first, that the irreducible unit of political legitimacy is the autonomous individual; and, second, that only the total and equal alienation of the rights of all citizens to the whole community can guarantee a sovereignty in which the subjects, in obeying all, obey themselves. The consequent oscillations of focus between the individual and the collective present considerable difficulties for Rousseauian theory. One finds Sartre, for instance, arguing at one moment that elections are a fraud because they force him to think thoughts not his own, and in the next breath stating that the only legitimate political unit is the spontaneous association in which the individual subsumes his autonomy in a collective solidarity. Rousseau's notorious paradox of forcing men to be free sums up the conundrum: the ends of autonomy can only be gained at the price of the surrender of autonomy. Or again, Rousseau's rules for the conduct of voting in a community capable of generating a general will specify that each citizen must be kept in rigorous isolation from other citizens organized to debate and persuade on behalf of particular legislation, that any mediation between the individual citizen and the collective sovereign is illegitimate and subversive: in short, autonomy is enforced to create a general will against which no individual may legitimately dissent.

This is not the place to pursue the paradoxes of Rousseauian sovereignty; I make no claims to refute the argument, only to point to some of its difficulties. It is important to point to these difficulties at this stage simply to indicate that the Rousseauian critique of representative democracy perhaps stands more usefully as a negative, rather than a positive argument. What it does tell us incisively is that voting for representatives is a means of both retaining and giving away sovereignty, or in a word, delegating sovereignty.

The mechanism of this delegation is the majority, or the plurality. But if the formation of the general will creates difficulties for direct democracy, so too the formation, and reformation, of majorities is no less fraught with problems for representative democracy. Indeed, it is one of the habitual arguments for federalism, that a federation tempers that "tyranny of the majority" of which Tocqueville and Mill warned so insistently.

The problem with arguments concerning the "tyranny of the majority" in representative democracies is the mythical quality of majorities. Majorities are really only statistical constructs of the electoral process. The majorities which voted, say, for Ronald Reagan in 1980 or for François Mitterand in 1981 constitute only a statistical category describing millions of persons who, individually, and for a wide variety of reasons, many of which were contradictory (as any opinion survey discloses) all carried out on a given day the similar act of marking a ballot for Reagan or Mitterand. This act constitutes the sole bond with all other individuals making up the "majority," and since the act of voting is solitary from the individual point of view, and from the social point of view, serialized rather than collective, this bond can scarcely be termed one of solidarity. Nothing else necessarily links the millions of the "majority" but this minimal, solitary, serialized act of voting for a limited choice of parties or candidates imposed upon the voter. Direct democratic theory, then, paradoxically discloses through its negative critique that one of the leading "problems" of representative democratic theory rests on flimsy foundations.

Of course, majorities do exist concretely in legislative bodies, if not in the people. And legislative majorities may believe themselves "mandated" by their electoral pluralities to do certain things. If the "tyranny of the majority" is redefined to focus on the majoritarian mechanism in the representative institutions, then constitutional limitations on the scope of governmental activity become highly relevant. Liberal freedoms (of thought, speech, association, the press, etc. are not merely guarantees for minorities, but are the sine qua non of a functioning representative democracy, the very procedural basis upon which legislative majorities can be formed by the collective decision of free individual choice (however confined by seriality and atomization). Thus all liberal democracies maintain checks on the scope of activity of legislative majorities, of varying quality and effectiveness. With regard to federal democracies, the question of checks becomes rather complex, given that national legislative majorities may be provincial legislative minorities, and vice versa. So too the nature of democratic sovereignty becomes complex in a federation. Yet this complexity is more apparent than real. The most incisive contributions to unravelling these complexities came at the moment of birth of the first modern (democratic) federation with the writing of the American constitution in 1787 and the debate which surrounded its ratification. It is to this debate which I now turn.

The prerevolutionary demands of the American colonists on Britain had been confronted by the 18th Century doctrine of the absolute sovereignty of Parliament. Thus, colonists wishing to restrict Parliament's power were compelled to argue that sovereignty was divisible, and to grope their way toward a new political order in which powers might be distributed among governments, each with a distinct sphere of activity. Conflicts between Parliament, through the Governors, and the local assemblies, led to a growing view that because sovereignty ultimately rested with the people, the attributes of governmental sovereignty could be divided and distributed. Bernard Bailyn concludes that the federalist tradition was "born in the colonists' efforts to state in constitutional language the qualification of Parliament's authority," so that the central government be kept from amassing a "degree of energy, to sustain itself, dangerous to the liberties of the people."[21]

The democratic and liberal thrust of revolutionary ideology, "radicalized" by British intransigence, is well known. The ideas of Jefferson's Declaration of Independence, although still a matter of interpretive controversy, are firmly on the side of the consent of the governed and the right of the people to alter or abolish a form of government destructive of the inalienable rights of individuals created equal – but this was in the form of a unanimous declaration of thirteen separate states, and sought to establish their right to be free and independent states, with full powers to do what "Independent States may of right do."[22] And in the Articles of Confederation, signed in 1781, it was explicitly affirmed that "each state retains its sovereignty, freedom, and independence, and every power, jurisdiction, and right" which was not expressly "delegated" to the Congress of the United States, and that the states were entering no more than a "firm league of friendship" for the common defence of their several liberties.[23] In other words, the first American constitution called for a classic confederacy of sovereign states, not unlike European federal leagues, and not incompatible with Rousseau's idea that sovereign communities could enter into limited 'international' agreements for mutual benefit[24] – although it should be noted that even the union of the Articles was "perpetual," and no right of secession was explicitly included.

This was a false start, and the real breakthrough in political innovation came at the constitutional convention of 1787. Some have denied that the federal system which emerged from this convention should be given the status of political theory, since it was the more or less accidental result of a patchwork of compromises: in the words of one critic, federalism was a *"pis aller ... the furthest point the delegates felt they could go in the destruction of the states without themselves inviting repudiation.*[25] It is true that some of the most eloquent defenders of the final settlement had gone into the convention opposed in principle to the federal system which emerged from the deliberations (Alexander Hamilton is a leading example), and that the much-praised theory of The Federalist was an intellectual rationalization of saw-offs and logrolling among delegates. But this is in no way a diminution of the achievement of the convention, nor of its public defenders. On the contrary. Out of political compromise, they fashioned an innovative, effective, and persistent set of political institutions and a powerful, persuasive and lasting theoretical defence of those institutions.

Among the problems of theoretical significance to democratic federalism with which the delegates grappled, two stand out: the question of size in a republic, and the question of checks and balances in a wholly popular sovereignty; the two questions were interrelated, and the answer was essentially the same for both.

The ancient wisdom had been that when republics became too large, they became imperial, leading to the corruption of their original republican virtue (e.g., Machiavelli's *Discourses* on Rome). Secondly, democracies were held to be inherently limited in size (from the Athenian polis to Rousseau's idealized Geneva). A large territory could only be governed imperialistically, and an empire demanded an emperor. Moreover, a democratic republic required a high degree of homogeneity in the citizenry or it would break down in factionalism. "In 1787," writes Douglas Adair, "the authority of scholars, philosophers, and statesmen was all but unanimous in arguing (from the experience of history) that no republic could ever be established in a territory as extended as the United States – that even if established for a moment, class war must eventually destroy every democratic republic."[26] How then did the founders manage to pull the rabbit out of the hat

A hint could be found in David Hume's 1752 essay, "The idea of a perfect commonwealth,"[27] where a kind of proto-federalism had been suggested for an indirect democracy (beginning at the county, successive levels of representatives voting for those at the next level). "Every county," Hume wrote, "is a kind of republic in itself," but the many levels beyond the county guarded against the dangers of excessive democracy: "Divide the people into *many separate bodies*; and then they may debate with safety, and every inconvenience seems to be prevented" (emphasis added). The "turbulence" of democracies, the dangers of the poor majority oppressing the wealthy few, of which philosophers since Aristotle had warned, could be contained or "refined" in a nation whose "parts are so distant and remote, that it is very difficult, either by intrigue, prejudice, or passion, to hurry them into any measure against the public interest." Thus large size is transformed from being a barrier to stable republicanism to a positive precondition. Although they were rather loath to admit an intellectual debt to Hume, who was in bad odour in late eighteenth American circles, it seems that some of the founders, James Madison in particular, were influenced by Hume's solution.[28]

The Constitution did not follow Hume's outline, as such. But it did something quite unprecedented: it created a "compound republic," neither national nor federal in the sense then understood and which had been embodied in the Articles of Confederation (what we now call a confederacy). Authorized in the name of "we the people," who desired "a more perfect union," it proceeded to specify two levels of government both elected by the people. What we now understand by the term "federalism" was, in effect, invented in 1787. This refinement of representative democracy into a federal principle was a key to unlocking the dual dilemma facing the founders.

There are some scholars who question the extent of the commitment to democracy in late eighteenth century America. While "republic" was a term favoured over "democracy," it is important to recognize that "pure democracy" was taken to be a Rousseauian direct democracy. As Madison put it in *The Federalist* No. 10, a "pure democracy, by which I mean a society consisting of small number of citizens, who assemble and administer the government in person, can admit of no use for the mischief of faction," since "a common passion or interest" will quickly turn on the minority. The problem with these regimes, which, when implemented, are "as short in their lives as they have been violent in their deaths," is that they are a merely political solution to a problem which is more than political: "theoretic politicians, who have patronized this species of government, have erroneously supposed that by reducing mankind to a perfect equality in their political rights, they would at the same time be perfectly equalized and assimilated in their possessions, their opinions, and their passions." Madison then counterposes to this "a republic, by which I mean a government in which the scheme of representation takes place" – and adds that the other great distinction of a republic, besides representation, is that it allows for a greater size.[29]

James Wilson told the Pennsylvania convention called to ratify the constitution that a sovereign power had to be located somewhere. Blackstone had located it in Parliament, the anti-Federalists wanted it to remain with the legislature of the states. But as the American Revolution demonstrated, sovereignty ultimately "remains and flourishes with the people" who are "the fountain of government." Or, as Hamilton put it in No. 22 of *The Federalist*, locating sovereignty in the state legislatures suggests a "compact" which further implied a unilateral right to repeal national laws or to revoke the compact itself. This possibility alone indicated "the necessity of laying the foundations of our national government deeper than in the mere sanctions of delegated authority. The fabric of American empire ought to rest on the solid basis of THE CONSENT OF THE PEOPLE. The streams of national power ought to flow immediately from that pure, original fountain of all legitimate authority." Wilson argued that without the idea of popular sovereignty, "we shall never be able to understand the principle on which this system was constructed:" both levels of government derive their authority as emanations of the power of the people. And even within one level, this principle had momentous consequences for the forms of government, "new and rich discoveries in jurisprudence." The Constitution stipulated a division of powers between the executive and legislative branches, and a division of the latter into an upper and lower chamber. But this in no way implied a reflection of British constitutional theory, in which the leading orders, or estates, of civil society were directly embodied in Parliament. In a distinct break from political thinking since Aristotle, the "democratic principle is carried into every part of the government," for as Wilson argued, "it is not necessary to intermix the different species of government. We have discovered that one of them – the best and purest, in which the supreme power remains with the people at large, is capable of being formed, arranged, proportioned, and organized in such a manner, as to exclude the inconveniences, and to secure the advantages of all three."[22]

This solution was intimately related to the question of faction and the tyranny of the majority. Madison saw that majorities were concrete threats to order in a "pure democracy," but that in a republic or a representative democracy, the *causes* of factionalism (the interests and the passions) would remain, but that their *effects* could be controlled. The extension of population and territory means a greater variety of parties and interests: "you make it less probable that a majority of the whole will have a common motive to invade the rights of other citizens; of if such a common motive exists, it will be more difficult for all who feel it to discover their own strength and to act in unison with one another ... The influence of factious leaders may kindle a flame within their particular States but will be unable to spread a general conflagration through the other States." Thus, in a federal republic, "whilst all authority in it will be derived from and dependent on the society, the society itself will be broken into so many parts, interests, and classes of citizens that the rights of individuals, or of the minority, will be in little danger from interested combinations of the majority."[31] Specifically, a large nation devoted to commercial pursuits fosters a host of divisive interests which are manageable, in that majorities can only be formed out of coalitions of particular wills; coalitions are forms of self-management of competitive interests. Yet more specifically, and here Madison made no effort to hide his own class perspective, divisions among the many would be fostered so as to protect the rich minority. In short, a federal representative democracy renders the very idea of a tyrannous majority doubtful, but serializing and atomizing the people into overlapping, competitive, and thus self-cancelling congeries of interests.

Federalism – as well as the separation of powers – was thus based rather paradoxically on the ground of democratic sovereignty. It was all too apparent that a copy of the British style of constitution by, say, setting aside an upper chamber to represent an "aristocratic" principle in government, would only present a target for popular agitation which might become radically democratic. The genius of the American constitution, and of its defenders, was to banish all notions of sovereignty which were not popular, and then to erect a complex of representative institutions, dividing and subdividing jurisdictions and responsibilities, so that the "people" would be divided against itself, so that each citizen could only represent his interests through voting for a multiplicity of offices in separate jurisdictions, which would, as governments, develop their own set of interests, often in contradiction with those of other jurisdictions. The American federation then, was not a "mixed regime" in the ancient sense: it was a democracy, refined and filtered through an artful maze of governmental institutions so designed as to powerfully discourage the formation and expression of a general or majority will. Thus the dangers of direct democracy and the problems of large size were thought to be greatly diminished, and democracy and federalism/separation of powers reconciled in the "compound republic."

Two other points should be made about this theoretical justification of the Constitution. First, federalism could be seen not only as a means of dividing the people against itself, and thus reducing the dangers of majoritarianism, but it could also be a means of limiting the dangers of government oppressing the people, by dividing the state against itself. This was a not unexpected argument from a people which had just fought a war of independence against abuses of power by the British state. The liberal antistatist argument has been a more common defence of federalism than the argument from self-limiting democracy, perhaps because the rapid triumph of democratic ideology rendered the latter argument suspect. Of course, the two arguments are interconnected, through the mechanism of the electoral process: majorities of voters elect legislative majorities which control governments. The point is that in either version, the original theoretical justification of democratic federalism rests heavily on liberalism, and is ambivalent about democratic legitimacy.

The observation is strengthened by the second, and more general, point about early American political theory. Gordon Wood, in his *Creation of the American Republic*, speaks of an "American science of politics" which broke with classical teaching in its detachment of leading social forces from institutional seats in the state. This meant that "institutional or governmental politics was thus abstracted in a curious way from its former associations with the society." At the same time, the society became less differentiated and more competitive. Political equality set people free to compete economically with one another, with widely varying results. Economic inequality could now be judged an effect of *natural* inequality, when conventional inequality was limited. The disembodiment of government from society was reflected in a decline of the ancient republican idea of a civic virtue. "America would remain free not because of any quality in its citizens of spartan self-sacrifice to some nebulous public good, but in the last analysis because of the concern each individual would have in his own self-interest and personal freedom."[32] Democratic federalism which divided the loyalties of citizens, could only come to birth in a liberal, competitive society which no longer demanded a unique civic loyalty. The end of formal hierarchy and its static orders meant that competitive individuals could be compartmentalized according to particular interests and passions which found different channels of expression in a competitive society. Federalism was one constitutional and institutional formalization of this process.

There was an unresolved ambiguity in American federalism which over the course of the nineteenth century deepened into a near-fatal contradiction. Dividing the people against itself was all very clever, but the federal form of division was *territorial*, and historically determined. The states were the colonial jurisdictions which had gone to war against Britain, replete with their own traditions, identities and, as it turned out, their own regional modes of production. As well as territorially-based representation, modern states also admit of functionally-based representation (as in corporatism). Federalism does not deny the latter, but it formally gives institutional primacy to territorial divisions. In doing so, it fosters an inevitable tension between the claims of the national government to represent the citizens of the component states or provinces, and the claims of the provincial governments to be the primary voice representing the people of that particular territorial jurisdiction. When the national legislative majority has weak representation from a particular province or regions, and when issues which divide the regions over fundamental interests are at stake, the legitimacy question becomes acute – sometimes dangerously acute.

It is here that the newer democratic federalism begins to lose some of its distinctiveness in relation to the older, predemocratic confederalism. Hence the potential, apparently inherent, in democratic federalism for provincial governments to redefine the federation as a compact between provinces. There are good reasons to expect that the democratic mandate of a national government could not in itself be proof against provincialism. As Hamilton presciently suggested in *The Federalist* No. 15, the very existence of government being premissed upon the fact that "The passions of men will not conform to the dictates of reason and justice without constraint," governments themselves can be no exception:

In every political association which is formed upon the principle of uniting in a common interest a number of lesser sovereignties, there will be found a kind of eccentric tendency in the subordinate or inferior orbs by the operation of which there will be a perpetual effort in each to fly off from the centre. This tendency is not difficult to be accounted for. It has its origin in the love of power. Power controlled or abridged is almost always the rival and enemy of that power by which it is controlled or abridged.[33]

Writing a half century later, from a less partisan centralist position, Tocqueville noted with some surprise the relative weakness of the national government and the strength of the state governments. In part, he ascribed this to the closeness of the state governments to their citizens, and the remoteness of Washington and the feebleness of its administrative instruments[34] (no small impediment for a large federation in the pre-industrial age of communications, and one which the authors of *The Federalist* failed signally to grasp).

The ambiguity in democratic legitimacy between the people of the provinces as national electors, and the provincial governments which they directly elect, may lead to an elision in the perception of mandated governmental authority, in which the national government loses its claim to representativeness to the provincial governments. The older image of a confederation as an alliance of preexisting sovereign bodies carries over into dual-mandated democratic federations. Montesquieu had written of a "république federative" as a "societé de societés," which was appropriate enough for what he was describing. Yet Hamilton in *The Federalist* No. 9 quoted Montesquieu approvingly, and at length, as if he had been referring to a federal government based on individual citizens, when in fact Montesquieu had specifically indicated that he understood a "convention par laquelle *plusieurs corps politiques* consentent à devenir citoyens d'un état plus grand."[35] Yet even after the innovation of 1787, a host of observers of democratic federations has persisted in formulations of the genre of a "community of States" (Calhoun), a "commonwealth of commonwealths, a republic of republics" (Bryce); a "federation of federations" (Proudhon), a "community of communities" (Laski).[36] This way of conceptualizing democratic federalism entails serious analytical difficulties inasmuch as focus is shifted away from the representative democratic mandate of both levels of government, and towards intergovernmental relations, in which the provincial level is implicitly – or sometimes explicitly – assumed to have a closer hold on the democratic mandate. As an American scholar has written, the Federalists may have believed that the popular basis of the Constitution undermined compact theories of federalism (since it was individuals grouped in states, rather than state governments, who ratified the agreement), but after 1800, the dominant view was that the ratification had been by sovereign states (the people under state governments) and the legal parties to the agreement were the states possessed of the democratic authority of their citizens.[37] The ambiguous consequences of this doctrine became more and more apparent as sectional conflict in the United States increased.

The American conflict between North and South is perhaps not a very useful paradigm for the internal contradictions of federations. Even divisions on linguistic, religious, and cultural lines are, in a sense, less serious and less profound than those which rent the American Union. In the American case, it was a division between two incompatible modes of production, capitalist and slave, and between two irreconcilable superstructures of political, legal and social values. Lincoln was right: America could not live half slave and half free, the conflict was irrepressible. Yet, even with these caveats, the sectional confrontation generated some original political theory of continuing interest to democratic federations.

The problem was a national one above all because of the contention over the settlement of the West, and the growing tendency of the capitalist North to rely on its greater demographic weight to use the national government as its instrument under the banner of national majoritarianism. As one writer has put it, this was a "drastic modification of the federal system. It involved taking an idea considered applicable to small groups and applying it to large ones," to the nation as a whole. To the South, this not only gave substance to the ancient fears about the tyranny of the majority, but the electoral mathematics of Northern majoritarianism led to a rethinking of minority rights along sectional, rather than state, lines.[38]

The theorist of Southern resistance to national majoritarianism was John C. Calhoun. That Calhoun was in fact defending slavery might seem to put him out of court at the outset as a theorist relevant to democratic federalism, but this would be, in effect, an *ad hominem* argument. Calhoun's theorizing of the "numerical" and "concurrent" majorities transcends, to a degree at least, the special interests he set out to defend. To call Calhoun the "Marx of the Master Class" may by hyperbolic, but his ideas are well worth examination.[39]

The framers of American federalism had not foreseen that the country could divide into "two great sections strongly distinguished by their institutions, geographical character, productions and pursuits," and federalism, as it was practiced, provided no answer to the sectional conflict.[40] Calhoun went back to first principles, which in his case turned out to be socialized Hobbesian assumptions about the basis of government. Man is self-interested, competitive and seeks self-preservation. But however nasty, he is not solitary. Rather man is by nature social and associative. This assumption allowed Calhoun to postulate the existence of communities as irreducible human units. Communities were givens, and within communities a simple, or "numerical" majority would be the principle of rule. But if government is necessary to contain and manage social conflict, it is itself a danger – even when it rests on the sovereignty of the people: "the right of suffrage, by placing the control of the government in the community, must, from the same constitution of our nation which makes government necessary to preserve society, lead to conflict among its different interests." The answer to the abuse of government was itself Hobbesian: his intention was "to explain on what principles government must be formed in order to resist by its own interior ... the tendency to the abuse of power ... Power can only be resisted by power – and tendency by tendency."[41]

The American republic had to be reshaped as its institutions could not any longer afford the checks and balances promised in the Constitution. *The Federalist* had worried about factionalism and the tyranny of the majority, but had erroneously believed that it had a solution. What was not foreseen was the role of parties in controlling legislative majorities on a numerical vote basis in defiance of minority sectional interests. All rulers oppressively aggrandize their power at the expense of their subjects, and the "people" embodied in the form of a national legislative majority was a despot in relation to minority communities or sections. A federal republican government could thus, through the mechanism of party and legislative majority, realize all the vices of a pure or direct democracy. Calhoun believed it necessary, not to repudiate democracy, but to refine it yet further so that not only numbers, but community interests should find representation. Thus the concurrent majority, which "regards interests as well as numbers – considering the community as made up of different and conflicting interests, as far as the action of the government is concerned – and takes the sense of each through its majority or appropriate organ, and the united sense of all as the sense of the entire community."[42] It is clear that Calhoun's use of "interest" differs from Madison's earlier usage in that the latter saw interests as essentially individual, while the former saw them as socially defined and territorially located. If Madison gave a federalist answer to a problem defined in liberal theory, Calhoun was beginning with a "federalist" problem and redefining federalist theory to encompass it.[43]

I said earlier that Calhoun's ideas transcend, to a degree, the interests of the slave South he was addressing. There is a hard class content to his argument, which he made no effort to hide. An advantage of the concurrent majority model is that it encourages the subordination of the poor to the leadership of the rich in the name of sectional interest, and secondly, it suggests cross-sectional accommodations between the wealthy elites in defence of their respective properties.[44] (Concretely, Calhoun was urging a double alliance – first, of rich and poor Southern whites in defence of slavery, and second, of Southern plantation owners and Northern capitalists against the poor in both sections.) Calhoun thus anticipated by a century the model of "consociational democracy" or "elite accommodation," with this significant modification – unlike twentieth century theorists, he was blunt about the class interests which were to be served.

Whether or not one shares Calhoun's enthusiasm for the preservation of wealth and privilege, his theoretical contribution to federalism is considerable. The dangers of the partiality of the national numerical majority in regard to regional interests must be recognized in any functioning federation – at the peril of escalating conflict and the loss of legitimacy of the national institutions of government. And the counter-position of concurrent to numerical majorities serves to point out an inherent contradiction in dual-mandate democratic federations: national majorities may be provincial minorities and vice versa, but both national and provincial legislative majorities have equally legitimate popular mandates. Continually to override provincial majorities by the national majority is effectively to have a unitary state. To allow the national majority to be continually defied by provincial majorities is to have a confederacy, not a federation. Calhoun's prescription raises many questions, but his concept of the concurrent majority is valuable. I shall return to it later in an attempt to redefine it more usefully for democratic federations.

The final theorist of federalism to be examined is from a different continent and an entirely different ideological tradition. P.-J. Proudhon, anarchist antagonist of Marx, became in later life a messianic enthusiast of federalism. In Proudhon's *Du principe fédératif* there is a marriage of federalism with radical social and political thought quite unlike the more conservative views of the American defenders of the concept.[45]

France, in the nineteenth as well as the twentieth century, was an unexpected terrain to give birth to a celebration of federalism. Centralist and absolutist monarchy had given way at the French Revolution to Jacobin centralism, unitary nationalism, and finally Bonapartism. The Girondins opposed a vague "federalism" to centralizing Jacobinism, but this was easily dismissed as class opposition to Paris and its revolutionary masses; the "federalist revolt" of 1793 raised the spectre of secession in the service of reaction. Federalism became associated with the political Right while centralism and national majoritarianism became deeply identified with the Left.[46] Proudhon took a different tack altogether: the Jacobins may have been cleverer than their opponents, but they had betrayed the revolution with their "one and indivisible republic" and made "liberty impossible in France."[47]

Proudhon is not modest in his claims for federalism. All the divisions, conflicts and hostilities which bedevil political systems "will instantly find a definitive solution in the theory of federal government."[48] The reason for this messianism lies in his belief that federalism offers a unique synthetic solution to a dialectical contradiction between liberty and authority which underlies all politics. It is this contradiction which leads Proudhon to severe criticism of democracy, and of the masses. On the one hand, the masses by themselves are incapable of creative activity, and democracy might lead to decline, if not checked; on the other hand, the "people, too, form one of the powers of the state, one whose eruptions are the most terrifying."[49] His main objection, it seems, is to the mass democratic state, in which authority has made a particularly pernicious return and liberty is in decline: in different language he describes a Tocquevillean critique of "democratic despotism." Like Tocqueville, he is not against popular sovereignty, since there is no viable alternative, and instead strives only to limit its self-destructive effects. With universal suffrage there is a constant pull toward unity, uniformity. The trick is to insert diversity into the very best seat of sovereignty itself. "Federation is thus the salvation of the people, for by dividing them it saves them at once from the tyranny of their leaders and from their own folly." As Vernon aptly comments: socialist decentralism thus joins hands with the federalism of Madison.[50]

It would, however, be misleading to simply draw this analogy without further explication. Although Proudhon is much less an economic determinist than Marx, his federalism does have an economic base which distinguishes it sharply from that of Madison. Political federation is to be mirrored by "agro-industrial federation," the old anarchist mutualism within a quasi-market of producers' co-operatives. This is functional federation, while territorial federation reigns in the political sphere. Together they form a society which Proudhon characterizes as "progressive federation," a corollary of the first two.[51] The important point here is that while Madison's federalism was designed to protect property against the majority, Proudhon's federalism protects a different kind of property against the democratic despot – property decentralized into the hands of the people as producers. The people in their fictive but dangerous guise as sovereign of the mass democratic state cannot be trusted to recognize their own best interests as individuals. Political federation divides the sovereign people, thus allowing the federal principle to flourish in economic life. There is an ironic hidden kinship with Madison, although Proudhon perhaps more importantly offers a political critique of Marx. In either event, Proudhon's creative use of the concept of federation demonstrates both the durability and the continuity of the idea, as well as its adaptability to quite different ideological usages.

Not that Proudhon's argument is without difficulties. His central idea itself remains vague and problematic in its institutional form. Whether he was thinking of a dual-mandate democratic federation, or a confederal arrangement remains a mystery,[52] which his language does nothing to clarify. And the Marx of *The Poverty of Philosophy* would have had little difficulty in demonstrating the lack of any coherent programme for destroying the power of capital and building an agro-industrial federation as an economic base. There is about Proudhon's project an ineradicable aura of petty-bourgeois nostalgia and delusive romanticism, reflected in the vagueness of its concrete prescriptions. And yet, such a dismissal would miss much.

As Vernon suggests, Proudhon represents a return to a tradition which was older than modern federalism, and which American federalist thought denigrated: the concept of "civic humanism," as against the atomized competitiveness of a liberal society.[53] Proudhon emphasized the value of what a later generation would call "participatory democracy" and saw the value of federalism in offering a wider range of offices and activities for the involvement of citizens. In the tradition of civic humanists, Proudhon addressed himself to the problem of the corruption of the civic spirit, and the tendency of democratic republics to decline into centralized, bureaucratic authority. As Vernon suggests, "what corrupts virtue is passivity, lack of responsibility, dependence, all of which undermine the engaged concern for a common good which the democratic citizen is required to have."[54] Federalism is posited as a means of encouraging involvement. Proudhon is, in effect, attempting to rescue the individual from the atomization and serialization of mass representative democracy, without returning to the tyranny of direct democracy, by developing a politics in which the individuals begin in solitary social groups or associations and come together under the federative principle – this time not as unmediated subjects of the people-at-large, but as members of definite groups with social identities. Such politics pose an audacious challenge to democratic principles: citizens will have multiple, competitive loyalties. Proudhon adds an even more disturbing corollary: it is in the nurturing and cultivation of these multiple, competitive loyalties that true civic virtue lies. Finally, Proudhon poses a challenge to the entire tradition of political thought obsessed with sovereignty and authority: there can be no free society in which the "community" is already defined and holds priority. Instead the question of community (or communities) is open-ended and should be the result of the spontaneous strivings of associated individuals to define their community loyalties. All this, and a political centre of the federation as well – Proudhon, as we have said, is not modest in his claims. But neither is he without interest for the theory of federalism. Especially in his emphasis on participation, multiple loyalties and the open-endedness of the question of community, Proudhon elucidates some critical elements in any theory of federal democracy.

We have traversed a number of themes and a number of thinkers in the history of political thought in clarifying the relationship between federalism and democracy. It is obvious that this relationship is ambiguous, but I have argued that much of the ambiguity is inherent in the representative form of democracy itself. Federalism was justified on grounds of liberal checks against the tyranny of the many, as were checks and balances between branches of government and other forms of limitations on the majority developed within representative systems. If democratic federalism divided the people against themselves, it did not challenge the democratic principle itself, merely its form of expression. This led to a specific science of federalist politics, concerned with the relationship between the different majorities, national and provincial. This further raises the question of the definition of the democratic community. Lessons can be drawn from *The Federalist*, Calhoun, and Proudhon which may be incorporated in a contemporary theory of democratic federalism, despite the contextual limitations of all of these theorists. In this last section, I propose to look at contemporary federalism in the light of these historical theories, and to draw some tentative conclusions by way of a qualified defence of the concept.

I rest my reflections largely upon eighteenth and nineteenth century thinkers because in truth the twentieth century has not produced political theory of federalism of much significance. There has been, to be sure, a political science of federalism, with empirical study of federal constitutions, institutions and practices in comparative perspective. But this neo-Aristotelian literature has shown a marked disinterest in broader theoretical and philosophical issues. There has been some not very sophisticated attempts at linking federalism with "freedom" or "democracy," and some equally unsophisticated attempts at debunking these linkages. What is interesting is that this debate has been carried out almost exclusively in the context of the liberal side of democracy, to draw on C.B. Macpherson's terms. Franz Neumann's critique of federalism's relation to democracy, implicitly defined democracy in terms of the liberal freedoms alone. And he is not alone.

Instead of asking what federalism does for liberal freedoms, we might start the other way around, and ask what liberal freedoms do for federalism. Here, I believe the answer is decisive. It is impossible to imagine a functioning federalism in an illiberal polity. One might see the forms of federalism, but they could not be operated in a one-party state which has no free press, denies voluntary association and assembly, and prevents free expression. Indeed, the Union of Soviet Socialist Republics offers just such an example. Constitutionally, the USSR is a federation in which even the right of secession exists. Functionally, as one observer has recently written, "only a humorist" could call the actual situation "propitious to federalism."[56] The reason is not to be found in the constitutional provisions, but in the centralization of power through the mechanism of one-party rule. It is not possible to have co-ordinate jurisdictions without autonomy of power at each level. And it is difficult to conceive of the dispersal of power in an orderly, constitutional fashion without a foundation of liberal freedoms which allows competition of political elites.

If it is granted that liberalism is a precondition of functioning federalism, can the logic of the relationship be reversed? I believe that it can, to a limited extent. Democratic federalism involves elite competition to mobilize support from overlapping electorates. Moreover, governmental elites competitively seek support from organized economic interests. Finally, power is defended against intrusions by other jurisdictions, and power-holders seek to maximize the security of their possession of power by extending their reach, where possible, into areas held by other, competitive elites. These are Hobbesian and Weberian assumptions which can, I believe, be supported empirically. But the implication is that competitive political elites in a federal system of divided jurisdiction has a shared stake in maintaining liberal freedoms, to the extent that a liberal framework is in their own self-interest. This would seem to be particularly the case for provincial elites who have a great deal to fear from tendencies to authoritarian centralism. Authoritarian centralist tendencies may, of course, exist within provincial jurisdictions, directed against sections of the provincial populations. But a federation does create a system with at least some vested governmental interest in the maintenance of the minimum of liberalism necessary to sustain the power to compete freely with other governments.

This indeed may be one rationale for the creation of the German Federal Republic following World War Two – and here a linkage may be drawn between liberalism and a problem of democratic sovereignty. In 1933 the fall of the Weimar Republic was accomplished to the accompaniment of a "democratic mandate" to establish a fascist state. This "mandate" is not factually unambiguous under the circumstances of Nazi intimidation of the voters, but it does highlight a theoretical paradox: what if the sovereign people vote out representative democracy and vote in a totalitarian state? The sovereign by this act alienates its sovereignty to a leader, party, vanguard or whatever, in a manner much more definite than in merely voting for representatives. A democratic federation, by dividing the people into overlapping electorates and dispersing governmental power into different jurisdictions, offers a barrier (clearly not a guarantee) against such an act.

It would, of course, be absurd to argue that federations are inherently more liberal than unitary states. Obviously, unitary liberal-democratic states have powerful internal reasons for organizing themselves in the way they do, a logic in which democratic federations normally share, without regard to federal arrangements, as such. But it is possible to suggest that democratic federalism may be a positive factor contributing to the survival of liberal practices in a liberal democratic polity. This is a modest claim, it is true, but not an entirely inconsiderable one. And in the way the argument has been put, the claim requires no appeal to the values and civic spiritedness of individuals operating the system, merely their interest as political actors. Values follow, in the usual fashion in which virtue is made out of necessity. If this was not exactly a question to which Madison addressed himself, the claim is made in a Madisonian spirit.

There is another kind of argument advanced against federalism which does not distinguish between levels of government but suggests that federalism in general is inherently conservative, in that it makes change difficult and puts a premium on inertia. One might well pose a counter-question to this: where is the abstract model of innovation and efficiency which is assumed in the argument? Unitary liberal democracies display many barriers to change. One ought not to fall into the trap of formalism. Intergovernmental conflict is a highly visible instutionalisation of something that goes on in other forms in unitary states, as intragovernmental conflict and as pressures brought to bear by organized economic interests. As Sydney Tarrow suggests, even in unitary states there are regional and local administrative institutions, and "functional interests ... range themselves around both poles of the political system – centre and periphery – and use their territorial leverage to fight out their conflicts of interest."[57] Federalism formalises this process, but does not invent it.

Yet the conclusion to be drawn from the eighteenth and nineteenth century theorizing of federalism is that the critics may be correct after all, even if federalism blurs into unitary states in practice. The separation of powers, checks and balances, and the division of the sovereign people into overlapping territorial jurisdictions were predicted upon the notion of creating lasting barriers to the capacity of national majorities to legislate against minority (wealthy) interests. Even if it is true that federalism cannot be singled out as a unique case of governmental inaction and conservatism, it is the case that federalist institutions do act as brakes on both national and provincial legislative majorities. If they did not do so, one could only surmise that there was no longer a functioning federalism in operation. From Madison to Proudhon, federal theorists were in agreement at least on that point. Moreover, federations do create relatively autonomous bureaucratic-political concentrations of power which become, in an age of complex legislation and pervasive interaction between state and economy, vested interests in themselves, often of formidable weight. In their emphasis on intergovernmental relations at or near the centre of things, federations add a further dimension to the transformation of democratic politics into bureaucratic forms of elite accommodation, and the attenuation of the ideal of popular sovereignty. This happens everywhere, but the characteristic complexity, induced by federalism, of a maze of intergovernmental and interbureaucratic forums for federal-provincial co-operation removed by many stages from electoral responsibility to the voters, reduces democratic input even further than in unitary states.

The earlier theorists of federalism did not anticipate that federalism would not merely multiply the number of governments, but would actually compound the growth of the state through proliferating mechanisms for co-operation and for conflict between levels of government. But then these same theorists did not anticipate the growth of the capitalist state. Proudhounian federalism in particular, seems to suffer in comparison with late twentieth century reality. Conservatives may be relatively content with federalism's fostering of big government, because it is government divided against itself, and because it may seem to give more space to private economic interests to play off levels of government against each other. Left-wing observers may be less complacent, and even tempted to become partisans either of national majoritarianism or, where strong provincial communities exist, of provincial autonomy or of secessionist movements.

Many of the objections of democratic socialists to federalism are, in reality, objections either to the liberal capitalist state or to representative democracy. It is a basic characteristic of representative democracy that citizens are separated from the decision-making political elite in all but the most generalized sense of the mass electoral mandate as a mechanism of responsibility. It is true that federalism further dissipates this already weak and doubtful control by diffusing the popular mandate into different jurisdictions. But the essential separation between citizen and government is created by the act of representation; the forms of representation are merely secondary. Only a romantic could believe that provincial jurisdictions in a federation represent communities in which the Rousseauian direct democratic ideals prevail[58] (of course, provincial jurisdictions may represent communities in a linguistic, cultural or ethnic sense of nationalist identity but that is a different matter). All jurisdictions are organized on representative democratic lines, and share in the same characteristics. The question to be addressed squarely is: should one's response to the limitations of representative democracy be modified in a federal state? My answer to this is a qualified "yes," but it is necessary to approach it in a somewhat roundabout way.

The essential organizational principle of federalism is territoriality. There are other conceivable ways of dividing the popular electorate, the most obvious being functionalism, probably taking the form of corporatist organization of the people into functional or economic sub-divisions. Federalism as a system of representation remains formally silent about the economic and class content of the nation, but is predicated along the axis of space and its political organization.The provincial units thus always subsume within their jurisdictions a range of economic interests, and a particular mix of classes and class fractions. If this mix (constituting, along with other factors, a culture) were in all cases an exact replication of that of the nation as a whole, one would have to assume that federalism was unnecessary and its institutions a mere shell to be readily sloughed off. Federalism must assume a certain reality in the provinces' separate identities. Whether or not these identities are cultural/ ethnic/linguistic or essentially economic, whether or not they are pre-existant or a historical construct of the federal arrangement itself, remains a matter of indifference. What is essential is that multiple territorial identities coexist within the same nation, and within the same citizenry. At the same time federalism also involves multiple governments, multiple bureaucracies and multiple, autonomously-based, political elites. These latter phenomena are partially, but not entirely linked to the former. They can never be identical, for the same reason that representative democracy always involves a separation between sovereign and legislator, between voters and their representatives. The danger is that in federalism, even the thinly democratic elements of representative government will be further diluted by a progressive substitution of intergovernmental relations for direct responsibility (however limited this may be) to the voters. Succinctly, federations have a tendency to emphasize the government of governments, rather than the government of people.

Two ways out of this dilemma are either to centralize and turn the provincial units into mere delegated administrations, or to actively seek the balkanization of the federation into small, loosely associated sovereign entities. Such options are more likely the result of historical forces, than of philosophic choice – although this should not prevent us from judging the results and developing standards for such judgements. Politically, both the centralist and decentralist opinions simply avoid the essential problem, which is that humanity inhabits spaces, in communities necessarily discontinuous and overlapping in organization. Political units of large territorial extent pose inherent difficulties, as the transition from the polis to the Alexandrine empire demonstrated in its undermining of the social base of classical political philosophy, and its posing of a whole new set of political questions. The centralist solution in a large nation must, in one way or another, suppress the communitarian discontinuities, or at least limit their political expression. The balkanization option is equally evasive: first, because short of regress to the individual or the family, no territorial unit, however local, can avoid being inclusive of communitarian difference; second, because economic and security considerations dictate that states cannot be too small, or that if they are, they must seek some form of association with other states, which will again raise some of the same questions as federalism. My point here is not that everyone should be federalist. It is simply that non-federalist states do not solve the problems to which federalism is addressed, by virtue of not being federalist.[59]

Let us assume that the federalist answer is worth exploring as a possible avenue. If it is, the intergovernmental bias of federal states, posed above, must be tackled. Can federalism be democratised, or can its elitist and statist tendencies be minimised?

Democracy in a federation must be defined differently than democracy in a unitary state. Democracy's mechanism of expression is the majority, and representative government, effectively the legislative majority. In a democratic federation, the sovereign people are divided into different but overlapping electorates, and there can be, by definition, no single majority voice, or single legislative majority, but rather an overlapping plurality of majorities. Here Calhoun's argument for "concurrent majorities" is highly relevant.

Yet Calhoun's theory was distinctly elitist and antidemocratic in practice. Can the expression of regional majorities be rescued, in a post-Calhoun age of the capitalist state, from simply being another argument for intergovernmental, interbureaucratic barriers to change? It must be admitted that intergovernmental elitism cannot be banished. The impossibility of drawing watertight constitutional compartments and the complexity of modern legislation and administration ensure that national-provincial governmental interaction will account for the expenditure of considerable political resources. Concurrent majorities, if governments are substituted for people, can simply become a reinforcement of intergovernmental elitism: provincial governments hold veto power over national governments with deadlock the result in, in a more extreme version, a "compact theory" of federalism is advanced in which the national government is reduced to a mere creature of the provincial governments and federalism is transformed into a confederacy or league of sovereign states. Federalism is undermined if only the legislative majorities of the provinces are considered. Democratic federations operate on national majorities, as well as on provincial majorities. Without the grounding of national institutions of government in the majority of the people, as people, rather than provincial states, sovereign power concentrates in the provincial units. Yet if the division of the nation into territorial sub-units reflects a reality of national life, that is to say, federation is not an empty superstructure, but reflects a federal society, the concurrent majority must be recognized as well.

Is this but a version of squaring the circle? Perhaps federalism is a Sisyphean epic of squaring the circle. As Dicey wrote long ago, the essential condition of federalism is the existence of a "very peculiar state of sentiment" among a people: "They must desire union, and must not desire unity."[60] Beginning with such a condition, it is certain only that federalist institutions and processes will be messy, and the despair of those seeking geometric, Platonic solutions to political problems. Even amid the untidiness, however, some guidelines can be suggested. To base national government solely on national majoritarianism is to pit two levels of government against one another in a manner highly unsafe for the future of the federation. In a regionally divided society, national legislative majorities are drawn from electoral coalitions which will likely, for the same reasons which differentiate regions, be based on regional concentrations. Ruling parties tend to reflect regional groupings with varying degrees of unevenness. The more this is the case, and it is always a danger, the regions concentrated in the legislative minority will tend to view the majority as not a democratic national majority but as an instrument of the domination of one group of regions by another, and therefore as lacking in legitimacy. One way of dealing with this problem is to attempt to harness together at the national level both majorities, the national and the concurrent. In the American Congress, this is done by basing the lower house on population, and the upper on equal representation from each state. While the President is representative of a simple national majority, the congressional system allows considerable input from senators. Parliamentary systems present more difficulties, but an upper chamber based on region or province rather than population, and holding effective veto power over any legislation entered by the cabinet in the lower house with federal-provincial implications, would in theory wed the two majorities. One proviso is that this upper house be directly elected, and not a body appointed by provincial governments, as in the West German upper house. In the latter case, intergovernmental elitism is simply extended into the internal structures of the national government which is to erode further direct responsibility to voters, and to lengthen the reach of one set of vested governmental interests at the expense of others.

Another way of maximizing electoral responsibility is to have recourse to referenda for constitutional amendments, so long as such referenda are themselves based on the concurrent majority, that is, on a regional veto. Again, leaving amendment to elected officials is to leave the federal system itself as simply a creature of intergovernmental elites.

There is a paradox in advising a maximization of electoral responsibility at the national level. The wider the electorate, the greater the atomization and serialization of individual electors. However, there seems no way out of this dilemma when federal structures are superimposed on representative democracy. The concrete alternative, after all, is not directly democracy, but elite domination and elite conflict at levels well removed from popular responsibility. Moreover, in a federal system, people also are voters in the smaller provincial units, where the communitarian fragmentation and diversity may be less.

Lurking behind this entire discussion of federalism in the twentieth century is the question of community and of citizenship. What are we to make, after all, of this notion of dividing the people against themselves? There was no doubt about the political point which *The Federalist* was making in this regard, although Proudhon does bring quite a different perspective to bear on this arrangement. But is it not inherently undemocratic to raise a constitutional structure which systematically divides the people into separate bodies and moreover divides each citizen between membership in at least two political communities?

Such a system would be undemocratic were the question of community inherently self-evident. That the claims of community are manifestly not self-evident is apparent from the political turmoil of nationalism in this century. Or, again, the claims of community in the abstract may be accepted while the question of the embodiment of these claims in concrete political manifestations as sovereign states with power over individuals is always an open-ended matter of controversy and division. The artificiality of nationalism, the manipulation of symbols of nationality by great states as a substitution for face-to-face community, when subjects are spread out over vast territorial expanses, is matched by the persistence of movements of cultural separatism and mass alienation from governmental institutions. The development of the democratic nation-state with its powerful mutual reinforcements of nationalism and popular sovereignty may have suppressed counter-tendencies at particular moments, but the resurgence of minority nationalist movements, the renewal of cultural enclaves, and apparently increasing individual political alienation in the late twentieth century, all suggest limitations to the solvent of national "self-determination." At some point in the argument for the priority of community there has to be an arbitrary decision: this is the community which will cover this territory and this is its definition; dissenters must submit or leave (although leaving generally means as individuals, not as a territory). Yet if such decisions – like the act of violence which is at the foundation of democratic republics – may be necessary, they can never be definitive.

This suggests another dimension of the arbitrary in democratic politics: the definition of citizenship. Who are the "people" which constitute the sovereign? The most decisive answer to this question lies in the arbitrary drawing of the borders of states. Such boundaries are invariably the result of past acts of violence and the culmination of historical accidents. True, those born into a particular state are taught to identify themselves with it, but this is merely to say that the nation-state has to work at recreating the conditions of consent in each generation, which only underlines the arbitrary nature of the definition of citizenship. Moreover, democracy, whether direct or representative, has always been pragmatic as to the exclusion of categories of persons resident within the national territory from full participation as voting citizens. All democratic states exclude children, which is no doubt noncontroversial, although the age cut-off point is not. Not all residents are citizens, and in many western countries it is possible to be a long-term resident and taxpayer without ever being able to become a naturalized citizen. These and others might be considered as exclusions marginal to any fundamental theoretical point about democracy, but they are symptomatic of something deeper. America in the nineteenth century was a democratic federation in the sense that most of those qualified to be citizens, e.g., white adult males, could vote. That women and blacks were excluded (indeed, that slavery was the economic base of an entire region) did not prevent Tocqueville from distilling his penetrating observations about democracy from his American experience. Ancient Athens was a democracy, even though women, slaves and the foreign-born were excluded – indeed, within the confines of the definition of the free adult male, Athens was more democratic, in the sense of a direct democracy, than any representative democracy today. And we ought not to forget that even the greatest theorist of direct democracy, Rousseau, founded his sovereign on a number of exclusions, among which one could cite exclusion by narrowly restricting boundaries and the rigorous exclusion of half the population (women) within these narrow boundaries not only from participation in the general will but from all public presence.

A possible objection to this line of argument is that such exclusions are merely transitional stages on the road to a definitive democratic citizenship. I think not. The theory of the sovereignty of the people must rest on a definition of the term "people." All definitions are, *ipso facto*, exclusionary; they define by excluding what is "not-X" from what is "X." The very notion of a sovereign people is that of a *community* of people capable of exercising collective political choice. As Rousseau says, "before examining the act by which a people elects a King, it would be well to examine the act by which a people is a people."[61] It is a democratic paradox that the more exclusionary the definition of the people, the less heterodox, diverse and conflictual the people become, the better democracy works. The wider the definition, the fewer the exclusions, the weaker the putative community constituted by the people, the more problematic the presence of the people in the politics of the state.

Federalism does not offer a solution to this paradox, but it does suggest a way of evading the horns of the dilemma. It does this by being agnostic about community. Of course, it is true that federations simply multiply the arbitrary decisions about community and citizenship. One is told in France that one is French; one is told in Alberta that one is a Canadian and an Albertan – yet the boundaries of the Albertan "community" are as arbitrarily drawn as the boundaries of the Canadian or French "communities." But a double arbitrary division creates the basis of doubt. Is one acting as an Albertan or as a Canadian? If the answer is "both," as it usually will be in a functioning federal society, the question of community has, in effect, been opened up again. If federalism is to be a more than institutional formalism, it must keep that question open. That may be very untidy and the bane of rationalists, it may make federations difficult to operate, but it demonstrates that federalism is not merely compatible with (representative) democracy, but may offer one of the better institutional frameworks for coping with some of the inherent problems of democracy. As Rousseau continued in a very different context: "it is the very vices that make social institutions necessary that make their abuse inevitable."[62]

NOTES

1 Alexis de Tocqueville, *Democracy in America*, Vol. 1 (Henry Reeve text, edited by Phillips Bradley, New York, 1954), 6.

2 From amongst many examples of democratic theorists who pay little attention to federalism, I might cite two. C.B. Macpherson, although a Canadian and an author of a classic study of a provincial political movement in Canada (*Democracy in Alberta* (Toronto, 1953)), makes no reference whatever to federalism in his theoretical works on democracy. J. Roland Pennock, in a recently published justification of American-style democratic politics, just passes 500 pages when he remarks, "Of the federal system little need be said," noting merely that federalism contributes to "dispersed leadership" and "loose, weak" parties, which he believes are conducive to the most satisfactory operation of democratic institutions. J.R. Pennock, *Democratic Political Theory* (Princeton, 1979), 503.

A notable recent exception to this disinterest among democratic theorists are the contributions of Robert Dahl ("Federalism and the Democratic Process") and David Braybrooke ("Can Democracy Be Combined with Federalism or with Liberalism?") to J.R. Pennock and J.W. Chapman, eds., *Liberal Democracy* (New York, 1983), the twenty-fifth number of the NOMOS series. Unfortunately, these pieces only appeared as I was revising the final version of this paper, but Dahl in particular makes a number of succinct points with which my own argument here is in substantial agreement.

Among writers on federalism, a corresponding disinterest in democratic theory is easy to discern. The classic institutional work on federalism, K.C. Wheare's *Federal Government* (London, 1945) sees no need to cite democracy as even a qualifying condition of a functioning federalism. Gilles Lalande's *Pourquoi le fédéralisme* (Montreal, 1972) lists ten arguments against federalism, which he then proceeds to refute. None of these arguments have anything to do with democratic theory.

3 For arguments indicating how descriptive analysis of democracy turns into functionalist justification of restrictions on democracy see, inter alia, Carole Pateman, *Participation and Democratic Theory* (Cambridge, 1970), and Quentin Skinner, "The Empirical Theorists of Democracy and Their Critics: A Plague on Both Their Houses," *Political Theory* 1 (1973).

4 *Politics of Johannes Althusius*, translated by F.S. Carney (Boston, 1964) is incomplete, but the only English translation presently available. An excellent modern source on Althusius' federalism is Thomas Hueglin, "Johannes Althusius: Medieval Constitutionalist or Modern Federalist?" Publius 9, no. 4 (1979): 9–42. Less useful is Patrick Riley, "Three Seventeenth Century German Theorists of Federalism: Althusius, Hug and Leibnitz," Publius 6, no. 3 (1976).

5 *The Politics*, 64–7.

6 Ibid.

7 M.M. Goldsmith, "Hobbes's 'Mortall God': Is There a Fallacy in Hobbes's Theory of Sovereignty?" *History of Political Thought* 1, no. 1 (1980); 40–1.

8 Hans Kelsen, *General Theory of Law and State* (New York, 1945) and *Pure Theory of Law and State* Berkeley, 1967).

9 Attorney-General of Nova Scotia v. Attorney-General of Canada (1951) SCR 31, Rinfret CJ at 34.

10 Harold Laski, *Studies in the Problem of Sovereignty* (Yale, 1917), 283.

11 K.W.B. Middleton, "Sovereignty in Theory and Practice," in W.J. Stankiewicz, ed., *In Defence of Sovereignty* (Toronto, 1969).

12 W.J. Ree, "The Theory of Sovereignty Restated," in Stankiewicz, 209–40.

13 A.V. Dicey, *Introduction to the Study of the Law of the Constitution* (London, 1908) 157.

14 Bertrand de Jouvenel, *Sovereignty: An Inquiry into the Political Good* (Chicago, 1957).

15 Yves Simon, "Sovereignty in Democracy," in Stankiewicz, *In Defence of Sovereignty*, 160–4.

16 Dicey, *Introduction*, 76,79.

17 Jean-Paul Sartre, "Elections: A Trap for Fools," in Sartre, *Life/Situations: Essays Written and Spoken* (New York, 1977), 202.

18 Ibid., 207–8.
19 *Du contrat social* in J.J. Rousseau, *Oeuvres complètes* (Pléiade ed., Paris, 1964), 111: xv, v. 3, 428.
20 Robert Paul Wolff, *In Defence of Anarchism* (New York, 1970), especially 27–34.
21 Bernard Bailyn, *The Ideological Origins of the American Revolution* (Cambridge, Mass., 1967), 209–28, quoted at 229.
22 See ibid., 160–319; Carl Becker, *The Declaration of Independence: A Study in the History of Ideas* (New York, 1942); Gary Wills, *Inventing America: Jefferson's Declaration of Independence* (New York, 1978).
23 R.B. Morris, ed., *Basic Documents in American History* (New York, 1956), 32.
24 "Extrait de projet de paix perpetuelle de monsieur l'abbé de Saint Pierre" and "Jugement sur le projet de paix perpetuelle," J.-J. Rousseau, *Oeuvres complètes*, v.111, 563–600; Patrick Riley, "Rousseau as a Theorist of National and International Federalism" *Publius* 3, no. 1 (1973): 5–17. As Carl Friedrich has pointed out, Rousseau discussed "national" federalism in his "Considerations sur le gouvernement de Pologne," but that due to his rejection of *representative democracy*, he was caught by the problem of size, and could have "no searching insight ... into the real functioning of a democratic federal order." C.J. Friedrich, *Trends of Federalism in Theory and Practice* (New York 1968), 24.
25 John P. Roche, "Republicanism and Democratic Politics at the Constitutional Convention," *American Political Science Review* 55 (1961): 816.
26 Douglas Adair, *Fame and the Founding Fathers* (New York, 1974), 116.
27 David Hume, *Essays Moral, Political and Literary*, vol. 1. T.H. Green and T.H. Grose, eds., (London, 1882), vol. 1, 480–93.
28 Adair, *Fame and the Founding Fathers*, was the first to note this. Garry Wills, *Explaining America: The Federalist* (Garden City, NY 1981) makes the most of the connection. James Moore, "Hume's Political Science and the Classical Republican Tradition," *Canadian Journal of Political Science* 10, no. 4 (1977): 833–9 discusses the connection. Theodore Draper, "Hume and Madison: The Secrets of Federalism Paper No. 10." *Encounter* 58, no. 2 (February, 1982): 34–7, explores the reluctance to admit a Humean influence.
29 *The Federalist Papers*, no. 10, Rossiter edition (New York, 1961), 81–2. The late Martin Diamond has done most to elucidate the degree to which *The Federalist* is, in fact, democratic: "Democracy and *The Federalist*: A Reconsideration of the Framer's Intent," *American Political Science Review* 53 (1959): 52–68; "The Federalist," in Leo Strauss and Joseph Cropsey, eds., The History of Political Philosophy, 2nd ed. (Chicago, 1972), 631–57; "The Separation of Powers and the Mixed Regime," *Publius* 8, no. 3 (1978): 33–43. Diamond's most vociferous critic is Paul

Eidelberg. *The Philosophy of the American Constitution* (New York, 1968) and *A Discourse on Statesmanship* (Urbana, Ill., 1874), but this reader, for one, does not find Eidelberg's criticisms very compelling. Nor does Paul Peterson, "The Meaning of Republicanism in *The Federalist,*" *Publius* 9, no. 2 (1979): 43–75, who supports Diamond.

30 Gordon S. Wood, *The Creation of the American Republic 1776–1787* (Williamsburg, Va., 1969), 530–1, 603–4: James Wilson, "Lectures on Law," in R. Green McCloskey, ed., *The Works of James Wilson* (Cambridge, Mass., 1967), I, 303; *The Federalist*, No. 22, 152.

31 *The Federalist*, No 10, 83–4; No 52, 324. This idea was later picked up by Lord Durham in his report on the British North American colonies. In recommending the establishment of elective municipal offices, he remarked that the "True principle of limiting popular power is the apportionment of it in many different depositories." *Lord Durham's Report*, Lucas edition vol. 11, (Oxford, 1912), 287.

32 Wood, *The Creation of the American Revolution*, 606, 612; See also J. Pocock, *The Machiavellian Moment* (Princeton, 1957), 519–26.

33 *The Federalist*, No. 15, 111.

34 Tocqueville, *Democracy in America*, 398–433.

35 De l'Esprit des Lois 9, no. 1 in Montesquieu, *Oeuvres complètes*, vol. 11 (Pléiade edition, Paris, 1951), 369; *The Federalist*, No. 9, 73–6; Martin Diamond, "*The Federalist*'s View of Federalism" in G.C.S. Benson, ed., *Essays in Federalism* (Clarement, Calif., 1962), 31–2.

36 J.C. Calhoun, *A Disquisition on Government and Selections from the Discourse*, C.C. Post, ed. (Indianapolis, 1953); James Bryce, *The American Commonwealth* (New York, 3rd ed. 1870) vol. I, 15; P.-J. Proudhon, *The Principle of Federation*, translated by Richard Vernon (Toronto, 1979), 57; Harold Laski, *Studies in the Problem of Sovereignty* (Yale, 1917). Aficionados of Canadian political rhetoric may note that Laski's "community of communities" formulation predated that of a former prime minister by over sixty years.

37 W.H. Bennett, *American Theories of Federalism* (Alabama, 1964), 124. Such an interpretation was strengthened by the amendment procedures which stipulated ratification by three quarters of the state legislatures or by conventions convened by the state governments for that purpose.

38 Roy F. Nichols, "Federalism vs. democracy," in Roscoe Pound *et al.*, *Federalism as a Democratic Process* (New Brunswick, N.J., 1942).

39 This was Richard Hofstadter's famous characterization of Calhoun in *The American Political Tradition* (New York, 1948), 68–92, where tribute was paid to his "arresting defence of reaction, a sort of intellectual Black Mass" (69). On Calhoun's theory more specifically, see Ralph Lerner, "Calhoun's New Science of Politics," *American Political Science Review* 57 (1963): 918–32.

40 Calhoun, *Disquisition*, 100.

41 *Disquisition*, 14, 10–11.

42 *Disquisition*, 23.

43 Lerner, "Calhoun's New Science," points out that in the end, Calhoun can be considered a liberal theorist after all, since he assumes that the only common good is the process of government. There are no ends, only an "agreement to continue the game."

44 *Disquisition*, 36–43.

45 On Proudhon, I have found the best source to be Richard Vernon's introduction to his translation of *The Principle*, ixlvii, and his "Freedom and Corruption: Proudhon's Federal Principle," *Canadian Journal of Political Science* 14, no. 4 (1981): 775–96; this account follows Vernon closely. See also Bernard Voyenne, "Le fédéralisme de Proudhon et ses disciples" in G. Berger, *et al.*, eds., *Le Fédéralisme*, (Paris, 1956), 87–128; and, less usefully, Preston King, *Fear of Power: an Analysis of Anti-Statism in Three French Writers* (London, 1967), 43–68.

46 G. Vedel, "Les grands courants de la pensée politique et le fédéralisme" in Berger *et al.*, *Le Fédéralism*, 50–1; Ralph Nelson, "The Federal Idea in French Political Thought," *Publius* 5, no. 3 (1975): 7–62; Albert Soboul, *The French Revolution 1787–1799*. Vol. 2, *From the Jacobin Dictatorship to Napoleon* (London, 1974), 317–19.

47 Proudhon, *Principle*, 78–81.

48 *Principle*, 7.

49 *Principle*, 28, 61.

50 *Principle*, 62, Vernon, "Freedom and Corruption," 785

51 *Principle*, 74.

52 Vernon, Introduction, xxii–xxiii.

53 Introduction, xxv–xxvi; "Freedom and Corruption," 781–78.

54 "Freedom and Corruption," 781.

55 Felix Morley, *Freedom and Federalism* (Chicago, 1959). Franz Neumann, "Federalism and Freedom: A Critique" in A.W. MacMahon, ed., *Federalism, Mature and Emergent* (N.Y., 1962), is rather uncharacteristically one-dimensional in his attack on the federalist case.

56 Hélène Carrère d'Encausse, *Decline of an Empire: The Soviet Socialist Republics in Revolt* (New York, 1979), 124, and in general, 121–55.

57 "Introduction," S. Tarrow *et al.*, *Territorial Politics in Industrial Nations* (New York, 1978).

58 A contemporary Proudhonian federalist who appears to fall into this romantic category is George Woodcock. See his interventions in Canadian federalist politics: "Political horizons," *Canadian Forum* (April, 1972): 15–47 and *Confederation Betrayed!* (Vancouver, 1981).

59 See Robert A. Dahl and Edward R. Rufte, *Size and Democracy* (Stanford, 1973) for an extended empirical discussion of the relationship between

size and the viability of representative democracy. They conclude that neither the classic city-state nor the modern nation-state ought to be seen as an "optimum" size. "Rather than conceiving of democracy as located in a particular kind of inclusive, sovereign unit, we must learn to conceive of democracy spreading through a series of interrelated political systems, sometimes though not always arranged like Chinese boxes, the smaller nesting in the larger. The central theoretical problem is no longer to find suitable rules, like the majority principle, to apply within a sovereign unit, but to find suitable rules to apply among a variety of units, none of which is sovereign" (135).

60 Dicey, *Introduction*, 141.
61 *Du contrat social*, I: v, 359.
62 *Discourse sur l'origine de l'inégalité*, 187.

CHAPTER SEVEN

Democracy and the Canadian Constitution

This essay, less theoretical than its predecessor, is addressed specifically (and polemically) to the controversy over the Trudeau government's unilateral patriation of the constitution following the defeat of the Quebec referendum on sovereignty-association in 1980. It was published in an important collection of essays on the 1982 Constitution Act titled, significantly enough, *And No One Cheered*.

I was particularly critical of the undemocratic and elitist nature of the BNA Act and of the persistence of these elitist attitudes in the debate over the new constitution in 1980–81. Drawing on the theory of the previous essay I was also insistent that democracy must be redefined in the Canadian context away from the national majoritarianism of more unitary states.

Looking back on this essay from a post-Meech Lake perspective, I think I was right about one very important thing, although perhaps wrong about some others. My stress on the undemocratic nature of the process, as well as the result, of the 1980–81 patriation saga did not find a lot of echoes at the time, but this theme swelled to a popular chorus over the Meech process. The populist demands for democratic control of the constitutional process in the last year of the Meech debate went beyond anything I had anticipated. The Meech fiasco demonstrated decisively that the old ways of elite accommodation are dead and buried. Unfortunately, Meech also showed that no alternative, positive voice of democracy had developed.

This failure to move beyond negativism points to what I now see as an error in my treatment of the so-called democratic aspects of the 1982 process. The Charter of Rights does have some democratic aspects,

Reprinted with permission from Keith Banting and Richard Simeon, eds., *And No One Cheered: Federalism, Democracy and the Constitution Act* (Toronto: Methuen 1983).

especially as it relates to the empowerment of previously subordinated minorities. But the political discourse of rights that has emanated from the subsequent experience of the charter in many ways contributes to a fragmented "constitutional minoritarianism" (to use Alan Cairns's phrase) which may actually undermine rather than strengthen democratic solidarity. In retrospect it is striking that Trudeau's call for amendment by popular referendum generated almost no spontaneous popular endorsement (and was consequently dropped), while the charter turned out to be an effective way to mobilize support for the Liberal package, as groups sought to define and redefine rights in their own image. In short, the people as a collectivity roused little enthusiasm, but the people in their particularity was an effective rallying call. This was all too apparent in the populist cacophony against Meech Lake.

Another mistake: I passed far too lightly over the exclusion of Quebec from the 1982 constitution. This was the real Achilles's heel of 1980–81. Moreover, the very rights discourse generated by the charter encouraged a new liberal-universalist Canadian nationalism which was intolerant of the collective rights of Quebec. Subsequent events, especially the 1988–89 controversy over Quebec's language law, have since convinced me that using the notwithstanding clause to override the charter may in certain instances be a very good thing – as I argue in the last essay in this collection.

Canadians, we are told, are not very interested in the great constitutional debates which have so animated the politicians in recent years. Perhaps. Yet if ordinary Canadians are not much interested in the constitution, it has been equally true that the constitution has not been much interested in Canadians.

The constitution of Canada has been, from 1867 onward, an arrangement between elites, particularly between political elites. Constitutions are normally arrangements between people and their governments. The American constitution, for example, begins: "We, the people, in order to form a more perfect union" and then goes on to regulate the relations between people and the governments they were instituting. The preamble to the constitution of the Fifth French Republic (1958) begins: "The French people solemnly proclaims its attachment to the Rights of Man and the principles of national sovereignty as defined by the Declaration of 1789" and goes on to state that the community shall be based on "equality" and "solidarity," that the republic shall be "democratic," and that "national sovereignty belongs to the people, which shall exercise it through its representatives and by way of referenda." The Basic Law of the Federal Republic of Germany (1949) begins with a preamble indicating that the "German people ... are called upon to achieve in free self-determination the unity and freedom of Germany," and then immediately in the first nineteen articles recognizes "inviolable and inalienable human rights as the basis of every community" and binds the state to "respect and protect" the enumerated basic rights. The British North America Act of 1867 was, as I shall presently show, almost entirely innocent of any recognition of the people as the object of the constitutional exercise.

If we go back further, we find that the seventeenth century social contract theorists such as Hobbes and Locke saw the fundamental basis of government as resting on an arrangement to maintain social peace between the individual members of a community. Canada may be the only country where the primary role of the constitution is to maintain peace between governments rather than between people, or between people and their governments.

The British North America Act ignored individual Canadians, except as they qualified through membership in a church or a language group. The BNA Act was itself never submitted to a popular referendum for ratification, except when Newfoundland was asked if it wanted *in*, and when Quebec was asked if it wanted *out*. But to make matters worse, almost all of the commentary – whether political, judicial, or academic – on the nature and reform of the constitution has tended to ignore the question of the relation of people to government, or of people to each other, in favour of persistent attention to the relation of government to government, or of Crown to Parliament, or of Canada to the British Parliament.

This obsessive orientation has not only had the effect of making constitutional questions appear tedious and irrelevant to most Canadians, but it has contributed to one of the least attractive qualities of Canadian public life – a general level of illiteracy in political philosophy. That a major debate over constitutional revision in the 1970s and early 1980s should take place in apparent ignorance (apart from a few glimmerings from a few participants) of the profound questions of liberty, equality, authority, and obligation, which any significant change in a national constitution must raise, is a sad commentary indeed. The irony is that these questions *are* inevitably involved. Canadians simply tend to sleepwalk their way through while remaining unconscious of the implications of their words and actions.

This is not some peculiar Canadian variant of original sin which we are fated to carry in our genes. It is a product of history and circumstance, and hence open to change. Indeed, there were faint indications in the great constitutional debate of 1980–82 that people are beginning to be included. It is said that a proverbial Irishman, coming upon a donnybrook in progress on a Dublin street, tapped one of the contestants on the shoulder and politely inquired: "Is this a private quarrel, or may anyone join in?" It is about time that the private quarrel of eleven governmental elites was extended to one which anyone can join in. But to do this it is necessary to retrace some of the roots of this mentality with regard not to the legalist language in which it has comprehended itself, but rather in the language of political ideas.

I propose to concentrate on the idea of *democracy*. We are told that we are a democracy. This is supposed to demonstrate our superiority to other systems, which are totalitarian or dictatorial or communist or barbaric – but certainly never democratic. When Paul Henderson scored the winning goal in the last minute of the final game of the first Canada-Russia hockey series, he confessed that he suddenly understood the "meaning of democracy." Lacking that luminous epiphany, the rest of us may still need guidance on the point, especially in Canada.

First of all, "democracy" has been reduced, in the Canadian case, to *representative* democracy; we exercise our sovereignty only to choose our governors. Of course there is an underground or dissenting tradition in this country of direct, populist democracy, evident in the farmer and progressive movements of the early twentieth century and in the extra-parliamentary, direct action, and citizen group activities of the last two decades, to give but two examples. But these have been sporadic and marginal to general practice. The United States has been much more given to such exercises of direct democracy as referenda, with "Proposition Thirteen" simply being a particularly spectacular example of a general tendency rarely followed in Canada. Prime Minister Trudeau, in his earlier, philosophical guise, even raised our practice to the dignity of theory: "at each election ... the people assert their liberty by deciding what government they will consent to obey."[1] Rousseau, two centuries earlier, was more sardonic on the subject of English parliamentary government: "The English people thinks it is free. It greatly deceives itself; it is free only during the election of the Members of Parliament. As soon as they are elected, it is a slave, it is nothing. Given the use made of these brief moments of freedom, the people clearly deserve to lose it."[2] The theory of direct democracy has never been given full constitutional form in a liberal democracy, but some constitutions do recognize some elements of direct democracy, usually in the form of referenda.

Representative democracies formally substitute the national majority for the Rousseauian general will. But even this concept has its limits in a country like Canada. National majoritarianism as the legitimate expression of the popular will, resonant as it is in relatively centralized and unitary states, tends to become weakened and uncertain in a federal context. Obviously a national majority may here represent the enforced supremacy of one province or region over others. As long ago as the 1840s, John C. Calhoun began exploring the dangers of majoritarian democracy to sectional interests in his *A Disquisition on Government.*[3] As a Southerner, Calhoun formulated a theory of "concurrent majorities" to defend against a Northern anti-slave majority. In the event, the North ignored such theory and put the South's peculiar institutions to the torch in the Civil War. At the same time, Calhoun's argument raised another dilemma often associated with sectional defences against national majorities: the argument may actually be on behalf of a sectional majority wishing to deny rights to a sectional minority, in this case slavery of blacks. Suffice to say at this point that the tempering of majoritarianism with federalism introduces deep ambiguities and contradictions into democratic discourse – or at least ambiguities and contradictions peculiar to federal societies.

However complex the problem, it must be recognized that an acceptance of the federal principle does necessarily enforce distinct limitations on democratic theory. Any federal system worthy of the name, by dividing powers between co-ordinate governments and by recognizing or creating sub-national jurisdictions on regional lines (especially where such jurisdictions overlap more or less with distinct regional, ethnic, religious, or linguistic cleavages), has in effect denied the universal efficacy of the national majority as the embodiment of the sovereign democratic will. In the Canadian case, federalism actually meant a more specific limitation on an older, non-democratic principle of sovereignty – the British doctrine of the supremacy of Parliament. By dividing powers between legislative jurisdictions in a written constitution, the BNA Act limited both the supremacy of any Legislature and the scope of national majority will.[4]

We will return later to the special case of federal democracies. But to assess Canada's place as a representative democracy, we will at this stage confine ourselves to a consideration of the principle of universal adult suffrage. By this yardstick, Canada today seems unexceptionable. Virtually all adult citizens can exercise their franchise to choose their governors. Exclusions from the franchise are relatively marginal. In the Canada Elections Act of 1970, all franchise restrictions on citizens eighteen years of age and over have been eliminated, save for convicts, the mentally incompetent, federal judges, and electoral and returning officers. It would be a brave reactionary indeed who would today dare publicly to urge the disenfranchisement of any group of citizens.

This democratic orthodoxy is, however, of comparatively recent origin. Native Indians were first allowed to vote in 1960. Canadians of Japanese origin were enfranchised for federal elections as recently as 1948. It was only in 1940 that the female population of Quebec was permitted to vote in provincial elections. Despite the rhetorical tendency of present-day politicians and commentators to read back into the past current conventional wisdom, Canada's origins have little to do with democracy and a great deal to do with a consciously anti-democratic ideology. Somewhere between the British North America Act of 1867 and the 1914–18 War (when Canadians were exhorted to die to "make the world safe for democracy,") *democracy* as a term of political discourse changed from a bad word to a good word. Such a change in discourse normally indicates an important change in the ideological structure of politics. In the case of Canada, it indicates a transformation in the relationship between citizens from hierarchy to at least formal equality. It also involves a crucial question about the legitimate source of sovereignty in the body politic.

The problem is that we have continued into the late twentieth century with a constitutional framework expressing eighteenth and nineteenth century British notions of sovereignty as derived from the Crown-in-Parliament, combining the three traditional elements of authority: the Crown (monarchy), the Lords (aristocracy), and the Commons (representative democracy). It was believed that a balanced constitution, mixing these three legitimate principles, was the wisest form of statecraft.

The earliest forms of government in the British North American colonies as drawn up by the British Colonial Office reflected a deep British distrust of the democratic potential inherent in American republicanism, a distrust hardened by conflict with the Americans and by the spectacle of a social and political revolution in France in 1789 and the subsequent Napoleonic wars. The influx of loyalist refugees and the determination of the British colonial administrators to build a "better America" as revenge for the loss of the thirteen colonies to the south meant that English Canada began its constitutional history in an atmosphere which could only be described as distinctly anti-democratic. The paternalistic colonial frame-work of authority was always present in the official ideology of loyalty to the British Crown. Within the colonies, the executive was crushingly dominant, backed by appointed officials from the local oligarchies, and not held responsible to the elected assemblies, which were themselves based upon a limited property-holding male franchise. To complete the picture, local strivings for self-government, such as American-style town meetings, were not only discouraged, but sometimes violently repressed. And in Lower Canada, ethnic conflict further deepened elite distrust of man in the mass, in this case involving a French-speaking majority facing an economically and socially privileged English-speaking minority.

The particular conditions of Canada's colonial genesis did much to contribute to a deeply-ingrained anti-democratic strain among the political elites, a strain reinforced by the decisive turn of the Americans towards democracy in the early nineteenth century, the War of 1812, and the American Civil War and its implications for Canadian autonomy. But Canadian elite opinion was only reflective, in a particularly sharp focus, of educated opinion in Britain. Not only was democracy an American and thus un-British aberration, but it was an ideological battle cry increasingly to be associated with the emergent urban proletariat spawned in the "dark satanic mills" of the industrial revolution. Trade unions and radicals challenged the stability of the bourgeois order and England's hegemony in the world economy, based as it was on starvation wages and vast capital accumulation. This image of democracy as a spectre haunting the middle classes led even such a fair-minded and liberal thinker as John Stuart Mill to devise elaborate franchise schemes for containing the potential influence of the lower orders. In this suspicion of democracy, conventional opinion was backed by the full weight of the respectable tradition of political philosophy, all the way back to Aristotle's espousal of the mixed regime as the best possible among imperfect men.

It should be specified that in the Canadian case, there was a kind of special populist twist to this anti-democratic argument. The idea that persons who sold their labour to others or who owned no property were not free and autonomous citizens and thus could not be trusted to exercise the franchise in a responsible fashion was widely accepted. On the other hand, it was a piece of more or less conventional wisdom in colonial Canada that by contrast to Europe, land was cheap and labour dear. The consequence was that propertyless immigrants found it relatively easy to become small farmers. In becoming small farmers, even if heavily indebted to merchants and banks, they were likely to qualify for the property franchise. Thus, the anti-democratic ideology did leave open the possibility that in frontier North America hard work could elevate those from the lower orders to the status of citizens participating in the public realm.

The actual situation in the various colonies before Confederation with regard to the franchise is difficult to summarize. Each colony had different rules; actual statistical information on the proportions of the adult populations that could vote is extremely difficult to come by, and the socio-economic structure of colonial society was itself always changing, thus altering the overall impact of the legal qualifications. It does seem likely, however, that as the century wore on, as the number of poor immigrants increased, and as land was more and more accounted for, the enfranchised proportion of the population actually declined. But this was subject to local variations and is not backed by conclusive empirical evidence.[5]

At the first federal election following Confederation in 1867, about 15 percent on average of the total population of the four original provinces was eligible to vote. By 1882, the last federal election held under variable provincial franchises, this proportion ranged from a low of 11 percent in British Columbia to a high of 35 percent in Manitoba. In 1891, all provinces except British Columbia showed enfranchised populations from one-fifth to one-quarter of the total. By the turn of the century, the progressive enfranchisement of adult males was slowly, but apparently inexorably, proceeding. Yet when the demand for *female* suffrage was raised, there was no shortage of anti-democratic arguments to justify the restriction of the vote to male heads of households who alone disposed of property and thus possessed true citizenship. Finally, however, following the war to "make the world safe for democracy," women were admitted to the franchise, and in the 1921 election the electorate accounted for 50.6 percent of the total population.[6]

This question of the extent of the franchise is a good index of the dominant political theory of the elites. It indicates that throughout the nineteenth century, there was a long ideological rearguard action fought against what Alexis de Tocqueville in the 1830s had described as the "irresistible," "universal," and "providential" rise of equality, a trend which was in his eyes endemic to modernity and impossible to reverse.[7] Moreover, an examination of the political discourse of the elites suggests that until very late in the century it was not even perceived as a rearguard campaign at all. Sir John A. Macdonald appears to have been blandly confident that democracy was just another American aberration, which sound and sensible British institutions would override. Indeed, Sir John – of whom his secretary wrote he had always held repellent the idea that a man should vote just because he breathed – once delivered himself of perhaps the most aphoristic distillation of the conservative anti-democratic view to be found anywhere: "The rights of the minority ought to be protected, and the rich are always fewer in number than the poor."[8] Nor was the Grit opposition to Toryism notable for its democratic sentiment. There was some such sentiment among the *Rouges* of Quebec, although here democratic sentiment can also be read as the nationalism of the French-speaking majority. The Ontario Grits sometimes sounded themes such as the famous "rep by pop" rallying cry, but on examination this had much more to do with asserting the primacy of Protestant English-speaking Ontario over Catholic Quebec, with the method of representation a handy weapon in the struggle. Representation of the "people" was thus distinctly secondary to representation of the interests of particular regional economic groupings, or the interests of particular religious, ethnic or linguistic groupings.

Let us now take stock of the distant relationship between democracy and the constitutional arrangements of 1867. First, the actual language of the British North America Act itself is revealing. Many constitutions use a preamble as a vehicle for discussion of the general political principles of the nation in question. Ours limited itself to noting that the *provinces* have "expressed their desire to be federally united into One Dominion," that such a union "would conduce to the Welfare of the Provinces and promote the Interests of the British Empire," and that it is thus "expedient, not only that the Constitution of the Legislative Authority in the Dominion be provided for, but also that the Nature of the Executive Government therein be declared." No mention of people, only of governments. Thus was set a theme which is carried through the rest of the exercise with only minor deviations.

People did make a first tentative appearance in section 14, where it is stated that, "if Her Majesty thinks fit," the Governor-General might appoint any persons to be his "Deputies," but this was quickly revealed to refer to those who held office. Governments, it appears, are actually composed of persons, but their importance derives from their office alone. This became obvious in the curious discussion of the House of Commons. Section 37 indicated in its original form that 181 members shall be "elected," but apart from an involved discussion of the respective weight of the provinces in the House, and even some detailed instructions on the distribution of seats geographically within provinces, there was little indication of *who* was supposed to elect the representatives of these provincial and geographic areas. Whatever franchise qualifications already existed in the provinces were to be adopted *holus bolus* by the new Dominion government, except for a clause in section 41 which boldly declared that at any election for the District of Algoma, "every Male British Subject, aged twenty-one years or upwards, being a Householder, shall have a Vote."

Section 51 dealt at length with the problem of "readjustment of representation," but solely in terms of balance between provincial contingents. Population changes were to be considered in relation to provincial strength, but such changes bore no relationship to the numbers of actual *voters*. In other words, people counted as components of provincial weight, but not in and of themselves.

Some of the legislative institutions were deliberately designed to be quite undemocratic. The non-elected Senate was to be Macdonald's safeguard for the wealth minority. The property qualifications for a senator were highly specific: 4000 dollars of *net* worth in land and an equal amount in "Real and Personal Property." Given that the average annual income of a fully employed mechanic in the 1870s was about $450 *before* expenditures on food, clothes, and accommodation for his family, it becomes apparent that the Senate certainly deserved its popular attribution as "rich man's club." Just to rub it in, section 31 specifies that if a senator loses his property or becomes bankrupt, he is to be removed.

Another sort of special privilege was written into the constitution with the provision for a second, non-elected chamber, the Legislative Council, in Quebec. Although the reason why Quebec, alone of the provinces, should have been saddled with a second chamber is not spelled out in the BNA Act, it is clear from the context of the debates. The Senate was to protect the wealthy minority, and the Legislative Council was to protect the English Protestant minority of Quebec. That similar councils were not set up to protect, say, the Catholic minority in Ontario speaks volumes about the nature of the bargain struck.

The concern about the Protestants of Quebec also led to one of the closest brushes with recognition of people to be found in the original Act. Section 93 speaks of protection of the "Rights and Privileges" of Catholic and Protestant subjects in education, of appeals to the national government against provincial Acts affecting the educational rights of religious minorities, and of "remedial Laws" to be made by the Parliament of Canada where such rights are judged to have been so affected. Without touching upon the tortuous and troubled history of this section in relation to Manitoba and Ontario, it might simply be noted that this unusual sign of recognition of the rights of citizens was not on the basis of individual citizenship at all, but rather on the basis that individuals had rights only as bearers of a recognized collective identity – in this case membership in a particular church. Similarly, section 133 gave limited recognition to the place of the French as well as the English language in the Legislature, laws and courts of both Canada and Quebec; once again, the singling out of Quebec among provinces indicates that it was actually the anglophones of Quebec who were the main objects of this attention. Once more, individual rights were given indirect and limited recognition through individual membership in a group – English or French speakers.

This brief inventory pretty well exhausts all evidence of apparent interest in the citizens of the new nation on the part of the BNA Act. For the rest, one has to suppose when taxes and revenues are discussed that they are to be derived from citizens, but the major thrust is to specify the fiscal relations between the provinces and the national governments in loving, and sometimes ludicrous, detail, including interest rates on outstanding intergovernmental liabilities fixed at 5 percent, and New Brunswick's right to continue to levy lumber duties.

If the BNA settlement were merely a document drawn up in a language which only inadequately expressed the reality of Canadian political relationships, we might pass over the matter in embarrassed silence. In fact the language of what was our fundamental constitutional document for over a century faithfully reflects the political philosophy of the political elites responsible for Confederation. That no popular ratification of the settlement was ever sought, indeed that any referendum or other such recourse was deliberately avoided, is a clear indication that the sovereignty of the people was a principle consciously rejected by the elites. Sovereignty was to continue in an unbroken chain of tradition in the person of the British monarch, to be exercised through her deputy in Canada with the advice of her ministers and the consent of the Commons and the Senate, and with certain powers further entrusted to Lieutenant-Governors and their provincial advisors: in short, the Crown-in-Parliament in a federal system of co-ordinate spheres of jurisdiction.

This traditional British concept of sovereignty has, to be sure, its own antiquarian charms. Yet even in England this ancient Whig notion has about as much relevance to the real world of today as the pomp of a royal wedding has to Britain's industrial decay. The rise of universal suffrage, political parties organizing the mass electorate, executive domination of policy making, and other familiar aspects of twentieth-century life have emptied the concept of its original content. The Crown is limited to a largely ceremonial role, the Lords do an odd bit of sniping here and there on behalf of corporate interests, and even the Commons is normally subservient to the Cabinet and the higher civil service. These observations are the mere commonplace of current political science. Yet the theoretical implications for the theory of the "sovereignty of Parliament" are too often ignored by romanticists of the British way of life and the Mother of Parliaments. The fact is that the people exercise a kind of sovereignty by choosing every few years which lot of politicians they wish to put in, and which out. Once in, a party governs with an eye to a number of factors – from how their actions are going down with the business community to the public opinion polls. If this form of government should be raised to the dignity of a philosophy of sovereignty, which it perhaps ought not to be, then the best label one can attach to it may be the doctrine of majoritarian populism. The people are assumed to have a will which is expressed through the election of governments with legislative majorities.

The same changes have also taken place in Canada, with the equivalent transformation of the original, borrowed notion of sovereignty enshrined in the BNA Act. Thus, when Sterling Lyon, former premier of Manitoba, spoke with unaccustomed eloquence against the proposed federal Charter of Rights at the constitutional conference of September 1980 by invoking a traditional view of the supremacy of Parliament, he was in fact engaged in a deceptive discourse. Apart from the fact that federalism puts into question *which* Parliament is supreme, thus rendering the idea somewhat irrelevant in the first place, Lyon's words took on a double meaning. Formally, he was speaking of an old, pre-democratic concept of sovereignty; practically, he was engaged in a majoritarian populist argument that the Legislature of Manitoba should have an unimpeded jurisdiction over minorities, limited only by the conscience of the majority. This latter argument is by no means a traditional conservative view; rather, it is a particular kind of democratic argument, although one which many more liberal democrats would reject.

My point here is that when the content of the traditional notion of sovereignty has been transformed by the rise of universal suffrage and the acceptance of formal equality between all citizens, the retention of the trappings of the traditional constitutional structure tends to mystify and confuse the real political issues involved. This is not to suggest that parliamentary government is outmoded or inferior to presidential systems. It is simply to affirm that a lot of rubble has to be moved away to gain a clearer view.

Another aspect of the BNA settlement which has crucial relevance today is its particular concept of nationality. As a federal country with two main ethnic, linguistic, and religious communities, it is now obvious that Canada could never have been a unitary nation such as France or even, perhaps, a relatively centralized federation such as the United States eventually turned out to be after the unpleasantness of a civil war. Yet it is also the case that the highly undemocratic nature of the Confederation settlement reinforced the centrifugal forces already at work. Sir John A. Macdonald and his Tory colleagues wanted a federation *more* centralized than that of the Americans. Whatever the Judicial Committee of the Privy Council later did to stand the division of powers on its head, there can be no serious argument that Macdonald's intention was to do other than to build as centralized a nation as was practicable. The award of all the important economic powers and all the important sources of revenue to the national government, the powers of reservation and disallowance, the declaratory power, and numerous other aspects of the BNA Act establish this tendency.

It is an old chestnut of examinations in introductory courses in Canadian politics to ask why a constitution, which on the surface is so centralized as to lead some students of federalism to deny that Canada can even be called a federation, has resulted in perhaps the most decentralized federation in the world, rivalled only by Switzerland. I do not want to go over the standard historical answers to this question. I do want to suggest, however, that the concept of building a national state was a peculiar and peculiarly limited one, and that some of its limitations are connected to its undemocratic nature.

Nation-building rested on two main foundations: formally, on the concentration of economic powers and fiscal resources at the national level along with the federal mission to colonize the prairies and integrate them into the national structures; informally, on the putative attraction of the various elites to accommodate each other on the prospect of mutual economic benefit. The relationship between the CPR, the Conservative party, and westward expansion is highly illustrative of the political economy of a centralized federalism. The limitation of this lies precisely in its reliance on elites and on their exclusively economic motives. Even a federation – perhaps *especially* a federation – needs some mass attachment of an emotional or sentimental nature to the national level. A functioning federal state must strike some stable balance between regional, provincial, or subcultural identities, and an identity of citizens *qua* citizens with their national state. The recognition of the principle of the sovereignty of the people is a way of encouraging such attachment over more limited identities.

The Americans began with the notion of "we the people," and certainly this deeply-held belief in popular sovereignty has been associated with that powerful sense of American nationalism which has long since overridden sectional loyalties. Few Canadians perhaps would want to emulate that example, with its attendant intolerance of "un-American activities," its expansionary aggressiveness, and its self-righteous evangelism. Nor is it at all likely that even the best will in the world could ever have sponsored a replica of American-style populist nationalism in the hostile conditions of British North America. What is not open to question is that the distinctly undemocratic nature of Confederation did nothing to encourage a potential sense of mass nationalism, and perhaps did much to discourage it. Certainly provinces, regions, and above all, linguistic-cultural communities became the most persuasive centres of sentimental attraction, *faute de mieux*. Worse yet, the seating of sovereignty in the British monarchy and the powerful emotional attachment to Britain and the Empire, which had always been so strongly encouraged in English-speaking Canada, was increasingly viewed in French Canada as a device for symbolically reinforcing anglophone Protestant hegemony over Catholic French-speaking Canada. The monarchy was thus at one and the same time a unifying symbol to one community and a divisive one to the other. On the other hand, the recognition and endorsement of differences has always been at the root of French Canada's demands on the national political system. It is hence a uniquely Canadian achievement to possess a symbol of unity which divides, and a division which unites. In neither case, however, is there any real sense of a sovereign Canadian people.

The burden placed on economic nationalism as a focus for attraction to the national government revealed a crucial weakness: economic relationships change with technological changes and transformations in production. In Canada this has meant that Macdonald's dream of national unity based on a national bourgeoisie and national political elite bound to the nation by fundamental economic interests has attenuated over the twentieth century as changing economic interests have drawn elites into attachments to provinces, regions, and even to north-south continentalist links with American capital and the American state.

All this is an historical parallel with the circumstances in which the federal government's constitutional initiatives of 1980–81 were brought forward. Coupled with the major economic initiative of the

National Energy Program and a renewed interest in regaining national fiscal capacity and autonomy in federal-provincial economic relations, the constitutional proposals suggested concerted and purposive moves on the part of the federal government on a series of fronts, the like of which has not been seen for some time. In effect, the Liberal Party – shut out of office in every single province, and with only one provincial member elected in the four Western provincial Legislatures – had perforce taken on the nationalist mantle of Macdonald's nineteenth century Tories at the national level. The defeat of the Parti Québécois' sovereignty option in the Quebec referendum of 1980 and the inability of the premiers in the same year to agree upon a constitutional formula for renewed federalism gave the Trudeau Liberals the historic opportunity to act unilaterally. And they seized the opportunity with the same determination which has characterized their attempted re-assertion of federal dominance over energy policy and fiscal federalism. In Trudeau's vehement rejection of Joe Clark's "community of communities," his passionate assertion that Canada is "more than the sum of its parts," and his government's national initiatives since its re-election in 1980, one can discern the elements of a new National Policy in the late twentieth century.

How does the constitutional reform fit into this renewed assertion of federal domination? In part – and it is this part which is relevant to our concerns – it does reflect a dawning, if imperfect understanding of the connection between the relatively low level of legitimacy of the national government and the weak constitutional basis for popular sovereignty in the BNA Act and in our constitutional practices since 1867.

The most controversial aspect of the initiative taken by the federal government in the fall of 1980 was its unilateralism, its assertion that a joint address to the British government by a simple majority in Parliament, with or without substantial provincial support, would suffice to create a new constitution. Much of the criticism of the method rested on the grounds of the violation of liberal procedural justice, a source of criticism to which Pierre Trudeau ought to have been especially sensitive given his philosophical convictions. Yet the government never argued that it was a *good* method, merely that it was a *necessary* one, all other avenues having been exhausted. Finally, when the Supreme Court handed down its judgement of Solomon on the matter, thereby sending all parties back to the bargaining table, the final compromise reached in November of 1981 indicated that perhaps unilateral patriation had always been more of a bargaining position than a final strategy in itself.

Whatever the Liberal government's motives and intentions, it is worth examining the opposition to unilateralism. This arose partly from traditionalism. In part, the provinces – including, no doubt, a substantial number of people as well as governments – saw the federal government as fundamentally unrepresentative of regional opinion, especially in the West, where the Liberals have very little support. This certainly weakened the legitimacy of a national government based on a national plurality of votes heavily skewed towards central and eastern Canada acting unilaterally on a matter so fundamental as constitutional revision. A question of concurrent majorities in a federal society is inescapable under the circumstances. On the other hand, the fact that the same forces bitterly opposed to unilateralism tended to be equally bitterly opposed to a popular referendum on the constitution raises another question of motives. Even a minority of the New Democratic Party, as well as some left-wing political observers,[9] argued that the proposed method was *undemocratic*. This calls for some discussion.

The argument that the bypassing of provincial government consent was undemocratic involves a curious definition of democracy. The consent of the governed is transposed to the consent of governments. This is squarely within the Canadian tradition, but seems of doubtful relevance to questions of democracy. Unilateral patriation *was* undemocratic, but so has been every other amendment of the BNA Act inasmuch as only governments, never people, have been consulted. And so was the final compromise, applauded by most of those who had fought unilateralism. The agreement hammered out in the kitchen of the conference centre was made by Messrs. Chrétien, Romanow, and McMurtry, not by the people of Canada, who have not even been asked to ratify the agreement through any form of popular consultation. Finally, it must be said that there were some significant aspects of the proposed constitutional package which did recognize at least some elements of popular sovereignty. The federal and provincial oppositions sometimes ignored, but in many cases positively opposed, those elements, and in the end they succeeded in eradicating most of them. A strange victory, this.

Before examining each of the democratic elements of the constitutional proposals in turn, I should like to begin with an alternative model of democratic federalism to clarify the contrasts with the existing system. I assume a federal *society*, that is, one in which provincial diversity is not merely the reflection of provincial governmental activity and interest, but results from regional economic, cultural, and linguistic bases which would persist in some form or other whatever the constitutional superstructure. National and provincial governments are co-ordinate, with their own spheres of jurisdiction. The main difference between the two types of government, apart from the specific allocation of powers and resources between them, would in my model rest on the two different electorates. The provincial mandate awarded to a party victorious in a provincial election would be the symbol of the sovereignty of the people of that province, just as the national mandate would be the symbol of the sovereignty of the Canadian people as a whole. Both would be equally legitimate within their respective spheres, and both equally illegitimate when extended unilaterally into the other sphere.

Two implications follow from this. First, it is clear that a constitutional framework must, of course, order the specific division of powers and thus act as the final recourse over jurisdictional disputes. Here the familiar apparatus of federal-provincial conferences and judicial review of constitutionality will continue to be operative in much the same way as always. At the same time, however, the constitution should concern itself at least as much with the relations between citizens and the state. Here the framework must be national, universally applicable to all citizens, and concerned with relations with all governments, national or provincial. A clearly specified set of rights and obligations of citizens will act as a guide to legislators at all levels, but in the final analysis the courts alone can be the final judge, as they are already with the division of powers between the governments. This does not involve the intervention of the national government *qua* government in the sphere of provincial jurisdiction, but merely the subjection of all governments to common standards of behaviour *vis-à-vis* their citizens and a common recourse for citizens against the actions of any government.

A second implication is that the national government is not a "government of governments," but a government of citizens. That is to say, it should be representative of the national electorate of a federal society. It should seek to maximize its *direct* representativeness of the constituent elements of this electorate through whatever institutional devices appear appropriate (proportional representation, a regionally representative second chamber, decentralized administration are some ideas). But it should minimize the interposition of provincial governments as "representatives" of provincial or regional citizens. Intergovernmental relations will continue on matters of federal-provincial concern, but within their own spheres governments should be in direct relationship with citizens only.

Some provincial proposals for constitutional change have been in direct conflict with the model. The Parti Québécois' White Paper on sovereignty-association suggested a transfer of powers from the federal government to a series of non-elected commissions and other bodies which would be responsible not to electorates, but to governments. The Quebec Liberal Party's Beige Paper on renewed federalism recommended a second chamber in Ottawa replacing the Senate, with members appointed by the provincial governments. This latter suggestion, echoed with variations by some other provinces, would not only substitute governments for people, but would also introduce a radical asymmetry into federalism since no equivalent intrusion of federal government representatives into the institutions of provincial government has been contemplated.

There were three elements of the federal constitutional proposals which could be cited as democratic, by contrast with the views of the provincial governments, or by contrast with some of the federal opposition as well. Two of these are in the text itself, and one in the process whereby the proposal was arrived at.

First was the Charter of Rights and Freedoms. Quite apart from liberal arguments for guaranteeing individual rights, especially against administrative and judicial abuses, an entrenched Charter performs a basic democratic function of regulating relations between governments and citizens which was never performed by the BNA Act. That it does so by clearly and decisively enunciating the equality of all citizens in their rights and freedoms is a major step forward. Section 3 of the new Charter at least spells out that "every citizen of Canada has the right to vote in an election of members of the House of Commons or of a legislative assembly and to be qualified for membership therein." Even if this actually will not change anything, it at least gives a constitutional sanction to the fundamentally democratic nature of the Canadian political system.

Prime Minister Trudeau has for some time been an advocate of such a Charter, on traditional liberal grounds, of course, but as well on grounds specific to Canadian federalism – that a federally-guaranteed Charter of Rights offers a protection for individual Canadians which would tend to bind them directly to the national government, thus counteracting to some degree the centrifugal attractions of provincialism. This is equally true of his 1960s strategy for federal bilingualism to draw francophones to Ottawa as well as Quebec City, of his government's promotion of multiculturalism, and of his argument that minority language rights are best protected by federal guarantees to individuals. This is why he had opposed provincial suggestions that provinces be allowed to "opt out" of the Charter. It would, after all, utterly undermine the concept of a national guarantee of individual rights of citizens if some citizens

could have their protections waived by their provincial governments. Or so the prime minister argued – until the last moment.

The Charter does seem to command wide support among Canadians. A Gallup poll in the spring of 1981 indicated that 62 percent
agreed that a Charter of Rights should be included in the patriation
plan, with only 15 percent opposed. Support was pretty uniform
across all regions.[10] Such support may, in part at least, reflect
another democratic aspect of the constitutional debate, this time
having to do with process. The televised and widely-reported
hearings of the Special Joint Committee of the Senate and House of
Commons attracted wide attention from various Canadian citizens
and groups who testified, particularly on the Charter. Very extensive revisions were made, incorporating many of the suggestions
concerning weaknesses and omissions from the initial draft. This
popular consultation of a government with its citizens could be
widely appreciated – in contrast to the views of the Progressive
Conservatives in Parliament, who had bitterly opposed the closure
of parliamentary debate and the referral to the committee as the
"death of democracy." Why the consultation of people by the
politicians should be considered undemocratic in contrast to debate
among politicians is a question best left to opposition MPs.

One might also ask some questions about the result of the
discussion over rights. While clearly identifiable groups – women,
native people, handicapped persons, cultural minorities – are given
various forms of recognition, the Charter is quite deficient in what
might be termed *social* rights. A number of European constitutions
drawn up with the participation of socialist and Communist representatives at the end of the war (Italy and the Fourth French Republic being the best examples) induced such constitutional provisions as the right to strike and the right to a job, or the right of
workers to participate in the decisions affecting the conditions in
which they work. These social rights are notably absent from the
text and even from the discussions and debates, within Parliament
and without. That the Charter should reflect an image of liberal
rather than social democracy is not particularly surprising given the
structure of Canadian society, and the philosophical make-up of the
governing party. What is rather more surprising is that the New
Democratic Party, despite its vaunted alliance with the Liberals over
the constitution, failed to force, or even to demand, any such
concessions from their allies. Nor was it on these grounds that the
Saskatchewan rebels broke ranks with the NDP caucus. The Canadian Labour Congress remained virtually silent during the debate,
in part for fear of alienating its nationalist-minded Quebec wing.

The NDP did win a negative concession when the entrenchment of property rights was withdrawn in the face of an NDP fear that such a provision could enable judges to prevent federal or provincial governments from nationalizing private corporations. On the whole, however, and even to the NDP and the CLC, democracy in Canada seems pretty well defined by liberal limits.

The final point to be pursued in this connection, and the one which had perhaps been most hotly contested by the premiers and other opponents, was the device of the referendum to amend the constitution. Carefully employing the same amending formula for provincial government approval (Ontario, Quebec, two Western and two Atlantic provinces) the referendum avoided the anti-federal dangers of majoritarian democracy, but for the first time instituted a recourse to direct popular consultation, something which had, as we have seen, been rigorously excluded from the original constitution-making process.

It is striking that it was this provision which drew the sharpest fire of the leader of the opposition and the premiers. The idea that provincial governments could be bypassed for direct consultation with the people was treated as almost an unthinkable suggestion contrary to our constitutional traditions. There is no doubt that it *is* contrary to our constitutional traditions. The point is that not all traditions are worth cherishing, and in this case there is an excellent case for dispensing with it. The case has been made best by the prime minister in a speech to law students at Osgoode Hall:

Right now, alas, the fount of our sovereignty lies in the United Kingdom. When it comes home where will the fount of sovereignty lie? Will it be an assembly of 11 first ministers as Mr. Peckford claims, as I'm afraid Mr. Blakeney claims too? Or will it be the people of Canada? And if you are a democrat it seems to me the answer is clear. It is not the institutional leaders elected at a point of time. It is the people of Canada and, if the people of Canada are not prepared to assume that burden and duty of speaking their will over the heads of their elected premiers and prime minister, then I say they are not a nation.[11]

The tradition opposed to this is that politics is an affair for governments and politicians alone, a Canadian tradition perhaps, but not a very admirable one, not one that has done much to strengthen popular support for and attachment to the Canadian nation.

That the referendum procedure and machinery would have rested in the hands of the federal government was, in my view, entirely appropriate, as it is the only government that represents all Canadian citizens. Provincial fears that this would, somehow, have allowed the federal government to manipulate impressionable citizens were exaggerated to say the least. First, if elections are merely manipulation, then the provincial premiers owe *their* alleged right to monopolize the expression of provincial opinion to their ability to manipulate their voters in provincial elections. Secondly, the idea that voters can be browbeaten by clever manipulation of the referendum questions shows a deep contempt for voters – one which is not borne out by the result of the Quebec referendum on sovereignty when the Parti Québécois' own convoluted and ambiguous question was rejected by 60 percent of the voters. Nor is it borne out by the experience of the federations of Switzerland and Australia, which employ popular referenda as a means of amending their constitutions and have discovered that voters are generally very conservative about change and often tend to vote contrary to the desires of their national governments.

There was one glaring weakness in the Liberal government's espousal of the referendum device as an amending procedure, in fact the Achilles heel of the whole process. If Trudeau really had had the courage of his democratic convictions, the entire constitutional proposal should have been submitted to a national referendum, to be counted on the same regional basis as the original amending formula. Despite the Supreme Court ruling, if such a referendum had been passed by the concurrent popular majorities of all regions, any possible obstinacy or interference in Westminster would have been rendered wholly illegitimate and would have constituted nothing less than the gravest of insults to the Canadian people.[12] To be sure, such a course of action might have involved considerable risks; one or more regions might have voted "no," and the package would have sunk. To assess the extent of the risk involved, however, we must consider the compromise text which actually emerged from the final federal-provincial First Ministers' Conference.

It is hard to escape the conclusion that the final text reflects more concessions on the part of the federal government than on the part of the provinces, Quebec being the exception in all cases. From my present point of view, it is most striking that it was the democratic elements of the federal proposal which were bargained away. Although the prime minister did at one point suggest submitting two versions to the voters in a referendum – an option which gained momentary support from Quebec Premier René Lévesque – he just as quickly dropped it in face of unanimous disapproval from the English-Canadian premiers. There followed a compromise which, among other matters, included: (1) carving out some of the provisions of the Charter of Rights and then subjecting most of the remaining provisions to a legislative override, whereby Parliament or the provincial Legislatures might legislate "notwithstanding" the provisions of the Charter; (2) excising all references to referendum procedures for amendment; and (3) substituting a new formula for provincial ratification of amendments. Each of these will be examined in turn.

The *non obstante* or override clause is a compromise which raises considerable question whether Canadians actually will have an entrenched Charter of Rights at all. At best it is a quintessentially and uniquely Canadian device which in effect says we have entrenched rights if necessary, but not necessarily entrenched rights. The override is admittedly hedged with checks, and much is left, in effect, to public opinion to prevent Legislatures from using the power. The effects are therefore not all that easy to predict. Moreover, "democratic," "mobility," "language," and "educational" rights *are* entrenched, without potential override. "Democratic" rights, however, include no more than a statement that every citizen has a right to vote in federal and provincial elections, and provisions for the number of sittings and terms of the Legislatures. The "fundamental freedoms," "legal rights," and "equality rights" are all subject to legislative override. To the extent that the override is used, we will have witnessed a triumph of the Canadian tradition of elitism – governments over people. Even if it is sparingly employed, it constitutes a kind of potential constitutional denial of individual rights.

This contrast of perspectives was dramatically highlighted when the ten consenting first ministers (without exception male and white) cynically decided to jettison native rights and some important aspects of sexual equality from the Charter. In this case the spectacle was too much, even for Canadians. There followed one of the most extraordinary exercises of direct, spontaneous democratic pressure on governments that has ever been seen in this country. The campaign by women on both levels of government was partially successful, that of native groups less so. But here at least was ample evidence that elected politicians cannot and ought not be allowed to arrogate to themselves the exclusive right to speak in the name of the people, that a functioning representative democracy requires constant pressure by citizens directly if it is to remain truly representative. The point was brought home forcefully when Sterling Lyon, perhaps the strongest opponent of an entrenched Charter of Rights, was unceremoniously defeated by the voters of Manitoba within a week of arranging the Accord emasculating the Charter.

Yet the new constitution allows precious little scope for popular participation. The removal of the referendum procedure for amendment means that there will never be in the future any popular consultations for change. At most one might envisage one level of government calling an "advisory" referendum to make a point against the other level on a dead-locked attempt at change. But this would have no formal authority. Again, Canadian tradition has been vindicated – at the expense of democratic sovereignty.

Finally, something should be said about the new amending formula itself. The Trudeau proposals had recognized a *regional* basis for what were, in effect, concurrent majorities necessary for any constitutional change. Partly out of western indignation that Ontario should get a veto, the opposing premiers finally agreed upon a counter-proposal for amendment by two-thirds of the provinces representing at least 50 percent of the population. For reasons which remain obscure, Premier Lévesque agreed with this proposal, which withdrew Quebec's veto. When Trudeau finally agreed to accept the counter-proposal in the final agreement, Lévesque cited the denial of a Quebec veto as a major reason for refusing to sign the Accord. Exasperation at Lévesque's bargaining tactics ought not blind one to the dangerous implications of the loss of a Quebec veto. Given the binational character of Canada, and given the central role of Quebec in French Canada (Trudeau himself has described Quebec as *"le foyer et le centre de gravité de la nation canadienne-française"*), it is a direct challenge to the very essence of any notion of democratic federalism to deny Quebec a veto and thus potentially subject Quebec to a national majority will repugnant to it. To be sure, there are now "opting out" provisions for provinces which do not like a constitutional amendment approved by seven of their sister provinces; and in the case of changes touching on educational and cultural matters, fiscal equivalents will be granted to any province exercising this right. This clearly constitutes a tacit recognition of Quebec's "special status." In addition, contrary to some Quebec critics, the new constitution does recognize Canada's cultural duality in terms of the entrenched language and education rights – a duality of *individuals* as members of linguistic groups, although certainly not a duality of *states* as between Canada and Quebec. Having said all that, the fact remains that a constitution which does not recognize a concurrent majority in Quebec is a constitution which leaves a festering wound in the Canadian body politic.

One improvement which the final agreement did make over the federal text had to do with the Senate. Despite the democratic tendencies in the Liberal proposals, they had rather cynically agreed to offer the Senate a veto over changes to its character in order to smooth passage of the Resolution through that chamber. The Senate, that apotheosis of all that is undemocratic in our past, was not only spared change in the constitutional revision, but was to have its status further strengthened. Giving the senators a veto over Senate reform was the equivalent of putting alcoholics in charge of a detoxification centre. Happily, this' vicious provision was dropped, given the interest of several premiers in major Senate reform. In the event, the senators did not dare restore the claude, perhaps sensing their lack of popular legitimacy.

Virtually all the recent proposals for a reconstituted second chamber have turned on the need for regional representation, given the growing unrepresentativeness of the national government when no political party can command support in all regions. That the Liberals can govern on the basis of a majority in Quebec and Ontario while excluded from the West reflects a serious deficiency, and one which could be partially alleviated by a second chamber with particular responsibilities for the federal-provincial questions. The idea of such a chamber being appointed by the provincial governments is not only undemocratic, but subversive of the national government's exclusive sphere of jurisdiction as well. More appropriate is direct regional representation within the national structures of government. One intriguing possibility here would be an *elected* Senate, chosen on a basis of provincial or regional equality as in the American case. Such a Senate could be elected on a basis of proportional representation, leaving the Commons as a constituency system. Party representation would be more reflective of actual popular support, meaning that a few Liberals would come from Alberta and a few Progressive Conservatives from Quebec. Thus, in the two Houses of Parliament the two kinds of representative principle appropriate to a democratic federation could be harnessed together: the national majority in the Commons and the concurrent, provincial majorities in the Senate. A recent national survey by the Canada West Foundation shows that almost two-third of Canadians would favour an elected Senate, and that less than one in three preferred the present Senate.[13] This may very well be one of the priorities for change now that the new constitution is in place.

In conclusion, the balance-sheet on the democratic basis of the new constitution is mixed to poor. The original federal proposals fell far short of an ideal democratic federal constitution, but at almost every point of difference with the BNA Act they must be judged as being more democratic. That it would be genuinely difficult to imagine them as less democratic is itself quite a comment on our constitutional history. Yet the premiers and the Progressive Conservative opposition in Ottawa revealed in the course of the debate apparent views about the sovereignty of the people which accord poorly indeed with that ritual rhetoric about "democracy" so familiar to political discourse. In the final crunch, with the encouragement of the Supreme Court, the Liberals compromised away most of the democratic content in order to get an agreement (*any* agreement?). Canadian traditions were preserved.

Of course, there are many other equally legitimate ways of judging the process of constitutional change. This way has the virtue of helping illuminate some of the unstated assumptions of political philosophy held by participants in the debate. The picture thus revealed is perhaps not all that flattering.

NOTES

1 Pierre Trudeau, *Approaches to Politics* (Toronto: Oxford University Press, 1970), 77.
2 Jean-Jacques Rousseau, *The Social Contract* (London: J.M. Dent, 1973), Book 3, chapter 15.
3 (New York: Poli Sci Classics, 1947).
4 I have explored these questions at greater length in "Federalism and Democratic Theory," paper presented to the Canadian Political Science Association, 7 June 1982.
5 F. John Garner, *Franchise and Politics in British North America 1755–1867* (Toronto: University of Toronto Press, 1968); Fernand Ouellet, *Lower Canada 1791–1840*, tr. Patricia Claxton (Toronto: McClelland and Stewart, 1980), 24–6.
6 Norman Ward, *The Canadian House of Commons: Representation* (Toronto: University of Toronto Press, 1950), 211–32; Gregory S. Kealey, *Toronto Workers Respond to Industrial Capitalism 1867–1892* (Toronto: University of Toronto Press, 1980), 330, 267–8n.
7 *Democracy in America*, ed. J.P. Mayer and Max Lerner, tr. George Lawrence (New York: Harper & Row, 1966), Vol. 1, Introduction.
8 Quoted in Bruce Hodgins, "Democracy and the Ontario Fathers of Confederation," in Ontario Historical Society, *Profiles of a Province* (Toronto: Ontario Historical Society, 1967), 88.
9 For examples of such left-wing criticism, see John Richards, "Populism: A Qualified Defence," *Studies in Political Economy* 5 (Spring, 1981): 23–5, and Norman Penner, "The Left and the Constitution," *Canadian Forum*

(June–July, 1981): 10–13. Similar criticisms were raised by dissenting delegates to the NDP's national convention, July 1981.

10 Canadian Institute of Public Opinion, *The Gallup Report*, 13 May 1981.

11 Quoted in the *Toronto Globe and Mail*, 6 February 1981, 10.

12 Edward McWhinney makes this democratic argument strongly in *Canada and the Constitution 1979–1982* (Toronto: University of Toronto Press, 1982), ix-x, 102–14.

13 *Toronto Globe and Mail*, 31 December 1981, 9.

PART FOUR

Democracy and Community

CHAPTER EIGHT

Federalism, Democracy, and the Canadian Political Community

This, as well as the subsequent essay, shifts away from political theory toward political practices and away from federalism as such toward relations between state and society. It was written for a volume which addressed the question of political and economic integration, both within Canada and in the wider international context. I argue that the social forces making for accommodation that underlay the crisis-laden appearance of Canadian politics may prove stronger than the divisiveness of the political elites. This was a very optimistic article, published just as the Liberals went out of office and the Mulroney Tories came into office with majorities in every province, including Quebec, and trumpeted a new era of co-operative federalism. I am afraid that I would now be much more pessimistic.

Was my analysis in 1984 wrong? I think not. Indeed, I would stand firmly behind some of the main points I made in this essay. The dialectic of territory and function that I pointed out seems to me to be a significant analytical tool for understanding the dynamics of integration-disintegration. Moreover the synthesis I suggested of political economy and neo-institutionalism has, I think, stood the test of time. What has changed the prognosis away from the optimistic tone of 1984 is the effect of the politics and policies of the Tory era. A neo-conservative government dedicated to enhancing the power of corporate capital by degrading the public sector has gone a long way toward delegitimating the national government. The advent of Free Trade in 1989 has, I believe, gravely weakened the east-west economic linkages and done considerable damage to the will and capacity of the constituent parts of the country to hold together. This

Reprinted with permission from J. Pammett and B. Tomlin, eds., *The Integration Question* (Toronto: Addison-Wesley 1984).

234 Democracy and Community

deterioration was depressingly demonstrated in the debacle of Meech Lake, which has driven Quebec far from the rest of Canada. Of course, it would be a partisan exaggeration to suggest that continentalization started in 1989. Free Trade was a culmination of one track of Canadian development which has been with us since the very beginning. Nevertheless the Free Trade Agreement has decisively, perhaps irreversibly, set the seal on the victory of the north-south axis. The implications of this for the very question of integration at which this essay was directed are profound.

Yet even if the optimism of this essay may seem dated, it does point to some enduring strengths of the federation that can be too easily forgotten in the more threatening climate of the 1990s. Although new political forms and new definitions of sovereignty may have to be devised in the future, the pregnant implications of the quotation from Northrop Frye with which I begin the essay should be pondered seriously. As William Morris craftily implied a century ago, *News From Nowhere* may signify more than meets the eye.

One of the derivations proposed for the word Canada is a Portuguese phrase meaning "nobody here." The etymology of the word Utopia is very similar, and perhaps the real Canada is an ideal with nobody in it. The Canada to which we really do owe loyalty is the Canada we have failed to create.
                                              – Northrop Frye, *The Modern Century* (1967)

The halls of academe have been echoing in the past twenty years with cries of alarm and despair over the fate of Canada: *Lament for a Nation, Divided Loyalties, The Roots of Disunity, Unfulfilled Union, Canada in Question* (now in its third edition!), *Quebec in Question, Bleeding Hearts ... Bleeding Country, Confederation Challenged, Confederation Betrayed!* When three academics recently wrote a history of postwar Canada that began with the statement "Canadian history is a success story," some reviewers were scandalized.[1]

Of course, this despairing tone is not confined to Canadian writers. American political scientists and sociologists have turned to generating books on *The Irony of American Democracy*, and Britons now read about *The Breakup of Britain* or ask themselves *Is Britain Dying?* What is unique to Canada is the particular emphasis on separatism, regionalism and other territorial threats to national unity, which the 1970s have brought to the fore. If the international crisis of capitalism has generated Reaganism and Thatcherism in the US and Britain, and socialist nationalism in France and Greece, it has in this country only given further point to the old joke about the essay contest on the "elephant" among children from different countries – to which the Canadian can only respond by writing "The elephant: a federal or provincial responsibility?" As a concession to Canadian duality, I should point out a Quebec variant of this joke: an international school class is given blank sheets and told to write about anything that interests them. The American child writes about making money, the German about making war, the Italian about making love, the French about making dinner – the Québécois draws up a draft constitution.

I wish to examine this question of the relation between national unity and regional disintegration in a historical context, so as to place the current "crisis" in relief against the time dimension. Integration is more generally seen as a spatial problem; the temporal dimension makes the *spatial* conjuncture more meaningful – and perhaps rather less alarming.

Before entering into a historical analysis, there is one important theoretical distinction I would like to make. There are basically two ways of organizing political power in a representative system of government: power may be based upon *territory*, or upon *function*. Early Western political theory emphasized function alone (Plato, Aristotle) but this was merely a reflection of the historically limited phenomenon of the *polis*, soon to disappear. Since the Greeks, the spatial or territorial organization of political representation has been predominant, at least at the formal level. Whether in the form of the single-member constituency or in a federal form that institutionalizes territorial power around provincial or regional governments, liberal democracies have constitutionally favored territory over function. The realities of the political process, however, have been quite another matter. The emergence of clearly class-based political parties early in the twentieth century seemed to many observers by the 1950s and 1960s to signal the decline and fall of the territorial principle. These predictions have proven quite unfounded. Yet, as Sidney Tarrow has recently argued, the trick is to avoid seeing these two principles as polar oppositions (in the Aristotelian sense) and to see them as interrelated: "Functional interests thus range themselves around both poles of the political system – centre and periphery – and use their territorial leverage to fight out their conflicts of interest."[2]

The historical oscillations of centralization-decentralization, and the ever-changing relationship between integration-peripheralization, which have characterized Canadian developments, must be seen in this light. Political integration in the form of "national unity" and cultural regionalism in the form of "provincial rights" may signify both less, and more, than meets the eye. Less, because they are themselves ideological constructs or vehicles of political rhetoric. More, because they serve to mask shifting alliances of functional interests coalescing around territorial poles.

It is well known that the intention of a number of the leading framers of the British North America Act, and of Sir John A. Macdonald in particular, was to create as close an approximation of a unified, centralist state as was possible in the conditions of British North America. Indeed, Macdonald looked confidently forward to the disappearance of localism and sectionalism as the new nation "stiffened in the mould."[3] In hindsight, the remarkable aspect of this prediction is not that it failed to come about, but rather that it could ever have been made. It bespoke a one-dimensional vision of *homo oeconomicus*, a vision that even in its own terms proved defective.

Consider the elements that went into the Confederation settlement. Here was the antithesis of what happened in the drawing up of the American Constitution. Without a break from the past in a revolution, Confederation was simply another stage of evolution in continuity with the past, and in continuity with the British Empire. But this continuity was more than an external form. It defined and encompassed the political theory of Confederation. There was no shift of sovereignty from Britain to Canada, neither in the formal sense of state sovereignty, nor in the pregnant political sense of a shift of sovereign power to the *people* of Canada. Thus the new Confederation lacked the formal and informal attributes of nationality.

Much has been made of the ideological background in English Canada, especially by the Hartzian school.[4] Whether or not one chooses to view the pre-Confederation political culture of English Canada as a tory fragment, a liberal fragment, a liberal fragment admixed with a "tory touch" or some other arcane mixture of flavors, may, in one sense at least, be irrelevant. Tory or liberal or whatever, English Canada was dominated by a hegemonic ideology of loyalism – by which I mean something much broader than the narrowly defined tradition of United Empire loyalism. Both Tories and Reformers could protest their equal loyalty to King and Country, even if the Tories wrapped themselves more effectively in the Union Jack.[5] Loyalism is a culturally sterile ideology, whose greatest success is to boast of letter-perfect imitation. From nineteenth century Canada to Protestant Ulster, loyalism has been a quintessentially anti-intellectual ideology, bleakly discouraging original thought by the ritual reiteration of borrowed symbols. It is only at those moments when the Motherland shows signs of flagging Imperial solicitude that loyalism is sometimes forced into short bursts of irritated innovation (as did happen from time to time in the course of

Britain's disengagement from Empire). Northrop Frye's "garrison mentalities," spread out across a thin line of spatial settlement, were an early, persistent, and monotonous feature of the Canadian cultural and ideological landscape.[6] This offered little positive material indeed for a new national cultural identity or for developing a nationalist ideology that, as could be seen in the United States in the early nineteenth century, might be a real, material force in national development. Nor was there in Canada the spirit of innovative political inquiry exemplified in *The Federalist*.

Another aspect of the loyalist creed was its distinctly *antidemocratic* cast. Tories and post-1837 Reformers found a largely shared value in distrust of man in the mass and a determination to evolve political structures that effectively excluded the principle of "one-man, one-vote" (not to speak of women) and sought artfully, or sometimes brutally, to limit the participation of the many in the affairs of state. The BNA Act not only refuses to follow American practice by authorizing itself in the voice of "we the people," but goes on to virtually ignore the existence of people throughout the rest of the text, contenting itself with regulating, not the relations between people and government, but the relations between governmental elites. The antidemocratic ideology was, for the most part, a principled conservatism of the elite; there is no point in applying retroactive condemnation from the democratic present. What must be emphasized, however, is the objective effect this ideology had in undermining a collective support basis for a new nationality.

Of course, there were other compelling reasons for the weakness of the new nationality. Foremost among these was the strongest factor forcing a federal form of government: the obstinate survival of the Catholic French-speaking community. Post-1960s rhetoric about two founding nations and a historic obsession with English-French relations are not especially helpful in disentangling the strands of this particular Canadian circumstance. First of all, in the nineteenth century, the religious cleavage between Catholicism and Protestantism in many ways overshadowed the linguistic cleavage. This is reflected in the language of the BNA Act. Moreover, the accommodation made with Catholic Quebec was a peculiarly asymmetrical bargain, one that reflected the original "accommodation" of the English conquerors with the defeated population of New France. Specifically, this had involved a tacit, informal arrangement between the English administrators and merchants on the one hand, and the Catholic hierarchy and landowners, on the other. Succinctly, "culture" (religion, education, language, and civil law) was traded for "economics" (development of the commercial empire of the St.

Lawrence). The political deadlock that had taken hold in the United Canadas from 1840 to 1867, with the virtual 50:50 balance ("double majorities"), was to be broken in Confederation by a renegotiation of the old arrangement. "Culture" would be left to the provincial governments, "economics" largely to the national government. To be sure, Catholic Quebec would have to be accommodated within the political structures at Ottawa, but even this would be along the same lines: major economic portfolios in the Cabinet would be informally, but rigorously, reserved for English Canadian ministers (an arrangement continued for almost a century).

This attempt to delegate all the divisive or contentious issues to the provinces (a prospect that deeply delighted George Brown and helped gain Ontario Grit support for the plan), may have been motivated by an irritated English Protestant desire to be rid of the claims of French Canadian Catholicism, but the distribution of powers between Ottawa and Quebec also applied equally to Ottawa and Toronto, Halifax, Fredericton, and all the later provincial capitals. Jurisdiction over some of the primary potential areas of emotional, affective loyalties lay with the provinces.

The allocation of fiscal resources and economic responsibilities between Ottawa and the provinces was strongly one-sided. In the context of the economic practices of the late nineteenth century, Ottawa was not only to be predominant, but the provinces were to be virtual fiscal tributaries. There is a sense, only slightly reductionist, in which Confederation was a large-scale debt consolidation for the benefit of the London bond merchants. But its "collateral" was its promise of future profitability through continental development, and the national government was to be the instrument of this development. *Accumulation* in the developmental context of a new nation may in fact come to be very close to *legitimation*. If we are to seek the real core of popular consent to the new nation and its national government, it will have to be found here.

It was no accident that railways were central to this legitimation through continental economic development. The economic historians long ago pointed out the critical significance of communication to a country whose population is so thinly and unevenly stretched out across a vast terrain. Canada may well be the only country in the world whose constitution specifically mentions railways. It may also be the only country in the world to raise the construction of a railway to the high mythic dignity of "The National Dream." Perhaps the real source of philosophical inspiration for Confederation is to be found in T.C. Keefer's *Philosophy of Railroads* (1849). This mythic integrative symbolism ought not to be dismissed; even in the age of

jet travel, any tampering with rail service or the ancient and vener-
able Crow's Nest rates raises a reaction so vituperative as to suggest
that more than an economic ox is being gored. Yet, as Frye has
pointed out, all this concern over railways, roads, bridges, canals,
steamships, airlines, etc., points not only to a peculiar genius for
deficit financing in the sacred cause of moving our natural resources
to the imperial centres, but in a cultural sense, to an obsession with
the "inarticulate forms" of communication. At its best, this obsession led Innis to some searching and difficult examinations of *The
Bias of Communications* and of *Empire and Communications*. More
typical perhaps is that the leading Canadian star of international
pop culture in the 1960s should have been a communications guru
whose slogan was "the medium is the message," a quintessential
Canadianism. From the beginning, Canadians showed a deep concern over the *means* whereby the sections of the country communicated with each other, but the *content* of that communication was
distinctly secondary.[7]

An obsession with achieving the technical groundwork of communications was not unnatural in a group of colonies on the edge of
empire. And it was the imperial framework that was transposed, as
a kind of constitutional metaphor, to the arrangement of powers
between the Dominion and provincial governments. The general and
residual grant of powers to the Dominion was matched by a restrictive listing of provincial responsibilities. The federal power of
disallowance: the power of reservation by the lieutenant-governor of
the provinces (appointed by Ottawa); the federal declaratory power
to bring provincial works under national jurisdiction; the power of
the federal government to act as the guarantor of the educational
rights of religious minorities, including the power to pass remedial
legislation; control by Ottawa of judicial appointment to what is, in
effect, a unified judicial apparatus; and, finally, the fiscal superiority
already noted – all these suggest an inferior, "colonial" constitutional status for the provinces, not unlike the relationship of British
colonies to the Imperial Motherland. One observer has recently
described the arrangement as "imperial federalism."[8] Macdonald,
moreover, confidently expected that as Conservative prime minister
he could work the operational political levers of this system in such
a way as to integrate the sections by means of a unified Ottawa-
dominated Conservative party ruling by proxy in the provincial
legislatures through the mechanism of national Conservative patronage. In other words, an effective one-party state would politically
integrate the sections on the same hierarchical model of the constitutional distribution of power and of the Empire as a whole.

The logic of this position was reinforced by the second phase of national integration and development, the National Policy of 1878. This spelled out the economic logic of the constitutional arrangement of a decade earlier. Tariff protection for Canadian-based industry and completion of the east-west railway within an Imperial trade framework meant the protection of central Canadian industry (whether genuinely indigenous or American branch-plant was irrelevant) and the development of the West as a staple resource-producing hinterland and market for the protected manufactured products of central Canada. This was reinforced by the terms upon which Saskatchewan and Alberta were created as provinces in 1905, with an inferior constitutional status in regard to jurisdiction over natural resources. Moreover, the National Policy was also a device for strengthening the Conservative party, as manufacturers paid for tariff protection with campaign funds, and the Conservatives used the national treasury to encourage the development of a national bourgeoisie centred in Montreal and Toronto. Again, the model of economic development was essentially hierarchical and imperial. I am not suggesting that there was a better, practical model of development then available; there probably was not. The point, however, is to indicate the precise nature of the concept of integration involved in both the constitutional and the economic development schemes.

What happened to this clearly and consistently conceived model of development? There was once a school of thought in this country that argued that a handful of old men in the Judicial Committee of the Privy Council in Britain, meeting infrequently over a number of years to consider various court cases arising out of the distribution of powers, perversely stood the intentions of the Fathers of Confederation on their heads and made Canada into a balkanized crazy-quilt presided over by a pack of parochial provincial warlords united only by their determination to rob the Ottawa treasury blind. This image is not entirely without substance, even if it is mainly hyperbole, and the decisions of the JCPC did effectively reword the constitution. But it no longer seems defensible to argue that the cause of growing decentralization was judicial review.[9] Much deeper causes than this were at work. Above all, it can be shown that the original centralist model was itself radically defective in terms of the empirical realities of British North America: like so many other Canadian national dreams, it left out the people.

The Imperialist analogy had high legitimacy in loyalist ideology, but the replication of metropolitan-hinterland relations within the new nation was not only unoriginal, but poorly thought out. Above all, Ottawa lacked the ideological and cultural hegemony over the provinces that London exercised by habit and tradition over the white-settler colonies and Dominions. There was no Canadian nationality, no national culture; even the weak expression of common colonial identity had been in the ambiguous terms of British North America. Instead, there were the existing local and traditional identities of the individual colonies, extremely strong and tenacious in the case of Catholic Quebec, but not without reality in the case of the other provinces as well.

In the place of cultural hegemony, the federal government's dominance was posited on its leading role in continental economic development, with cultural integration to follow. (If nothing else, the Fathers of Confederation were decisive economic determinists.) The problem with this was twofold. First, it now seems extraordinarily naive, in the light of subsequent comparative experience, to believe that cultural identity would simply follow the dollar. Certainly in the case of French Canada, Lord Durham's faith of 1840 that a liberal political system offering scope to individual ambition would ultimately wear down the integrity of French culture and foster long-term, peaceful assimilation, was misconceived.[10] Confederation offered no better avenue toward this goal than had the legislative union of the Canadas, especially since a provincial jurisdiction had been created with a French Catholic majority and powers over cultural and educational matters. Moreover, Quebec's role as guarantor of French Canadian culture has always acted as a barrier against cultural nationalism in regard to the other provinces. To the extent that a common English Canadian cultural identity was actually forged out of colonial elements, the process would have to take place at the level of civil society, at least until well into the twentieth century.

The second, and perhaps more serious, problem was that economic development, in terms of the model adopted, was a decidedly double-edged sword. The very creation of provincial jurisdictions, however inferior in constitutional theory, would create an institutional differentiation in the state along territorial lines, around which particular economic interests might coalesce to pressure the national government or simply to extend rivalry with other interests. To the extent that provincial jurisdictions overlapped with distinct regional economic interests, this tendency was to become a pronounced and permanent feature of federalism, even when the specific players changed roles and sides from time to time. To this extent alone, the provincial governments would become autonomous and dynamic forces, with implications both for the formal constitutional division of powers, and for the form of national integration when there were competing institutional foci for organizing the attachments of citizens. And with the gradual democratization of the franchise at both levels, the popular legitimacy of provincial governmental decisions cut deeply into the formal constitutional superiority of Ottawa, resulting in a progressive atrophy of the will to exercise the quasi-imperial prerogatives of the BNA Act, as well as radically undermining the supremacy of the national over the provincial wings of the political parties, which Macdonald had so mistakenly projected.[11] It is no accident that the first formidable counterattack to federal domination was mounted not by Quebec, but by Protestant, English-speaking Ontario, and that the doctrine of provincial rights and the compact theory of Confederation – the ideological constructs put into political and juridical battle with centralist Ottawa – were at first shaped more by Ontario's economic demands than by Quebec's cultural peculiarity. It was not possible to assign one level of government economic responsibilities as a watertight compartment in a federal system.[12]

If the strength of the provincial governments had been underestimated, so too had the strength of regional, provincial, or sectional division in the national institutions themselves. Almost immediately after 1867, the social divisions, supposedly delegated to the provincial level, reproduced themselves within the party system, the Cabinet, and the policymaking apparatus in general. While this process was most visible in the case of the accommodation of Catholic Quebec within the Conservative party and Cabinet until the 1890s when the Liberals took over the same role, a similar process was taking place with other provinces and sectional groups as well. (None of this, of course, is incompatible with pluralist theory, even in a nonfederal state.)

The replication of sectionalism within the national structure was an asymmetrical process, however, and in this asymmetry lay a grave weakness in the integrative capacity of national institutions. One theoretical model for a functioning federal democracy is a derivation from Calhoun's concept of concurrent majorities – that each section must assent specifically to a national policy or be able to nullify its effect in that section.[13] This could take the form of veto power by provincial governments (compact theory and some versions of executive federalism) or it could take the form of sectional interests within the national government holding effective veto power. In Canada, the superimposition of British parliamentary institutions over a federal system has meant that national decision-making is only indirectly structured by regional interests – effectively, through the balance of regional forces reflected in the party forming a Cabinet. Given the unequal composition of the provincial components of Confederation, the massive economic and demographic weight of Ontario and Quebec, and a model of economic development that could only deepen the power discrepancy between centre and periphery, party government and party discipline would effectively shut out much of the voice of protest from the smaller, economically less developed provinces. In short, the national majority legitimating the actions of the national government would be asymmetrical, thus lending a structural imbalance to political representation. Regional alienation, increased focus on intergovernmental conflict and a breakdown of the national two-party system – the rise of provincially based protest parties, and, more recently, the impasse of the two major national parties being locked into distinct, increasingly exclusive, territorial enclaves, have flowed from this asymmetrical structure of representation.

Perhaps my tone has been too harsh in judging the shortcomings of the original Macdonald-style centralist vision. The problem was not that of individual failings. Indeed, Macdonald's vision was in many important respects farsighted and successful. The railway was built, the west settled, industrialization engendered. A half century after Confederation many of the original economic aims had been achieved. All these were remarkable, even extraordinary accomplishments in the face of history, geography, and the alleged laws of economics. The point at issue here, however, is the unanticipated *political* consequences of this single-minded pursuit of national economic development. Nor are we yet done with these consequences – in this chapter, or in this country.

The exclusively economic basis of national development did not escape the notice of Canadians of the Victorian and Edwardian eras. Ideologically, the forty years or so from Confederation to the First World War were dominated by the national question. Major schools of thought contested the meaning and content of Canadian nationality, even as provincialism proceeded apace within the sphere of federalism. Looking back over this great debate, one is struck by an extraordinary convergence, at the structural level, of all the arguments, however opposed they may be in content.

The Imperialists, whether moderate and pragmatic Conservative politicians, or enthusiastic zealots of the Imperial Federation League, saw Canada's future as part of the larger British Empire. Even if, as has been convincingly argued, they were expressing a genuine Canadian nationalism through a practical anti-Americanism, and even if they looked to a leading Canadian role in the Empire, the fact remains that their concept of nationality was British and the institutional framework for national expression was an Empire of which Canada was only a part. The archrival of Imperialism was continentalism. The highest expression of this was Goldwin Smith's *Canada and the Canadian Question* (1891), which argued in favor not only of continental union with the US, but of a "moral federation of the English speaking people." Both Imperialism and continentalism denied the legitimacy of the culture of French Canada, and through the manipulation of symbols of English domination, drove French Canadians into defensive groupings. The French Canadian nationalism of Henri Bourassa, denounced as disloyalty in English Canada, alone among national ideologies of this era actually posited an independent, autonomous Canadian state, but went on to posit a binational cultural basis for this state.

There was an underlying structural similarity in all these arguments. The nation and the state were not coterminous concepts in Canadian discourse. The concept of cultural nationality and the concept of political or state sovereignty were distinct and analytically separate. Moreover, the idea of differing cultural nations coexisting under a wider political sovereignty – whether French and English within Confederation, or Canada within a wider Empire, or the moral federation of the English-speaking peoples – was at the root of most thinking about the national question. Integral nationalism in the European sense, or even in the American sense, in which state sovereignty is synonymous with a single cultural, ethnic, and linguistic nationality, never took decisive shape in this country.[14] Need I add that Canada has, for the first fourteen years of her second century, been governed by a prime minister who previously made an academic and journalistic reputation by a sustained philosophical attack on the concept of the nation-state?

This concern with the national question itself fell under increasingly severe attack in the early twentieth century in the face of class and regional discontent generated by the very economic successes of the National Policy. The creation of an agricultural hinterland in the West also created a regional concentration of farmers opposed to the discriminatory tariff and railway policies of Ottawa as well as to the predatory corporate capitalism fostered in central Canada. Industrialization spawned an industrial working class, which had begun organizing into trade unions and contesting the unchecked prerogatives of employers and their allies in governments.

The 1911 election, with its defeat of free trade with the United States, seemed a reconfirmation of the National Policy. The Borden government did indeed exemplify a twentieth-century version of nationalized politics, a stance to which the enforced centralization of the First World War profoundly contributed. The Union government of 1917 represented the highest stage of this apolitical, business image of government. While establishing a merit system in the public service, inaugurating a universal income tax, and carrying out various other rationalizations and reforms, this government ended by disclosing the limitations of nationalist politics. The imposition of conscription led to revolt in French Canada and the reinforcement of a Liberal Quebec. "Rationalized" freight rates helped to destroy indigenous industrialization in the Maritimes, and engendered a Maritime Rights movement. Continued tariff and other economic policies favoring central Canadian manufacturers inspired farmer parties who rose to office from Ontario to Alberta. Anti-labor policies helped rouse workers into actions ranging from independent labor candidates to an unprecedented level of strike activity in 1919. The net result of the renewal of National Policy centralism under Union government was the near-eclipse of the Conservatives in the 1921 election, the breakdown of the two-party system, and the emergence of class and sectional politics on a scale never witnessed before.[15]

This crucial point in the political evolution of Canada must be more carefully examined. Too often the rise of the farmers' parties at the end of the war, and the regrouping of third party politics in the 1930s around the CCF and Social Credit, have been interpreted in terms of regionalism. What was happening to the political culture of Canada can, in part, be understood in terms of territorialism, but only one-dimensionally. Quebec's reversion to the Liberal party most closely follows the territorial model, but third-party movements generally followed a functional, rather than territorial, model. The analysis of the political economy by the Progressive and farmer theorists was almost always a functional analysis – and at the level of prescription, it bordered on corporatism, which is to say on the suppression of parliamentary territorial representation in favor of formalized functionalism. Similarly, the CCF saw itself as a farmer-labor national alliance, and Social Credit maintained a highly functionalist analysis of the deficiencies of finance capitalism. It is true that the Progressives were strongest on the prairies – where wheat farmers were ascendant – that the CCF found a provincial base in Saskatchewan, and Social Credit in Alberta, and that there was thus an *appearance* of regional protest. To a large extent it was a case of functional interests regrouping around territorial bases, with regionalism accentuated by an electoral system which rewards territorial concentrations of support, but punishes more thinly spread nation-wide support.[16]

In the face of this general revulsion against National Policy centralism and the willingness of at least some groups to turn to third parties to break the hold of central Canadian business interests over national government, there came into being on a piecemeal, haphazard basis, generally under Liberal auspices, what has been called the "Second National Policy." This sometimes uncoordinated set of expedients was characterized by a turning away from nation-building and a new emphasis on redistributive policies. This might take the form of universal social services (old age pensions) or more likely the form of regional pork barrelling or payoffs to assuage this or that complaining group.[17]

Redistributive politics were greatly strengthened by the effects of the Second World War and its immediate aftermath in the early years of the Cold War. First of all, the national government dis-covered that it could achieve supremacy in federal-provincial relations through its superior fiscal power, without changing the constitution. Second, Keynesian economics provided a systematic rationale for redistribution as an effective form of stabilization and thus as a support for accumulation. Finally, massive American capital investment in Canada, in direct resource extraction and in branch-plant industrialization, provided an economic surplus that allowed a margin of redistribution. Two waves of redistributive social programs contributed to this system: during the latter years of the Second World War, and in the mid-1960s, during the greatest post-war boom.

Within this context, various predictions were launched by politi-cal scientists that Canada was set on an inexorable path to greater centralization, that modern technology and the imperatives of modern economic planning and management were bound to under-mine the antiquated forces of provincialism and regionalism. It is obvious that this has not happened, but it is less obvious why it has not. Explanations that cite Quebec nationalism, Western alienation or, simply, regionalism as the bases of disintegrative tendencies are scarcely useful, since most of these factors have been constants throughout Canadian history. More useful attempts to explain decentralist tendencies include the province-building argument, which rests on a political economy explanation of functions of capital grouping around regional or provincial bases and spurring the provincial states into autonomist development policies. Some-times this is seen to involve specific class groupings organizing themselves within the provincial state apparatuses (e.g., the "new middle class" in Quebec) or simply the support of fractions of capital for province-building policies (the *arriviste bourgeoisie* of Alberta).[18] Another explanation is a "neo-institutionalist" view, which stresses the autonomy of governments from civil society and sees federal-provincial conflict more in terms of the antagonistic institutional goals of competing governments.[19] Finally, there is what one might call the normative approach, that decentralization is essentially superior to centralization and is winning the hearts and minds of Canadians.[20]

The political economy and neo-institutionalist approaches are not incompatible. Marxist arguments on the "relative autonomy of the state" suggest that, especially in a federal system, one may find class and intraclass conflicts carried on by sections of the state. On the other hand, neo-institutionalist analysis has to explain *why* provincial governments have grown so dramatically in the past twenty years or so, although not before. I suspect that some synthesis of these approaches is the most fruitful method to follow. Certainly, it seems the growth of the state at the provincial level – much more rapid in fact than the more publicized size of the federal bureaucracy – constitutes the most important variable in the last two decades of federal-provincial relations. In this context the ideology of decentralization appears in quite a different light than the rhetoric of its enthusiasts would suggest.

Let us take the most difficult case first, that of Quebec. Granted the linguistic and cultural specificity of Quebec, and without denying the importance of the linguistic and cultural demands generated by this national grouping, there is nevertheless a profound problem with all attempts to develop a simple explanatory equation of national distinctiveness with the drive to sovereignty – without the intervention of some very important variables. An ideology of national autonomism was well developed before 1960, and the cultural basis of a separate national identity was no weaker then. The most acceptable explanation of the Quebec economy and society is the emergence of a new professional, technical middle class (or a new secular *intelligentsia* in the broad sense), which attached its interests to a positive *étatiste* nationalism, which in turn broke down the culture-economics tradeoff that had underpinned English-French relations since the Conquest and gave a mighty thrust to the growth of the Quebec state. There are loose ends in this explanation, and the questions multiply as we approach the present,[21] but it answers more effectively than any other the question of the specific forms that Quebec autonomism has taken. And it makes some sense of the ideological shift from French-Canadian to Quebec identity: the new nationalism is a distinctly *statist* ideology. That is not to say it is necessarily socialist, or even social democratic. But even when it takes private enterprise forms, it is private enterprise organized around the territory of the Quebec state. This is what seems to set it inexorably on the road to political sovereignty. Or so it might have appeared, from 1976 to 1980.

The argument for Quebec sovereignty was phrased in significantly different ideological terms than the demands for greater decentralization coming from the English-Canadian provinces, but there are some similarities. Someone has suggested that while the Quebec government sought political sovereignty with economic association, some English-Canadian premiers wanted economic sovereignty with political association. Yet even if the demand for formal sovereignty has not been voiced (except for the Western separatist groups), the more aggressive and wealthy provinces have been demanding some of the same kind of economic powers the PQ was seeking through its more elaborate and formal scheme. For example, the Quebec White Paper on Sovereignty-Association proposed a series of commissions to coordinate aspects of the economic association, with equal representation from Quebec and Canada – in other words, a mechanism whereby the 30 percent of the population of Canada in Quebec could achieve parity of negotiating power with the 70 percent who resided elsewhere.[22] The often-voiced demands of the premiers of Alberta, BC, and Saskatchewan for equality of fiscal and economic power with central Canada can be seen in the same light. The Compact Theory has taken on a thrust in the age of province-building. During the recent constitutional debate, the government of Alberta stated as its official position that each province is a sovereign entity, and the premier of Newfoundland stated as his view that the federal government was merely the creature of the provinces, with only so much power as they were willing to delegate to it.

This rhetoric is obviously not without significance. The argument on behalf of the provincial view is that Ottawa has failed to fulfil the role it proclaimed for itself at the end of the Second World War, as guarantor of national economic stability and growth. As the national government has fallen victim of the international crisis of capitalism, its economic legitimacy has suffered. Given the near-exclusive *economic* basis of national integration, from the first to the second National Policies, this delegitimation was bound to have particularly severe effects on the standing of the national government. When provincial demands are fueled by a massive province-building drive, once pioneered by Ontario alone, but now spread from

Alberta to Newfoundland, the disintegrative effects are deepened. When the old English-Canadian ideology of loyalism has given way to a dominant liberalism premissed upon individual economic reward – a transformation in values that goes back to the nineteenth century, but that really gained momentum after the First World War, the economic crisis clearly strikes deeply indeed at national integration in the traditional sense: it is the provincial governments that seem more and more to be the guarantors of individual economic welfare.

The economic argument has a certain surface plausibility. The *ideology* of decentralization is, however, much more of a mystification. The rhetoric that surrounds that attack on Ottawa generally takes the form of an attack on big government, rigid bureaucracy, and waste and inefficiency. Giving more power to the provinces is, on the other hand, seen as giving power back to the people, standing up for the local community against the interventionist bureaucrats in far-away Ottawa. There is even a dash of Canadian Reaganism in all this, as when Premier Lougheed informed the Prime Minister at a recent First Ministers' Conference on the economy that government is, by definition, incapable of creating jobs, except at the cost of inflation. The irony is that the basis of this ideology is itself big government – the growth of provincial states, the rate of which has far outstripped that of the national government. There is the further irony that within the provinces, the clear trend has been toward greater centralization, with local communities increasingly falling under the interventionist sway of Edmonton, Quebec City, Queen's Park, etc. In another sense, of course, the ideology of decentralization is little more than the free enterprise rhetoric of the interests that have grouped around the provincial states, directed against a competitive level of government. Territoriality and functionalism are, as always, dialectically interrelated.

It is too easy to allow appearances to crowd out realities. The present level of verbal hostility between Ottawa and the provinces is not new. Oliver Mowat was not above implying Ontario's secession in the late nineteenth century. In the 1930s and early 1940s, Messrs. Hepburn and Duplessis carried on a vituperative conflict with Ottawa, which makes present relations between first ministers seem the very soul of civility. Clearly the economic basis of provincial power is stronger today, and this has shifted federal-provincial relations into a new stage, but that this should mean apocalypse now seems a bit far-fetched.

I suggest that the best grounds for dismissing fears of the imminent breakup of Canada lie in shifting attention away from governments, and toward the civil society. This is, by the light of the Canadian Constitution, a somewhat heretical and unCanadian statement. It is also heretical in the light of some of dominant academic analyses of Canadian political integration, such as executive federalism, or consociational democracy, which stress elite accommodation as the key mechanism in integration, and suggest a high degree of aversion to popular participation in the process of government.

When I emphasize civil society, I am not so naive as to confuse this with "the people" in general. There are good indications, however, that the most economically powerful sections of civil society do not always find it in their interests to support the disintegration or balkanization of Canada. On the contrary, Bob Blair of Nova Corporation begins in Alberta but ends in building national pipelines and spreading a nationalist gospel. Jack Gallagher of Dome Petroleum begins in Alberta but moves on to the Beaufort Sea, making a major play for oil in federal lands, voicing support for the National Energy Program, and ends a major corporate welfare case for the federal government. The federal and Alberta governments after months of public posturing come to an oil-pricing and revenue-sharing agreement – in part because the Bob Blairs and Jack Gallaghers want and require such an agreement, and both governments have a stake in compromise.

Just because the public style of bargaining has become more open, as each government tries to enlist public opinion on its side, does not make the eventual necessity of conflict resolution any less pressing. The Prime Minister recently suggested that an era of cooperative federalism was giving way to one of competitive federalism. I strongly suspect that one of the underlying causes of this shift is that intergovernmental relations are becoming, in effect, more democratized than in the past. A federation differs from a confederation in that both levels of government have direct popular mandates from their overlapping electorates, or, taking it from the other direction, citizens are divided in their participation in government into both national and provincial identities. Many of the provincial governments would, of course, like to establish some modern version of the Compact (confederal) Theory whereby they hold the sole legitimate right to represent their (provincial) citizens, thus reducing the federal level to a government of governments, rather than a government of citizens. Arguments on behalf of a Senate appointed directly by the premiers would serve as a partial triumph of the principle, establishing an effective provincial government veto over federal decisions. It we are to take the idea of the federal principle in a democracy seriously, however, we must be prepared for constant competition between governments for the support of the same electorates as a weapon of intergovernmental conflict.

The BNA Act would appear to have minimized the scope for this kind of competition with its distinctly undemocratic philosophy of government-citizen relations. Presumably the spectre of the slide of democratic federalism in the US, first into bitter sectionalism in the 1840s and 1850s, and finally into a bloody civil war in the 1860s, was an active discouragement to the Fathers of Confederation. However, good economic determinists as they were, they might have reflected on the *structural* basis of that conflict, rooted as it was in two incompatible modes of production and two correspondingly incompatible societal superstructures. In any event, the gradual democratization of the franchise in Canada did change the basis of national integration, first by buoying up the legitimacy of the provincial governments. In the late twentieth century, this democratic legitimacy question is being played out in a different way.

A dramatic indication of this was the Quebec Referendum. First, it was highly significant that a majority vote on sovereignty-association was seen as the necessary, if not sufficient, condition of forcing English Canada to recognize Quebec's "right to national self-determination." A majority alone would constitute the effective power to the Quebec government to bring English Canada to the bargaining table. And it does seem that for all the discussion about the legality and constitutionality of secession, English Canada was prepared to accept the obligation implied by such a decision. Political elites were less willing than ordinary citizens to spell out the natura of response,[23] but this can be explained by an understandable unwillingness to give away bargaining tactics in advance. A democratic expression of the will to become sovereign was essentially unanswerable in the power conjuncture of the late twentieth century. (What sort of economic association might have been negotiated is, of course, something else again.)

More interesting than the fact of the failure of this appeal to the people is an examination of the underlying reasons. This is a complex question to which definitive answers are unlikely at this point. There is, however, a great deal of data upon which informed speculation can be based. One generalization that appears to stand up is an apparent unwillingness of a majority, including a majority of francophones, to make a definitive choice between two levels of government to which they remained, by and large, attached.[24] The PQ's problem was that an identification with Quebec (or French Canada) as a cultural or sociological notion did not translate on a wide enough scale into a rejection of federalism. Put another way, nationalist aspirations, the logic of which were predicated upon the Quebec *state* alone, failed to convince a sufficient number of nationalist-inclined francophones to result in a referendum majority. A number of surveys have yielded the observation that francophone Quebeckers actually show higher degrees of satisfaction with the federal government than do the populations of many English-Canadian provinces.[25]

This paradox, why separatism has gained the strength it has in Quebec as compared to other provinces, must have a more specific cause than cultural/linguistic distinctiveness and a separate national identity, if Quebeckers as a whole do not demonstrate the degree of hostility to federal institutions and symbolic that one might otherwise expect. Again, the answer would seem to lie in *class* – in this case, in the distinctive ideology developed by the intellectuals in Quebec (taking intellectuals in the broad sense as all those who make a living through words and concepts, including bureaucrats, teachers, journalists, artists). Intellectuals are at the heart of the *indépendantiste* movement and demonstrate a degree of alienation from federalism and support for independence that far outpaces that of any other group.[26] And the PQ is the party par excellence of this group. Of course, intellectuals wield an influence disproportionate to their numbers; in Quebec, at least, they seem to have the capacity to define much of the agenda of political discussion. The fact that only a minority of Quebeckers are committed *indépendantistes* indicates, in this case, more than meets the eye. Yet it is also true that even though the *péquiste* intelligentsia has generally exercised an ideological hegemony over the society that exceeds any comparable example of intelligentsias in English Canada, they have so far signally failed to persuade the majority to follow them to the logical conclusion: the project of sovereignty.

This disjuncture between elite and mass has some interesting implications, especially for some widely accepted theories of how English-French relations are supposed to operate in this country. The consociational model posits deep cleavages between the subcultures at the mass level, with national unity saved by liberal elites who overcome differences through mutual accommodation.[27] Yet a survey of Montrealers on the question of the PQ language law showed a striking divergence within the francophone community on the basis of education and income: the poorer and less educated the francophone respondents were, the *more liberal* their attitudes to allowing modifications in the language law as it affected the educational and other rights of the anglophone minority.[28] A CBC survey of Anglo-Quebec opinion elicited the oft-repeated comment that anglophone anxieties and resentments were not against the ordinary francophone people, but only against the PQ elite. Moreover, there is some fragmentary – albeit conflicting – evidence that English-Canadian public opinion outside Quebec may not match the degree of intolerance that the much-publicized "anti-bilingual backlash" would seem to indicate.[29] It has also been argued that much of the anti-bilingual opinion in the West was less anti-French sentiment than extreme irritation at a federal government that appeared to be promoting a central Canadian concern while refusing to recognize the special grievances of the West.[30]

French-English relations may be much more complex than the consociational model would indicate. One section of the Quebec elite – federal Liberal MPs – do work at accommodation, but the elites surrounding the PQ actively work at undermining accommodations. Yet it is not at all clear that this latter elite can carry their population with them; the appeal for a democratic mandate, initiated by the PQ, turned out to be a more effective weapon for the federalists. In short, from the point of view of national integration, the antidemocratic implications of consociationalism seem unnecessary; consultation with the masses may not be a cause for instability.

There is another irony as well. Some observers have pointed to the existence of a separate political jurisdiction in Quebec with a francophone majority as an institutional encouragement to eventual separation. Certainly the opportunity for a relatively clean break (abstracting from the problem of the English-Canadian minority) is much greater than in countries with mixed populations inhabiting unitary states (Belgium, Ulster). Yet this may also provide the very institutional basis of continued association within Confederation. The capacity of the Quebec state to legislate, for example, priority to the French language within its borders, offers a considerable escape-valve for tensions that might otherwise build up to explosive levels.

It is perhaps premature to accept at face value the argument that the cultural and linguistic cleavage between English and French Canadians is such as to automatically call into question the continuation of the political association between Quebec and Canada. It is my suspicion, based both on the findings of survey data and on the political events of the past few years, that the long-held views of Prime Minister Trudeau that the emotional, sentimental attachment of francophones to Quebec does not replace economic or functionalist attachments to Canada, which are cooler but nevertheless tenacious, may not be far wrong. The economic failures of the federal government seem to have impinged less on the loyalties of Quebeckers than they have on Westerners; perhaps this is a recognition that, after all, Confederation has not been so bad for central Canada.

When one turns to survey data on English-Canadian provincial opinion, one glimpses the other side of the Quebec paradox. At the level of national identification and of common cultural symbols, English Canadians seem more nationalist than regionalist (with the exception of Newfoundlanders who, after all, have only had some thirty years experience at being Canadian). Yet Western Canadians tend to show higher levels of dissatisfaction with the national government than Quebeckers, and English Canadians seem readier than Quebeckers to judge their provincial government as better serving their interests than the federal government.[31]

Quebec is obviously not a province like the others, but neither is it simply a nation ready to assume the full plenitude of sovereign powers (although that clearly remains a possible outcome). But the PQ image of an English Canada inexorably driving toward centralization – a view spelled out at great length in the PQ's White Paper on Sovereignty-Association – is a grotesque misreading. The history of this country is not such as to warrant any such view, and survey data on public opinion on Canadian identity offers no support for it.[32] It is true that Albertans have no linguistic, ethnic, or even cultural (in the narrow sense) discontinuities with the people of, say, Ontario. And it is true that this gives a different tone to the cause of Alberta provincialism, as opposed to Quebec nationalism. Yet on a number of specific criteria, Albertans appear more alienated than Quebeckers from the institutions of the national state.

Why should this surprise us? Why should we consider culture an independent variable, but not economics? Why should we have placed so much weight on English-French relations, while neglecting the unfolding of localisms, provincialisms, regionalisms based on the economic and geographic course of Canadian development? That these questions can still be posed is itself an indication of a certain bias in Canadian political science and political sociology. Those who have tried to see Canadian integration exclusively in terms of English/French cultural duality have recognized only one axis of a more complex set of cleavages in interrelationships. And those who have looked to an either/or scenario of centralization/integration vs. peripheralization/disintegration within English Canada have failed to recognize the dialectic of functionalism and territoriality in a system that has placed heavy priority on economic development as the mechanism of integration, while fostering (perhaps inevitably) a dispersed, regionalized, unevenly developed economy with strong continental tendencies pulling against the east-west axis. The institutional division of a federal system into territorial jurisdictions reinforces the conflictual tendencies – but it may also reinforce, in an untidy but generally flexible manner, tendencies to resolve conflicts, through institutionalized channels for playing off functional and territorial interests.

This is not to suggest that these institutional channels are working as well as they might, nor that specific improvements might not be made. Chief among these is the lack of genuine representation from the Western and the Atlantic provinces in the institutions of the federal government itself: a point to which I will return presently. But the federal system has a paradoxical quality: it works better than it *appears* to work. The complexity of the societal cleavage patterns in Canada, the uneven reinforcement of these patterns by the institutional structures of government, and the increasingly noisy and clamorous quality of debate as competing governments appeal to their electorates, all tend to enhance an appearance of chaos and disintegration that is scarcely justified by the practice of compromise and accommodation.

One of the striking observations of recent research on public attitudes in Canada is that ordinary Canadians show both a relatively (and perhaps, given general levels of alleged public ignorance about government, unexpectedly) high degree of sophistication in their perceptions of how federalism works, at least insofar as the division of powers operates between governments,[33] and also reflect in their political identities a subtle image of the allegiance of a genuinely federal *society*. As David Elkins points out, Canadians have both federal and provincial loyalties, but except for Quebec *indépendantistes*, provincial loyalties are not negatively related to national loyalties (nor, it seems, for francophone Quebeckers as a whole). As Elkins concludes:

Successful federations, by their structure, require and encourage multiple identities and loyalties. There is no logical reason why there must be a hierarchy of feelings such that nationalism blots out regional attachments, or vice versa. Particularistic identities are nurtured within a context provided by the nation as a whole. It is ... not even necessary that all people or groups share the same images of that whole within which they are unique parts ... there can be for most Canadians no pleasure in being forced to choose between one identity or another. Multiple loyalties can have, therefore, a civilizing result, since they encourage us to reject absolute choices and teach us to give assent and express dissent in graduated and qualified terms.[34]

There is another point here as well. Canadians retain strong regional identities, but they demonstrate overlapping and sometimes contradictory ideas of what their "region" constitutes.[35] Provincial governments can thus scarcely be seen as *exclusive* voices of the regions; indeed, province-building and the growth of institutional interests around provincial states may be antithetical to regionalism, as such.[36] There is a space here, I suggest, for diverting some of the zero-sum rhetoric of competitive federalism, built up around governmental actors, into less territorially based forms of conflict, within a democratic polity where electorates and organized economic interests are being mobilized by both levels of government. To the extent that the interests and loyalties of the elements of civil society are not delineated strictly along lines of governmental jurisdiction, but overlap and crosscut, then this mobilization will lead to the "victory" of neither integration nor disintegration, but will reinforce tendencies to compromise.

Some changes in the institutional/constitutional structure would assist this tendency. A strengthening of the federal government, interpreted not as an increase in powers, but as greater direct regional representation, seems imperative. If Canadians demonstrate the characteristics of citizens of a federal society, the political institutions of the national level of government reflect the federal principle more poorly than do many countries less federal in social and cultural terms.[37] If the national government is to be a legitimate government of citizens – equally legitimate with the provincial governments – it must break the (correctly) perceived equation of the national majority with a Central Canadian majority. This is, needless to say, not merely a problem of the Liberal party, but a problem for the country. Some means should be found for institutionalizing recognition of the concurrent majorities of the regime.[38] A step in this direction would be the provision of an elected Senate, based on equal provincial representation. As an elected body, such a Senate would have the legitimacy to do much more than the present body, but it would also embody the principle of concurrent majorities, along with the national majority represented in the House of Commons.

The recent conversion of the federal Liberal government to economic nationalism, at least in energy resources, parallels its attempt to reassert its national position in fiscal federalism, its attempt to act as guarantor of individual linguistic and civil rights through the constitutional charter, and its attempts to raise its visibility with individual taxpayers.[39] Its economic nationalism, through Petro-Canada and the National Energy Program's Canadianization provisions, appears to be favored by people generally, although not by business.[40] Moreover, there has been a clear trend in the past decades for Canadian aversion to continental integration to steadily increase. In 1965, one-fifth of the population favoured political union, and one-half economic union, with the US by 1980, but at the height of the Western separatism flurry, only 3 percent of Westerners favoured union with the US while 90 percent wished to remain part of Canada.[41]

Yet the federal government also runs the risk of replicating the fate of the Union government of 1917–21: centralist nationalism can so exacerbate regional differences as to be itself a disintegrative force. It can avoid this fate only to the extent that it comes to be perceived not as a partial instrument of one region's domination over another, but as a genuine government of citizens. Thus, any strengthening of the federal level must be a strengthening of its regional representativeness, not of the power of Ottawa over the regions. This should not be in contradiction to the democratization of public life, but an expression of the democratic principle in genuinely federal society.

The great constitutional debate of 1980–81 and its final resolution seem to offer both hope and disappointment in this regard. Certainly, the legitimacy of a national parliament controlled by a party with virtually no representation from the West attempting to unilaterally patriate and alter the constitution was deeply suspect. On the other hand, the federal proposals contained some democratic innovations in Canadian constitutional practice, notably the entrenched charter of rights and the (regionally based) popular referendum procedures for amendment. Unfortunately, given the means available for elite domination of the process, the provincial premiers were able, in the end, to eliminate (in the case of the referendum) or to greatly modify (in the case of the rights charter) these democratic elements. The final compromise was in many ways a strengthening of the hold of the provincial governments (opting out of constitutional amendments) without any equivalent strengthening of the regional representativeness of the national government (no Senate reform).

And yet the attempt of both sides to mobilize popular support for their positions had unexpected consequences. The conspiracy of first ministers to undermine rights provisions on women and native peoples, won earlier by popular representations, resulted in a massive grass-roots lobbying campaign, which forced the heads of government to partially retreat. The women's and native people's causes were genuinely *national*, in the sense that they adhered to no regional power cluster, yet they were in no way seeking the aggrandizement of one level of government at the expense of others. Their partial victory should be taken as a heartening sign of the effect of popular mobilization on depolarizing federal-provincial conflict.

Another example is the 1981–82 struggle between Ottawa and the provinces over federal-provincial fiscal arrangements. To the extent that this involves a conflict between vested governmental interests over revenues, people are the losers (especially users of medicare services and post-secondary educational institutions). A federal parliamentary task force that opened up the process to a wider consultation with the public came to conclusions that differed from those of the federal government.[42] The *public* interest in such questions is that governments can score victories over other governments at the expense of services to the public. The more the process is opened up, the greater the pressures on governments to compromise.

A final observation is that the pessimism and alarmism noted at the beginning among observers of Canadian political life may be overdrawn – at least so far as the prospects for continued federal integration. This is not to assert that hopes of egalitarianism and social justice are likely to be met by the Canada of the 1980s; it is simply to suggest that Canada as such is likely to remain viable. And in one sense at least this is a not inconsiderable prospect. The very conflict which so alarms observers is a sign of healthy democratic clamor in a diverse society. The dialectic of territoriality and functionalism is being played out more clamorously in other Western countries as well these days, including some that have few institutional means of coping with decentralizing tendencies. Canada may well prove particularly resilient in the face of these pressures.

Canadians, paradoxically, persist in seeing themselves through borrowed spectacles. Imported models of how an integrated "nation" is supposed to look and behave continue to set the framework within which Canada is observed and evaluated. This is itself a Canadian characteristic. I began with a quotation from Northrop Frye, and I will close with one from another Canadian cultural institution, the comedy team of Wayne and Shuster, interviewed recently by the *Financial Post*:

Is there enough Canadian sentiment or whatever to hold things together? I think that's the most preposterous thing of all in this country. Why are we so dedicated to finding a cliché? We were once interviewed by Barbara Walters. She said: "What is Canada? Is it a mosaic or is it a melting pot?" And I said we're a country terribly in search of a metaphor. The only problem is that the national animal of Canada is not the beaver, it's the copycat.[43]

NOTES

1 Robert Bothwell *et al, Canada since 1945: Power, Politics, and Provincialism* (Toronto: University of Toronto Press, 1981).

2 Sidney Tarrow, Peter J. Katzenstein, and Luigi Graziano, *Politics in Industrial Nations* (New York: Praeger, 1978).

3 Ramsay Cook, *Provincial Autonomy, Minority Rights, and the Compact Theory 1867–1921* (Ottawa: Queen's Printer, 1969).

4 Kenneth McRae, "The Structure of Canadian History," in Louis Hartz, ed., *The Founding of New Societies* (New York: Harcourt, Brace and World, 1964), 219–74; Gad Horowitz, *Canadian Labour in Politics* (Toronto: University of Toronto Press, 1968); David Bell and Lorne Tepperman, *The Roots of Disunity* (Toronto: McClelland and Stewart, 1979).

5 Dennis Duffy, *Gardens, Covenants, Exiles: Loyalism in the Literature of Upper Canada* (Toronto: University of Toronto Press, 1982).

6 Northrop Frye, *The Bush Garden: Essays on the Canadian Imagination* (Toronto: Anansi, 1970).

7 Ibid.; Frye, "A Summary of the Conference," *Options* (Proceedings of the Conference on the Future of the Canadian Federation) (1977): 435–48.

8 Douglas Verney, "The Reconciliation of Federalism and Parliamentary Supremacy," *Journal of Commonwealth and Comparative Politics* 16, no. 3 (1983): 22–44.

9 Alan Cairns, "The Judicial Committee and its Critics," *Canadian Journal of Political Science* 4, no. 3 (1971): 301–45.

10 David Cameron, *Nationalism, Self-Determination and the Quebec Question* (Toronto: Macmillan, 1974); Janet Ajzenstat, "Liberalism and Nationality," *Canadian Journal of Political Science* 14, no. 3 (1981): 587–610.

11 J.R. Mallory, *Social Credit and the Federal Power in Canada* (Toronto: University of Toronto Press, 1954), 18–19; Christopher Armstrong, *The Politics of Federalism: Ontario's Relations with the Federal Government 1867–1942* (Toronto: University of Toronto Press, 1981), 61–2.

12 Cook, *Provincial Autonomy, Minority Rights*; Armstrong, *The Politics of Federalism*.

13 Donald V. Smiley, "The Structural Problem of Canadian Federalism," *Canadian Public Administration* 14, no. 3 (1971): 328–43.

14 Reg Whitaker, "Images of the State in Canada," in Leo Panitch, ed., *The Canadian State: Political Economy and Political Power* (Toronto: University of Toronto Press, 1977), 48–9.

15 John English, *The Decline of Politics: The Conservatives and the Party System 1901–1920* (Toronto: University of Toronto Press, 1977); David Jay Bercuson, ed., *Canada and the Burden of Unity* (Toronto: Macmillan,

1977); E.R. Forbes, *The Maritime Rights Movement* (Montreal: McGill-Queen's University Press, 1979).

16 Alan Cairns, "The Electoral System and the Party System in Canada," *Canadian Journal of Political Science* 1, no. 1 (1968): 55–80.

17 V.C. Fowke, "The National Policy – Old and New," *Canadian Journal of Economics and Political Science* 18, no. 3 (1952): 271–86.

18 Garth Stevenson, *Unfulfilled Union* (Toronto: Macmillan, 1979); John Richards and Larry Pratt, *Prairie Capitalism* (Toronto: McClelland and Stewart, 1979); Kenneth McRoberts and Dale Posgate, *Quebec: Social Change and Political Crisis*, 2nd ed. (Toronto: McClelland and Stewart, 1980).

19 Alan Cairns, "The Governments and Societies of Canadian Federalism," *Canadian Journal of Political Science* 10, no. 4 (1977): 695–726.

20 George Woodcock, *The Rejection of Politics* (Toronto: New Press, 1972); Woodcock, *Confederation Betrayed* (Madeira Park, BC: Harbour Publishing, 1981).

21 Jorge Niosi, "The New French-Canadian Bourgeoisie," *Studies in Political Economy* 1 (1979): 113–61; Gilles Bourque, "Class, Nation and the Parti Québécois," *Studies in Political Economy* 2 (1979): 129–58; Pierre Fournier, "The New Parameters of the Quebec Bourgeoisie," *Studies in Political Economy* 3 (1980): 67–92.

22 Gouvernement du Québec, *La Nouvelle entente Québec-Canada*, 1979.

23 M.D. Ornstein and H.M. Stevenson, "Elite and Public Opinion before the Quebec Referendum," *Canadian Journal of Political Science* 14, no. 4 (1981): 745–74.

24 Jon H. Pammett, Harold D. Clarke, Jane Jenson, and Lawrence LeDuc, "Political Support and Voting Behaviour in the Quebec Referendum," in Allan Kornberg and Harold D. Clarke, eds., *Political Support in Canada: The Crisis Years* (Durham, NC: Duke University Press, 1982).

25 *Le Devoir*, 17 May 1980; David Elkins and Richard Simeon, *Small Worlds: Provinces and Parties in Canadian Political Life* (Toronto: Methuen, 1980); Clark, Jenson, LeDuc, and Pammett, *Political Choice*.

26 Maurice Pinard and Richard Hamilton, "Le Référendum québécois," *Policy Options* 2, no. 4 (1981): 39–44.

27 Kenneth D. McRae, *Consociational Democracy: Political Accommodation in Segmented Societies* (Toronto: McClelland and Stewart, 1974).

28 *Le Devoir*, 19, 21 September 1981.

29 M.D. Ornstein *et al*, "The State of Mind: Public Perceptions of the Future of Canada," in R.B. Byes and R.W. Reford, eds., *Canada Challenged* (Toronto: Canadian Institute of International Affairs, 1979).

30 David Smith, *The Regional Decline of a National Party: Liberals on the Prairies* (Toronto: University of Toronto Press, 1981); Raymond Breton

et al, Cultural Boundaries and the Cohesion of Canada (Montreal: Institute for Research on Public Policy, 1980), 290.

31 Elkins and Simeon, *Small Worlds*, 20.

32 Ibid.; Mildred Schwartz, *Public Opinion and Canadian Identity* (Berkeley: University of California Press, 1967); Mildred Schwartz, *Politics and Territory: The Sociology of Regional Persistence in Canada* (Montreal: McGill-Queen's University Press, 1974); R. Manzer, *Canada: A Socio-Political Report* (Toronto: McGraw-Hill Ryerson, 1974).

33 Clarke, Jenson, LeDuc, and Pammett, *Political Choice*, 77–85.

34 Elkins and Simeon, *Small Worlds*, 25–6.

35 Clarke, Jenson, LeDuc, and Pammett, *Political Choice*, 42.

36 Roger Gibbons, *Prairie Politics and Society: Regionalism in Decline* (Toronto: Butterworths, 1980).

37 Fred C. Engelmann, "Reforming Canadian Federalism," in Larry Pratt and Garth Stevenson, eds., *Western Separatism* (Edmonton: Hurtig, 1981), 229–42.

38 Donald V. Smiley, "Territorialism and Canadian Political Institutions," *Canadian Public Policy* 3, no. 4 (1977): 449–56; Richard Simeon "Regionalism and Canadian Political Institutions," *Queen's Quarterly* 82 (1975).

39 G. Bruce Doern, "Spending Priorities: The Liberal View," in G. Bruce Doern, ed., *How Ottawa Spends Your Tax Dollars: Federal Priorities 1981* (Toronto: Lorimer, 1981), 1–55; Doern, "Liberal Priorities 1982: The Limits of Scheming Virtuously," in G. Bruce Doern, ed., *How Ottawa Spends Your Tax Dollars: National Policy and Economic Development 1982* (Toronto: Lorimer, 1982), 1–36.

40 Larry Pratt, "Energy and the Roots of National Policy," *Studies in Political Economy* 7 (1982): 27–60.

41 R.J. Zukowsky, *Intergovernmental Relations in Canada: The Year in Review 1980*, vol. 2 (Kingston: Queen's University, 1981).

42 Richard Simeon, "Fiscal Federalism: Review Essay," *Canadian Tax Journal* 30, no. 1 (1982): 41–51.

43 *Financial Post*, 23 January 1982, 4.

CHAPTER NINE

Between Patronage and Bureaucracy: Democratic Politics in Transition

This essay was written for a special issue of the *Journal of Canadian Studies* on political and other forms of patronage in Canadian life. Political patronage, long a staple of Canadian politics, has been a key factor mediating the relations between state and society throughout our political history. Its use and abuse have characterized Canadian development in ways which are unique: neither American nor British development parallels the Canadian historical trajectory.

By the mid-1980s, political patronage had become a very bad term. Still practised quietly, patronage was an orphan when it came to the public discourse of parties. The disjuncture between public protestations of purity and the privately enduring habit has been yet another source of the alarming alienation and disaffection of citizens with politicians and political institutions so evident by the end of the decade.

It is, I argue, the democratization of Canadian society in the late twentieth century that is transforming the political process and progressively undermining basic structures of the political system, however, necessarily replacing the elements of the old order with viable democratic alternatives. The legitimacy crisis in politics and the public realm is not then simply a reaction to a particular set of venal or incompetent politicians. Rather it must be seen as a deeper effect of a democratization process which has yet to find its appropriate institutional forms.

Writing in 1906, the French political scientist André Siegfried noted that the relationship between politics and bureaucracy being different in Canada than in France, elections were different phenomena:

Reprinted with permission from the *Journal of Canadian Studies* 22, no. 2 (Summer 1987).

The Canadian government, not having the Napoleonic bureaucracy at its back, is not able to exercise its influence after the fashion of ours. Its influence is called into action rather by its office-holders, who hold out promises in its name. "Vote for the government, and you shall have such and such a subvention, new railway or appointments." These are the words you will hear uttered by the ministerialists – no attempt to disguise the nature of the market transaction (as with us). The Opposition, instead of protesting, retaliate with promises of what they will do for their supporters should they come into office. Thus both sides call into play the powers of the state in order to catch votes.[1]

Some eighty years earlier, Robert Gourlay in his *Statistical Account of Upper Canada* had written that "ministers seem to have no idea of holding Canada but of enfeebling the people: ruling over them by a wretched system of patronage and favouritism ..."[2] Some eighty years later, the general election of 1984 reverberated to charges of political patronage; patronage was one of the election issues covered most in the press (only the economy and national unity gained significantly more attention), yet three-quarters of voters polled thought that all parties would use patronage in the same way as the party in power.[3]

There can be no mistaking the centrality of political patronage to the practice of Canadian politics, from the earliest colonial beginnings to the present day. Serious analysis of this phenomenon has, however, been somewhat sporadic in the literature. One problem has been a tendency to moralize, to dismiss patronage as mere corruption or as a primitive anachronism whose passing should be hastened. Another has been a tendency to view the Canadian practice in isolation, rather than within a wider comparative framework.

There are exceptions to these tendencies, to be sure. There are the political-anthropological studies of patronage associated with Vincent Lemieux in Quebec which have extended into a wide-ranging comparative framework.[4] There have also been a number of studies of patronage associated with the broad context of political modernization, tracing the not always smooth transition from traditional local patronage-oriented political cultures to more modern cultures in which redistributive relations are bureaucratized and nationalized, often within a context of class or regional dependency.[5]

Modernization theory has its limits. Certain phenomena are generally characteristic of all modern Western societies: urbanization, industrialization, mass politics, etc. The problem with using these as explanations for particular political developments is that the specificity of particular institutional arrangements and particular mixes of political cultures cannot be satisfactorily accounted for. Thus, analyses of the changing nature and place of patronage transactions within the Canadian political process which stress the universal factors of modernization cannot explain a problem which comparative study immediately suggests: patronage in the Canadian system (nationally and regionally) has always played a role which is distinctive and specific to Canada by comparison with our nearest neighbours from whom we have borrowed much in the way of forms and ideas. There is no historical trajectory which a particular nation must follow, for at no time in the past has the Canadian experience been identical to that of its neighbours (and erstwhile models), the United Kingdom and the United States, either earlier or later.

One of the crucial variables in comparative political development is historical timing. Similar developments may take place in different countries, but in different order or in different conjunctures. The result may be quite distinctive national experiences, and specific institutions and processes which reflect these distinctive experiences. In the case of patronage, processes of national mobilization and bureaucratization of political life were closely connected with the forms and prevalence of patronage relations, but these developed in different patterns and rhythms in the three English-speaking countries of the North Atlantic. In particular, bureaucratization was distinctly tied to the democratization of politics. By political patronage I mean transactions in which inducements derived from control of the state (jobs, contracts, favours) are given or promised by a political party or its representatives in exchange for political support by a client. By bureaucratic redistribution I understand policy outputs of the state which are directed to universally defined categories of citizens. I am using democratization as a description of the construction of a mass electorate in the nineteenth and twentieth centuries.[6] If in the end mass electorates were constructed in all three countries, the paths followed were separate and perhaps the electorates themselves, although superficially similar at a structural level, are not exactly the same political actors.

Tocqueville opened his *Democracy in America* with the reflection that is was "evident to all alike that a great democratic revolution is going on among us, but all do not look at it in the same light." He supposed it inevitable that his native France would eventually arrive at the same equality of condition as that of the Americans, but he hastened to add that "I do not conclude from this that we shall ever be necessarily led to draw the same political consequences which the Americans have derived from a similar social organization. I am far from supposing that they have chosen the only form of government which a democracy must adopt."[7] History has indeed born out Tocqueville's supposition.

In America, adult white male suffrage had become virtually universal by the early nineteenth century. Although women had to wait for another century to vote and blacks were not only unenfranchised but still enslaved, the effective elimination of property and class qualifications within the potential citizenship category of adult white males was not without considerable democratic consequences for American politics. The triumph of Jacksonian Democracy in 1828 was celebrated as a democratization of the distribution of public office. The spectacle of General Jackson dispensing patronage to his followers from a table in a Washington tavern was more than an exercise in partisanship: it was also a social revolution in public participation in political life. Since this democratization of patronage long preceded the emergence of the modern bureaucratic state, democratic redistribution was fixed on the party system rather than on the state. By 1840 mass parties manipulating mass electorates were as characteristic of conservatism as of radical democracy, but the rewards to be dispensed were in either case restricted to the "spoils of office" – jobs, contracts, tariffs.

In the post-Civil War era of continental capitalist development and mass immigration, new electorates were incorporated into the political process through the instrument of party and the means of patronage. The immigrants, for instance, were integrated not through state welfare programmes, which scarcely existed, but through the big city political machines, which themselves dispensed "welfare" in the form of patronage and socialized the newcomers by means of the party. By the early twentieth century, social reformers who began to look to the state as the efficient mechanism of change turned against the party machine as corrupt, venal and ineffective. Inevitably, the bureaucratization of the public policy process which was the thrust of the Progressive platform was also an attack on the democratic nature of patronage: taking "politics" out of administration by removing offices from party control and installing the merit system of appointment was a middle-class assault on one of the few avenues of upward mobility for working-class and ethnic Americans. Nor was it that effective a rallying cry. The bureaucratic welfare state has, by any number of measures, been slower to develop in America than in other Western nations, which is at least partially attributable to the lower salience of an organized lower-class lobby for social welfare policies. While many explanations for this rest at the level of the political economy, the party system is central. Unprogrammatic mass parties, with relatively classless appeals to their mass electorates, are both a legacy of pre-bureaucratic democratic patronage and a cause for the persistence in American politics, federal and state, of greater patronage resources at the disposal of the parties than obtains in most other Western democracies (including, as we shall see, Canada). American parties exhibit relatively lower levels of coherence in relation to policy but relatively high levels of partisanship in patronage appointments.[8]

Britain, by contrast, followed quite a different historical trajectory. Prior to the democratization of the electorate, the oligarchic patronage and corruption which had prevailed in the eighteenth and early nineteenth centuries began to give way to a degree of bureaucratization. The Reform Act of 1832 broadened the electorate to elements of the middle class, and the middle class continued to expand its influence through the state and judicial apparatus throughout the nineteenth century. The underlying philosophy continued, however, to be consciously and decisively anti-democratic. Major civil service reform succeeded in the 1870s; in this same era there was a dramatic decline in corruption in local constituency contests.[9] There are a number of explanations for this sequence: the administration of the Empire and the need to manage growing international economic and political competition from European imperial rivals required effective bureaucratic mechanisms; the emergent challenge of working-class demands for incorporation into citizenship called forth in part bureaucratic means of maintaining middle- and upper-class hegemony through state policy administered by responsible and respectable civil servants; and finally, British universities were already producing trained administrators. In fact, education was the key to maintaining upper- and middle-class control over entry into the administration, and was reflected in the division of the civil service into three tiers of administrative, executive and clerical classes.[10]

Reflecting these changes, the Liberal and Conservative parties began competing in the 1870s and 1880s to organize and mobilize their electorates through constituency organizations which were policy rather than patronage oriented. In the first decade of the twentieth century the Liberals took the lead in introducing state welfare programmes (old age pensions, and sickness, disability and unemployment insurance). When the Labour party took a leading role in advancing the demands for extension of the franchise to the working class – that extension came to fruition with the Representation of the People Act of 1918 – it was not only rewarded with the support of the majority of voters of that class but also it was active in structuring the new electorate on programmatic social democratic lines. The Tory-Socialist class politics which has dominated British political life over the past six decades has not eliminated patronage entirely, especially at the local council level, but the programmatic and ideological tone of British politics contrasts with that of American politics. As a reflection of this difference, British public servants are allowed much greater scope than their American counterparts for partisan political activities. The relative partisan neutrality of the British stale allows this, while in the American case a higher degree of partisanship in appointment requires more stringent controls upon civil servants when in office to preserve a degree of administrative efficiency.

Canada stands apart from both the British and American paths with regard to the democratization of the electorate against the background of patronage and bureaucracy. By treating the Canadian experience in comparison to the US and Britain it is possible to cast more light on the significance of patronage in Canadian politics than is possible by studying Canada in isolation.

An excellent start in this regard has been made by the American historian Gordon Stewart in a series of articles and a recently-published book, *The Origins of Canadian Politics*.[11] It would do a disservice to the richness and variety of Stewart's insights to reduce his work to a few simplified points, but for our purposes here the following observations are especially pertinent. Employing the British terms for eighteenth-century political discourse, Stewart discerns a strong "Court" tendency in nineteenth-century Canada in contrast to the more "Country" Whiggism of America. An emphasis on a strong executive is found to be characteristic to both Tories and Reformers; central control of patronage was key to this political enterprise which was prone to the domination of party by strong leaders (of whom Sir John A. Macdonald was by far the most successful). Government's reach into society was largely through the mechanism of party patronage (and "corruption") rather than bureaucracy. Centralized power in Ottawa was checked not by a "Country" opposition but by rival "Court" government in the provinces, themselves relying on extensive control over patronage. Paradoxically, although patronage was employed in the service of stability and political integration during a period of continental nation-building, it actually promoted the long-term persistence of localism and petty partyism. Patronage was distributed from the centre in such a way as to integrate local elites into the national network of party, but the means did not transcend the differences of local community, province, language or religion by substituting common national symbols of loyalty; rather, they only reinforced the degrees of localism and provincialism already in existence. Neither a national ruling class (as in Britain) nor a national ideology (as in America) emerged in Canada. The result was a unique mixture of executive dominance and persistent localism.

Stewart's insights are most stimulating, and lead directly to an appreciation of the broader context of John English's outstanding analysis of the paradox of Borden Conservatism at the time of World War One, when the drive for national integration and bureaucratic rationalization ran headlong into the stubborn particularities of locality and identity – and class.[12] There are, however, some difficulties in Stewart's analysis which emerge more clearly when we turn to the twentieth century and to the (sometimes unfulfilled) extrapolations which Stewart's theorizing on the nineteenth century would suggest. First is a tendency to downplay somewhat the economic basis of politics in favour of a more idealist "political culture" reading. The second is a missing dimension: the democratization of the electorate. These two factors are in fact closely interrelated, as I hope to show.

As is well known, the Canadian political elites remain strongly (and fairly unanimously) anti-democratic in principle throughout most of the nineteenth century. Property and gender qualifications on the franchise continued into the twentieth century, finally being swept away in the early 1920s. Thus party patronage was deeply entrenched long before the construction of mass electorates. Parties were classic "cadre" formations originating in the legislature and reliant on the distribution of state offices and rewards to organize locally, as Stewart shows. As a nation-building instrument, the Macdonald Conservative party not only relied upon elite accommodation arising out of the existing networks of patron-client relations but embodied a project to help construct a national capitalist class in central Canada. This was what the National Policy was all about politically: the Tory party formed the linkage between business interests and public policy. The mechanism of this linkage was what Frederick Gibson called "corporate patronage," as opposed to the older small-scale "staple patronage" of low-level jobs and petty contracts: "tariff adjustments and trade treaties to protect particular industries and firms; government guarantees for corporate bond issues; subsidies and subventions for iron and steel, for railways and shipbuilding; tax concessions; and preferential access to natural resources."[13] This corporate patronage system, crucial to the financing of the Tory party's operations, had specific *class* and *regional* implications. The anti-democratic philosophy still prevalent in the late nineteenth century was given material form in national policies which favoured the bourgeoisie of central Canada at the expense of farmers and workers and the western and maritime hinterlands.

The alacrity, and efficiency, with which the Laurier Liberals took over the Macdonald National Policy after 1896; the successful dumping of the Liberals by big business in the reciprocity election of 1911; and finally the Union government of 1917 were all landmarks along the road to the challenge to the two-party system which boiled over at the end of World War One. It is important to recognize that the challenge to the two-party system was not merely a rejection of the Liberals and Conservatives on policy grounds. It was very much a challenge to partyism itself. Party patronage was identified by the farmer and Progressive movements not as a mere means employed by the old parties, but as part of the problem itself. The new movements wanted to reorient politics around a new public policy agenda in which bureaucratic redistribution superseded patronage transactions. In the theory of group government, parties disappeared altogether to be replaced by producer groups which would negotiate distributive issues directly.

In discussing the primacy of patronage and partyism in Canada, Stewart fails to account for a persistent strain of anti-party and anti-patronage thinking which was embodied in the relatively successful farmers' movements at the end of the war, but which had much deeper roots in the nineteenth century. In the first decades of Confederation, anti-party sentiment was particularly strong among those who looked to a new national ideology which they believed should transcend the narrowly economic self-interest which seemed to underly elite accommodation. Canada First and the Imperial Federation movement both rejected patronage politics in favour of pursuing programmatic (if rather vague) policy outside the instrument of party. These strivings toward national ideology, however, had no firm or coherent material base in class. With the political upheavals in the aftermath of the war, however, this was no longer true. The protest movements of this era did not, of course, succeed in throwing off parties, and indeed where they were elected (in Ontario, Alberta and Manitoba), they themselves governed more or less as parties. Yet they also played an important part in reorienting the national policy agenda toward what has been called the second National Policy with a greater emphasis on bureaucratic redistribution, and were among the sources of the programmatic third parties of the 1930s and 1940s (the CCF and Social Credit).

To recapitulate: patronage politics were rooted in the predemocratic elitist politics of the nineteenth century. Unlike the case of the

United States in the same period, party patronage was not democratized, and thus lacked some of the strength and resilience which is exhibited in the USA. Since patronage was employed by parties which were themselves very much elite organizations which were not addressing themselves to mass electorates but rather to restricted networks of local notables and influentials,[14] its pervasiveness and centrality, as stressed by Stewart, were perhaps misleading guides to its actual strength. For as the electorate gradually expanded in the late nineteenth century (from something like 15 percent of the total population in 1867 to about one in four at the end of the century) until it suddenly exploded to near-universal adult suffrage in the 1920s, patronage politics generated strong opposition from those elements seeking more democratic forms of public representation.

Canada differed from the British experience in significant ways as well. The bureaucratization of politics and the decline of patronage in Britain had been accomplished essentially prior to democratization by an alliance of the old ruling class with elements of the new middle class seeking incorporation into the British state. The already programmatic focus of politics was then turned leftward when the Labour party led the struggle to democratize the franchise. In Canada, the conjuncture of democratization and the attack on patronage created a more complex web of relationships. Elements of the governing Conservatives during the war say that national mobilization and rationalization of economic resources required that the old localism of patronage politics had to be overcome. Local, traditional interests were rejected, but the newer forms of corporate patronage which had emerged out of the National Policy era were not undermined – indeed they formed the material basis for the Tory programme of nationalism. These in turn were vehemently rejected by class, regional and, in the case of French Canada, national interests which together brought about the severe political chastisement of the Conservatives in the election of 1921.

These complexities are best illustrated in the background to civil service reform in 1918. The Tory promise in the election of 1911 to institute a merit system of appointment stemmed directly from a meeting between Borden and a group of key Toronto capitalists who offered to shift their previous support for the Liberals to the Conservatives in return for certain policy pledges. Among these were the merit system under an independent Civil Service Commission, and end to subservience to "Roman Catholic influences in public policy or in the administration of patronage," and a strengthened department of Trade and Commerce with an apolitical mission to sell Canadian products abroad.[15] At first glance this might seem to be an unlikely mixture, but the three points hung together quite logically. Leading elements of corporate capital wanted a more efficient, meritorious state to advance its interests; French Canada was perceived as the strong bastion of the old localism and pre-corporate patronage which stood in the way of the renovation and modernization of the capitalist state. Borden took his time in meeting this expectation, but by 1918 a Union government had proved unable to administer patronage in the traditional manner, and civil service reform offered a way out – as well as responding to a national business programme with which Borden was in substantial agreement, given opportune political conditions.

French Canadians were net losers from civil service reform since (along with the persistence of anti-French prejudice) the Catholic education system did not prepare francophone candidates as well for the merit system of appointment and promotion. The educated middle class in general were beneficiaries at the expense of the less educated. There was a lengthy battle in the 1920s and 1930s between the Civil Service Commission and Members of Parliament – some from French Canada but many from traditional islands of localism in English Canada – over the boundaries between patronage and merit. By the 1940s, however, the battle had essentially been won by the forces opposed to patronage. The famous mandarinate of the senior public service which reached its golden age in the 1940s and 1950s was the most positive evidence of the success of the merit principle.[16] This mandarinate provided the technical expertise to effectively administer a total war mobilization and to carry out a relatively centralized management of the postwar economy, as well as to oversee a vastly expanded Canadian role abroad. Keynesian fiscal policy and elements of welfare state programmes were both better developed in Canada than in the USA, and less developed than in Britain. Specialized bureaucratic forms were relatively highly developed by contrast to the American state in this same era, which continued to rest to a greater degree on partisan appointment and of officials who moved in and out of the state and private sectors with greater frequency than their Canadian counterparts. By contrast, the Canadian state was somewhat less differentiated from partisan politics than the British state: the continued insistence on rigorous prohibitions on partisan activities by public servants under Canadian law and practice indicated a greater sensitivity to the lurking presence of patronage on the margins. The party system in Canada also reflected the distinctive position of Canada between the American and British models. Neither as thoroughly programmatic as British parties, nor as thoroughly unprogrammatic as American parties, Canadian parties constituted, from the mid-1930s on, a hybrid system of strongly policy-oriented third parties, which on occasion achieved office provincially, with traditional parties grafting patronage and localist politics together with bureaucratic policy orientations. The Liberals were the pre-eminently successful party at the national level from the mid-1930s on, and they based their success on a combination of traditional patron-client relations at the local level with dependence upon the policy inputs of the senior civil service.[17] In other words, the construction of a mass Canadian electorate had the effect of partially displacing the centrality of patronage politics in Canadian public life so characteristic of the nineteenth century. The relatively greater presence of the state in Canadian life by contrast to the USA has been explained on widely different grounds, ranging from theories of "defensive expansionism" to ideology and political culture, but from this perspective the historical timing of democratization in relation to the party system is not without considerable significance.

Another major difference between the Canadian and American experiences lies in the connection between the patronage-oriented political machine and the political socialization of immigrants. In the United States, in the words of one writer, the classic big city machines "would probably not have been possible, and certainly would not have been so prominent a feature of the American political landscape, without the immigrant ... Thus it was the succeeding waves of immigrants that gave the urban political organizations the manipulable mass bases without which they could not have functioned as they did."[18] The insecurity of the immigrants in a new land (particularly before the elements of government social security programmes came into being) and the predemocratic cultures from which many of them emigrated combined to offer the party bosses the raw material for building durable patron-client structures within a democratic electoral system.

In Canada, the connection between immigration and patronage is much weaker, and here again the main reason rests with historical timing. In the United States, the era of mass immigration effectively came to an end in the 1920s (although internal migration from poorer rural areas such as the South continued to offer some new fodder for the Northern city machines after the 1920s). In Canada, there were two crests of mass immigration: the first occurred during the first three decades of this century; the second followed World War Two, peaking in the 1960s and early 1970s. These waves of migration had a very different social and political impact on Canada than immigration had on the United States.

The first wave was primarily rural, and was encouraged initially by the Laurier government as agricultural settlement for the prairies. Immigration law and policy were geared to farmer settlers. Rural immigrants were much less "manipulable" by political machines because they were more dispersed and more self-sufficient than the urban immigration of the late nineteenth and early twentieth centuries in America. While the prairies were by no means free of patronage-oriented political machines – the Saskatchewan Liberal machine described in the 1930s by Escott Reid turned out to be a highly durable organization, and ethnic clienteles were a continuing part of that organization – the overwhelming fact remains that it was precisely the prairies which gave birth to many of the third-party protest movements of the first half of the twentieth century. These policy-oriented movements challenged not only the platforms of the two mainstream parties, but their political *practices* as well, and even the very idea of party politics. In part at least the class position of petty bourgeois commodity producer in relation to the monopolistic credit market and rigid mechanisms for the marketing of grain overrode the particularistic politics of ethnic insecurity to produce a more policy-oriented, bureaucratic politics.

The one city in this era which felt a major impact of mass immigration was Winnipeg; here the old political circles proved so incapable of building anything like an American-style political machine that uncontrollable class tensions between workers and capitalists boiled over into the Winnipeg General Strike of 1919. In the aftermath of the strike, ethnic North Winnipeg became a bastion of third-party (social democratic and, to a much lesser extent, Communist) politics.

The second, postwar wave of immigration has been almost entirely urban, but it postdated both the democratization of Canadian politics and the emergence of the welfare state. Provision of services to immigrants was already a bureaucratic, not a political, process. Moreover, the postwar immigrants have been on the whole far better educated and more attuned to contemporary urban life than their predecessors of the pre-World War One era.[19] Big city machines have not been a prominent feature of the political landscape in Canada (the Drapeau machine in Montreal, now defunct, being a partial exception, but one in which immigrant politics played a limited role).

The distinctive features of the Canadian mixture of patronage and bureaucracy have undergone further refinement and clarification in the 1960s and after. The Quiet Revolution in Quebec involved the compressed modernization of Quebec society under bureaucratic auspices.[20] The Lesage Liberals moved toward a more centralized corporate form of patronage than the more traditional Union Nationale,[21] while drawing many welfare functions, from education to social security, out of private church hands into the control of the secular state. At the same time the Quebec government made serious demands on the distribution of powers between federal and provincial levels of government and raised challenges to the federal role which were statist, rather than traditional, in nature. These demands eventually escalated into the sovereignty programme of the Parti Québécois in the late 1970s. English-Canadian provinces, especially Ontario and the West, constructed their own bureaucratic rivals in Ottawa in the 1960s and 1970s. Just as centralized patronage in Ottawa in the late nineteenth century generated rival patronage machines in the provinces, centralized bureaucracy generated rival provincial state apparatuses in the latter half of the twentieth century. Competition for mass electorates tends to be waged on the ground of bureaucratic outputs rather than on the distribution of patronage, which is more restricted to the level of rewards to corporate supporters and to elite party activists. Indeed, executive federalism puts a premium on non-partisan elite accommodation between bureaucracies as the prime mechanism of stability, and leads to serious strains between federal and provincial wings of the same political party.[22]

The growth in the size and complexity of government penetration of the society and the fragmentation of government functions into myriads of special-interest programmes and regulatory agencies each with specialized clienteles[23] has led to the diffusion of power downward to middle-ranges of the bureaucracies, both federal and provincial, where accommodations are made with private interest associations outside of partisan political control. While it is undoubtedly true, as Paul Pross has recently pointed out, that power diffused is power confused, and that Parliament may paradoxically be regaining leverage where coordination is needed, or where accommodations among the "policy communities" at the bureaucratic level prove impossible,[24] it is notable that the re-entry of Parliament is on the terrain of bureaucratic policy output, not on that of party patronage. Indeed, the reawakened interest of pressure groups in parliamentary committees stems above all from the opportunities which committees provide to focus the attention and mobilize the opinion of interested publics on particular policy outcomes. The construction of a mass electorate and the fragmentation of that public into a more diffuse and variegated complex of special interests has bypassed the instrument of party in favour of more direct, unmediated relations between citizen (as manifested in the partial form of particular interests or particular identities) and state (as manifested in the partial form of specialized department, agencies, divisions or programmes).

Parties themselves have attempted, with very limited success, to reconstruct their own organizations in order to come to terms with this new reality. Characteristically this has taken the form of overt attempts to "democratize" party structures, and, in particular, to involve the membership in policy formulation. The Liberal party under Pearson and, initially, under Trudeau developed elaborate participatory mechanism surrounding regular policy conventions.[25] In part, these can be seen as attempts to mobilize participation of urban middle-class people resistant to the (declining) inducements of small-scale patronage on the basis of the more "psychic" rewards of policy-centred participation.[26] The so-called "new politics" also had the unintended – highly damaging – effect of alienating regional party wings outside Toronto by emphasizing national majoritarianism in a country where policy was a divisive, rather than a unifying, force.[27] In any event, the party as a channel for policy formulation has proven to be largely irrelevant when a party is in office and forced to play bureaucratic-interest politics. It is also a source of difficulty when a party is in opposition and seeking to maximize its vote-gathering leverage with the mass electorate in relation to public opinion polls and public relations advice rather than the policy preferences of its own, highly restricted and unrepresentative, membership.

Parties do, however, retain not-unimportant patronage powers, even if they have proven to be weak channels for bureaucratic policy formulation. Parties are, after all, the mechanism for staffing elective offices and thereby the appointments which remain the prerogative of the Governor-in-Council. There are about 350 prestige positions normally named by the Prime Minister: lieutenant-governorship, senate seats, ambassadorships, deputy ministerial posts, heads of important agencies.[28] Some of these, however, are not normally treated as party patronage rewards, other are hedged in by the need to consult provincial governments and even on occasion the Official Opposition in the Commons. An American president will normally dispose of many more such high-level appointments on a freely partisan basis.[29] There are also some five hundred judicial appointments, and many more part-time contracts to lawyers to act as Crown prosecutors or do other legal work for government agencies, or for architects, engineers or other professionals on government business. These are traditional areas of party patronage, closely tied to previous partisan activity or financial contributions to the party. Ironically, the expansion of the state in the postwar era into broader policy areas and more extensive bureaucratic interventions has also expanded the scope for patronage appointments available to federal cabinet ministers. There are now estimated to be well over a thousand appointments to advisory councils and boards housed under department jurisdiction, and positions on the boards of over four hundred Crown corporations and agencies.[30] Many of these latter reflect state interventions into areas once thought to be private. Bureaucratic expansion has carried with it a small echelon of patronage riders which expands along with the growth of governmental functions, rather like markings on the surface of an inflating balloon. Thus, as traditional small-scale patronage has declined with the progress of bureaucratic modernization, new forms of patronage have arisen to take its place. There is, however, a crucial distinction between old and new forms. While old patronage was never as democratic in scope in the American sense, it was diffused much further down the income and status scale than the new patronage which is decisively middle class in nature and available almost exclusively to people with professional or business qualifications. The growth of the capitalist welfare state has "classified" party patronage at the same time as it has bureaucratized redistributive relations for the lower class.

These developments can be glimpsed in greater detail by looking at the political socialization of the immigrant vote in metropolitan areas, to which I alluded earlier. Ethnic politics in the major urban centres of contemporary Canada included well-organized elite support for party organizations and a certain amount of bloc voting (especially for the Liberal party in Toronto and Montreal), Patronage in the old sense, however, is pretty much confined to elite "spokesmen" and does not penetrate down very far into the ethnic communities. Even the patronage which does exist is largely centred around a new kind of bureaucratic policy output: *multiculturalism*, with its various appointed councils and subsidy programmes. More importantly, the major role of the Member of Parliament from metropolitan ridings in relation to his or her immigrant constituents now appears to be as a link between the constituent and the bureaucracy.[31] The MP makes government programmes known to people perplexed by an array of services, and often fronts for constituents experiencing problems with access to the faceless bureaucracy (immigration problems concerning relatives still abroad tend to be high on this list, but making sense of particular circumstances in relation to complex governmental social assistance programmes is a perennial difficulty). This personal link recalls some of the functions of the old machine politician, but the analogy is strictly limited. For one thing, there is no particular need for the MP to be on the government benches to fulfill the role. Opposition MPs can be just as effective, given that they are not offering particularist patronage, as such, but merely facilitating access to the universalized benefits of the bureaucratic welfare state. If opposition MPs discover problems in the administration of government programmes, the government is usually eager to solve the problem to avoid bad publicity resulting from inaction. The point is that the resources are mainly under bureaucratic, not party, control. Patronage in the older sense is mainly a resource for building links between the party and the ethnic group only at the elite level. Once again we find that political patronage exists mainly as a mechanism of elite accommodation, but has only very limited purchase on mass constituencies.

The bureaucracy is itself increasingly resistant to political controls and hints of patronage. The professionalization of the public service, and particularly the unionization of public servants, have created strong barriers to the exercise of patronage from within – so much so that a special government Committee on Personnel Management and the Merit System reported flatly in 1979 that "the likelihood of any return of political patronage is about nil."[32] Public servants and their unions have mounted court challenges to the restrictions on their individual rights to participate in elections on behalf of parties – restrictions which seem to reflect the fears of an earlier era of patronage.[33]

There are clues here to the increasing odium in which patronage is surrounded in public discussion. The introduction of the patronage question in the 1984 election was of a very different order than its place in elections before World War One. In the era of the National Policy, elections were *about* patronage in a structural sense, but patronage was rarely an election *issue*, as such. In 1984 it had become an issue precisely because it was seen as morally problematic. When bureaucratic redistribution dominates political discourse, patronage is seen as anachronistic, inefficient, and deplorable. Patronage runs counter to the logic of the dominant discourse and its defenders have enormous difficulties in justifying their actions in terms acceptable to the public and the media – as witness the public agony of John Turner after making the Trudeau-directed appointments of seventeen Liberal MPs (one sixth of the Liberal caucus) to posts ranging from the Embassy in Portugal to the Livestock Feed Board, or the defensiveness of the Mulroney Tories in the face of a hostile press as they have moved to replace Liberal incumbents with Tory appointees.

Parties face a genuine dilemma. They are organizations which must compete with both the state and the private sector to attract human resources, yet they can offer few of the material incentives which corporations or bureaucratic agencies can provide in the form of high salaries, career advancement, pensions and other fringe benefits. By contrast, they offer much more job insecurity. Parties neither produce goods or services for sale in the market, nor draw directly on tax revenues; they have few resources of their own to deploy. Parties exist to contest elections. Only if they are successful can they provide supporters with real rewards – appointments, contracts and other favours from the state sector which the winning party partially controls. Yet these rewards are relatively few in number and parties face a storm of censure when they do fill them. Moreover, given the apolitical bureaucratic orientation of the state sector, many of the patronage appointments are lost to continued partisan activity once they enter state employment. It is possible to imagine parties which rest on relatively stable class bases with strongly programmatic positions, which would finance and staff their organizations on the basis of motivations associated with policy, but this certainly does not describe the actual Conservative and Liberal parties of today, and perhaps only very imperfectly describes the NDP.

Rumours of the decline of party may be exaggerated, especially when a mythical golden age of the past is counterposed to the present.[34] But in this one instance at least parties have declined in significance as they rest uneasily suspended between the old patronage politics and the new bureaucratic politics. Neither as programmatic nor as ideological as British parties, yet with far fewer patronage resources than their American counterparts, Canadian parties are in search of a role and an enduring foundation.

Their problem, and the increasing odium surrounding party patronage, may be merely another symptom of the decline of elite accommodation as the dominant mode of Canadian politics. The democratization of Canadian life has been in process for many decades at the social and cultural level. There are numerous examples of this which can be indicated, but two may suffice here. University education (pointed to a number of years ago by S.M. Lipset as a sign of Canadian conservatism and elitism by contrast to the more democratic United States) has not only become a much more general phenomenon in the population since the 1950s, but is actually more "democratic" than American higher education in that there is no stratum of elite universities à la Harvard, Yale, MIT, et al.[35] The second example is the emergence of previously underrepresented or unrepresented sections of the population seeking direct public representation (women, gays, old age pensioners, etc.) outside the traditional elite structures, as well as the emergence of issue-oriented "public interest" groups (ecology, peace, pro- and anti-abortion, and so on). Traditional forms of elite accommodation, so characteristic of Canadian politics in the past, have come under increasing strain.[36] Patronage was always a central mechanism of elite accommodation. The practice of patronage has now been identified decisively as a privileged field of reward for political elites whose legitimacy is failing in terms of the democratic discourse of recent decades.

The widely reported scorn for politics and the low esteem with which the public views politicians coincides, paradoxically, but logically enough, with an increasing focus on the public realm for the satisfaction of wants and demands which previously had been considered private, even personal.[37] The politicization of society finds its realization in the bureaucratization of politics. The progress of the democratic principle, which in Canada was first defined, at least in part, in opposition to the politics of patronage, has slowly eroded the practice of patronage and thereby weakened the institution of the political party. It has not, however, replaced that instrument with any functional equivalent mediating between the dispersed and fragmented interests and identities of the society and the diffuse and fragmented apparatus of the state. Classic democratic theory might suggest that the political party could be the means whereby the people express their solidarity around an egalitarian programme to harness the forces of privilege and wealth through state action. Mired in their democratic origins, parties have not been able to free themselves from their past. Nor have the fragmented democratic publics been able to improvise means to transform their diverse interests into coherent expressions of solidarity.

The age of patronage is gone. That of bureaucrats, lobbyists, and PR specialists has succeeded. Alternative democratic politics still lie beyond the horizon.

NOTES

1 *The Race Question in Canada*, 2nd English ed. (Toronto, 1966), 121.
2 Robert Gourlay, *Statistical Account of Upper Canada*, edited by S.R. Mealing (Toronto, 1974), 61.
3 Allan Frizel and Anthony Westell, *The Canadian General Election of 1984* (Ottawa, 1985). 65, 106.
4 Vincent Lemieux, *Parenté et politique: l'organisation sociale dans l'Île*

d'Orléans (Québec, 1971); *Le patronage politique: une étude comparative* (Québec, 1977); Lemieux and Raymond Hudon, *Patronage et politique au Québec: 1944–1972* (Sillery, 1975).

5 John English, *The Decline of Politics: The Conservatives and the Party System 1901–1920* (Toronto, 1977); Reginald Whitaker, *The Government Party: Organizing and Financing the Liberal Party of Canada, 1930–1958* (Toronto, 1977); David Smith, *The Regional Decline of a National Party: Liberals on the Prairies* (Toronto, 1981) and "Party Government, Representation and National Integration in Canada," in Peter Aucoin, ed., *Party Government and Regional Representation in Canada* (Toronto, 1985), 1–68; Ralph Heintzman, "The Political Culture of Quebec: 1840–1960," *Canadian Journal of Political Science* 16, no. 1 (March 1983): 3–60.

6 I am relying here on a crucial article by Martin Shefter, "Party and Patronage: Germany, England and Italy," *Politics and Society* 7 (1977): 403–51, in which the effects of historical sequences of state bureaucratization and electoral democratization on party systems and modes of party politics are analysed, and on a recent article by Ann Shola Orloff and Theda Skocpol which sets this within the context of comparative state policy "Why Not Equal Protection? Explaining the Politics of Public Social Spending in Britain, 1900–1911, and the United States, 1880s–1920." *American Sociological Review* 49, no. 6 (December 1984): 726–50.

7 *Democracy in America*, vol. 1 (New York, 1954), 3, 14.

8 This generalization may have to be partially modified in relation to the somewhat greater policy coherence recently exhibited by the Reagan Republicans: see Thomas Byrne Edsall, *The New Politics of Inequality* (New York, 1984), and "Republican America," *New York Review of Books* (24 April 1986): 3–6.

9 John P. King, "Socioeconomic Development and the Incidence of English Corrupt Campaign Practices," in Arnold J. Heidenheimer, ed., *Political Corruption* (New York, 1970), 379–90; William B. Gwyn, "The Nature and Decline of Corrupt Election Expenditures in Nineteenth Century Britain," in ibid., 391–403.

10 Colin Leys, *Politics in Britain* (Toronto 1983), 233–6.

11 "Political Patronage under Macdonald and Laurier, 1878–1911," *American Review of Canadian Studies* 10 (1980): 3–26; "John A. Macdonald's Greatest Triumph," *Canadian Historical Review* 63 (1982): 3–33; "The Origins of Canadian Politics and John A. Macdonald," in R. Kenneth Carty and W. Peter Ward, eds., *National Politics and Community in Canada* (Vancouver, 1986), 15–47; *The Origins of Canadian Politics: a Comparative Approach* (Vancouver, 1986).

12 English, *The Decline of Politics*, 8–30.

13 Frederick W. Gibson, ed., *Cabinet Formation and Bicultural Relations*, Studies of the Royal Commission on Bilingualism and Biculturalism (Ottawa, 1970), 172.

14 This was noted by contemporary observers. Lord Bryce visited Canada after the completion of his monumental study of *The American Commonwealth*. In Canada, Bryce wrote: "Neither in the Provinces nor in the Dominion does a party victory carry with it a distribution of 'good things' among the minor politicians. To win an election is of course a gain to the leading politicians on the look out for office and for those few underlings who expect sometime or other to receive favours at their hands, but these places are trifling in number compared for those that have to be fought for as spoils of victory in the United States": *Canada: An Actual Democracy* (Toronto, 1921), 21.

15 J.E. Hodgetts, William McCloskey, Reginald Whitaker, V. Seymour Wilson, *The Biography of an Institution: The Civil Service Commission of Canada 1908–1967* (Montreal, 1972), 46–47.

16 J.L. Granatstein, *The Ottawa Men: The Civil Service Mandarins 1935–1957* (Toronto, 1982).

17 Whitaker, *The Government Party*.

18 Elmer E. Cornwell, Jr., "Bosses, Machines and Ethnic Groups," *The Annals of the American Academy of Political and Social Science* (May 1964). 353: 28–9.

19 Peter Oliver's *Unlikely Tory: The Life and Politics of Allan Grossman* (Toronto, 1985), 144–73, has some extremely interesting reflections on the political significance of the postwar immigration to Toronto.

20 Hubert Guindon, "The Modernization of Quebec and the Legitimacy of the Canadian State," in Daniel Glenday *et al.*, eds., *Modernization and the Canadian State* (Toronto, 1978), 212–46; Kenneth McRoberts and Dale Posgate, *Quebec: Social Change and Political Crisis*, rev. ed. (Toronto, 1980); William D. Coleman, *The Independence Movement in Quebec, 1945–1980* (Toronto, 1984).

21 Lemieux and Hudon, *Patronage et politique au Québec*, speak of "le gros patronage" and "le petit patronage."

22 Donald Smiley, *Canada in Question: Federalism in the Eighties*, 3rd ed. (Toronto, 1980), 120–57.

23 Alan Cairns, "The Embedded State: State-Society Relations in Canada," in Keith Banting, ed., *State and Society: Canada in Comparative Perspective*, Research Study of the Royal Commission on the Economic Union (Toronto, 1986), 53–86.

24 Paul Pross, *Group Politics and Public Policy* (Toronto, 1986), 46–83.

25 Joseph Wearing, *The L–Shaped Party: The Liberal Party of Canada, 1958–1980* (Toronto, 1981); Stephen Clarkson, "Democracy in the Liberal Party," in Hugh Thorburn, ed., *Party Politics in Canada*, 4th edition (Toronto, 1979), 154–60.

26 This was first pointed out with regard to urban reform clubs in the US Democratic party in the early 1960s: James Q. Wilson, *The Amateur Democrat* (Chicago, 1966).

27 Smith, *The Regional Decline of a National Party*, 72–89.
28 Christina McCall-Newman, *Grits: An Intimate Portrait of the Liberal Party* (Toronto, 1982), 358.
29 Martin and Susan Tolchin, *To the Victor ... Political Patronage from the Clubhouse to the White House* (New York, 1971), 254. The patronage powers available to a president pale beside those available to some state governors: an incoming governor of Pennsylvania disposes of some 50,000 partisan appointments. No political executive in Canada, federal or provincial, past or present, has ever exercised this kind of scope for patronage.
30 McCall-Newman, 358–9.
31 This has not been studied extensively. See David Hoffman and Norman Ward, *Bilingualism and Biculturalism in the Canadian House of Commons*, Documents of the Royal Commission on Bilingualism and Biculturalism (Ottawa, 1970), 57–120.
32 Committee on Personnel Management and the Merit System (Ottawa, 1979).
33 A judgment in the Federal Court of Appeal in the case of Barnhart *et al.* vs. the Queen and the Public Service Commission in 1986 partially upheld the existing restrictions on partisan activity, but an appeal is being brought before the Supreme Court.
34 John Meisel, "The Decline of Party in Canada," in Thorburn, *Party Politics*, 119–35.
35 S.M. Lipset, *The First New Nation* (New York, 1967), 297.
36 Khayyam Z. Paltiel, "The Changing Environment and Role of Special Interest Groups," *Canadian Public Administration* 25, no. 2 (1982): 198–210.
37 Cairns, "Embedded State" is an eloquent and cogent statement of the pervasiveness of this tendency.

CHAPTER TEN

Quebec and the Canadian Constitution

In this essay, written especially for this volume, I take stock of some of the major changes which have occurred in Canadian politics over the past fifteen years and assess the impact of these changes on the future of Canadian democracy. The conjuncture of an increasingly rights-based liberal discourse as the dominant form of political argument in post-charter Canada along with the ascendance of free-market conservatism, the turn to continentalism under free trade, and the re-emergence of serious tensions between English and French Canada over the language issue and the Meech Lake failure have intersected to form a compounded crisis whose resolution will certainly demand radical answers.

Above all the Meech Lake disaster has recentred the national question. In the wake of Meech, Quebec is moving sharply away from the rest of Canada. As well, the Oka crisis dramatically displayed the other national problem, that of the first nations. In the end, questions of nationalism have the greatest capacity to challenge the fundamental elements of the political community. The nationalizing effects of the charter and the politics of equality have by and large stopped at the Quebec border. This is not to say that gender, sexuality, ethnicity, and class are not playing themselves out in Quebec as in the rest of Canada (not to speak of the rest of the world), but they play within a *Quebec* framework, not a Canadian one. Similarly, the native peoples are demanding self-government and sovereignty as the basis for their own political and cultural development.

It may be a simplification, but there is a sense in which Canadians may soon have to distinguish very clearly and decisively between those who want *in* and those who want *out*. This is a great paradox of democracy. The more the people become conscious of themselves, the more they become conscious of those who constitute the *other*. There is a problem with communities: they all have borders and boundaries – some belong, others do not.

Canadians have made much of the ambiguity of sovereignty. We have distinguished, sometimes carefully, sometimes not so carefully, between state and nation and divided our loyalties between country, region, province. There is something virtuous in this, as I have tried to show in some of these writings, but perhaps it was always making a virtue of necessity. The Quebec challenge of the early 1990s is really a challenge to what we used to call "English Canada," or what we might now call "the rest of Canada," but what may be, at the end of the day, simply *Canada*. This is why the title of this essay is a deliberate inversion of the title of Ramsay Cook's 1966 book *Canada and the French Canadian Question*. In the quarter century since then, the French-Canadian question became the Quebec question, and then the Quebec question became the Canadian question. English Canadians used to ask, in the title of another book of the 1960s, *What Does Quebec Want?* Quebec's sense of purpose and its firm identity now insist that the rest of us consider another, more complex and difficult, question: "What does Canada (with or without Quebec) want?" This surely is the challenge of the 1990s.

"ROLLING THE DICE ..."

In early June of 1990 the eleven first ministers of the Canadian federation were closeted behind closed doors in Ottawa for seven days and seven nights to prevent the country from breaking apart. Three years earlier the first ministers had unanimously agreed to the Meech Lake accord, with its constitutional recognition of Quebec's status as a distinct society within the Canadian federation. Despite this agreement, the accord was now within weeks of expiring since Manitoba had failed to ratify and Newfoundland had de-ratified.

From time to time the ministers emerged to address television cameras before a curious gaggle of spectators waving banners and cheering or jeering. On the final night, the television cameras were allowed behind the doors of the conference room. Each of the ministers spoke in turn of an agreement finally to implement the accord. They sang a ragged version of *O Canada* and the little Greek chorus of spectators dispersed. A scientifically selected sample of the much larger but silent group of spectators sometimes called the citizenry of Canada but perhaps more accurately described as the television audience was subsequently consulted by polsters as to its views. A similar national sample had previously indicated that by and large they understood very little about this constitutional agreement but that, whatever it was, they emphatically rejected it. Now they indicated they still thought it was a bad thing, but that it was important it be ratified so that the country would not break up.

The television audience had to wait for the finale of this three-year-long epic. The entire fate of the agreement, and the recognition of Quebec as a distinct society, rested on a vote of the members of the legislature of the second smallest province in the country – until a lone native member of the Manitoba legislature succeeded by procedural devices in preventing that body from coming to a vote on the issue by the deadline. At the same time, the premier of Newfoundland, in a fit of pique over federal manoeuvres, cancelled the promised vote in his legislature on the eve of the deadline. The accord thus died on 23 June 1990.

To an observer from another planet, or even from another country, this spectacle must have seemed bizarre. It appeared equally strange to many Canadians – and even more so when the immediate background was considered. Ten years earlier, in a referendum, the people of Quebec had rejected the constitutional option of independence from Canada. National bilingualism was accepted in principle by all federal parties and seemingly by substantial numbers of people from both communities. A new constitution, enacted in 1982 without Quebec approval, was to have been completed with Meech Lake's 1987 recognition of Quebec's status as a distinct society. It seemed that Canada had gone a long way toward solving the problems associated with its binational character. Indeed, by comparison to many other countries plagued with divisions along linguistic, cultural, or ethnic lines, Canada seemed to be singularly blessed.

Yet within less than two years, what had appeared to be a skilfully woven web of accommodations had unravelled. By 1989–90, Canada appeared in the media of the wider world as a country riven by fierce communal hatreds, facing separatism and dismemberment.[1] Within Canada, polls showed an increasing majority of Québécois declaring support for sovereignty, and surprising numbers of English Canadians agreeing that they ought to leave. In Montreal schools, edits were threatened forbidding children to speak English to one another on playgrounds, while city councils in Ontario passed resolutions declaring themselves to be English-only municipalities. Quebec businessmen publicly toyed with the idea of abandoning Canada altogether, while sober, respectable opinion leaders in English Canada sorrowfully intoned the doom-laden end of the country we had loved.

The negotiations themselves were a kind of Monty Python hostage drama: the dissenting premiers kidnapped and held in Ottawa by nine desperate first ministers who insisted on their signatures before letting them go. It was reported that an attempt by the premiers of Newfoundland and Manitoba to walk out of the conference was prevented when another premier, a former professional football player, physically stopped them from passing through the doorway. The final death seen on television was, all things considered, a loony spectacle. The prime minister brightly summed up the process as "rolling the dice."

All this does not add up. How could Canada, such a sober, moderate, cautious, sensible kind of country, end up looking like Daffy Duck on a drunken binge, while the world watched with a mixture of bewilderment and head-shaking sympathy?

The easy answer to this question, and the one chosen by many Canadians, is to blame the politicians. Although comparatively little attention had been paid to the undemocratic nature of constitutional politics in the 1980–81 patriation battle,[2] by the late 1980s the elitist, closed-door nature of the Meech Lake affair had become a common complaint of journalists, echoed in innumerable person-in-the-street interviews and open-line shows. But if easy answers are tempting, they rarely account for the whole truth.

Old-style elite accommodation certainly failed. The ludicrous public convulsions of June 1990 were the visible manifestations of a set of discredited political elites trying desperately but ineffectually to paper over their own lack of legitimacy. Insistence on senate reform as an integral part of constitutional change is another symptom of the same malaise. Even the old, unreformed, and unelected senate has roused surprising support by blocking or delaying unpopular legislation from the elected House of Commons. Many groups with strong-held political demands have bypassed the so-called "representative" institutions of government and turned to the appointed and democratically irresponsible court system for redress of their grievances through Charter of Rights litigation. Representative institutions are in trouble.

Yet it would be intellectually dishonest to argue that the answer to Canada's difficulties is simply more democracy. If democracy is a necessary condition, it is by no means a sufficient one. It must be frankly acknowledged that democracy is itself part of the problem, as well as part of the solution.

There are at least three fundamental questions which must be decided in a democracy. First, who are the "people?" Who are included, who excluded? Second, what are the institutional mechanisms for implementing the "will of the people?" Third, how are minorities protected against the oppression of the majority while avoiding a tyranny of the minority? Canada's failure to make up "its" mind about the first issue has led to conflicting sets of institutional arrangements. This in turn has led to a particularly perplexing conundrum associated with the third problem: because it is unclear who constitutes a majority and who a minority, the rules of conduct governing the relations of majorities and minorities are hopelessly confused.

At the heart of these fundamental conundrums of democracy is the national question. Democracy works most easily when "the people" are sharply and distinctively defined by nationality, and those who fall outside this definition are too few and too unthreatening to challenge the dominant definition. History and circumstance have forced Canada to follow a more difficult path, on which two linguistic and cultural communities (one of which is itself deeply riven by regional divisions) have tried to maintain an uneasy and shifting accommodation. The traditional method of maintaining some national equilibrium has been, more or less consciously, to de-emphasize democratic process and rely on the mutual interaction of elites to keep the system together at the top. This system of elite accommodation is inherently conservative, both socially and politically, and discourages democratic control from below. The system has been deteriorating since the 1960s – and the Meech Lake fiasco was an exclamation point loudly marking the close of this phase. Everyone agreed that the process of Meech Lake was unacceptable and should never be repeated. Few, however, could agree on an alternative democratic process to put in its place.

The lack of a clearly articulated democratic alternative is not simply the result of a failure of imagination. As democratic pressures grew and elite domination declined, very different democratic visions, based on differing definitions of "the people," differing conceptions of the majority and minority, and differing conceptions of the institutional arrangements necessary to give voice to the popular will came into focus. While English Canada is not united on these issues, the major division is between Quebec and English Canada. Thus Meech Lake, the "Quebec round" of constitutional change, proved to be the flashpoint for deep antagonisms that were rooted in contradictory democratic visions.

PEOPLES AND NATIONS

The states of Europe imposed national uniformity on diverse peoples, cultures, and languages within their national territories. America began as an idea and Americans then constructed nationality out of ideology. The Declaration of Independence and the Constitution of the United States were ideological constructions which later became symbols of nationalism. The title of a recent book nicely described the founding of American institutions – it was a case of *Inventing America*. The Constitution opens, "We the People, in Order to form a more perfect Union ... do ordain and establish this Constitution."

France was not invented; it was imposed upon other languages and cultures within the territory we now call France. The French Revolution and the Napoleonic empire that followed provided a political discourse for the construction of a France one and indivisible. In the case of both France and America, the role of "the People" is central, both as democratic and national legitimation, even though both come to this point from opposite directions, as it were.

The case of Canada is historically ambiguous. Suspended as always somewhere between Europe and America, Canada began neither as a distinct idea nor as a distinct nationality. The idea of Canada was that it was *not America*. Ideologically, Canada was a space defined negatively by an absence. America was a democratic experiment, founded on a revolutionary rupture with Europe and the European past. The positive ideology of America was a force for the construction of a powerful American nationalism. What Canada stood for ideologically was loyalty to empire and continuity with the past. Yet the sense of nationality which these things presupposed was both borrowed from abroad and divided from within. An irony of Canadian history is that instead of reinforcing one another, ideology and nationalism have played against each other. First the conservative ideology of loyalism divided Canadians between British and French nationality. Then, as a more liberal and democratic ideology displaced the older conservative elitism, the growing sense of popular participation in public life and self-determination emphasized that two mutually exclusive images of "the People" were in contention.

Another irony: the constitutional and institutional framework of Canadian federalism pits ideology and nationalism against one another in a way that constantly displaces democratic aspirations onto the terrain of power struggles between governments.

QUEBEC NATIONALISM AND
CANADIAN DEMOCRACY

The evolution of Quebec nationalism, from the outset of the Quiet Revolution in 1960 through the sovereignty-association referendum of 1980, shows this process of displacement at work. The Quiet Revolution was both the expression of a modernized and thus more positive and effective Quebec nationalism and an internal renovation of Quebec society and politics. In the latter aspect, it represented a highly compressed liberalization and democratization of a society which had been held too long under conservative elite domination from within, as well as domination from without. The effects of the Quiet Revolution in hastening the decline of the ideological and cultural influence of the church and the traditional elites are well known. What is less well known, and certainly not often noted, is the somewhat perverse effect the democratic renovation of Quebec had upon Canadian democracy in general.

The dominant discourse of the new Quebec nationalism in the 1960s and into the 1970s was *statist*. Sometimes confused by politically illiterate right-wingers in English Canada with socialism, this statism was simply a logical response to the dominant position of English-Canadian and American capital in the private sector. To become *maîtres chez nous* it was necessary for francophone Québécois to utilize the instrument of the Quebec state, the only instrument in the early 1960s that could be under francophone control. This turned out to be a passing phase of nationalism. Although the Parti Québécois retained a social democratic and moderately statist cast when they arrived in office in 1976, the PQ proved in practice to be a transition stage toward the thoroughly neo-liberal market nationalism which came to dominate Quebec under the Bourassa Liberals in the 1980s. In the early 1990s Quebec has clearly become a society which is more market-oriented and less statist than English Canada – a complete reversal of the situation of the 1960s. Yet even now Quebec governments are concerned with defining a more autonomous political space within which the new Quebec bourgeoisie can flourish.

Post-1960 Quebec nationalism, *positive* by contrast with the negative and defensive nationalism of the Duplessis era which preceded it, found its way blocked by the fiscal and administrative power of Ottawa. In order to fulfil its agenda for Quebec it was necessary to reconstitute federalism, to make demands upon Ottawa for new powers (or old powers usurped by Ottawa, it makes little difference). Thus for English Canadians the impact of the Quiet Revolution was felt mainly in the insistent demands of the government of Quebec for more power. Rather than being posed as a social question of relations between English and French Canadians, it became a question of *intergovernmental affairs*. As such it quickly resolved itself into elite bargaining and bureaucratic negotiation. Thus the famous concept of *executive federalism*. Later other provinces picked up Quebec's cue and joined in an increasingly complex process, but Quebec, where a province-building agenda was reinforced by powerful nationalist drives, has remained at the centre of the dynamic. Thus in both its statist and market phases Quebec nationalism has had the same inadvertent but perverse effect on Canada, that of reinforcing the old political and bureaucratic elitism.

It is perhaps paradoxical, but quite in keeping with contemporary experience elsewhere in the world, that as Quebec modernized and thus became less distinct in its cultural identity at the mass level and more integrated into international popular culture, its political identity as a distinct nation solidified. As traditional bonds of authority and order (religion, patriarchal family, the local notables, patronage) waned, the *imagined community*[3] of the sovereign nation waxed. But the insistence on the presentation of Quebec to the external world (including the rest of Canada) as a unity struggling for the symbols and the instruments of political sovereignty inevitably reinforced the statist and thus elite-driven response of the other constituent units of the Canadian political community.

Democracy in Quebec has been viewed above all as national self-determination. What are certainly democratic demands have often been couched in the language of the constitutional and fiscal powers of the Quebec state. The response from English Canada has been to re-jig the terms and mechanisms of executive federalism. Thus the official discourse of Canadian politics has been permeated with reification. "Quebec," "Canada," "Ontario," "Alberta" appear as collective actors, leviathans whose constituent parts – individuals, classes, genders, ethnic groups, cultural and religious communities – have often been given scant attention.

Nationalism in Quebec generated a dialectic of opposition from within, and Quebec anti-nationalism extended onto the national stage with the arrival of Pierre Trudeau as prime minister in 1968. Despite Trudeau's liberal federalist philosophy, in practice his government set out another statist alternative: a federal government strengthened by "French Power" and national bilingualism as a counter-pole of attraction to an emergent semisovereign state of Quebec.

THE QUESTION OF SOVEREIGNTY-ASSOCIATION

These competing statist visions came to a head with the sovereignty-association referendum of 1980. What is particularly ironic about this is that in certain respects the referendum was a landmark in the evolution of Quebec democracy. The PQ's decision not to move down the path toward independence without the explicit approval of the people was both prudent and courageous. It was prudent because separating the act of voting PQ and opting for sovereignty allowed the PQ to come to office in the first place; yet it was also courageous because it submitted the party's very *raison d'être* to the independent will of the people, a proposition whose riskiness became all too apparent in the result. The referendum campaign, despite the deformations inevitably placed upon such an event in the age of media manipulation, was a moving example of a people collectively making a crucial decision about the nature of their political community. Never before or since in Canadian history have the people been taken so seriously by the political elite, and in general they responded with a dignity and gravity befitting such responsibility.

English Canadians outside Quebec were mere spectators to this event. Yet the very fact of the referendum and its place within the wider Canadian political context demonstrates that the power of democratic legitimacy transcended the rules of constitutional law and the confines of executive federalism. A crabbed and narrow definition of the rules might suggest that there was no "legal" way for a province to separate. Just such a definition had once driven the United States into a savage civil bloodletting and the enforcement of national unity by bayonets. By the time of the Quebec referendum campaign it was already quite clear that, whatever the outcome, the will of the Quebec people would be unanswerable, by either the Quebec or the federal government. If Quebec voted "yes," the federal government and the other provinces would have no choice, like it or not, but to commence negotiations for Quebec's eventual accession to sovereignty. In the event, sixty percent voted "no" and it was the *indépendantiste* government of Quebec which had to accommodate itself to an unpleasant but clear verdict. Democracy won.

And lost. The problem with democracy as practised in societies too large for face-to-face contact of citizens is that choices, even if left to the decision of the people, are structured by elites. In representative democracy, it is parties which structure the choices available to voters. Referenda are in one sense more directly democratic in that people make choices unmediated by party representatives. But the form of the question put in a referendum powerfully structures how the public can express its will. This was striking in the devious manner in which the PQ composed its all-important question.

The referendum itself did not pose the question of independence clearly. The PQ insisted – an insistence which went back to the party's founding – that it would present the idea of political sovereignty for Quebec only in association with some continued form of economic association with Canada. In fact the original grouping which became the PQ was called the *mouvement souveraineté-association*. This was clearly done for reasons of political expediency, to mollify fears of economic disruption and loss of capital attendant upon a sudden political shift toward separation. But it perhaps also expressed a dominant understanding among *péquistes* that independence was to be understood only in a political sense, while economic independence was a relatively meaningless concept in a world of increasingly internationalized capital. This suggests that the PQ was in no way a vehicle for a socialist or state-centred nationalism that might have posed at least a theoretical alternative to capitalist interdependence and interpenetration. The PQ clearly did not share a Marxist belief that economics were the foundation for a political superstructure. Rather the spheres of politics and economics were separate, although interrelated. They appeared to believe that political sovereignty would be a superior position from which to bargain for a better set of economic relationships with the rest of Canada.

The PQ proposition, in a nutshell, was that an economic community could be maintained at the same time as the political framework of that community was being demolished. This runs counter to the fundamental basis of the modern state. If the PQ had envisaged some fundamental alteration in the form of the state, such alternative visions of political order might have been possible. But this was not part of the PQ agenda. Instead they adopted an entirely conventional notion of the state and political system: citizenship in the conventional liberal state involves a set of reciprocal rights and obligations shared with fellow citizens, economic rights in the welfare state are matched with some economic obligations through redistribution, and redistribution in a federal state should take place between provinces and regions.

The PQ's referendum proposition did two things: it asked if people wanted sovereignty but it tied this sovereignty to a promise of a particular form of economic association with Canada. The essential problem with this is that while the PQ could certainly ask the first question, they had no business promising the second as a corollary of the first. In their pre-referendum statements of how they envisaged this association (a document called, significantly, *Égal à égal* and their White Paper on sovereignty-association) they argued that they could in fact establish not the same relationship they had previously enjoyed under federalism but a *better* one, that is, one more advantageous to Quebec. To this end they projected a series of commissions to regulate the association, on which Quebec would have equal, or near equal, representation with Canada. These commissions, it should be noted, would be appointed and thus at yet one further remove from democratic accountability than the existing institutions of executive federalism.

What claims does Quebec have to equal representation with Canada when it represents roughly one in five of the Canadian population? Here we have to uncouple the two parts of the referendum proposition. If Quebec were not to separate from Canada (if the answer to the first part of the question were no), then the second part would have to be answered in the context of the existing rights and obligations obtaining among members of the Canadian community. Arguments for binationality, special status, a distinct society, etc., which would have the effect of enhancing Quebec's representation beyond its demographic proportion (and beyond the other provinces) have been made, and have even been realized to a limited extent – but within the context of existing constitutional relations. Certain claims can be made by French Canadians or by Quebec on historical grounds (e.g., minority language rights, which cannot be legitimately advanced by other linguistic groups such as Ukrainian or Hindi speakers, or special status to control old age pension funds, which cannot be claimed by other provinces), but these claims are related to obligations accepted by francophones, such as paying taxes to Ottawa, and by the government of Quebec in accepting the legitimacy of a federal government which is elected by a majority of anglophones. Claims for more than proportional representation would have to be assessed according to a kind of prudential calculus involving constitutional law, historical precedent, relative bargaining power, and political expediency and the structure of rights embedded within the existing community.

If the answer to the first part of the question were yes, however, the situation is radically altered. The effect of a yes vote would be that Quebec was renouncing its obligations by asserting a unilateral right. This right is self-referential only and is realized by breaking away from the reciprocal rights and obligations of the wider community. Having thus snapped the bonds of the community, or signalled its firm intention to do so, which amounts to the same thing, Quebec loses its capacity to argue its claims in the same language and by the same calculus that it can use when the answer to the first part of the question is no. A different set of rules must now come into play, those that normally govern the relations between independent sovereign states. There is of course an abstract equality which exists between any two sovereign states that negotiate with one another bilaterally: there are two sides to the bargaining table and two signatories to a bilateral agreement. But it requires little analysis to conclude that this equality is merely formal and is often a highly misleading guide to the actual balance of power between the two. For instance, Canada is an "equal" partner with the US in the Free Trade Agreement; but no one could seriously believe that there is substantive equality between two states whose populations, power, and wealth are so unbalanced.

Relations between an independent Quebec and a Canada without Quebec, and thus the specific form of economic association, would be based on relative bargaining power and political expediency but *not* on constitutional law, historical precedent, or mutual rights and obligations embedded within the existing community structure. Negotiations based only on relative bargaining power and political expediency are driven by the moral calculus of self-interest and concern for consequences. Concretely, as a Canadian citizen I would look quite differently upon Quebec claims in the latter case than in the former. I would specifically deny that citizens of Quebec any longer had valid claims upon me as a citizen. My concern as a citizen would now become a concern that my government conclude a bargain most favourable to me and my fellow Canadians. To be sure, enlightened self-interest would dictate that any bargain struck be fair, so that it would not rebound against the position of my own community, and thus against myself (i.e., that it not force an eventual backlash on the other side). But my calculation of fairness would be quite different than a calculation of fairness made in the case of relations between fellow members of the same community. In practice, it is highly doubtful, given the disproportion in population, resources, etc., that negotiations with an independent Quebec would result in the degree of substantive equality between Quebec and Canada which the PQ promised.

The PQ referendum question, by refusing to recognize this distinction, was presenting a dishonestly posed choice to Quebec citizens. It was attaching a unilaterally formulated promise of a particular form of economic association, which it could not keep, to its assertion of political sovereignty, which it could make unilaterally. But if the latter were premised upon the former, that is, if Quebec voters had chosen to demand independence *because* they were convinced it would result in precisely the form of association promised by the PQ, then even the assertion of a will to be politically independent would itself have been tainted and uncertain.

An honest approach would have been quite different. The Quebec government would have posed a simple question: do you wish to form an independent, sovereign Quebec? Armed with a clear mandate based upon an expressed will of the majority for independence, the Quebec government could then have initiated negotiations with Canada.[4] This would of course have been politically chancy, but sixty percent of the electorate rejected even the qualified, tortuous, and dishonest question which was posed. If most of the people who did vote yes were actually voting for sovereignty, *tout court*, for which there is some empirical evidence, then a "clean" question would have armed the PQ with the support of a substantial minority upon which further political mobilization might build.

THE TRUDEAU CONSTITUTION

Intellectual dishonesty was certainly no monopoly of the yes side. Proponents of the no side took great pains to present their position as positive rather than negative. Thus a no vote was said to be a vote *for* a "renewed federalism." The no side quite brilliantly captured the ambivalence of Quebec citizens about their political community with campaign buttons which declared *"Je suis fière d'être Québécois et Canadien."* But what was this renewed federalism which was promised in exchange for rejecting sovereignty-association? Claude Ryan was at the head of the no side, and his Quebec Liberal party had earlier published the so-called "Beige Paper" outlining the Liberal view of a renewed decentralized federalism in which Quebec held a position of virtual equality with the rest of Canada. But it was not Claude Ryan and the Quebec Liberal party who were in a position to realize a new federalism after the referendum. It was Pierre Trudeau and the federal Liberal party. Their vision of a renewed federalism proved to be something rather different.

The Trudeau vision did not deny that Quebec was, as Trudeau himself once put it, *"le foyer et le centre de gravité de la nation canadienne française."* But what Trudeau wished to avoid was the conflation of French Canada and/or "Quebec" with the government or state of Quebec. The concern with francophones outside Quebec reflected in the policy of national bilingualism was not, as some have claimed, an attempt to deny the social reality of Quebec identity but rather an attempt, in a typically Trudeau manner, to constitute a political counterweight to the dynamic of Quebec nationalism which he believed would, if left uncontested, eventually find political expression in a separate state and the breakup of Canada. As Trudeau has written recently, "we were very aware that Quebec nationalist thinking tends both to identify the interests of the French-Canadian collectivity with the province of Quebec and to confuse language with ethnicity, which gives rise to expressions like 'the two founding nations of Canada' and 'Quebec, the founding state of French Canadians.' "[5] His answer was to enhance the position of individual francophones through constitutional guarantees of language and educational rights across Canada.

This fit very well with Trudeau's liberal philosophy, but it failed to appreciate that what he calls "Quebec nationalist thinking" is in fact more widespread and pervasive than he would like to admit, and that it was this and not the Trudeau alternative which was presented to Quebec voters in the referendum campaign. A renewed federalism surely meant some sort of special constitutional status for Quebec that recognized that it is not a province *comme les autres* but constitutes a distinct society or nation within the framework of federalism. Pan-Canadian individual rights do not speak to the Québécois sense of collective identity and the need to protect this through the one collective instrument clearly under their control, the government of Quebec. This special status was not recognized in the Canada Act, and it is hardly surprising that Quebec refused to sign. Much was made at the time and later about this being inevitable since the government of Quebec was separatist. Yet it is highly unlikely that any Quebec government, separatist or federalist, would or could have signed the 1981 deal. The unfinished business of 1981 was to find an appropriate balance between the national pan-Canadian orientation represented in the Charter of Rights and the need for distinct status for Quebec.[6] Despite Trudeau's later attack on Meech Lake as antithetical to his own conception of constitutionalism, Meech Lake was already latent in the 1981 deal in the latter's pregnant silence about the fundamental claims of Quebec.

THE CHARTER OF RIGHTS

If Trudeau's constitution failed to answer the question to Canada posed in the no vote in the Quebec referendum, it succeeded beyond its framers' wildest dreams in its impact upon English Canada. The inclusion of the Charter of Rights was a clever political tactic in the prolonged struggle over patriation in 1980–81. By mobilizing groups from across Canada to argue about how the charter should be strengthened, it thus undermined those who opposed the patriation package as a whole. But in practice the charter has proved to be much more than a tactic. It is no exaggeration to say that, for good or ill (probably some of each), the charter has helped effect a veritable revolution in the political culture of English Canada, whose effects will continue to be assessed for some time to come.

The American political sociologist Seymour Martin Lipset, who has been studying comparative political values in Canada and the United States for a generation, concludes in a recent book that the charter "probably goes further toward taking the country in an American direction than any other enacted structural change, including the Canada-U.S. Free Trade Agreement."[7] "Americanization" may not be the best way of understanding the impact of the charter, but the depth of the change in political values it reflects can no longer be seriously in question. Some have criticized this impact severely, while others have praised it extravagantly. What is certain is that political life after the charter is very different from life before the charter. Some have gone so far as to suggest that Canada is becoming a "rights society." Canadians have adopted the language of rights as a means of expressing their sense of their own value and dignity as citizens. The use of this language has profound implications on how people relate to their governments and to each other.

To capture the full flavour of the enthusiasts for the charter, we can do no better than to turn to the words of the charter's most immediate parent, Pierre Trudeau:

In the grand tradition of the 1789 Declaration of the Rights of Man and the Citizen and the 1791 Bill of Rights of the United States of America, it implicitly established the primacy of the individual over the state and all government institutions, and in so doing, recognized that all sovereignty resides in the people ... In this respect, the Canadian Charter was a new beginning for the Canadian nation: it sought to strengthen the country's unity by basing the sovereignty of the Canadian people on a set of values common to all, and in particular on the notion of equality among all Canadians.[8]

As so often with Mr Trudeau's eloquent rhetoric, one is tempted to riposte: "Yes, but ..." The theory linking a constitutionally entrenched Charter of Rights with the concept of popular sovereignty is clear enough: the people constitute government for certain specified purposes but reserve certain matters to themselves out of reach of government. So too the linkage of the charter with equality: individual rights are universal attributes of citizenship and thus belong equally to all. That, as they say, is the theory. Practice is another matter.

First there is the inclusion of s.33, the famous "notwithstanding" clause permitting legislatures to override parts of the charter. Rejected by some as a contradiction to the very idea of a charter,[9] and lauded by others as striking an appropriate balance between parliamentary supremacy and the constitutional regime, s.33 does set the Canadian charter apart from the American Bill of Rights, which contains no such derogatory clause.

Then there is the awkward problem of the prominent role of the judiciary and the concomitant decline of elected institutions. Rights claims must be submitted to the courts. Judges are appointed officials not subject to popular control, yet the effect of charter litigation may well be to transfer power away from those institutions which do fall under some popular influence (legislatures) to these democratically irresponsible officials. Some have written of the "judicialization" or "legalization" of politics as an anti-democratic trend, leading to demobilization of popular struggles and their transmutation into expensive battles of lawyers and judges carried out in a discourse inaccessible to ordinary people.[10] Others, perhaps proceeding from a less radical perspective, have raised concerns about a so-called "rights society" in which litigious Canadians advance rights claims as trumps against other claims; they wonder about an emphasis on rights without an acceptance of obligations.[11]

These are serious objections which carry much force. But the books are not closed on the argument. As I have argued elsewhere, one of the problems which critics of the charter have not properly addressed is the elitist nature of the representative institutions and their inability to cope with the needs of minorities.[12] Alan Cairns has suggested that the charter may be the means by which "the citizens of a fragmented society may achieve an integrating collective sense of themselves from their common possession of rights and the availability of a common language of political discourse."[13] Certainly the charter offers an avenue for previously marginal groups left out of the majoritarian institutions of representative democracy. It is not so much the actual route of charter litigation which may be most important but rather, as Cairns suggests, the "availability of a common language of political discourse." In this regard it would be a mistake to see the charter as the *cause* of changing political values; rather it is both a contributing cause and an *effect* of deeper changes which have been going on for some time in Canadian society. Taken together, those have led to a more expansive and inclusive definition of democratic citizenship.[14]

Trudeau himself has declared, and many observers have concurred, that a major effect of the charter has been to develop a new basis for attracting citizens to the national government.[15] If this was the long-range strategy of the Trudeau Liberals in attaching the charter to the patriation package in 1980–81, it has already succeeded, at least in part. One can now discern a new concept of political community taking firm hold in English Canada. It is one in which individual and group rights are guaranteed by a constitution identified above all with the national state. Traditional mechanisms of elite accommodation and executive federalism tend to decline in legitimacy as groups assertively raise claims on the national stage.

Whether this development heralds a greater degree of national unity or national integration is unclear. It may indeed only serve to intensify conflicts and heighten the degree of fragmentation which has always characterized Canadian society, while – and here is the rub – disabling some of the available mechanisms for bridging and accommodating differences. This was already evident at the time of the debate over the charter in 1980–81. While the charter sparked significant popular mobilization, the thrust of this mobilization was almost entirely around special interests and particularist identities. What *united* people about the charter was what *divided* them as Canadians. On the other side, there was little if any public support for the one element of the Trudeau constitutional package which emphasized the democratic collectivity, the referendum procedure for constitutional amendment. A new, more rights-conscious Canada left the old elite mechanisms in place but lowered their legitimacy: a prescription for future disaster soon to be filled at Meech Lake. The 1981–82 constitutional process demonstrated the strength of group liberalism more than that of democracy.

The charter represents and symbolizes a political discourse which extends traditional liberalism to a wider number of constituencies. But it speaks more weakly to the compromises and mediations required by a common citizenship. The language of rights has a marked tendency to be stridently principled and thus uncompromising. The bitter and irreconcilable abortion struggle, couched in terms of the right to choice versus the right to life, bears fierce witness to just how passionate and hateful a rights-as-trumps debate can be. No doubt the abortion controversy is the worst-case scenario, but even rights debates with lower levels of intensity bear signs of the same uncompromising quality.

By far the most serious deficiency of the "rights society" engendered by the charter is that it has been largely limited to English Canada, with serious consequences for Canadian unity. This is by no means to suggest that Quebec is less liberal or interested in the rights of individuals than English Canada. It is a mark of Quebec's maturity as a liberal democratic society that guarantees of human rights are at least as well entrenched as they are in other provinces.[16] Nor is there any evidence that Quebec opinion is any less liberal on matters of civil liberties and civil rights than English Canadian opinion. But the charter as a force for national unification is mainly, if not exclusively, an English-Canadian phenomenon.

For English Canadians, the charter has provided a common language (even if, ironically, that language may itself be divisive) and a common focus, a sense of shared universality and equality. The Québécois did not require, and have firmly resisted, any such externally imposed direction. Here we come again to the fundamental division of the "people" into two distinct nations. This would not be a matter of great significance were it not for the impact the charter has had on upsetting the equilibrium between the two peoples. The universalist language of the charter does not easily permit or tolerate such concepts as distinct societies or special status. And the distinct identity of Quebec does not easily permit or tolerate what appears as an invasive imposition of externally derived values and rules. These differences became most painfully apparent in the conflict over language rights which broke out in late 1988.

LANGUAGE AND POLITICS

If there were any lingering doubts about the profound impact of the Charter of Rights on Canadian politics, they should have been removed by the Supreme Court's decision on the constitutionality of Quebec's language law (Bill 101).[17] Citing the charter and the Quebec Human Rights Code, the court ruled that Quebec could not prevent the use of English on commercial signs. Within a week of the decision, the largest and most militant nationalist demonstrations in over a decade swept Montreal, and the Quebec government felt compelled to override both the charter and its own code in reenacting and amending 101 (now 178). Three anglophone Quebec cabinet ministers resigned in protest. This crisis really began the derailment of the Meech Lake constitutional accord. A handful of judges armed with the charter showed that they could turn Canada upside down.

Expressions of regret, or even outrage, at Quebec's use of the notwithstanding clause to override the Charter of Rights, have been nearly universal throughout English Canada. Not only is this in rather strange contrast to the insistence on the inclusion of this clause by the provincial premiers in 1981, but it is also in strange contrast to the near-universal silence which greeted the use of s.33 by the Saskatchewan government of Grant Devine a few years earlier in a bill legislating striking provincial employees back to work.

The sign provisions of 101 were strongly supported by the majority in Quebec. This is partly for reasons intrinsic to the purposes of the language law. If French is to be secure within the boundaries of Quebec, it is important to maintain an urban landscape of signs and symbols that reinforces the predominance of French and clearly indicates to immigrants the linguistic character of the province.

Nowhere else in Canada or North America is there a secure base for the French language; only Quebec has the capacity to legislate the external reassurances that it is truly *home* to Francophones. This may be symbolism, but it is deeply important symbolism that the majority will not allow to be snatched away – especially by a federal court sitting in Ottawa. In fact, the Court itself recognized that the maintenance of a *visage linguistique* (the Court used the French phrase even in its English text) is a valid purpose of public policy, which could even justify the legislation of the "marked predominance" of French over English in commercial advertising.

The visibility of French in Quebec is also symbolic in another, related sense. The Supreme Court's ability (in the absence of the override power) to threaten the integrity of the sign provisions of 101 raised the spectre of further legal challenges to the more important parts of the language legislation. That the legislative guarantee of the French language might be insecure is clearly intolerable to a linguistic majority in Quebec which is also a tiny majority in an anglophone North America. The security provided by 101 has underwritten Quebec's continued adherence to Canadian federalism – as some honest anglophones in Quebec have admitted, although more often in private than in public. The corollary of this proposition is obvious: if the notwithstanding clause did not exist to protect the language law, independence would once again become a necessary option.

On grounds of political prudence, both the existence of s.33 and its use by the Bourassa government seem amply justified. But the anti-Quebec clamour which broke out in English Canada explicitly eschewed reasoning based on political prudence. Instead the issue has been debated as a question of *rights*. More precisely the question has been couched as a conflict between "collective rights," claimed by Quebec and rejected by English Canada, and "individual rights," claimed by English Canada and rejected by Quebec. Premier Bourassa explicitly noted that in coming up with an amended version of 101 he was compelled to make a "difficult adjudication" between individual and collective rights.

Yet even if it is taken at face value, this philosophical debate fails the first test of political relevance: it does not deal with the facts. To hear English-Canadian politicians talk, one would think that the primacy of individual rights had been (to quote one resigning Quebec minister) "imbibed with their mother's milk." Memories are short: at the time of this controversy, the Charter of Rights was less than seven years old! Collective rights are much older and more deeply entrenched in our constitutional and political practices.

In the BNA Act of 1867 there is no reference to individual rights, as such. There are, however, clear references to collective rights with regard to language and religious education. The language provisions (s.133) state that laws, parliamentary debates, and court proceedings may be in either English or French at the federal level – and in Quebec. The latter was the only province of which bilingualism was demanded and it is clear from the context that the object of s.133 was to protect the collective rights of the anglophone minority. For the same reasons, Quebec alone was saddled with an appointed upper chamber of its legislature (abolished only in the 1960s), the purpose of which was to protect the anglophone Protestants of Quebec from the francophone Catholic majority. Similarly, the premise of s.93, dealing with minority education, is the collective rights concept: separate schools are guaranteed for the "Queen's Protestant and Roman Catholic subjects" where they form minorities. This provision, recently upheld by the Supreme Court in the Ontario separate schools reference case against a challenge based on the charter, is as forceful a statement of collective rights as can be imagined. Again, in the context of the 1867 act, it is clear that the main object was to protect the Protestant minority in Quebec.

In short, the concept of collective rights is an original element of the Canadian constitution, one which is arguably better entrenched than the more recent concern with individual rights. It is ironic that collective rights were largely designed to serve the anglophone Protestant minority of Quebec, the very minority which now claims the primacy of individual rights against the threat of the collective rights of the francophone majority.

Of course, much in the nature of Canadian society and politics has changed since 1867 to alter the contextual meaning of "rights" in the late twentieth century. A new rights-consciousness is expressed in terms of individual rights and in the growth of what may be called "group rights." The latter lie somewhere between collective and individual rights in that they acknowledge disabilities and unequal treatment of certain groups (women, visible ethnic minorities, disabled people, etc.) without investing these rights in any collective bodies. The group concept is recognized in s.15, the equality rights section of the charter, along with its provision for affirmative action programs for disadvantaged groups. In these cases, claims must be made by individuals, but on the basis of group discrimination. The "distinct society" clause of the Meech Lake accord, on the other hand, seemed to reaffirm the older collective rights notion, in that the Quebec government was designated as bearing the right, and obligation, to advance the distinct character of

Quebec society. The case of native people, to the extent that their claims have been embodied in constitutional discussions, seems to have more closely followed the model of collective rather than group rights. As the debate over Meech proved, this mixture was volatile.

A second, and crucial, contextual factor is the rise of the new Quebec nationalism and the renegotiation of the fundamental bargain which has underlain the relations between English and French Canada. This bargain began to unravel over the bilingual signs issue. Like many important political accommodations that strike a delicate balance between conflicting social forces, it is the essence of this bargain that it is tacit and not articulated in the clear and unequivocal language of constitutional principles. In societies divided along lines of linguistic and cultural community, universalist principles may only deepen divisions. Skilful compromises that do not speak their name are usually wiser, although difficult to sustain.

The language sections of the Charter of Rights were designed by Pierre Trudeau in the name of individual rights. The Parti Québécois launched Bill 101 in the name of collective rights. Irreconcilable principles? In practice, not at all. Individual language rights actually presuppose collective rights: two language groups, English and French, are recognized as having a historically privileged priority, one not accorded to other linguistic groups. The Liberal view was not as far away from the PQ position as the rhetoric indicated. And indeed, in practice the Liberal position was much more flexible than might have been anticipated.

As for the PQ position, its apparent hard line defence of collective rights was by no means as illiberal as many have assumed. Even the philosophical defence of 101 on its first introduction in the National Assembly by Dr Camille Laurin – always considered the most culturally nationalist of PQ ministers – was rather liberal in inspiration. French, argued Dr Laurin, was at a distinct disadvantage in North America and it was the obligation of the government of Quebec to intervene so as to right that disadvantage and thereby guarantee equality of opportunity for francophones. In keeping with this liberal perspective, the traditional rights of the anglophone minority were protected by 101. Indeed, every aspect of English language use that touches upon freedom of expression as traditionally understood (but not commercial signs) was protected: anglophones are free to express themselves in their own English-language media and institutions of education, as well as to receive health and social services in their own language.

However tempered with liberalism, the legislative intent of 101/178 is at bottom concerned with sovereignty – but not necessarily sovereignty in the sense of independence. Rather, language is a sovereignty issue in Quebec in that it revolves around the sovereign right of the Quebec community, through those political institutions under its control, to legislate the priority of the French language within the boundaries of the community. The historical irony is that the PQ's very success in framing and implementing a clear, effective, and relatively liberal language law – arguably its major achievement in two terms in office – was also the single act which did most to undermine the PQ's own option of sovereignty-association. If Quebec could exercise sovereignty in legislating language within the framework of the Canadian federation, perhaps it did not require sovereignty in the full political sense. Here indeed was the very basis for a tacit accommodation between the Liberal federalists and the PQ *indépendistes*. The protection of the essentials of 101 could underwrite Quebec's continued membership in the federation.

Despite the apparent antagonism between the Lévesque and Trudeau governments, including language provisions in the Charter of Rights in 1980–81 constituted a compromise between the spirit of national bilingualism as an individual right and the collective right of Quebec to make the French language secure within its jurisdiction. S.23 of the charter, on minority language educational rights, was drawn up in such a way as to prevent any possible challenge to one of the key provisions of 101: the requirement that immigrants to Quebec have their children educated in French. Along with the language of work, this is perhaps the most crucial part of 101, given the demographic threat to a francophone majority in Montreal posed by the previous tendency of immigrants to opt for English-language schooling. In effect, the Trudeau government secured this section of 101 from a charter challenge. Moreover, on equality rights s.15 did *not* include "language" as one of the explicit grounds upon which individuals could claim they were suffering from discrimination. Although this may not be enough to prevent a challenge to the language of work sections of 101, it would make such a challenge more difficult to sustain. Interestingly enough, the silence of the federal charter equality sections regarding language stands in contrast to Quebec's human rights charter which boldly states that "Every person has a right to full and equal recognition and exercise of his human rights and freedoms, without distinction ... based on [among other categories] language."

These little-heralded compromises suggest a deeper compromise. There was no desire to actively undermine 101 once it was recognized that to do so would be subversive of the federalist position in Quebec. In the end, the collective rights position and the individual rights position dovetailed. After taking office in 1984, the Mulroney Tories seemed to assume the main lines of Liberal language policy.

Of course neither side could publicly admit what had happened in practice. Trudeau was unwilling to admit that to win his struggle to keep Quebec in Canada, he had to give way on the principled ground of individual rights. The PQ would not admit that sovereignty had been rendered less attractive by their own achievement in securing the place of the French language. It would be wrong to suggest any explicit understanding, as such. Historic compromises may sometimes be easier if neither party draws up a list of demands for negotiation, but each allows the force of circumstance to determine them.

Such compromises are also of course inherently unstable, as conditions change. The PQ, especially once it was out of office, was increasingly disposed to welcome the weakening of 101 by judicial review so as to encourage a revival of separatist sentiment. For its part, the federal position had an Achilles' heel in regard to the position of the francophone minorities outside Quebec. It is the essence of this tacit accommodation that no facile equation can be made between majorities and minorities in Quebec and the rest of Canada. The francophones of Quebec are a majority only in that province, but a weak and threatened minority in the larger picture. Extraordinary measures are required to protect the French language within the sole jurisdiction where French is the majority tongue. Francophone minorities outside Quebec are doubly vulnerable and deserve some constitutional protection and an attitude of liberality on the part of the anglophone majority, which is in no way threatened in the security of its language. The case of the anglophones of Quebec is *not* analogous to that of the francophone minorities outside Quebec: Quebec anglophones constitute a minority tied to an overwhelming linguistic and cultural majority outside the province, which, moreover, enjoys an institutional network of support within Quebec (English education from primary school to university; English language TV and radio stations and newspapers, guaranteed English-language health services, etc.) which is unparalleled among linguistic minorities in Canada. But these facts are not recognized or acknowledged in English Canada. Polls show conclusively that English Canadians believe that the francophone minorities outside Quebec are *better* treated than the anglophone minority within Quebec.[18] There is only one rationale for this manifestly absurd belief (other than sheer ignorance): English Canadians tend to see anglophone Quebecers not as a minority but as part of a pan-Canadian English-speaking *majority*. To the extent that this is true, the language controversy has revealed a fundamental incompatibility between the Canadian and Quebec ideas of political community.

Thus the Supreme Court, in one blunt and imprudent action, threatened a delicate and complex balance between individual and collective rights, or perhaps hastened the collapse of a balance already coming unstuck. Granted that the Bourassa government was able, by invoking the notwithstanding clause, to protect the language law. This crisis indeed illustrates the wisdom of having such a clause. It may be the only way to temper the political havoc which could otherwise be wrought by the rationalist application of individual rights without regard to circumstance – especially in a society divided by language and culture. The political reality however is much more devastating. The English-Canadian reaction was so monolithic, and so condemnatory, and so reflective of a double standard that the damage to Quebec-Canada relations was extensive, and probably irreversible. There were simply two irreconcilable worlds in conflict. English Canadians in their majority were convinced that universally applicable individual rights are trumps against any collective rights of the minority community (Quebec) – rights which the Québécois were ready to defend with at least equal, if not greater, passion against a threatening majority (English-speaking North America).

Quebec is a more rounded, confident civil society than ever before. But underneath the confidence there is a deep insecurity having to do with being a tiny French-speaking island in a vast English-speaking sea in North America. The language law controversy struck directly at that insecurity and English Canada demonstrated considerable insensitivity in the face of the Quebec reaction.[19] It is a matter of deep irony that this demonstration followed almost immediately on a demonstration by Quebec of great insensitivity toward English Canada's own profound national insecurity. I refer here to the Free Trade election of 1988 in which Quebec voters played a crucial role in bringing about the defeat of a resurgent Canadian nationalism. But first it is necessary to retrace some of the steps to this result.

"BABBITRY WITHOUT OPTIMISM": THE RISE OF THE NEW CONSERVATISM

In the course of the 1980s the national party system, largely unchanged for half a century, was transformed. The Conservatives became the new dominant or "government" party. Not since the days of Sir John A. Macdonald have the Tories been able to do what Brian Mulroney did in 1988: win a second consecutive majority government. This constitutes a genuine realignment. The Conservatives have made themselves the unchallenged party of business and the dominant party in Quebec. In so doing they have challenged the very identity of the Liberals and called the role of the NDP into question.

Canada used to have a two-party system so far as business was concerned. For decades the Liberals and the Conservatives split the support of Bay Street. Of course Liberals were congenial to business. But, more to the point, they played the "responsible reformer" role by co-opting the left into a safe middle way between socialism and unregulated capitalism. To this we owe most of the elements of the Canadian welfare state.

The Liberals also held a virtual stranglehold on the votes of Quebec. They did not usually have to work very hard at keeping their lucrative property, but when they were challenged they rose to the occasion. The reason Quebec was (and is) so valuable is the perspicacity of its voters since the mid-nineteenth century when they have intervened in politics beyond their provincial borders. They usually permit themselves the luxury of partisan divisions in provincial politics, but not when it comes to presenting a Quebec face to the outside world.

The Liberals dominated Quebec in most elections from 1921 to 1984, but with the departure of the commanding figure of Pierre Trudeau in 1984 and the near-certainty of a Tory sweep of the rest of Canada, Brian Mulroney became the inheritor of the Quebec *bloc*. Unlike John Diefenbaker, who briefly held a Tory majority in Quebec from 1958 to 1962 but lost it due to his inability to comprehend Quebec, Mulroney has devoted himself to cultivating his native province.

Business abandoned the Liberals before the Quebec voters did. Bay Street thought they had found a political ally in the Clark government of 1979. The sudden return of the Liberals in 1980 was accomplished with little support from big business. The *Financial Post* did a survey of corporate executives in 1980 and found that they had become monolithically Conservative. For their part, at least some Liberals returned to office with the view that since business had done little for them, they had little obligation to business. Canada under Trudeau in the early 1980s lurched in the opposite direction to Thatcher's Britain and Reagan's America. The National Energy Program, the Foreign Investment Review Agency, regional development funds, and a series of other initiatives together gave the impression of a renewed burst of interventionism and central control – just as Canada's neighbours were striking out in the direction of privatization, deregulation, and the "downsizing" of government.

By the end of the Trudeau era, even these initiatives were in disarray. But to Canadian capital, the die had been cast. By 1984 the Conservatives had become like the US Republicans or the British Tories – *the* party of business. And when the PCs, in the twilight of the Trudeau era, had the foresight or good luck to elect as their leader a man who was at one and the same time the chief executive of the Canadian branch of an American multinational corporation and *un p'tit gars de Québec* (as much at home in colloquial French as in his English mother tongue), the Bay Street–Baie Comeau alliance was born.

The Mulroney Tories came to office committed to the business agenda and they have remained as faithful as the exigencies of electoral politics will permit. But Mulroney knew that Canadians would not accept a neo-conservative agenda if it were presented frontally and unadorned. There was the example of the Social Credit "new reality" restraint program in BC which deeply divided the province and brought about something approaching a general strike. Consequently the approach to enacting Reaganism was indirect, crab-like. In Mulroney's first term this lent some credence to the image of the Tories as "soft," given to flip-flopping in the face of public disapproval.

However one judges the record of the Mulroney Tories, his has *not* been a government which has failed to act decisively. The Free Trade Agreement of 1988 is perhaps the most significant single act of any government in this century and represented a perilous and complex undertaking; the Tories rammed it through against the wishes of the majority of the Canadian electorate. The Meech Lake constitutional accord if enacted would have represented a major restructuring of federalism and especially of Quebec-Canada relations. The severe impact of its failure is a reflection of a very high-risk strategy. The Goods and Services Tax, which fundamentally restructures the tax system to make it even more regressive than it is already, was put through Parliament against the opposition of every province and a clear majority of voters across the country. Its implementation represents a unilateral imposition on fiscal federalism unparalleled in the sixteen years of Trudeau's supposedly confrontational and centralized federalism. None of this suggests a cautious government. Mulroney's Tories are in many ways the most radical force to come out of Ottawa in years.

But what is the vision which animates this radical party of conservative reform? It is not a *national* vision, because it sees the trappings of Canadian national sovereignty as anachronistic impediments to doing business, barriers to the free play of market forces. It is not really a *political* vision because it has systematically sought to undermine the very mechanisms of a public sector through privatization, deregulation, and curtailment of social programs and regional subsidies. It is a *privatized* vision of a Canada (or more precisely of that geographical space called "Canada" on maps) in which there are enhanced opportunities for some individuals to make money with minimal interference from the state.

As befits someone who built his career as the executive of an American branch plant, Mulroney's ideology aspires to the status of a branch plant version of Reaganism. At the heart of Reaganism is George Babbit, the man whose highest aspiration is to make money but who has no idea of what money should be used for. But Babbit is wrapped in the Stars and Stripes, which cloaks his inner emptiness in an alluring if misleading glitter of red, white, and blue. At the heart of Mulroneyism also lies George Babbit – the same Chamber of Commerce verities, the same certainty that life is measured in dollars – but this time Babbit unadorned.

Perhaps it is even worse than this. Long ago, when diplomat and diarist Charles Ritchie returned briefly to his native Nova Scotia from the intense, high-pitched "Siren Years" in wartime London, he sadly pronounced that he found a surface layer of American babbitry but a "peculiar brand of babbitry without optimism."[20] I think this judgement holds for Canada as a whole, now as well as then. Canadian business, despite its sycophantic celebrants among journalists and academics, lacks the cultural self-assurance and single-minded panache of its American counterpart. The same goes for its political expression.

Another, nastier, characteristic of neo-conservatism is an increasing emphasis on coercion to enforce the upward redistribution of resources entailed in the market-driven economic policies and the reduction of social programs. Here too the Tories have followed suit. Increasingly under Mulroney the Ottawa government has become a law-enforcer and tax collector.[21] Legitimation expenditures such as social services, health care, and education are mainly under provincial control, while Ottawa steadily cuts back financial support. By 1990–91 Mulroney had even brought Canada into its first war in forty years and was increasing military spending. Finally, neo-conservative regimes have sought to undermine if not eliminate the kind of popular associations which mediate between the welfare state and its clients. Citing budgetary restraints, the Tories have cut back funding for women's and native groups and their activities. Thus, despite initial hesitations, the Mulroney Tories have conformed by and large to the Reaganite and Thatcherite models. Just as Thatcher rolled back Labour policies and Reagan reversed Democratic liberalism, Mulroney has significantly transformed the public agenda of a Canada shaped by years of Liberal centrism.

Quebec is crucial in the disorganization of the opposition which allows conservatism to remain dominant. In party terms, so long as the Liberals held Quebec the centre-left of the political stage could afford the luxury of a social-democratic third party in English Canada. The NDP could even be useful to the Liberals, when from time to time they lost their majority and had to rely on a centre-left alliance. With the Tories holding Quebec, the objective effect of the NDP's presence in English Canada has been to divide the centre-left, thus keeping the Tories and their right-wing agenda in office. If the Tories continue to hold Quebec, opposition to conservatism cannot tolerate two competing parties.

The Tory position, however commanding, concealed a double vulnerability around the national question. Tory support in Quebec was built in part around strong Quebec nationalists, including many adherents of the yes side in the 1980 referendum. The support of these people for the federal system, let alone the Tory party, was always somewhat conditional. Moreover, there was the possibility of serious divisions with traditional Tory elements in English Canada. And then there was the Tory weakness in regard to Canadian nationalism. This became glaringly evident during the great free trade debate of 1988.

FREE TRADE AND CANADIAN NATIONALISM

The election of 1988 was the English-Canadian equivalent of the 1980 sovereignty-association referendum in Quebec. The issue in both cases was national sovereignty. Nationalism reached a peak as it came to the supreme test, and in both cases it lost. Or so it might appear. In 1980 the sovereignty option failed the electoral test but survived to rise again within a decade. In 1988 Canadian nationalism won a moral victory but was cheated of real victory by the machinations of the electoral and party systems. Both contests were structured by the manipulation and intimidation of the forces of wealth and power and yet constituted moving and sometimes magic moments of democratic self-government when the people debated and made choices about the nature of the good society.[22] Although separated by time and place, the two events did not move on unrelated tracks. Once again the ancient *Doppelgänger* effect of Canadian history appeared, as these two great moments of democratic national self-determination served only to define more sharply the differences between the two peoples and to drive them against each other.

The economic arguments surrounding the Free Trade Agreement (FTA) can be debated by economists. From a political point of view, the economic arguments scarcely mattered. What was at issue in 1988 was the nature of Canada and its future as a political community. The Tories of Sir John A. Macdonald's day had built an east-west economy as the basis for a separate political community north of the United States. It was this Canada which they defended against Liberal continentalism in the free trade election of 1911. The Tories of Brian Mulroney's day have definitively abandoned any attachment to the east-west economy, which they have indeed assiduously set about dismantling, in favour of the extension of unimpeded "free market forces" across the Canada-US border. As Canadians have usually realized, one cannot retain political sovereignty without an economic substructure to sustain it.

The political effects of free trade were in fact far more immediate in 1988 than ever before. In 1911 it was tariffs which were at issue. The National Policy was pre-eminently a tariff policy. By the late twentieth century, tariffs were no longer a leading or even important instrument of national sovereignty. Three-quarters of Canadian trade with the US was already tariff-free. The evolution of interventionist capitalist states has today reached the point where so-called "non-tariff barriers" to trade have become the major impediments to cross-border market forces. Non-tariff barriers are discriminatory state regulations, incentive and subsidy programs, tax manipulations, and other devices which together have the effect of advantaging a state's own private producers at the expense of international competitors. These could only be reduced or eliminated by severe restrictions upon national sovereignty and the legislative competence of both Parliament and provincial legislatures.

Unlike the many countries of the Common Market, Canada under the FTA stands alone against a superpower ten times its size in population and greater yet in terms of economic clout, a superpower whose corporations have already made substantial and far-reaching inroads into Canada in terms of ownership and control of large parts of the Canadian private sector. There are no transnational alliances possible to offset this power, and thus little scope for negotiation. It is surely no accident that the FTA was the greatest single issue to animate Canada in at least a generation, while on the other side of the border most Americans have never even heard of it. The imbalance is structural.

One survey suggested that there were really two different Canadas confronting the free trade issue. One Canada looked to individual economic well-being as the standard for judging policy; national and cultural sovereignty were only important if they contributed to individual economic betterment. This Canada was the Canada of Mulroney Toryism and the Canada of big business (much of it American branch-plant). This Canada was predominantly for free trade (although a minority feared the economic consequences). The other Canada saw national and cultural sovereignty as goods in themselves and viewed free trade as a threat to the nation. It was to this second Canada that Liberal leader John Turner made his appeal when he stated that even if there were a price to be paid for being Canadian, he was willing to pay that price.

The second Canada faced a heavy array of forces. The combination of the Canadian and American governments, as well as eight of the ten premiers, was formidable enough. But equally important was the intervention of big business, both to sell the deal with tens of millions of dollars of "non-partisan" advertising and to intimidate opposition with threats of the dire economic consequences were the FTA to be defeated. The Pro-Canada Network, put together as a popular coalition to fight the deal, was able to raise a mere $600,000. Yet this group had an influence far out of proportion to its resources.

The Tories tried to sell free trade by painting it in regionally divisive terms. Anti-free trade sentiment, they insistently argued, was a plot by Ontario to deny the rest of Canada the benefits already enjoyed by the wealthiest province. Yet except for Quebec, every region of the country actually rejected free trade. Indeed, opposition was weaker in Ontario than it was in Saskatchewan, BC, and the Atlantic provinces.

If regionalism was not a line of division over this issue, *class* certainly was. Never in Canadian history was a national election fought so clearly along class lines. Business was nearly unanimous. Except for a handful of dissenters, medium-sized and small business were out in force under the leadership of big business. Nor were there any apparent splits between the American-owned branch-plant sector and the indigenous Canadian-owned sector. Class war from above became the rule in the last days of the campaign when corporations directly threatened their employees with the loss of their jobs if free trade failed at the polls.

The appearance of class war from above is hardly surprising when the hidden agenda of the FTA is considered. Reaganite or Thatcherite neo-conservatism had failed to come off as an open political project in Canada; but neo-conservatism could be delivered to business if it were entered through the back door under the guise of impersonal continental market forces operating within a North American free trade zone. There was even the prospect that under the FTA various social and regional programs which business disliked, but which boasted powerful political support in the country, could be ruled out as unfair subsidies to Canadian production. This was no doubt very much on the minds of the blue chip Business Council on National Issues when it engineered the introduction of free trade onto the national agenda during the mid-1980s.[23]

Across the class lines were the forces representing the other Canada. The Pro-Canada Network had strong labour support but the class conflict spotlighted by the free trade issue brought together far more elements than this. It is the unprecedented broadness of the coalition which remains perhaps the most interesting feature of the entire experience. As well as labour, the anti-free trade coalition included women, senior citizens, farmers, environmentalists, artists, and less categorizable Canadians simply concerned with the survival of the country. There has been much debate in recent years in left-wing circles about the emergence of "new social movements": have they modified the classic Marxist contradiction of capital and labour? In the mobilization of opposition to free trade this argument moved out of the realm of theory into political reality.

In another sense the anti-free trade coalition represented the crystallization of an indigenous Canadian strand of ideas. In the early 1970s the Waffle wing of the NDP had argued for the close identity of nationalism and socialism. Eventually expelled by the NDP leadership, the Waffle had withered and died as a movement. Yet fifteen years later the left-nationalist vision of the Waffle was reborn in the struggle against free trade. Business and Toryism had openly abandoned even a national capitalist road and had opted for outright, unmystified, continentalism. Opposition to the control of the political agenda by business was necessarily now a defence of the integrity of the Canadian nation, and vice versa. It would be an exaggeration to suggest that the anti-free trade coalition was socialist (despite what business propagandists may have asserted), but what is clear is that in a class-divided context Canadian nationalism represented a left, progressive face, defending the welfare state against market-driven attacks, while the continentalists spoke for a neo-conservative agenda.

Nationalism is always a chameleon, taking its specific colouring from its surroundings. It is always a mistake to characterize nationalism as either progressive or reactionary. It may be one or the other, or both, or first the one and then the other – depending upon the circumstances. Reaganism and Thatcherism have relied heavily, and rather paradoxically given their "anti-statist" pretensions, on particularly virulent and aggressive forms of nationalism as legitimation.[24] Given the historical binational character of Canada, waving the flag and calling up tribal demons is a risky and divisive, rather than unifying, procedure. In short, while nationalism has been largely appropriated by the political right in America and Britain, Canadian nationalism had become, de facto, a liberal and progressive force in 1988. On the other hand, Toryism, the political expression of big business, has failed abysmally to develop a workable nationalist basis for a conservative agenda. There was thus much scope for the centre and left (ranging all the way from reform Liberals to radicals on the left of the NDP) to draw on Canadian national sentiment in 1988. John Turner, in his memorable exchange with Mulroney in the televised leaders' debate, briefly but potently exploited this identification.

Nationalism has always been weak in Canada but in 1988 it grew out of association with the political left, just as the left, also traditionally weak, grew by association with the nation. More to the point, given the often dark and discouraging history of exclusionary nationalisms, 1988 was Canadian nationalism's finest hour. This was a nationalism which was generous, liberal, and compassionate. Unfortunately, it was also thwarted and, in its manipulated defeat, it would shortly lose its progressive cast and become something narrower, more inward-looking, and less admirable.

The defeat of Canadian nationalism in 1988 tells us much about the limitations of democracy within the straightjacket of the present institutional forms. The Tories were originally set to enact the FTA without acquiring any public approval, even though they had never promised such a sweeping deal while winning the 1984 election. Given the profound significance of the agreement, this was an astonishing affront on their part. The only reason it was ever allowed to become a contested issue was the unelected Senate's refusal to approve the deal without an election. But even though an election was called in which free trade became the central issue, an election is not a referendum. This was the fatal flaw on the anti-free trade side. In a referendum, attention can focus exclusively on the issue; in an election, the choice is directly between parties and only indirectly between issues. Even though free trade "lost" 1988 *as a referendum*, it "won" as the result of the party system. The anti-free trade side was represented by two parties and the pro-free trade side by one. Since the Liberals and the NDP failed entirely to sink partisan differences in the national interest, the anti-free trade vote was fatally divided. The 42 percent of the votes across the country became magically transformed into a Tory majority government, with a mandate from the process, although not the people, to implement the FTA. Never has the legitimacy of the parliamentary system of government looked more suspect.

But there was another problem for Canadian nationalism which went well beyond a biased and inappropriate process. I have used the image of the two Canadas facing the free trade issue. Yet there were actually more than two Canadas at play. Quebec stood entirely outside the passions generated by Canadian nationalism. Historically, Quebec (shielded perhaps by language) has never shared English-Canadian apprehensions about American domination.[25] By 1988 Quebec was a business-oriented society which took its cues from a francophone economic elite who had become the new cultural heroes. Quebec opted overwhelmingly for the Tories and free trade. It was unmistakeably their votes which made the difference in electing a Tory majority. Outside Quebec only Albertans actually gave a majority of their votes to the Tories. Everywhere else the anti-free trade Liberals and NDP received clear combined majorities of the popular vote. Obviously, the nationalism of English Canada had few if any echoes in Quebec. Indeed among some Quebec nationalists there may even have been an element of vindictiveness in helping to defeat the Canadian national dream, just as their own had been defeated in 1980 – although in the latter case it was the votes of Quebecers alone which were determining. Certainly the role played by Quebec in the great free trade election did not escape the notice of bitter English-Canadian nationalists.[26]

The fallout from the stolen victory of free trade was doubly acrid: the process treated the verdict of the people with contempt, and it insured antagonism between Canadian and Quebec nationalisms. Both issues subsequently boiled over in the Meech Lake fiasco.

THE MEECH LAKE FIASCO

As everyone has admitted, the *process* of constitutional change followed in Meech Lake was a disaster. The 1987 negotiations were apparent triumphs for elite accommodation and Mulroney's co-operative federalism. Meech Lake 1987 was the highpoint for Mulroney's rather old-fashioned style of politics as deal-making.

Meech Lake post-1987 is a graphic illustration of why that kind of politics is outmoded.

Quebec governments have always had a somewhat schizophrenic view of English Canada. On the one hand Quebec nationalists have yearned for a single, monolithic English Canada with which Quebec can bargain on a basis of equality. On the other hand, Quebec bargainers have sought to form alliances with other provinces against the federal government to gain strength by exploiting divisions within English Canada. With Meech Lake it appeared momentarily to Quebec that the two images of Canada had come together. English Canada was united, but along decentralist lines. And nine English Canadian premiers and the prime minister of Canada had approved the recognition of Quebec as a distinct society along with Quebec's other minimal demands for adherence to the constitution.

The agreement was apparent, not real. Once again Quebec had misunderstood the nature of English Canada. Perhaps there was a time when the signature of the prime minister and the nine premiers would have simply delivered English Canada. But no longer. For Quebecers, despite passionate internal debates, there was enough sense of collective identity that the signature of the premier of Quebec could be taken for what it claimed to be – a promise of agreement on behalf of the people. What Quebec politicians did not understand was that English Canada was no longer the kind of country where twenty million people could be delivered by the signatures of ten politicians. As the deal unravelled on the larger stage, Quebec politicians spoke of a betrayal of trust, of a broken contract. To many English Canadians, the breach of trust was between them and their politicians, not between English and French Canada.

The problem with the Meech Lake process was not simply that it was elitist but that the bargainers lacked the courage of their elitist convictions. If the bargain struck in 1987 had been subject to ratification by the legislature within weeks, the mechanism of parliamentary majorities could have closed the deal. Of course this might have led to lingering legitimacy problems but the deal would have been done. Instead the process agreed upon was the worst of all possible worlds. Three full years would be given for ratification. This would allow time for public hearings, but these hearings, it was made clear, could not result in any change. As Robert Bourassa kept saying, not a single comma or semicolon could be altered or the deal, from Quebec's point of view, was off. The three national parties contributed to this atmosphere by in effect conspiring together to suppress debate. In the 1988 election, for instance, Meech was a non-issue because no party would raise it (except for the Tories who exploited it for partisan gains in Quebec).

In short, the old elite accommodation process was exposed for all to see. The public could say anything it wanted, believe anything it pleased, but none of it would make the slightest difference to the politicians. This was a prescription for disaster. The prescription was soon filled when governments were changed by the electorates of Manitoba, New Brunswick, and Newfoundland and new premiers, unbound by the deals of their predecessors, came into office. Populist paranoia about what "They" were doing to "Us" had been fed by elite contempt for popular input. And of course ill-informed but deep resentments in English Canada about how "They" were selling out to Quebec were only fanned by the process. The appearance on the scene of anti-Meech premiers thus provided tribunes for the people.

The popular backlash was paradoxical. Anti-Meechism too had its elite and mass expressions, which differed considerably. At one level one might have discerned something like the anti-Free Trade coalition: feminist groups, native peoples, ethnic Canadians, left-nationalists, some trade unionists, all found common expression for their specific interests in opposing Meech. Indeed, in the last weeks before the deadline, something like the pro-Free Trade business coalition of 1988 also took shape to back Meech. Like the anti-free trade coalition, the anti-Meech campaign found no common ground whatever with Quebec counterparts. One of the more bizarre elements of the debate was the argument advanced by spokespersons for (anglophone) feminist groups that the distinct society clause could be used by the Quebec government to repress the rights of Quebec women, despite the fact that Quebec feminists angrily repudiated this contention.

Spokespersons for the various groups and interests clustered around the anti-Meech campaign may have been sincere in their protestations that they were not anti-Quebec, but the larger public opposition is less clear. Public opinion surveys, and the more anecdotal evidence of letters to the editor, open-line shows, and person-in-the-street interviews, suggest that popular opposition was fundamentally premised upon a rejection of Quebec's right to distinct status.[27] Québécois perceptions that they were rejected by English Canada do have substance, despite the disclaimers of elite Meech opponents.

At least the people may have been more realistic than their elite spokespersons. Meech Lake was after all the "Quebec round"; they were responding to this in their own way. Anti-Meech leaders, on the other hand, raised a host of demands for symbolic recognition of other groups: women, native people, ethnics, etc. This is the problem with symbolic politics: there is never any end once symbolism is placed on the negotiating table. The idea of a projected "Canada Clause" to reflect the distinctive elements of the country apart from Quebec offered the altogether alarming prospect of circus-like hearings across Canada in which every group with a self-professed claim to symbolic status would insist upon inclusion. Mercifully this mischievous idea died with Meech.

Quebec at least had its own house more or less in order. English-Canadian opinion was ambiguous. On the one hand the reluctance to grant Quebec distinct status seems to have been associated with a certain idea of Canada as a society in which universally applicable individual rights must supersede any special status or collective rights for particular groups. This was certainly the premise of those who cited Bill 178 in Quebec as an argument against the distinct society. On the other hand, much of the opposition came from particular groups who demanded the extension of special status or symbolic dignity to themselves. Here again *rights* seem to have been central, but in this case not individual but group rights aspiring to collective rights status or, in the case of the native peoples, collective rights seeking equal recognition to that accorded Quebec. The language of rights unleashed on English Canada in the 1980s has been powerful in its impact but diffuse and confusing in its implications. The Meech debacle shows that much greater care and thought is required to sort out the various and contradictory elements gathered in riotous assembly under the great umbrella of rights. What *is* crystal clear is that English-Canadian society, with its particular view of rights, could not accommodate the special status of Quebec as a distinct entity. Those Meech opponents who claimed that their quarrel was not with the distinct society clause but with the failure of the accord to extend this notion to other groups or peoples were in practice rejecting Quebec, since they could offer no credible or remotely consensual notion of a workable extension of Meech. No wonder the Québécois threw up their hands in exasperation and despairingly asked "What does English Canada want?"

Meech has let the genie back out of the bottle and Meech's death does nothing to get it back inside. The old elite accommodationists will no doubt sagely declare: "We told you so." But the two communities were hardly about to tear each other apart at the mass level while nation-saving elites struggled to bridge the gap at the top. The elites were themselves part of the problem, as they have been since the 1970s. Some tried to accommodate, others strove to foster disunity to achieve other purposes. And the growing divergence between the two communities at the mass level was perhaps in part based on mutual antagonism but more importantly on the evolution of divergent democratic visions. English and French Canadians speak different languages, in more ways than one.

"THE VISION THING ..."

US President George Bush, taxed with a lack of national vision in the face of the profound changes in the world at the end of the 1980s, referred in some bewilderment to the "vision thing." The "vision thing" is, at the opening of the 1990s, a yawning abyss for America's northern neighbours. Granted Canadians have never suffered from American delusions of imperial grandeur. But even small and modest countries require some small and modest national vision – especially when they face severe internal and external identity crises.

Like George Bush, Brian Mulroney represents a conservative philosophy of government that emphasizes markets over politics, the private sector over the public, and the devaluation of the state as an instrument for achieving greater equality among citizens. Unlike Bush, Mulroney cannot displace frustrations on external enemies like Saddam Hussein. And, unlike Bush, Mulroney cannot call up tribal demons to rally round the defence of the Flag as a substitute for a positive vision. Babbitry wrapped in red, white, and blue is tawdry enough, but babbitry naked is not a pretty sight.

Sir John A. Macdonald's Tory idea of nation-building was a businessman's idea, but it was *national*-capitalist in design. Laden with conservative assumptions about class, race, gender, and religion, it still possessed a sense of collective purpose, a national project, a sense of direction, and the will to reach a desired destination. Mulroney's Toryism has dismantled every vestige of Macdonald's vision, *but to what national goal?* Continental free trade and the removal of borders; Canada "open for business" to foreign ownership; federalism as a "Confederation of shopping centres" (to use Trudeau's memorable phrase); the national government as no more than a law enforcer, tax-collector, and flogger of public properties at firesale prices ... does this add up to anything of national or collective, as opposed to private, purpose?

Enrichissez-vous! was the slogan Balzac proposed for bourgeois France. Whether pursued with all due legal proprieties or crossing the line into corruption, private enrichment is not and can never be a compelling moral vision for the polity. If it is posed as a means to a greater end, it may at least be plausible, if not compelling. But short of such a moral calculus, private enrichment is mere babbitry.

For all its shortcomings, Pierre Trudeau's vision of Canada was national in scope and directed toward a sense of a public good. Instead of counterposing a conservative national vision to replace that of the Trudeau Liberals, the Mulroney Conservatives have systematically set about removing the public space where any national vision can flourish. After Free trade, the neo-conservative assault on the welfare state, the dismantling or impoverishment of national cultural institutions, and the insistence of government ministers that Canadians should properly direct their attentions inward toward their own self-enrichment, is it any wonder that the debates over language policy and Meech Lake degenerated into an orgy of petty selfishness, French against English, region against region, group against group? Or that by the sordid last days of the Meech affair, success was being measured by the strong-arm tactics and browbeating which could be mustered by the contending sides? When legitimacy fails, only coercion remains.

THE BIRTH OF TWO SOVEREIGN NATIONS?

The reaction in Quebec to the failure of Meech was decisive. In the winter of 1990–91 support for sovereignty among Quebecers rose to unprecedented heights. The Bourassa government created the Bélanger-Campeau Commission to examine options for Quebec's constitutional future, inside or outside Canada. This commission included both Liberal and PQ politicians as well as representatives of various sectors of Quebec society. In public hearings, francophone representations were strongly – although not unanimously – favourable to the sovereignty option. The ruling Liberal party appointed its own constitutional commission (Allaire). The Allaire report, ratified almost without change in a Liberal convention notable for its nationalist passion, envisages a sweeping transfer of powers to the jurisdiction of Quebec, leaving the federal government exclusive jurisdiction only over national defence, customs, debt management, and equalization. A broad bipartisan post-Meech consensus seemed to emerge: either radical changes to confederation must be made that would give Quebec virtual or functional sovereignty, or Quebec would move to break formally with Canada. To this end a referendum to provide a mandate for sovereignty if necessary would be called sometime in 1992.

Ironically, the rejection of Meech Lake by the rest of Canada passed the constitutional initiative to Quebec. By placing Meech and its distinct society clause on the table and then rejecting it, English Canada removed the last restraint on Quebec's bargaining position. Moreover, since the minimum position advanced by Quebec was now far in excess of what Meech had promised, and since Meech had been rejected by the rest of Canada as offering too much, it became increasingly difficult to construct realistic scenarios for compromise. With a referendum offering popular backing for sovereignty, it might indeed become impossible for Quebec leaders to back down. Mulroney rolled the dice: the result may prove to be far more decisive and fateful than he anticipated.

A significant evolution in Quebec society lay behind these surface events. Sovereignty was no longer an issue of a single political party but a movement with broad nonpartisan support in the larger community. Especially noteworthy was the emergent support of business. Although some representatives of very large capital with international investments expressed qualms about the economic risks of a separatist adventure, the clear majority of the Quebec business community had apparently come to accept sovereignty as both necessary and desirable.[28] The Bélanger-Campeau Commission was chaired by two leading business figures. Labour, significantly, was supportive of a business-led sovereigntist movement. Moreover, it was very striking that at the public hearings of the commission the only francophone groups or individuals to express any significant reservations about sovereignty, or any support for federalism, did so entirely in dollars-and-cents terms. Emotional or sentimental attachment to Canada was conspicuous by its absence. It is no wonder then that many Canadians were beginning to conclude that Quebec was already gone in spirit.

With Allaire and Bélanger-Campeau on the table, the choices were greatly simplified. Only two options seemed capable of retaining Quebec in some sort of relationship within Canada. Option one would be an extreme form of special status for Quebec, in which almost all spending and taxing powers would be transferred from the federal government to the exclusive jurisdiction of Quebec. The problem with this option is that Quebec would continue to send MPs to the House of Commons in Ottawa who would make or break Canadian governments (as Quebec voters have always done) and participate in passing laws which would be of significance to Canadians outside Quebec but of no interest to the voters of Quebec, where the provincial government would hold jurisdiction over almost all matters. This would simply not be acceptable to English Canadians, who have for some time been complaining (rightly or wrongly) about Quebec domination under existing federal arrangements.

Option two would be special status for all, involving a radical decentralization of powers to all provinces, including Quebec. Some have suggested an "opting-in" arrangement whereby provinces might elect to pass some of these powers back to the federal government on their own initiative. The result would be either a federalism so decentralized as to call into question the very notion of any coherent national integrity, or in the second variant, a patchwork quilt (or perhaps a crazy-quilt!) of a country in which there was no uniformity of treatment, no universality, and no national standards.

It is surely no accident that variants of option two have been advocated recently by neo-conservative economists who wish to reduce, if not eliminate, the role of government in favour of unchecked and unregulated market forces. A radically decentralized or patchwork Canada would make impossible the functioning of the kind of national and universal social programs, such as Medicare, which most Canadians support very strongly. It would at the same time erode, if not ultimately eliminate, the national sense of citizenship, founded on equality and universality, which many Canadians have begun to prize, especially since the advent of the Charter of Rights.

Options one and two represent far too high a price to be paid for what amounts to a legal fiction of retaining Quebec as part of Canada. It is highly doubtful that either option would find acceptance among Canadians outside Quebec. If either were to be imposed from Ottawa, the results would, sooner rather than later, lead to the breakup of the country – which was what was supposed to be avoided by these devices in the first place.

There is another option: sovereignty for Quebec. In 1980, when Quebec voters were deciding their future in the referendum on sovereignty-association, there was much anguish among Canadians outside Quebec about the possible destruction of the country. In the 1990s, after the Meech debacle, and with an enhanced sense of Canadian national identity, there was much less anguish about the possible end or radical reformation of a country which many more Canadians had come to see as an artificial construct. Perhaps a sovereign Quebec could be seen not as the "end of Canada" (*pace* the rhetoric of National Unity), but as the birth of a new Canada whose citizens could begin to live in their own skins, at greater ease with themselves, freed from a set of artificial bilingual and bicultural identities imposed by Ottawa. Perhaps the departure of Quebec could open up a more democratic political and constitutional agenda for Canada. The ancient pressures towards undemocratic elite accommodation as the means of resolving the differences between two peoples and two nations would largely vanish with the departure of Quebec. Many other problems would remain, of course, including the problem of regional discontent in a Canada where Ontario would suddenly represent one half the population. But the way might also be open for Canadians to resolve these problems on their own terms, without the constitutional agenda being driven by the quite different concerns of Quebec. In this sense, Quebec sovereignty might be seen not as an option for the death of Canada but for the birth of two new sovereign nations.

There are of course enormously difficult problems associated with transforming a nation which has existed for a century and a half into two countries. The economic costs in the short run should not be minimized, any more than the complexities and potential irritations of negotiating a satisfactory division of assets and liabilities. But the new reality of continental free trade, however mistrusted by Canadians outside Quebec, offers a favourable scenario for a post-separation economic arrangement which would avoid many, if not all, of the repugnant features of the PQ's sovereignty-association plan in 1980. Perhaps there would be little if any need for an overarching bureaucratic (and democratically unaccountable) layer of supranational government. Instead most economic relations could be regulated by treaty. The economic benefits of trade and investment could continue in the absence of an artificial and dysfunctional political arrangement. With the free movement of capital, goods, and people written into a fundamental treaty, the Maritimes would in practice be no more cut off from the rest of Canada than Alaska is cut off from the continental United States by an expanse of Canadian territory comparable to the distance across a politically sovereign Quebec between New Brunswick and Ontario.

"WE ARE THE PEOPLE(S)"

Perhaps there is an ironic lesson for Canadian democracy in the convulsions of Eastern Europe and the Soviet Union. The end of Communism in Eastern Europe and its apparent death-throes in the USSR have been accompanied, to general dismay and alarm in the outside world, by the emergence of often virulent outbreaks of nationalisms in the form of secession movements and communal violence. Even in as relatively stable and moderate a country as Czechoslovakia, tensions between Czechs and Slovaks have broken out just as democratic processes are being restored after forty years of authoritarian rule. And everywhere there is a tendency to look for minority scapegoats, a role for which the Jews seem familiarly, if lamentably, cast.

Just when the people are finally free to govern themselves, they revert to atavistic and particularistic identifications. Obviously this is no way to build a democratic community. But why this perverse reaction? One answer lies in the failure of the discredited Communist regimes of the past to overcome traditional communal divisions by replacing particularistic identifications with more universal identities. Worse, the devaluation of the universalist elements of Communist theory (radical egalitarianism, building a classless society, international solidarity of the oppressed, etc.) by the squalid police-state propaganda and official lies of Communist practice has, in the eyes of long-suffering subjects, served to discredit all universal values, including those of democratic citizenship in the larger community. Public space was in effect privatized by party elites that appropriated public office to the exclusion of the people. When universal values are distrusted, the legitimacy of the broader community comes into question. When coercion fails, as it did dramatically in the last days of the former Communist regimes of Eastern Europe (save Romania) and as it appears to be doing now in the USSR, there is a tendency for people to fall back upon those traditional, tested, habitual values associated with their most immediate and limited identities, their ethnic, religious, cultural, or linguistic groups. This too may be an expression of democracy (the assertion of the will of the people, as narrowly rather than broadly defined). Unfortunately this kind of democratic expression may, in its exclusionary thrust, turn ugly and oppressive toward minorities within or competitive majorities from without.

There may be a clue here to explain the upsurge of petty, restrictive, and exclusionary nationalisms in Canada at the end of the 1980s. The acrid language controversies set off by the Quebec language law affair in 1988–89 and the resurgence of anti-French and anti-English tensions in Canada and Quebec surrounding the Meech Lake affair seem symptomatic of a people deprived of a broader, more generous, and positive vision, turning inward and reverting to more basic but negative identities and values.

A generous, progressive national vision was threatened and galvanized by the spectre of free trade. This vision crystallized in the campaign against the Mulroney government and the free trade agreement in 1988. The stolen victory of free trade and the antinational project of the Mulroney government are at the root of much of the sourness of Canadian public life in the aftermath of 1988. A generous liberal nationalism, frustrated as the basis for a national vision, has been eroded and dismantled by egregious babbitry. Frustrated liberal nationalism has in too many cases turned inward and become narrow and divisive.

Wir sind das Volk (we are the people) chanted the East German demonstrators who brought down the Berlin Wall. It was a powerful democratic rebuke to a regime which had claimed, with consummate duplicity, to speak for the people. But soon these same people were chanting *Wir sind ein Volk* (We are *one* people) as an expression of pure German nationalism. When *das Volk* is not *ein Volk*, but two (at least), and there is no national vision, democracy itself becomes a divisive rather than a unifying factor.

Canadians can at least take comfort from the fact that they are not alone in the world in facing these problems. Canada retains resources and capacities which other divided countries do not command. There is a level of civility and tolerance which puts many other countries to shame. There is a rich experience of federalism on which to draw. But if Canadians are to come out of their present difficulties they will require greater clarity in their political ideas. And above all some coherent answer will have to be forthcoming to the question, "What, after all, does Canada want?"

NOTES

1 In 1989 pollsters had found that two-thirds of Americans surveyed thought it would be a good idea for Canada to join the US. After a year of the Meech Lake spectacle, support for union among Americans had dropped twenty points, to only 47 percent (*Maclean's* [23 June 1990]).

2 Although I made much of the undemocratic nature of the constitutional process of 1980–81 in an article published in 1983 (see chapter 7), this analysis elicited complete indifference or only mild support at the time.

3 I draw this phrase from a fascinating exploration of nationalism in another context to that of Quebec: Benedict Anderson, *Imagined Communities: Reflections on the Origin and Spread of Nationalism* (London: Velso, 1983).

4 This is argued in Kenneth McRoberts, *Quebec: Social Change and Political Crisis*. 3rd ed. (Toronto: McClelland and Stewart, 1988).

5 Pierre Elliott Trudeau, "The Values of a Just Society," in Thomas S. Axworthy and Pierre Trudeau, eds., *Towards A Just Society: The Trudeau Years* (Markham, Ont.: Viking, 1990), 366.

6 In point of fact it is not true to say that there are no elements of special status for Quebec in the Canada Act. The effect of s.23 is that Quebec is exempted from the obligation to allow the English-speaking children of immigrants to attend English-language schools. The provision (s.40) for fiscal compensation for a province opting out of a constitutional

amendment on cultural or educational matters was clearly designed with Quebec in mind since it is difficult to imagine any other province following such a course. In any event the Trudeau governments were not above making special deals with Quebec, as in the Cullen-Couture accord on immigration in 1976 which actually prefigures the immigration section of Meech Lake – except that Cullen-Couture is a pure example of special status only for Quebec, while Meech would have extended the arrangement to all provinces. After Meech, a far-reaching agreement for devolution of immigration power to Quebec alone was struck between the Mulroney and Bourassa governments.

7 Lipset, *Continental Divide: The Values and Institutions of the United States and Canada* (NY: Routledge, 1990), 166.

8 Trudeau, "Values," 363.

9 Brian Mulroney, in full oratorical flight, declared that the Constitution is "not worth the paper it is written on," because of the notwithstanding clause. House of Commons, *Debates*, 6 April 1989, 153.

10 This argument has been made with remorseless energy in Michael Mandel, *The Charter of Rights and the Legalization of Politics in Canada* (Toronto: Wall and Thompson, 1989).

11 The late Donald Smiley was one political scientist who had expressed some deep concerns along these lines and would have written more extensively about it had it not been for his untimely death in the spring of 1990.

12 "Rights in a 'Free and Democratic Society': Abortion," in David P. Shugarman and Reg Whitaker, eds., *Federalism and Political Community: Essays in Honour of Donald Smiley* (Peterborough: Broadview Press, 1989), 327–48.

13 Quoted in Smiley, *Federal Condition in Canada* (Toronto: McGraw Hill-Ryerson, 1987), 193.

14 See the studies by Alan Cairns and Cynthia Williams, "Constitutionalism, Citizenship and Society in Canada: An Overview" and Williams, "The Changing Nature of Citizen Rights," in Cairns and Williams, eds., *Constitutionalism, Citizenship and Society in Canada*. Vol. 33 in the series of studies for the Royal Commission on Economic Union and Development Prospects for Canada (Toronto: University of Toronto Press, 1985).

15 This is the burden of Rainer Knopff and F.L. Morton's study "Nation-building and the Canadian Charter of Rights and Freedoms," in Cairns and Williams, *Constitutionalism*.

16 The Quebec Human Rights Code is significantly more expansive than the Charter of Rights in that it covers private relations as well as the relations of citizen and state to which the federal charter is limited.

17 The argument in this section is adapted from my article "The Over-

riding Right: Why Quebec Was Right to Use the Notwithstanding Clause," *Policy Options* 10, no. 4 (May 1989): 3–6.

18 Paul M. Sniderman *et al,* "Political Culture and the Problem of Double Standards: Mass and Elite Attitudes toward Language Rights in the Canadian Charter of Rights and Freedoms," *Canadian Journal of Political Science* 22, no. 2 (June 1989): 259–84. In a 1989 national survey, 40 percent of anglophone respondents indicated their belief that "too much" was being done for francophone minorities outside Quebec, as against only 17 percent who thought "too little" was being done; on the other hand, no less than 72 percent believed that too little was being done on behalf of the English minority in Quebec. The Globe and Mail / CBC News Poll, *The Globe and Mail,* 23 October 1989.

19 For a persuasive case against the Trudeau bilingual policy see Kenneth McRoberts, "Making Canada Bilingual: Illusions and Delusions of Federal Language Policy," Shugarman and Whitaker, *Federalism and Political Community,* 141–72.

20 Charles Ritchie, *The Siren Years: A Canadian Diplomat Abroad, 1937–1945* (Toronto, 1974), 204.

21 Sharon L. Sutherland, "Federal Bureaucracy: The Pinch Test," in Michael J. Prince, ed., *How Ottawa Spends, 1987–88: Restraining the State* (Toronto: Methuen, 1987), 38–128.

22 This aspect of the election has been brilliantly captured in Rick Salutin's *Waiting for Democracy: A Citizen's Journal* (Toronto: Lester & Orpen Dennys, 1989).

23 See David Langille, "Corporate Statesmen: The Business Council on National Issues and the Canadian State," *Studies in Political Economy* 24 (Autumn 1987): 41–86.

24 I have made this argument at length in "Neo-conservatism and the state," in Ralph Miliband, Leo Panitch, and John Saville, eds., *Socialist Register 1987: Conservatism in Britain and America, Rhetoric and Reality* (London: Merlin Press, 1987), 1–31.

25 See Jean-François Lisée, *Dans l'oeil de l'aigle: Washington face au Québec* (Montreal: Boréalis, 1990).

26 See Philip Resnick, *Letters to a Québécois Friend* (Montreal: McGill-Queen's University Press, 1990). I can speak directly about the anger of election night 1988 for in the aftermath I was myself driven to take a public anti-Quebec position which I would later regret. In an article in *Canadian Forum* ("No Laments for the Nation: Free Trade and the Election of 1988," [March 1989]), I argued that "Quebec domination of Canadian politics has never been more obvious, nor more abrasive" and went on to suggest that Meech Lake should be killed in retaliation. Like many Canadian nationalists, I would judge in retrospect that I had let the passion of the moment overrun my reason.

27 A national survey in early 1990 shows that 60 percent of opponents indicated reasons such as "Quebec does not deserve better status" (20 percent); "gives Quebec too much power" (12 percent); "disagree with Distinct Society" (11 percent); "all provinces should be equal" (11 percent); "it's bad for unity" (6 percent). Fourteen percent thought the accord "generally bad," while 26 percent did not know why they opposed it or gave miscellaneous reasons. Toronto Star / CTV Poll, *Toronto Star*, 6 February 1990.
28 See the survey of opinion by Charles Macli, "Dueling in the Dark," *The Globe and Mail Report on Business Magazine* (April 1991): 29–38.

Index